By the Word of Her Testimony

365 True-Life Story Devotionals for Women

Director of Publications: David W. Ray
Managing Editor of Publications: Lance Colkmire
Editorial Assistant: Elaine McDavid
Layout Design: Michael McDonald
Cover Design: Amber Cleaver

ISBN: 978-1-64288-182-0

Acknowledgements

First, I acknowledge the idea for this book was God's, not mine. Thank You, Lord, for directing me to do this; and for having patience with my ignorance of the process as I literally answered, "Sure God, I'll do that! It doesn't sound hard!" I have a feeling You laughed. Sometimes ignorance truly IS bliss.

Thank you to my wonderful and supportive husband, Kip Box, and my children, Judson Box, and Madison and Noah Robinson.

Thank you to my dad, Lonnie Ray Whitehead, there in my hometown of Red Bay, Alabama, who has encouraged me so much.

Thank you to my dear friend Joey Tripoli, a writer and English teacher who spent hours of her time helping me prepare the manuscript.

Thank you to the staff of the Michigan Church of God State Office—Sonya Smith, Ernie and Michele Wright, and Tammy Lambert—for all their help preparing and promoting this project.

Thank you to Erin Candela, Leisha Brotherton, and Charla Terry who helped work on so many files.

Thank you to the following friends and pastor's wives listed in alphabetical order who helped gather women to submit their stories. There are SO MANY MORE, but these went above and beyond: Colleen Adams, Terri Casto, Jennifer Eller, Lisa Davis, Kelly Fader, Julie Faircloth, Susie Fleming, Danielle Fortune, Amber Grice, Mariah Haar, Mary Hamman, Peggy Jablonski, Marie Jacobs, Darlene Ramey, Rebeca Reyes, Monique Rogers, Rebekah Strom, Neoma Turner.

Finally, thank you to every single lady who took the time to tell your story. You will overcome by the blood of the Lamb and the word of your testimony you gave here!

About the Cover Artist

Amber Cleaver, who resides in St. Clair County, Michigan, is a self-taught artist who discovered her passion for painting five years ago. She is a wife, sister, mom, and a grandma. She and her husband have experienced the redemptive power of the Lord when He healed their marriage after seven years of divorce. Jesus Christ is the center and the foundation to everything she does and stands for. You know she has a passion for Jesus by the way she loves. Her brave and courageous obedience to the Father is shown everywhere she goes.

Amber is also a realtor, designer, and a new store owner. In her leisure time you'll find her enjoying all things outdoors. Her favorite saying is, "See what God has painted for us."

You can find some of her art at *Partner2Create* on social media.

Foreword

You are about to begin a journey that reveals the amazing grace of Jesus Christ. With each testimony you read, you will be made aware of the faithfulness and tender mercies of our loving Savior. You will be reminded that His grace extended to us is life-changing! You will experience through these heartfelt testimonies the power of His transforming love. And you'll be blessed abundantly as you are made aware that this same love is available to each of us regardless of the circumstances we face.

You may be in a place of pain. You may be broken and battered; wounded and weary; discouraged and depressed. But through the powerful stories of these women you will be able to see the reality of the redeeming love offered freely by Jesus Christ.

Perhaps you are battling pain because someone has hurt you deeply and the suffering feels endless. Maybe you are hurting because of wrong choices you've made and now the enemy is tormenting you with condemnation. You may be in a place of darkness because of circumstance that came unexpectedly and suddenly in your life due to sickness or sorrow. You may feel helpless and hopeless.

As you read of the transforming power revealed in each testimony, it is our prayer that your hope is renewed. Take your burdens to the Lord and allow His love and grace to turn your life around. And your testimony will be like one of these recorded in this book! It will reveal the always sufficient, always available and always amazing grace of Jesus is more than enough for any battle you may face.

God bless and keep you as you begin this powerful 365-day journey and experience the power of His redeeming love!

—*Rhonda Holland*

Introduction

Welcome to the true stories of God's redeeming love in the lives of women just like you. Some stories you will identify with, others you will marvel at, still others you will just read and glorify our Lord at His amazing grace. The underlying theme of every story is the same truth that Hagar, Sarah's handmaid, came to understand when she ran away and sat crying, wondering what to do next—God sees us!

God sees us and loves us personally. No matter the situation, we see God helped every woman who called on Him to save her. He still does that today! In fact, when these same sisters in these same stories call on Him, He still hears their call now. There are more volumes to be written of the times He has healed sicknesses, delivered financially, and caused situations that were absolutely impossible to be solved.

The thing that allows us to conquer Satan is twofold, according to Revelation 12:11. The first is the blood of the Lamb, Jesus Christ, that He shed on the cross of Calvary. Second is the word of our testimony. We must tell our story of what He has done in our lives. Combined with the power of the blood of the Lamb, this gives us power to conquer our enemy!

So read these testimonies, but don't stop there. Tell someone else how you have been saved, healed, or delivered. Conquer the enemy's plans in *your life* through the blood of Jesus and your word of *your testimony*.

Day 1

Today's Scripture:

"I will never leave you nor forsake you" (Hebrews 13:5 NKJV).

Today's Testimony:

God loves you, me, and others who suffer; just ask for His help. He answers prayer. I'm a witness in the name of Jesus. I was born to a married working-class couple with seven other children. Our family was caught up in a dysfunctional cycle of addiction including alcohol and gambling. When I was two or three years old, my seven siblings and I were abandoned at a foster facility. This began my journey of being orphaned. I entered into the foster-care system and spent eight years in ten different foster homes and many different schools. During this time, I was a victim of physical, sexual, and emotional abuse in most of these homes. Even though I was suffering, God always had me, and I realized later in my life that this journey was part of God's purpose for me. When I was twelve I couldn't read. I was so beaten and starved; I weighed only forty-three pounds. I felt worthless. One day in a desperate cry for help, I fell to my knees and asked God to find me an adoptive home. That day I made a deal with God that if He found me a family, I would become a social worker and help kids like me who were lost in foster care.

As faith would have it, just one week later my prayer was answered. I was given the gift of adoption from a couple who wanted to adopt a child. I finally had parents that loved me. They loved me unconditionally. They adopted me, fed me, and educated me—teaching me to read.

I went to college and received my master's degree in social work. I got my first job in the field working with kids who were hurt like I was. At this children's home, I met my husband who had a similar passion for helping others. I went on to work for thirty years as a social worker in the field of foster care and then with the elderly.

I presently have the privilege of giving care to my precious parents whom God used to rescue a hopeless twelve-year-old. My folks are aging now and are ailing. I am giving them love and dignity, which they gave me many years ago. My life has been blessed; I found that even through suffering, God is able. When I was thirty years old, I was even reunited with my seven siblings, the ones I was separated from in the early '60s, God actually made a way for us to find one another. This has also been a blessing in restoration. There is always hope for the lost and to those who cry out to God.

—Carrie

Today's Takeaway:

Carrie's story moves me to tears! Have you ever felt alone or abandoned? It's exactly what the enemy of our soul wants us to think—that we're alone and no one cares. Don't ever believe that lie. We are never alone. Just like God was with Carrie in the darkest time of her life; He is with you right now.

Day 2

Today's Scripture:

"Therefore thus saith the Lord God, Behold I lay in Zion for a foundation a stone, a tried stone, a precious corner stone, a sure foundation: he that believeth shall not make haste" (Isaiah 28:16 KJV).

Today's Testimony:

As a child I went to church with my grandmother. I loved Sunday school and church. When I was fourteen, I answered an altar call in response to a wonderful salvation message by the pastor. I remember telling him afterward, "It felt like a refrigerator was lifted off of my back." He just chuckled, but I felt as light as a feather, and that experience is with me to this day at age seventy-two. The Lord is faithful.

Have you ever felt sorry for God? Well, I did and I told Him so while standing on my kitchen rug at my sink doing dishes. I felt like a yo-yo, up and down in my Christian walk. It seems like I get up and excited in the Lord, then someone does something, or something negative happens, and the rug is just pulled right out from under me.

Then the Holy Spirit, in His understanding and gentle, yet affirmative manner, replied. "Plant your feet on the solid Rock, because nobody and nothing can roll that Rock out from underneath you." I was amazed and immediately recalled a song my grandma used to sing, by Edward Mote: "On Christ, the solid Rock, I stand; all other ground is sinking sand." That was many years ago, but I see it vividly in memory. I am living on that truth.

—Cindy

Today's Takeaway:

I'm laughing as I sit here thinking about Cindy feeling sorry for God. It makes perfect sense. He must get weary with us, constantly forgetting that He's powerful enough to see us through anything, forgetting that He's never failed us, that He's never left us and never will. The great thing is, He is a patient and loving Father who understands our weaknesses. So stand on that solid Rock today and remember that as long as you hold onto Him, *nothing* can roll you off of it.

Don't worry about God. He can handle things. He can handle you and all your problems. He can handle me and all of my problems—and somewhere on the other side of the world right now, God is handling some sister's problems there too. And He's not even a little stressed. He's got this!

Day 3

Today's Scripture:

"The Lord is my strength and my shield; my heart trusts in Him, and I am helped; therefore my heart exults, and with my song I shall thank Him. The Lord is their strength, and He is a saving defense to His anointed" (Psalm 28:7-8 NASB).

Today's Testimony:

I first claimed verse 7 as part of my testimony at age sixteen, when facing the amputation of my foot: "The Lord is my strength and my shield; my heart trusts in Him, and I am helped." Over and over, I whispered those words as fear of entering the operating room threatened to supersede the peace I held within. In the following weeks and months, I experienced the Lord's ever-abiding presence through moments of tremendous pain. I found Jesus to be the perfect faithful friend my life needed.

It didn't take long for me to add verse 8 and make these two verses my life's theme. God adds color to each person's life in various ways; for me it's been from one surgery to another. Through the years, doctors have performed a total of thirty-one surgical procedures on various parts of my body, with more expected, yet God's help remains just one plea away. I have rehearsed those two verses before every operation and throughout each recovery, weaving them as golden threads in the tapestry of my life.

Whenever I received another diagnosis, the enemy tried adding dark colors of despair and depression, but the Lord covered me with hope and joy by using my testimony to bless another. He scattered the broken pieces of another person's life within my path, to give me a purpose in being the one to help them put it together again. As I read His Word, I've come to know that I can rest in the hope of His promises. He faithfully forgives me, pulling out every wrong stitch I make and replacing it with strands of beautiful color.

My relationship with Jesus becomes more intimate through each unique experience. He graciously lavishes me with more blessings than I can count, and thankfulness swells my heart until it spills over onto others. Whether I randomly serve people here or go annually to serve those in Guatemala, I strive to continually offer my life as a song to my God and King.

Though I continue to live with chronic pain and health challenges, the Lord colors my life with such vibrant love that I can only choose to respond with praise. I will go on thanking Him for giving me the gift of writing to tell of all the marvelous works He's performed in my life. I desire to encourage as many people as I can, and I hope you are one of them.

—*Tricia*

Today's Takeaway:

No matter what we go through in this life, there's a loving Savior who knows all about it. He waits for us to give every care over to Him. I challenge you today, give everything you're facing to Him and see what beautiful thing He will do in your life, and trust when that picture is different than the one you had pictured in your mind.

Day 4

Today's Scripture:

"If you forgive those who sin against you, your heavenly Father will forgive you" (Matthew 6:14 NLT).

Today's Testimony:

Life with my biological mother was filled with belittling, name-calling, and outright discouragement. She filled my head with every negative thought imaginable. By seventeen, I thought I needed boys to fulfill me, not realizing that only Jesus could. I continued to look to men to fill a void in my life, and became intimate with one man while planning a wedding with another. Later, I spiraled down to the darkest moments of my life while in a relationship with a neo-pagan who was engaged in witchcraft. He pulled me into some dark, terrifying places until I finally broke away from him and his strongholds over me.

I started attending church, and one Sunday the pastor made a mid-sermon altar call. Too scared to respond, I told God, "You can't mean me, but if You do, then have the pastor say something again." At the end of the altar song, the pastor said, "Sing it again because someone needs to come down." This happened twice more. I told God, "If You mean me, call me by name. I need *You* to want me."

Ask and you shall receive. My cousin, who was on stage in the choir, came to me, grabbed me by the arm, and walked me to the altar. In the gentlest whisper, he said, "Adrienne, God told me to come and get you and to tell you that He loves you *so* much. It's time to come home, sweet daughter." At that moment, I decided to go all in. Jesus could have everything—the hurt, the bitterness, every hope, and every dream.

It was a long journey to complete healing, but I never again looked to anyone except Jesus for my comfort and acceptance. My relationship with God is so tangible now that it couldn't be taken from me for anything. Thinking back, as cliché as it sounds, my worst day with Jesus is still far better than my best day without Him.

—*Adrienne*

Today's Takeaway:

The things you go through in your childhood have a way of popping up in your life later, don't they? Sometimes that's a positive thing; sometimes not so much. The key to all of it is to rely on the One who can take away the pain that people inflict. The truth is, people who are hurting usually hurt others. Are you a victim of this? Are you inflicting pain on someone? Either way, there is a God who cares and can help.

I've been there and I can testify that He *does* help. Get alone and tell Him everything—all of it. Pour out your heart to Him and ask for His help to forgive. The next time you feel that hurt, do it again. I promise, He begins to apply a healing balm to your hurt and healing comes. I don't pretend to understand it; I just know it's real. Give it a try.

Day 5

Today's Scripture:

"By this all will know that you are My disciples, if you have love for one another" (John 13:35 NKJV).

Today's Testimony:

I was born in Paris, France. At the age of ten, I took my First Communion, then I made my Confirmation at a cathedral in Paris. My parents always saw that I attended church so I would learn all about the Bible. At that time, most French people were Catholic. I will never forget those days I spent going up those many steps to the cathedral all dressed up in my long white dress and veil.

When World War II was declared, everything changed. There were no more big gatherings anywhere. We were only able to get a little food and medication. Our shutters had to be closed. We could only use a blue light due to the bombings. This went on for a long time.

After the war, I met my "Prince Charming." He was an American soldier. We were married; then we came to the United States. We had four lovely children together. I wanted them to go to the Catholic church and Catholic school. Two of my boys went to public schools, and my other two children went to Catholic schools. Time went by, and soon, I'm ashamed to say, we weren't attending church at all. The children grew up, were married, and went their own ways.

Years later, one of my sons and his wife came home and told us they had been saved. We were happy. They began doing tremendous work in Haiti. They helped construct two schools. I am so proud of them to this day.

I then decided to attend church again, so I went to a couple of different churches at first. Soon I was baptized by my son at the YMCA. My husband came with me; I was so happy! My daughter and her husband were attending a local church, and their children were attending the Christian school there. I noticed the people were caring and showed love to everyone; I liked that. I began going there too. Eventually, my granddaughter married the pastor's son. It's amazing how small choices have a long-lasting effect on your whole family.

—Jean

Today's Takeaway:

Wow! I'm picturing Jean's pretty white dress and flowing veil being lifted by the breeze as she climbed the steps to the cathedral in Paris. She had learned a lot about the Word of God by then, enough to cause her to want to commit her heart to Jesus. Little did she know that World War II was headed her way. The Word that had been committed to her heart and the knowledge of who is ultimately in charge of it all would steady her through the coming difficulty. That's how it is with us. We need the Truth and the Life (Jesus Christ) to strengthen us for each new day.

Day 6

Today's Scripture:

"Therefore, if anyone is in Christ, he is a new creation; the old has passed away, and see, the new has come!" (2 Corinthians 5:17 CSB).

Today's Testimony:

I grew up in a middle-class home with my sister, my mom (who was a homemaker), and my dad (who worked at General Motors). We went on many family vacations, and my parents showed me how much they loved me every day. When I was a baby, I was baptized in the Catholic church. I was made to continue going to church every Saturday night with my mom and sister, and also take classes to make my First Communion.

Between the ages of six and seven, however, I was molested by a family member for at least six months. By middle school, I stopped going to church and all the classes. In school, I found out that I loved alcohol—from the very first time I tasted it. It made me be everything I wanted to be; it hid my emotions and my past very well. By the time I barely graduated from high school, I was a blackout drinker. I tried some college while I worked full-time, but I quit; I was always looking for the party. Partying continued through the years and progressed quickly, spiraling out of control.

I dressed provocatively to get into bars and found that the more skin I showed, the more free drinks I got. Unfortunately, I put myself in harmful situations where I was raped and got two DUI's. This doesn't include all the chaos—not only in my own life, but also the countless relationships I ruined. My second DUI forced me into Alcoholics Anonymous, where I finally got clean and sober.

This is where I met my now husband. Neither one of us was attending church at the time. We dated, moved in together, got engaged, had a baby, and then got married – all within two years of meeting each other. It seems like we barely got started in our life together, and it was almost over—life was spiraling out of control . . . again. There was verbal abuse toward each other, even in front of the kids. We both wanted control of our household, and neither one of us was willing to listen to the other. Our finances were up in the air; I was extremely fearful of not paying our bills on time. Things were a mess.

—*Tonya*
(To Be Continued in Tomorrow's Reading)

Today's Takeaway:

Whew! I'm exhausted just reading about what Tonya's life is like right now. She described it as "spiraling out of control." That sounds accurate. I've felt like I was in a tornado before, have you? There's one thing about it, we can't go forward until we deal with the past. We have to let God heal our hurts and give Him our hearts before we can have forward progress. That can be just you and God or involve counselors, but it has to happen. Build strong!

Day 7

Today's Scripture:

"Anyone who listens to my teaching and follows it is wise, like a person who builds a house on solid rock" (Matthew 7:24 NLT).

Today's Testimony *(Continued From Previous Day):*

My life was full, but I felt so empty on the inside. We went to some counseling; it didn't help much. Neither of us wanted to change. Our close friends repeatedly told us to find a church and get God into our lives. Ironically, our son was going to daycare at a church at the time; the pastor invited us to come one Sunday. Even though I knew we needed it, I put it off. Finally, after weeks we all went as a family. Everyone was so nice and welcoming that even though I was nervous at first, I felt comfortable. We continued going week after week; it became our home and our family.

It seemed like every week the sermons seemed to focus on how much Jesus loves me. I kept thinking, *How could Jesus love me so much? There are so many things in my past—people I have hurt, and who have hurt me that I can't forgive.* I felt so unworthy of His love for me. Finally, after going to church for about a year, I decided to let it all go. I remember praying, weeping, and asking for forgiveness for my sins. After service I told everyone I could that Jesus Christ is my Lord and Savior. It was so freeing to finally get those chains off that held me back for so many years.

I've been saved for about three years now and life is so much better than it was. I've been baptized as a public declaration that I'm a follower of Jesus Christ and was just recently baptized in the Holy Spirit.

We are told in the Bible that we will have trials and tribulations. The enemy has thrown some difficult situations my way in the last few years; I couldn't have made it through without God and my church family. I'm currently on the praise and worship team; I was appointed church treasurer about a year ago. On payday, the first check I write now is our tithe check . . . a lot different than before. I freely give as much of my time and talents that I previously didn't even know I had. One thing I pray for is that you too will hear the call, answer it, and see what amazing plans God has for your life.

—*Tonya*

Today's Takeaway:

As Jesus said of Zacchaeus in Luke 19, "Salvation has come to this house" (v. 9 NKJV). It's easy to see. There is a great change. Isn't it beautiful? One of the quickest ways to know someone has truly let go of their old ways of life is when they give God control of their money. Tonya used to be controlling with it; now she is eager to pay her tithes. It was the same for Zacchaeus—he used to rob people, charging them too much in taxes; afterward he repaid four times over. Salvation changes everything. Our perspective in every area of our lives changes. Praise God!

Day 8

Today's Scripture:

"And that from a child thou hast known the holy scriptures, which are able to make thee wise unto salvation through faith which is in Christ Jesus"
(2 Timothy 3:15 KJV).

Today's Testimony:

When I was four years old, I was watching a Christian station on Saturday morning. It played children's shows on Saturday mornings, and that is what I was allowed to watch. I clearly remember standing in the den, watching a show called *Kids Like You*. There were some turtle puppets who were talking about Jesus. They were telling us about how Jesus died for our sins and explaining what sin was. At the end of the show they led the prayer of salvation. I prayed with the turtles on TV and asked Jesus to come into my heart and forgive me from my sins. After praying with the turtles I went to find my mom and tell her all about it. I went to her crying, telling her that I sinned. I told her I get mad at her sometimes and that I told a lie. She started crying and asked me if I wanted to pray with her to ask Jesus into my heart. I told her I'd already prayed with the turtles, but I would pray with her to make her feel better.

My experience was so simple and innocent, yet so sincere and powerful. I found God when I was four years old. I used to wish I had a "better" testimony. I always thought that my story was kind of "lame." I didn't think it could reach people, but now I realize my testimony is very powerful. Just like it says in 2 Timothy 3:15, "And that from a child thou hast known the holy scriptures, which are able to make thee wise unto salvation through faith which is in Christ Jesus" (KJV). God has kept me from a lot of heartache and pain. I am so thankful to the Lord for where I am in my life and for all the things He has kept me from. I realize now that if I had a different testimony, I would have a completely different life. God is able to use me in all the different ways He does *with* the story that I do have.

Never think your testimony isn't good enough—God will use it for His glory. He has big plans for you.

—Jennie

Today's Takeaway:

This makes my children's pastor's heart burst with joy. I've written countless puppet skits over the years, and I love the fact that God used puppets to help lead Jennie to Christ. Her sweet four-year-old heart was ready to accept Jesus because she understood she had done wrong things and God could forgive her and live in her heart. Jennie is still living for God all these years later. She is a joy to be around. God has blessed her life. Tell *your* story, no matter what it is. God will use it to help someone else; I promise!

Day 9

Today's Scripture:

"Even to your old age, I am He, and even to gray hairs I will carry you.
I have made, and I will bear; even I will carry, and will deliver you"
(Isaiah 46:4 NKJV).

Today's Testimony:

I think most of us can make note of times or situations where evidence of God's intervention becomes very clear. Our Father God knows exactly when to step in and bring deliverance to the captives. Luke 4:18 says Jesus came "to preach deliverance to the captives . . . to set at liberty them that are bruised [oppressed]" (KJV).

Mine came in the early fall of 1976. I had been captive to postpartum depression, pushing toward psychosis. Suicide had become a major struggle in my head. That day in our baby girl's room, I made a declaration to the Almighty. With tears streaming down my face, I cried out in complete desperation, "I will kill this child or kill myself." The answer was immediate. An overwhelming peace poured over me. Immediately, I knew things would be all right for me and my baby girl.

It did take time, but deliverance had come and I was able to handle my emotions. Calm prevailed, and I know that is the day Christ's salvation came to me. I had been "churched" my whole life, but it was that day that Christ's sacrifice became very real to me. He set it in motion immediately as two women I knew invited me to Bible study almost within the same week. Amazing grace!

—*Trudy*

Today's Takeaway:

God sees us always and He hears us cry out to Him in times of desperation. Even if we can manage only a weak cry of "Help!" He hears us. Remember, God knows our every thought. He can hear prayers that you don't even speak out loud when you aren't able. Thankfully, Trudy remembered that her "help comes from the Lord." She called to Him and the answer came.

Don't be discouraged if your answer doesn't come immediately. Sometimes it takes time for solutions to our problems to come. God will send you strength to keep walking when He delays His deliverance. Trust Him that He's working even when you can't see the answer. Walking by faith and not by sight may be scary, but remember that you're not alone on the path.

Day 10

Today's Scripture:

"You will seek Me and find Me when you search for Me with all your heart"
(Jeremiah 29:13 NKJV).

Today's Testimony:

As I look back over my life, I can see the hand of God moving in every season. I remember as a little girl I found the most private place I could think of—a blue laundry bin; I hopped inside of it, and I prayed with all my heart. I asked God to save me and forgive me for all of my sins. I believed that prayer and believed in God. I read my Bible as a young girl and had dreams of singing and loved making up songs. The Lord taught me to sing worship songs when I felt afraid. The enemy must have hated that and jumped on his assignment to steal, kill, and destroy because shortly after my childhood awakening, my biological dad was taken out of my life and lies from the enemy loudly filled my mind.

I started feeling abandoned and unwanted. Self-image issues started shaking me to the core, and instead of sharing those things, I internalized them and isolated myself. When I prayed and asked God to bring my dad back and it didn't happen, I began to feel abandoned by God too. A spirit of fear started controlling my life, and my childhood was then marked by silence, sadness, and oppression. Though I was growing up in the church, I found myself distant from God as a teenager. All I was seeing and hearing was what not to do and it seemed like just a bunch of rules. I still maintained my belief in God, but I was far from *knowing Him*. My perspective was clouded by lies from the enemy. I even started fighting my parents about going to church. Though I was going in the opposite direction of God, He remained faithful to me always, sending people to minister to me and prophesy over my life. I entered a season of indifference and spiritual complacency as a teen. At this point of my life I began to question whether God existed at all.

—*Haven*
(To Be Continued in Tomorrow's Reading)

Today's Takeaway:

Oh, how the enemy of our soul *loves* to make God sound like nothing but a bunch of rules to people. He wanted to trick Haven into thinking that because God didn't bring her dad back into her life, He wasn't real. Remember, Satan is the "father of lies" for a reason. Are you listening to a lie? Believe only God! He is the One who gave His very life for you, not for rules—for *love*.

Day 11

Today's Scripture:

"Ask, and it will be given to you; seek, and you will find; knock, and it will be opened to you" (Matthew 7:7 NKJV).

Today's Testimony *(Continued From Previous Day)*:

Then things started to shake and change; my life suddenly flipped upside down in a good way. I walked into a new church that my stepdad picked out for us; immediately something was different. I felt the presence of the Lord. I walked in and saw love in the people and a love for God that I never knew existed. Not only that, but the pastor spoke messages as if he knew God personally. It was apparent he had a relationship with Him. The messages made sense to me and the Word of God started to capture my heart. I didn't know what was happening, but the Holy Spirit was ministering to me through the Word.

A holy conviction started enveloping my heart and highlighting sin I knew was keeping me from God. After weeks of seeing something that seemed so real, I decided I had to know if it was true. I called out to God in a time of worship and I said, "God, I have heard in Your Word that if I seek You with all my heart I will find You, so I'm going to seek You with everything I've got and if You are real, reveal Yourself to me." Then I set out to seek God—writing down Scripture, reading the Bible, listening to messages—and the Word of God came alive to me. I finally understood what the Bible was saying.

I repented, I worshiped; God revealed Himself to me. He spoke to me. I heard the voice of God; He pointed out that I was trying to fill a hole in my heart left by my biological dad. I was expecting a man to fill that hole, but God said, "I AM." I realized God was meant to fill that hole in my heart. Jesus Christ died for me and had amazing love for me. I rededicated my life to God, but this time I made Jesus the Lord of my life and everything *in* my life. I surrendered everything to God, and the journey He took me on afterward was the most fun and incredible time of getting to know Him and how He works. I was saved, baptized, filled with the Spirit, and discipled. I began serving, singing, and discovering the calling and purpose of my life. The lies that filled my mind prior were replaced with truth; sadness was replaced with joy, and heaviness was replaced with praise.

—Haven

Today's Takeaway:

What a change! There's such joy and peace now that the enemy of our soul has been replaced with the Savior of our soul. "Religion" is different from a *relationship*. Now that's what I'm talking about!

Day 12

Today's Scripture:

*"Jesus said, 'Let the little children come to me, and do not hinder them,
for the kingdom of heaven belongs to such as these'"* (Matthew 19:14 NIV).

Today's Testimony:

A dreary sky met my wonderings as I looked out my childhood bedroom window. I clearly remember watching raindrops drip off the pine tree's boughs. There were no lights on, so I stood alone in the dimly lit room.

Out of the blue, I had a matter-of-fact question I wanted to ask my nearby mom. I suddenly wanted to know what it meant to "ask Jesus in your heart." I don't remember how quickly she came; only that she did. I don't even remember her response; only that it made sense to me. It made so much sense that I knew it was what I wanted! A four-year-old little heart just wanted to be filled with Jesus. He was good. He loved me, and I just wanted to love Him too. I remember crying . . . feeling overcome.

Over the years, growing in God and in the church, I've never questioned that moment or its validity. It is just as real to me now, forty-one years later as it was then! When at times I have tried to compare it to other people's miracle conversions, I am surprised at the simplicity of mine. That the God of the universe moves the heart of a child as naturally as the rain fell that day . . . His Spirit fell on me. No bells. No whistles. No altar call. Quite literally, I was a child drawn by a still small voice and a simple knowledge that apparently whatever my mom told me was right. My spirit knew it.

Today, as I look back, my particular testimony offers me so much hope for our children and the world at large. Salvation experiences are as varied as the individuals who share them, but God knows how each one hears best. He can draw the youngest of children as well as the aged on their deathbed. Maybe He will use a church, a pastor, or another believer. Maybe He won't. He is big enough to speak on His own in the silence of a common day and change it forever!

—Angie

Today's Takeaway:

This brings tears to my eyes when I think of teaching children's church for four-year-olds, or leading the toddler nursery with Bible stories; they are so worth it! These children can know the Lord! Some people think young children can't understand, but I think back to when Jesus was riding into Jerusalem on the donkey's back and people were shouting praises; there were children praising Him that day. Jesus noticed them. God took notice of Angie that rainy day and He drew her by the power of the Holy Spirit. Thank God for a mother that knew the Lord and could lead her child to God. What greater privilege is there?

Day 13

Today's Scripture:

"He brought me up also out of an horrible pit, out of the miry clay, and set my feet upon a rock, and established my goings. And he hath put a new song in my mouth, even praise unto our God: many shall see it, and fear, and shall trust in the Lord" (Psalm 40:2-3 KJV).

Today's Testimony:

For me, the "miry clay" included a life with no purpose, no vision, and my justification of sins I deemed acceptable. As my life went on, those sins kept expanding. Gradually, compromise led me down a dangerous path.

I remember believing that as long as I wasn't the worst of the sinners in my circle of friends, then I was OK. Eventually, I found myself in a relationship that was getting more and more abusive. I had moved far away from family and friends to be with this person. I really believed there were no other options for me, and generally that summed up my life—until one day when I actually "heard" the Gospel message for the first time. I had grown up in a Christian home and school, so I am sure I heard the Gospel many times. But this was the first time I ever really *heard* it and realized what Jesus did was actually *for me*. I somehow grasped the seriousness and commitment involved. This wasn't a cheap Gospel. Jesus paid a high price. I knew this would change my life as I knew it. I guess I was counting the cost. If I jumped, I knew I would be all in, no turning back. So I withheld my decision for a short time. It didn't take long.

The day came when the abuse was particularly violent and I escaped to the bathroom toilet—the only place with a little privacy. From that humble perch I looked to Heaven and said, "God, if You are real, get me out of this." Instantly, a tangible power and courage filled me. I washed my face, went to the bedroom and started packing. My resolve was unshakable, supernatural. I didn't know the correct Christian terminology or Bible verses, but that was the point I was leaving behind my old life and was forging ahead toward God—even though I had no idea what that looked like or where I would go. He had, indeed, plucked me out of the "miry clay" and set my feet upon the "rock," which is Jesus.

—*Barbara*
(To Be Continued in Tomorrow's Reading)

Today's Takeaway:

Compromise is dangerous when it involves bargaining with our soul. If we compare ourselves with others, trying to feel better about our level of sin, things go south fast. We need only to trust our souls to Jesus and compare only to the Word of God. Thankfully, Barbara listened when she heard the Gospel. It gave her the strength she needed to walk away from the enemy's trap. If you are in a trap, look to the One who can strengthen you and empower you to live what He died for you to have—life, and that more abundantly.

Day 14

Today's Scriptures:

"He brought me up also out of an horrible pit, out of the miry clay, and set my feet upon a rock, and established my goings. And he hath put a new song in my mouth, even praise unto our God: many shall see it, and fear, and shall trust in the Lord" (Psalm 40:2-3 KJV).

"I cry out to God Most High, to God who fulfills his purpose for me" (Psalm 57:2 ESV).

Today's Testimony *(Continued From Previous Day):*

I finally had the strength to leave my abusive relationship due to giving my heart to Jesus, but I didn't know where I would go.

God began to provide for me right away. I had a car with a broken exhaust system that needed repair before I could physically leave. I had purchased the parts needed and was struggling to get it fixed myself. The "carpenter" who was working on our home saw me struggling and, while I wasn't looking, crawled under the car and fixed the exhaust for me. Jesus, the Carpenter, provided a carpenter to be my mechanic and get me on my way. I love that. As the verse above states, He truly did (and still does) "establish my goings."

There is no kind of "miry clay" too deep or too thick that He cannot pluck us out. I experienced that firsthand.

Now He has "put a new song in my mouth," a hymn of praise to our God, who is worthy of it all. I declare that many will see and put their trust in Him. This is now my purpose and vision.

—*Barbara*

Today's Takeaway:

I don't know if there is anything that hurts the heart of God deeper than abuse. God's Word declares He is love, and abusing another person is the absolute opposite to love. The difficult part is that many times the abused person can't see another way or doesn't have a way out. I assure you, Sister, God makes a way when there seems to be no way. Don't listen to any lie from the enemy who tries to tell you that you are at fault for abuse of any kind. If you or someone you know is being abused, it is time to act.

Just like God miraculously provided a way for Barbara to have her car fixed, He will provide for you. Just make the step. The national number for the abuse hotline is 800-799-SAFE.

Day 15

Today's Scripture:

"But he said to me, 'My grace is sufficient for you, for my power is made perfect in weakness.' Therefore I will boast all the more gladly about my weaknesses, so that Christ's power may rest on me" (2 Corinthians 12:9 NIV).

Today's Testimony:

Two of my earliest memories: Jesus and my ballerina lamp. What do the two have to do with one another; how is this my salvation story? Let me explain. My mom taught me how to talk to God, like she was teaching me my "ABCs." She taught me how to walk with Him, like she was teaching me to tie my shoes. She made it that simple . . . that important.

It wasn't until years later, though, that I realized by *what grace* I was truly saved. But before we go there, let me take you back to when I was just a toddler. I'd lie in bed and stare up at the light fixture above me. On it were beautiful little ballerinas, all in a graceful arabesque. I loved them. I wanted to be one.

In kindergarten, my dream became a reality. I got the slippers, the pink tights, and the leotard. I felt just like a ballerina. But that didn't last long. I never could become one of those ballerinas I had always dreamed about. I just don't have what it takes.

Like so many other things—and so many times in life—I just couldn't do it. I failed. I gave up. I fell short of the glory of God (Romans 3:23). This "dance" we call *life* is hard. It doesn't always look beautiful and I'm not always very good at it. Simply put, I don't have the *grace*. "But he said to me, 'My grace is sufficient for you, for my power is made perfect in weakness.' Therefore I will boast all the more gladly about my weaknesses, so that Christ's power may rest on me" (2 Corinthians 12:9 NIV). *This* is my salvation story, my testimony: Christ's power has given me life, though I am weak and unworthy. *I just don't have what it takes.* But He strengthens me, and His grace saves me—every day. I mentioned my mom taught me about Jesus, from the very beginning . . . and she continued until He took her home. One of the last things she ever said was, "It's all grace." She was talking about salvation. If not for the grace of God, we'd never make it home. That's what makes His salvation so wonderful, so completely undeserved . . . and so beautiful.

—*Joey*

Today's Takeaway:

It's a beautiful and rich heritage to look back and think of a mother who led you to know Jesus; it's one of the greatest treasures a daughter can own. But there is even a greater heritage to have—once you have accepted Christ, you then become the daughter of a King. You become a princess! I believe Joey *is* a real ballerina, because I believe if you took ballet, you're a ballerina for life, but much more importantly, she is a real daughter of the King of kings! And you can be too.

Day 16

Today's Scripture:

*"And Jesus said unto them, Because of your unbelief: for verily I say unto you,
If ye have faith as a grain of mustard seed, ye shall say unto this mountain,
Remove hence to yonder place; and it shall remove; and nothing shall be
impossible unto you"* (Matthew 17:20 KJV).

Today's Testimony:

My life began very early with a love for the Lord.

In a migrant workers' field, a local Christian woman came to share her faith with the gathered children; I was one of those children. It was then that I experienced Christ's presence in my heart. With her example of bubbles, which we saw as beautiful, she told about the beautiful love of Jesus Christ.

And with that, I thought being a Christian would be a beautifully easy life, but that was not His plan for me. Instead, it's been a struggle walking in His great plan for me. It's been great but not anything easy. I had to learn the difference between my will and His will. There lies the struggle for most of us.

I've been seriously ill for most of my life, and it's hard at times to keep strong faith. The past four years have been filled with surgery after surgery, all kinds of medications, and pain. It becomes overwhelming, frustrating, and tiring, but I cling to God's Word. I don't rely on man. It's been my mustard-seed faith that has brought me through. I know the mustard seed is the strongest, most resilient and prosperous little herb on the earth. This scripture has been my faith walk since childhood: "Now faith is the substance of things hoped for, the evidence of things not seen" (Hebrews 11:1-3 KJV).

My faith is in the Lord, who is my Healer and Savior. With the love and encouragement from everyone in my life—including my husband and church family, the voice of God continues to remind me that faith as a mustard seed always holds us stronger than anything we are going through. Let us cling to the truth, that the day of the Lord is coming, and His glory will be forever and ever.

—*Gloria*

Today's Takeaway:

Because of that Christian woman taking her faith to a group of migrant workers' children, Gloria was able to hear and understand the good news of the Gospel. With something as simple as blowing bubbles and talking about the beauty of Jesus' love, lives were changed. It really is that easy to tell someone how wonderful the Lord is and what He's done in our lives. Let's look around our world today and find someone to talk to. Who do you see daily? Who might be open to hear what God has done for you? That is sometimes all it takes to change someone's life.

Day 17

Today's Scripture:

*"For this is My blood of the covenant, which is being poured out
for many for forgiveness of sins"* (Matthew 26:28 NASB).

Today's Testimony:

One night as a child I spent the night with my grandparents; it was one of my favorite things to do as a child. I always felt unconditionally loved in their presence, which strategically positioned my heart to be soft and open to the love of Christ.

That Sunday, in a small church in West Virginia, we settled into our pews. I remember thinking about what a comforting feeling it was to have my hands around my grandma's arm. I don't recall any other hymns that evening, but this one I will never forget:

> Just as I am, without one plea,
> But that Thy blood was shed for me,
> And that Thou bidd'st me come to Thee,
> O Lamb of God, I come! I come!

My heart became full with the presence of the Holy Spirit. My dear, sweet grandma looked at me, and asked, "Baby, do you need to go to the altar?" I shook my head yes and with tears streaming down my face, I headed for the altar.

Although my body wasn't running, my heart was sprinting. I reached the altar and dropped to my knees. The pastor knelt down next to me and asked, "Would you like to accept Jesus as your Savior?" Although I had no concept of the ramifications surrounding my answer, I gave a resounding, "Yes." At that moment, I wanted to know Jesus more than anything in the world.

For over fifty-five years, I have been loved and guided by His Spirit. This journey continues to prove on a daily basis that "Yes" was the right answer. To God be the glory!

—*Tonya*

Today's Takeaway:

There's nothing better in this world than that feeling of pure love, safety, and security that you can experience with certain people. Children need this desperately. There are some who don't get to feel that due to circumstances out of their control. Tonya was blessed to have these great moments with her grandparents, and she's thankful.

If you were blessed to know this feeling as a child or not, there is a Savior who provides a far greater comfort than any sweet grandparent ever was able to give. I love the hymn that Tonya heard that night; I've sung it many times with tears streaming because of the thought that we can absolutely come just as we are without a hope of an excuse. And He's ready to forgive anything and everything. What comfort there is in that!

Day 18

Today's Scripture:

"I say to you that likewise there will be more joy in [the presence of the angels of God] over one sinner who repents" (Luke 15:7 NKJV).

Today's Testimony:

In my youth and young adult years, I was a very rebellious, angry, and reckless person. I didn't care who I hurt, including myself. I didn't care about making anyone else happy, other than myself. I made some horrible decisions in an effort to "make me happy." I spiraled into a frenzy of drinking and drug abuse, sexual perversion, self-harm—physically, mentally, and emotionally, and living on the verge of prostitution and suicide. I decided that the rules didn't really apply to me, so I barreled through my life, carelessly and aimlessly.

I came from a home where my mother openly prayed, attended prayer meetings, and served in her church. We went every Sunday, attended Sunday school, and were very involved in serving through the church. But that upbringing never sat well with me, because there was never a connection with God, or so I thought. I don't remember ever being led to seek the Lord for salvation or to establish a relationship with Him.

At an early age, my parents divorced; so, of course, I ended up with the all-too-cliché "daddy issues." I told myself, "I don't need a man in my life. My mother raised us by herself and I am just fine." My thinking led me to a very promiscuous lifestyle; I searched for someone who would cherish me, and love me—someone who would fill the void that I had really created for myself.

After many instances of indulging in reckless behavior, nights of not knowing how I got to where I was (both mentally and geographically), I began to realize it was a miracle I was still alive. Finally, after several serious abusive relationships, multiple partners, selling everything I owned for drugs and alcohol, and almost saying "yes" to sex for anything I needed, God asked me if I was ready to be done with it all. I can still hear Him saying, "It's time to come home."

— *Becki*
(To Be Continued in Tomorrow's Reading)

Today's Takeaway:

It is hard to imagine the kind of hurt that would cause someone to try to self-destruct, but so many people hurt so badly they'd rather mute the pain with greater pain than deal with it. Have you ever heard the line, "How do you make a headache stop hurting? Hit your foot with a hammer." That seems to be the idea here. It's almost as if Becki wanted to die. Thank God, He had a different plan! Tomorrow you'll hear the rest of the story, but understand that even at this point, God had been right there with her all along. He never leaves us nor forsakes us. He is patiently waiting for us to realize that everything we try to substitute for Him is worthless. He is matchless!

Day 19

Today's Scripture:

"His father saw him [the prodigal] and was filled with compassion; he ran and put his arms around him and kissed him" (Luke 15:20 NRSV).

Today's Testimony *(Continued From Yesterday)*:

Like in the story of the Prodigal Son, as I was exhausted from running, my praying mother dropped everything when her phone rang to come and pick me up and bring me home. I had finally surrendered, but not yet to God. I still didn't know what that looked like. I just knew I was tired.

After a time of rest, withdrawal, and safety, I met the man who is now my husband of twenty-eight years. He took me to church to meet his precious parents. I established an amazing relationship with the pastor's wife; and after experiencing God in a way I had never known was possible, I submitted my life to Jesus Christ. It really was that easy. I repented of all of my sin—all of my guilt, doubt, chaos, and unbelief; I totally surrendered.

I will never forget the peace I felt knowing I was forgiven and that I would learn to forgive myself. I now serve God with everything I am. I never thought I would end up being the worship leader at a church after using the gift God gave me in vain at bars and clubs. But here I am, because He is in my life.

—*Becki*

Today's Takeaway:

Wow! I love this story of total salvation and redirection. This is the plan of God taking hold of someone's life. Can you imagine how angry the enemy was when Becki realized the truth of God's forgiveness and left the horrible pit he had her in? When we compare the enemy's plan of misery, pain, and exhaustion to God's plan of peace, joy, and life—is there any comparison?

I love the fact that God picked Becki up, washed her clean, and called her to serve as a worship leader. I've heard her lead worship; there is a powerful anointing in her. I believe it's a spirit of gratefulness and joy within her, because she knows the pain of sin and how wonderful it is to be delivered. There is a price to her praise, and sadly she has paid it; but now, oh, there's only the joy of salvation and worship!

Day 20

Today's Scripture:

"And you will seek Me and find Me, when you search for Me with all your heart"
(Jeremiah 29:13 NKJV).

Today's Testimony:

My story begins when I was three. I grew up with a father who was an alcoholic and a mother who had to work evenings to pay the bills and put food on the table. Unfortunately, this was the perfect atmosphere for my sexual abuse to begin.

My father began abusing me at night while my mother provided for our small family. The abuse continued for two years and stopped only when my mother found out about it. As a result, one day soon, my mother packed up all that would fit inside of our station wagon and drove herself, my sister, and me to live with some family.

I remember not realizing what the move, at the time, would mean for me. Life seemed to become normal until my mother could no longer handle the guilt that came from my abuse and began turning to drugs. While my mother struggled to handle life's basic ups and downs, she bought toys and food to cover up her addiction and to show us "love." I believe the combination of not dealing with my abuse and turning to food began at that time. I had a love/hate relationship with food that continued throughout my life.

It was not until I was sixteen years old that someone told me about a God of love. I was told about the Gospel on a weekly basis and remember the pastor calling God a "Father." I can remember the word *Father* bringing back memories of my abuse. How could they use *that* word to describe a loving person? My teenage mind could not process that picture of a God, so I turned to drugs also. I began numbing my pain with drugs and sex to stop it from hurting so badly. I spent a year running from God. I had no idea how far God would go to save me.

—Jamie
(To Be Continued in Tomorrow's Reading)

Today's Takeaway:

It's hard sometimes for someone who endured pain from an earthly father to grasp a glimpse of the love their heavenly Father could possibly have for them. It would be like asking a blind man to describe the beauty of a sunset he's never seen—impossible, almost. The thing is, if you allow Him into your heart, you can feel His love, a little like the blind man can "feel" the warmth of the sunset. The Father is always waiting for you to turn to Him and allow Him to help. He's right there; don't run. Surrender!

Day 21

Today's Scripture:

"And you will seek Me and find Me, when you search for Me with all your heart"
(Jeremiah 29:13 NKJV).

Today's Testimony *(Continued From Previous Day):*

When I was seventeen years old, strung out on drugs, and crawling home on my hands and knees, I heard the voice of God calling to me: "Turn to Me or I will allow you to die in your sin." Those were the words I needed and the words I would learn to love. That day changed my life. I stopped the drugs and sex, and stopped hanging out with friends who were on that path.

I spent my senior year learning more and more about God. As I read and studied God's Word, Jeremiah 29:11 stuck out to me: "I know the thoughts that I think toward you, says the Lord, thoughts of peace and not of evil, to give you a future and a hope" (NKJV). This verse became my anthem. I quoted the scripture when my self-esteem was so low and friends were few. I'd scream it when my food addiction had the scale topping out at 363 pounds.

Through the help of wonderful church members, trained counselors, and a husband and family who loved me, I was able to overcome my eating habits. I discovered my weight was a shield I'd placed upon myself for protection. I realized it was time to let go and let God. Through prayer and guidance, I decided that weight-loss surgery would be a helpful tool I could use to regain confidence and understand portion control. I now know that God loved me at my highest weight, and He still loves me another eighty-six pounds lighter. My appearance does not determine how much love I receive from the Father.

God chose Jesus to bear all my sin on the cross. He was there calling me deeper when I was crawling on my hands and knees. He was sitting there in my pre-op room watching me change my weight-loss story. He is there in every good time, and every bad time; all you have to do is search for Him. Jeremiah 29:13 states "You will seek Me and find Me, when you search for Me with all your heart" (NKJV). I am grateful for my salvation in Christ alone.

—Jamie

Today's Takeaway:

The heavenly Father touched Jamie and saved her. Now that she has come to Christ, I'm so proud of her facing the pain she suffered as a child, which caused her to use food as a comfort. She is working toward her healing in so many ways. She is an overcomer!

There are times when our past has caused us to deal with pain in ways that Christ never planned. Are you there right now? God gives us Christian leaders and counselors that are gifted to help us through. Lean on their wisdom if you need it. That's not weakness; that's wisdom. Listen, sister. Healing is coming!

Day 22

Today's Scripture:

"I also tell you this: If two of you agree here on earth concerning anything you ask, my Father in heaven will do it for you" (Matthew 18:19 NLT).

Today's Testimony:

Many years ago, I felt a great void in my heart. God was tugging at me, and without knowing Him, I knew He was calling me. Soon I could no longer ignore His insistence. I visited a church nearby and made the most special and important decision of my life. I accepted Jesus Christ as my Lord and Savior, and didn't ask permission from anyone.

My husband, a drug dealer, demanded an answer: *Why make this life-changing decision without his consent or opinion?* He didn't agree, and had no interest in anything that had to do with God. I read that Matthew 18:19 tells us if two agree here on earth concerning anything they ask, then our Father in Heaven will do it for them, and thought to myself that unless he joined me in this decision, life would never change. We needed to be in agreement. My faith was in our bond. I was his wife, his friend; why wouldn't he listen? I became desperate and at times hopeless. I tried and said everything, and everything failed.

Then, the Voice that called me invited me to activate my faith and to release my husband into His hands, and so I did. Prayer became my weapon; I'd pray and pray again. Unashamed, I asked everyone I knew to join me in prayer for him. I was convinced prayer would work, and it did. Six months later, that hard-hearted man accepted Christ. My husband was free. Christ made him free. He was transformed by the Holy Spirit, and a drug dealer is now a bishop, a servant of the Lord, a man who's devoted to the Kingdom.

Today, I invite you to put your faith into action. Pray, and pray again. Feel free to ask others to join in your prayer. Prayer works! Remember 2 Corinthians 5:7, "Walk by faith, not by sight" (KJV). Salvation is coming to your home.

—Awilda

Today's Takeaway:

Many times when we are struggling with issues within our lives, our first instinct is to run and hide. I've heard friends say, "I'll come back to church when I get my life back together." This is exactly what the enemy wants us to do. When he can isolate us, he can attack us more easily. Think of the lion who attacks the herd of antelope—the first move is to isolate the weakest one, then move in for the kill. How sad!

We have to follow Awilda's example. When we have a need, we must swallow our pride and admit it. Do you think no one else struggles? It may be that your courage to ask your friend for prayer today may just free her up to share her need with you. Go ahead—unleash the armies of prayer warriors over your need and see what God will do!

Day 23

Today's Scripture:

"'For I know the plans I have for you,' declares the Lord,
'plans to prosper you and not to harm you, plans to give you
hope and a future'" (Jeremiah 29:11 NIV).

Today's Testimony:

God has always been faithful and good to me throughout my life. I was raised in a Christian home, but I didn't always follow Christ as I should have. Thinking I needed to experience and learn things on my own caused several challenges in my life. I remember as a child that being overweight wasn't acceptable in my family, and the comments that were made (intentional or not) affected how I felt about myself. Another major hurdle was realizing that people of my faith were looked down upon by many kids and their parents in the small town where I grew up. In addition, my father was strict and had very strong Christian convictions.

I became rebellious; I started running away, getting drunk, smoking cigarettes and marijuana, threatening to quit school when I turned sixteen; but one decision, surely not recommended, changed that self-destructive course I was on. After attempting suicide at the age of sixteen, I was admitted into a Christian crisis center for teens. This brought a change that led me to where I am today. Meeting other kids who were struggling and talking about my issues led to a foundation being laid, but the one thing that affected me most was getting to know the Christian college students who were employed there. I watched and talked to them; this allowed me to see how they were choosing to serve Christ on their own, plus, they accepted me. By the time my six weeks had come to an end, I accepted Christ into my heart.

I lived in a school district where none of my new church friends attended. After I returned home from the crisis center, a church family opened their home to me so I could attend school there. My life was a total turnaround. I felt accepted, loved, and that I belonged. That summer I attended church camp, and I received the gift of the Holy Spirit. The joy of the Lord and His Spirit, now alive within me, was springing forth in an outward witness of the relationship I was forming with God. My senior year was a super year. I graduated, received the "Co-op Student of the Year" award, and became engaged to marry the man I have now been married to for forty years.

—*Carrie*

Today's Takeaway:

The things we go through can hurt, can't they? How we choose to handle them can change the entire direction of our lives. Either we take it to Jesus or we pull it inside and it grows and gets more painful until we feel like we'll explode. Think about what hurts inside you right now and give it to God.

Day 24

Today's Scripture:

"Believe on the Lord Jesus Christ, and you will be saved, you and your household"
(Act 16:31 NKJV).

Today's Testimony:

I was a mean, unhappy wife, and mother of two sons. Mostly I was angry at their alcoholic dad of thirteen years; he was not abusive, just always drunk and drinking. One evening I cried out to God: "There has to be more to life than all my crying, arguing, and unhappiness." I was brought up Catholic; you stay married no matter what the situation. A short time after my prayer, a lady in town invited me to go to a musical event at the local high school. It was an evangelistic crusade. I had no idea what it was, but when the altar call was made, I went. Everyone prayed for me that God would change my life. Within the next few weeks, I felt like a different person. My friend took me with her to prayer meetings, Bible studies, women's studies, and baseball too. My husband began to dislike her because I was becoming a "Jesus freak" to him. I listened to Christian music and teaching tapes, pleaded the blood of Jesus over everything, and even thanked God for bringing him safely home at night. Later he told me he laid in bed quietly to hear what I prayed nightly.

One day my youngest son went with me and my friend to a women's study, and prayed for his daddy to know the Lord. Meanwhile, God was working on my neighbor to help. He gave my husband some records of Psalms music by Jimmy Swaggart. I'd never heard of such a thing—I saw my husband with beer in one hand and Bible in the other. Together we began searching the Scripture for the words to these songs. Together we wrote each word down, crying through them as we went. God was working! Shortly after this, my husband said he had to pull off the expressway on his way to work because he was crying to a song, "You Don't Need to Understand Just Take My Hand." A song he got from me.

One Sunday a few weeks later, he said, "I don't want to shock you, but I'm going to church with you and the boys." I wanted to jump up and down; the boys were very happy. I had received the word, Acts 16:31, for my household.

That year my husband handed out Christian flyers and candy for Halloween. Christmas came, and he didn't want to go to a family party because there would be alcohol. God changed him. It happened, with lots of tears and prayers. God makes all things beautiful in His time. "To God be the glory for all the things He has done."

—Blanca

Today's Takeaway:

This is a beautiful story of the triumph of salvation over sin. Blanca received love and shared it again and again until she eventually won her husband and household. Take hope from this. It didn't happen overnight. She didn't give up on her lost loved ones, and neither can you. Claim Acts 16:31!

Day 25

Today's Scripture:

"Enter by the narrow gate. For the gate is wide and the way is easy that leads to destruction, and those who enter by it are many. For the gate is narrow and the way is hard that leads to life, and those who find it are few" (Matthew 7:13-14 ESV).

Today's Testimony:

I walked into a local church one day. The motto was "Better Fathers, Better Mothers, Stronger Families." The sermon was on the wide path and narrow road from Matthew 7:13-14. I sat in awe, wondering if someone had called ahead to the pastor and told him, "You have a crazy Wiccan lady coming that's lost and broken, get the fire extinguisher ready." As I sat and listened to him, it was as if he was speaking directly to my soul, coring me of my existence and filling me with Jesus Christ. It was an "aha" moment for me. I literally felt him speaking to my soul in ways that I never knew was possible.

I began to read and try to understand the Bible at home. I started to search for scripture that would give me direction about whether it was wrong to continue down the prior Wiccan path again because I was still tempted all the time with Wicca. I remember one morning waking up and my son's brown leather Bible was open to the Book of Micah on the kitchen table. There was a napkin on the page underlining Micah 5:12, which says, "I will destroy your witchcraft and you will no longer cast spells" (NIV). To this day I have no idea how that happened; our children were with my husband at camp. This is still a mystery to me, or God's divine intervention perhaps? I sat at our kitchen table and read it over and over. That day it ended! I took my black hardcover *Book of Shadows* and everything that had anything to do with Wicca. I walked outside, put it in the burn pit and burned it all. I watched almost twenty years of my satanic life burn and I didn't have one uneasy feeling or concern. In fact, it gave me the feeling of freedom. What an epiphany!

The more I surrendered myself to Jesus, the more my family life began to fall into place. The more I began understanding the Word of God, the more healed I became. It wasn't until I completely surrendered it all to Jesus Christ that He wiped me clean and rebuilt me. He healed me and I was able to live again.

—*Angela*

Today's Takeaway:

The Lord knows the deepest secrets of our hearts. Everything is known to Him— and He still loves us. He loves us enough to put people in our path to tell us the truth and give us opportunities to turn from things that are opposite to His Word and plans for us. The key to it all is the Word of God and our surrender to the truth of it. He has so much ready to bless us, but He is holy; so we must cling to what is good and turn from what is evil—that means turning to the Word of God for direction to know the difference.

Day 26

Today's Scripture:

"Trust in the Lord with all your heart, and lean not on your own understanding; in all your ways acknowledge Him, and He shall direct your paths" (Proverbs 3:5-6 NKJV).

Today's Testimony:

Each one of us starts off life similarly. We first learn to crawl, then walk, and then run. As a parent, you are so excited when your child takes their first steps. These first steps are uneasy and may lead to a lot of falls. Eventually your child gets steady on their feet, and then they're off and running. My Christian walk has been the same.

I was raised in a Christian home until I was about seven years old. My parents divorced; after that, I couldn't attend church because it conflicted with parent visitation. Still, I always had a desire to seek God. My mom remarried shortly after the divorce and I knew immediately I would not like this new man. My childhood with him consisted of verbal, emotional, and sexual abuse. This led me to continue to seek God—on my own. I attended various Christian youth groups and churches, but never felt connected to God or to a church.

When I was twenty, I met my now ex-husband. In the beginning, he was charming and treated me like a princess; but as time went on, he became verbally, emotionally, physically, and sexually abusive. Again, I continued to seek God, but still without feeling any sense of connection. We divorced and I fell into an awful state of depression and anxiety. I was to the point where I just wanted to give up on life, but God had a better plan for me.

—*Candice*
(To Be Continued in Tomorrow's Reading)

Today's Takeaway:

It's no wonder Candice had a hard time feeling connected. She had been hurt and abused. She needed to be healed and heard but, instead, she married and was abused again. How painful! Depression and anxiety are the very real hallmarks of a person who needs healing. Thankfully, God specializes in binding up wounds and healing broken hearts. Even Humpty Dumpty has hope in His hands! I've seen the worst of cases (sometimes I've felt like the worst of cases) and nothing has EVER been too hard for our God to handle. Keep reading tomorrow and see what God does for Candice.

Until then, know that there is never anything too hard in your life for God to help you through. It may seem impossible right now because you're in the middle of it, but God says, "I am the Lord, the God of all flesh. Is there anything too hard for me?" (Jeremiah 32:27 NKJV). NO! There is nothing too hard for our Lord. You can trust Him with your situation.

Day 27

Today's Scripture:

"But he was wounded for our transgressions, he was bruised for our iniquities: the chastisement of our peace was upon him; and with his stripes we are healed"
(Isaiah 53:5 KJV).

Today's Testimony *(Continued From Previous Day)*:

After my divorce and sinking into depression, I met a friend who told me the only way to get my life on track was to get back to God. To be honest, I didn't want to hear it. I had been seeking God, on and off, my whole life and felt like He was never there. Finally, though, a year later I made the decision to give God one last chance, so I started attending church again. Within months I gave my life to Christ and was baptized. All the past finally started healing.

Although I had given my life to Christ, I still made mistakes. However, even with the mistakes, my life was finally changing. I signed up for a mission trip. This was not what I wanted, but I believed it was what God was asking me to do. But just two months before my trip, I was told I had HPV 16 and it was precancerous. I had to have surgery to remove the precancerous cells. I was scared, but God told me not to worry because He would heal me so I could go on the mission trip. God was true to His word. My doctor was amazed when he did the surgery because there were only a couple precancerous cells and he was able to remove them all. He said he had never seen anything like it.

Five months later, I had my annual doctor appointment and once again my doctor was amazed. Not only were all the precancerous cells gone, my body was fully healed—as if there was never even a surgery. God fully delivered me—from everything.

—*Candice*

Today's Takeaway:

Through divorce, abuse, depression, anxiety, HPV/pre-cancer—God brought Candice out and delivered her, because He had a plan for her life that was drastically different from the enemy's plan. There is nothing too big to take to our God. The Scripture says in 1 John 4:4, "Greater is He [our God] that is in you, than he [the enemy] that is in the world" (KJV). Our God is greater. Just remember today, your God is greater than all of your problems put together—sickness, financial, family issues, lost loved ones, job problems, depression (anything you can name)—He can handle it. Trust Him. Give it to Him in prayer. Tell Him everything.

Day 28

Today's Scripture:

"My flesh and my heart may fail, but God is the strength of my heart and my portion forever" (Psalm 73:26 NASB).

Today's Scripture:

At twenty years old, my husband and I had just transitioned into a new church, and the music director chose to step down. I had sung with my family for years, but had never led. I was asked to step into the position while trying to find someone to fill the role. I remember all the Sundays that I burst into tears as soon as I walked out of the church because I had no idea what I was doing. I was uncomfortable because we, honestly, were not very good, and none of that was enjoyable in the least. Long story short, I remained in that role for ten years.

At the end of that time, we felt God was leading us in a new direction and in a new state across the country. I was pregnant at the time. The good thing was they had a fully staffed worship team . . . emphasis on "had." Not long after my family and I joined the staff, two of the worship leaders also felt the call of God to move in another direction. I had plans to sit to the side, tend to my children, and worship from afar. But that's not what God had for me. Instead, there was a need that I willingly, though anxiously, walked into. From that willingness, my calling was revealed. When I was a young girl, my dad wanted me to sing in church, but I didn't want to. There was too much pressure. It was safer just to sit back. My dad saw through that, and just like any good dad, he made me do it anyway. Sometimes it went great, and I was on cloud nine. Sometimes it went terribly, and I vowed to never step foot on stage again. Nevertheless, every time, I grew. I learned something.

It was the same for me with God. "No thanks, Lord, I'm good right here in the safe zone. Yeah, nothing amazing will come from it, but nothing terrible will either." But when God opened the door and asked me, there was no refusing the loving God that only has plans for my good. When I think back on what would have happened if I said no, my heart aches. I encourage you today. Stop looking for the perfect path. Stop looking for the safest route. Instead, look for the need. Don't be afraid to step (*or fall*) into new things. God may see something that you don't.

—*Whitney*

Today's Takeaway:

It's so hard to be brave, isn't it? When God asks us to do something new, it may seem scary. I've been there, have you? Are you there now? Is He talking to you about doing something that you are struggling with? Keep in mind, He never asks you to do anything that He doesn't first equip you to do. You have the gifts and talents in place to do whatever He has asked of you. There's a great reward for obedience. Go ahead, girl, be brave!

Day 29

Today's Scripture:

"As far as the east is from the west, so far has He removed
our transgressions from us" (Psalm 103:12 NKJV).

Today's Testimony:

As a child, I felt like church was nothing special. As a teenager, I felt pressured to accept and submit to God, but I felt out of place in church. I felt as if I was different, like I was the only one that couldn't make sense of the lessons in the Bible, of the restrictions, the condemnation of religion, or the faith that people had to accept something they couldn't see. I felt angry, hopeless, and unworthy.

The enemy told me that I was nothing more than the total of all my sins, and that I couldn't be good enough for God's love. The enemy convinced me that some sins can never be forgiven. Over the years, that pain developed into rebellion, and I pushed away any mention of God. My heart was a constant battlefield between the part of me that was reaching for God and wanting to change, and the part that hid in the darkness afraid that I couldn't.

Broken and defeated, I finally reached out to God, surrendering everything. I prayed, "Lord, I'm afraid; I'm so broken and I have done terrible things. I'm afraid You won't love me." For the first time in my life, I felt a roar inside me, as God answered with, "My child, nothing you have done have I not known." Then He gave me the scripture from Psalm 103:12 that says, "As far as the east is from the west, so far has He removed our transgressions from us." For the first time ever, I decided to *live* for Christ. God gave me the wisdom to understand the things I could not before, and the grace I needed to push the enemy out of all areas of my life.

I have now been given the opportunity to serve the Lord by helping guide children through their spiritual journeys. God revealed to me that we need a revival that starts in our churches, and it can begin with children. Luke 18:17 says, "Truly, I say to you, whoever does not receive the kingdom of God like a child shall not enter it" (ESV). So here I am, being used by God in ways I never dreamed!

—Ariella

Today's Takeaway:

Talk about God choosing specific people to serve. Ariella started out as a child in church that just could not make a connection to receive; and now, not only has she received but is called by God to help other children connect with Him. Wow! I love that! I love the fact that when she surrendered all to the Lord, she allowed Him to "open her up" and begin such a great work in her that she began to see things she couldn't before and take responsibility for herself and her actions. Oh God! Help us all to open ourselves up like that to You everyday so that we can see past what we think we know to begin to think more like You.

Day 30

Today's Scripture:

"All praise to God, the Father of our Lord Jesus Christ. God is our merciful Father and the source of all comfort. He comforts us in all our troubles so that we can comfort others. When they are troubled, we will be able to give them the same comfort God has given us" (2 Corinthians 1:3-4 NLT).

Today's Testimony:

If you had known me as a child, you would've probably thought I was a very happy girl who was friendly and smiled all the time. I was affectionate and loving, but my outward appearance was different from the feelings and emotions that were going on inside. I had learned at a very young age how to mask all the pain, sadness, and hurt inside. Making people happy brought great satisfaction to my soul; therefore, I had to keep up my smiling happy appearance.

The two people I loved most in the world divorced when I was around six years old. I felt as though I was living in two different worlds from that point on. I was with my mom most of the time, and I would visit my dad on Wednesdays and every other weekend. My mom eventually married again to a wonderful man who became my step-dad. What I didn't know at the time was that the Lord had given me such a special gift to have two dads in my life—He knew that I needed them both. My dad began dating other women—some I liked and some I couldn't stand, but I gladly wore my content and happy mask.

I would visit my mom's parents quite often in those same years. I loved going to see them. They lived at the lake, and they owned a restaurant that had a gas station, hotel, bait and tackle shop, and storage sheds. I enjoyed my time on the lake. I loved to swim, water-ski, fish, and ride in the boat. I was definitely a water girl. What no one knew, though, was that at this same time I was being molested by multiple people, multiple times over several years. I was very good at hiding the pain I felt inside.

—Kami
(To Be Continued in Tomorrow's Reading)

Today's Takeaway:

It's hard to imagine—Kami's pretty, seemingly, happy face, being repeatedly abused in such a savage way. Tears sting my eyes as I write this; I want to get in a time-machine and go back to snatch her away before it can happen. She's so very wonderful, and I want to horse-whip every last abuser. Don't worry, dear sister, God sees and knows *all* things. He causes people to give an account for things they think they got away with. As for Kami, and everyone else like her who has suffered, there is a heavenly Father who is able to wipe away all pain and give strength to forgive the abusers. He is even a big enough God to dull memories into distant smudges in our mind's eye. Read on, tomorrow, and heal.

Day 31

Today's Scripture:

"Even when I walk through the darkest valley, I will not be afraid, for you are close beside me. Your rod and your staff protect and comfort me" (Psalm 23:4 NLT).

Today's Testimony *(Continued From Previous Day):*

Like I said, I was good at hiding pain. Being molested by multiple people for years caused me to just finally learn to mask and smile.

My dad's parents were always grounded in the church and loved the Lord with all their hearts. I would go see them every Wednesday and every other weekend when I would be with my dad. They always made sure I was in church every time the doors were open, and I was with them. Every Saturday night we would go to the living room and kneel down and pray. Mostly I would listen to them. Their prayers brought comfort to me; however, I cherish them much more now than I did back then.

One Sunday morning, as we were in church, there was a visiting evangelist who gave the invitation for those who wanted to accept Jesus into their hearts. I began to cry and feel the Lord tugging on my heart. I went down and knelt before Him and asked for His forgiveness, asked Him into my heart. I gave myself completely to Him. That day began a lifelong relationship. He became my Savior, my healer, my counselor, and loving Father. From that day forward, He began tearing down the brick wall that surrounded my heart. He showed me how to forgive those who had hurt me. He showed me how to open my heart to others and begin trusting them with everything I had held inside. He even showed me how to reach outside of my comfort zone and extend the love of Jesus Christ to others who were hurting and didn't know Him.

God has never left me, He's never forsaken me. He's always been there in my past, in my present, and in my future. He always had a plan for my life, and I'm grateful that He took everything the devil meant for my destruction and turned it around for His glory. My heart is completely open to Him forevermore.

—*Kami*

Today's Takeaway:

Thank God for the drawing power of His wonderful Holy Spirit that drew Kami to the altar to finally get His help. She surrendered her heart and let Him begin the work of healing all the pain and hurt she had inside.

There's no easy path for this. It's not a quick fix for years of suffering, so don't get discouraged if you can't feel complete healing or victory over your situation in one trip to the altar. These are things that you and the Father work through together, and if He brings a counselor or trusted leader into the mix, great. Follow the Word, give it to Him, and forgive. Kami forgave and God did something *wonderful* in her life—He's not finished with her yet, or with you.

Day 32

Today's Scriptures:

"Remember them which have the rule over you, who have spoken unto you the word of God: whose faith follow, considering the end of their conversation" (Hebrews 13:7 KJV).

"Come and see the works of God" (Psalm 66:5 KJV).

Today's Testimony:

When I was eleven, I was invited to my friend's birthday party. At the party I met a new friend and she asked me if I went to church. I told her that I did not. I explained that we used to go but we were not going at the time. She invited me to attend her church. I told her I would go wherever she went because I liked her.

My birthday friend's family began taking me to church with them. Very soon my entire family started attending. The pastor ministered and delivered a message of salvation. I gave my life to Christ in that little church. I loved going to church and I knew this was real. My salvation was followed shortly by my water baptism.

What great examples I had in my Christian walk. We began attending every Sunday morning, Sunday evening, and Wednesday night. My family was incredibly involved in the church over the years. We were active in Sunday school, youth group, singing, fellowship meetings, and I attended church camp every year. I loved it all. Jesus was and is real to me.

—*Barb*

Today's Takeaway:

How absolutely wonderful this story is to me! The responsibility of every Christian is found in Matthew 28:19, which says to "go . . . and make disciples of all the nations, baptizing them in the name of the Father and of the Son and of the Holy Spirit" (NKJV). When Barb was only eleven, she met a young Christian who was doing just that—making disciples. Because of her "birthday friend," Barb's entire family got in church.

I sit here right now, saved and ready for Heaven because someone invited my family to church—over and over until we came. Look out for the Lord to put a "birthday friend" in your path today—someone you can talk to about what the Lord is doing in your life, at your church, et cetera. See what happens. You never know, what you say or do may change the lives of an entire generation!

Day 33

Today's Scripture:

"But those who hope in the Lord will renew their strength. They will soar on wings like eagles; they will run and not grow weary, they will walk and not be faint" (Isaiah 40:31 NIV).

Today's Testimony:

As an infant, I was poisoned by carbon monoxide, due to the floor of a car rotting out from rust and gas seeping in. My parents didn't seem to realize I was sick or take any action to help me. It soon became apparent to relatives that my biological parents were mentally unstable and unfit to be parents, due to severe neglect and drug usage. Child Protective Services were called and my two older brothers and I were taken away. My eldest brother was adopted by our grandparents. Due to lack of room, my other brother and I were placed in a foster home.

I grew up to age four in the foster home with my brother. We were starved, abused, and neglected by our foster parents. I often ate dog food or raw potatoes to satisfy my constant hunger pains. The house we lived in was in ruins and falling apart. One night a thunderstorm blew the roof in and it collapsed on my brother. I saw his arm reaching out of the rubble. I ran over and began tearing the rubble off of him. I saw his face and he was breathing—he was alive. The Lord had protected him.

There was a godly couple who had been unable to have children. They were led by the Lord to look at foster homes. When they saw how malnourished and neglected we were, their hearts broke and they were moved to adopt us both. I was adopted at age four and my brother at age five. I started going to church and learning about God. I accepted Jesus into my heart when I realized I needed salvation from my sins. As I grew older, I realized that the Lord was the One keeping an eye on us in the foster home. He kept us safe and protected us from harm. He led my (adoptive) parents to snatch us out of that environment and to raise us right. He also later led me to find my biological parents and long-lost brother to fill in the missing gaps of our story. And that's how the Lord delivered me and saved me.

—*Leah*

Today's Takeaway:

I'll be completely transparent. This wrecked me. I had to walk away and get some air before I could finish typing. I had to stop and pray before I could write this, and now I can barely see through tears. I prayed and asked God to forgive me when I think my life is so hard, when I complain, when I'm selfish; and I asked Him to help me look around and see when people have needs that I can fulfill. My heart is broken to think about their suffering, but then I think about what God did: He lifted them out! That's what He does. He's our Savior!

Day 34

Today's Scripture:

"But be doers of the word, and not hearers only, deceiving yourselves"
(James 1:22 NKJV).

Today's Testimony:

Looking back on my life, I can give witness to the marvelous things God has done for me. I didn't grow up knowing the Lord. I didn't give my life to Christ until my late twenties. Did life change overnight? Unfortunately, it didn't. What it did for me was give me a glimmer of hope. I saw that beacon of light that my life could be better.

I would look at other women who possessed the aspects of the fruit of the Spirit and I wanted those in my life too. I asked and begged God for them, but I didn't see anything happen; life just seemed hard. Was that what it was supposed to be like? Then I heard a passage from James 1:22-25 that talked about being doers of the Word and not hearers only. That was when I changed. I started actually "doing" what God's Word said. If He said to have no anxious thoughts but give everything to prayer and petition to God, then I did that. I would give no place to the devil to allow anxious thoughts to keep manifesting.

As soon as the enemy would put a thought in my head, I would put it against God's Word and ask if it lined up with it and be a witness in my Spirit. If it didn't, I knew it was from the enemy. I had to immediately put it out of my mind and out of my thoughts. I choose to think on things that are lovely, pure, and of good report because God's Word says to do it.

My relationship with the Lord has been a continual work in progress. I am thankful that as I learn to deal with patterns, habits, and thoughts of my own past, He continually renews my mind and makes it new in Christ. My hope and prayer are to strive to be more like Jesus each and every day. He says in His Word to pray without ceasing. If every believer chose to grow so close to the Lord that their life radiated Jesus out of them . . . what a great world it would be to live in.

—Amy

Today's Takeaway:

Amy has discovered a *huge* truth from the Word of God, and because of it she is living a life of victory. First, we need to *hear* the Word; next, we need to *do* the Word. We apply it to every area of our lives to see how we should live. It will cause us to repent sometimes—change our words, attitudes, and thoughts. It will bless others and us. A doer acts and is blessed!

Day 35

Today's Scripture:

"He gives power to the faint, and strengthens the powerless. Even youths will faint and be weary, and the young will fall exhausted; but those who wait for the Lord shall renew their strength, they shall mount up with wings like eagles, they shall run and not be weary, they shall walk and not faint" (Isaiah 40:29-31 NRSV).

Today's Testimony:

I have been raised in church my whole life. As a matter of fact, my family pastored my church most of my life. I remember as a little girl going to church every Sunday and Wednesday. I remember prayer meetings and tent revivals that went *way* past my bedtime. At almost every service we were given an opportunity to accept Jesus as our Savior. I even remember saying "the sinner's prayer" with my church family, what seems like, a million times, but not really knowing or understanding what it meant. Then, one Sunday morning when I was six years old, I was eating my breakfast while watching one of my mom's favorite televangelists. The rest of my family was getting ready for church, so it was just me and the TV. I can't exactly remember what the minister preached that morning, but I do remember feeling like my heart was going to jump out of my pretty, little red dress if I didn't pray with him. From then on, my life was different. I knew I wasn't like everyone else. Later, at a church prayer meeting where we were all praying God would prepare our hearts for the tent revival the next week, I was baptized with the Holy Spirit at age nine.

There were two women who were truly my heroes in faith that prayed with me at that altar until I encountered God personally; it was life-changing. Since then, my whole life has been in ministry. I've taught every class, and scrubbed every toilet. And what I have learned is, God is always there. I've been exhausted physically, mentally, and spiritually. I have, at times, felt completely alone in this world. There have been times when I begged God to just let me not care anymore. But, I have always been reminded to wait on the Lord. When I am weak, He is much stronger. When I am tired, He will carry me. It is God alone who renews my strength.

—*Bekah*

Today's Takeaway:

Oh, how I love this testimony because Bekah was trained by godly women, including her mother, like the Scripture teaches us in Titus 2 which says the older women teach the younger women to live in a way that honors God (see vv. 3-5). Bekah's life does that. She is now a pastor's wife. God knew she would serve the Lord in that way, and her life is spent serving Him and His people.

Now look around, Are you older? Look for young women to teach. Are you younger? Look for older women to learn from.

Day 36

Today's Scripture:

"He comforts us in all our troubles so that we can comfort others. When they are troubled, we will be able to give them the same comfort God has given us"
(2 Corinthians 1:4 NLT).

Today's Testimony:

I began attending church when I was nine years old. My husband's grandfather was the pastor at that time. I started attending Sunday school with my next-door neighbor. Then, when I was ten years old, my brother was involved in an automobile accident and was killed. The pastor and his wife came to our house and ministered to us with such love and compassion, and even agreed to do the service for my brother. My parents were so impressed by the love the pastor showed during such a difficult time that it won my family to the church.

It wasn't long afterward that my mom rededicated her life to the Lord, and went on to become my inspiration to serve the Lord as well. And at eleven years old, I too accepted the Lord into my heart.

I remember that event so vividly because the Lord allowed me to see my brother walking with Jesus, which was such a comfort to me.

That same year I went to our church camp meeting in our state. I met the man who would become my husband there. Years later, my pastor performed the marriage ceremony for us.

We attended, and worked in church until my husband was called into the ministry. We began to evangelize for about two years, and then began a church. After seven successful years we transferred to another church, and have been pastoring there for the last forty-three years. God has truly blessed us—from pastors, to missions, to worship leaders—our entire family is serving the Lord today.

—Joyce

Today's Takeaway:

When tragedy strikes, there is never a better time to show the love of Jesus than at that moment. Joyce's family experienced pain on a level that I hope most of the world can be spared—losing a child. Speaking from experience, when you're in the dark place of grief and you feel the comforting touch of kindness and support around you—you never forget it. I'm talking about supplying basic needs like food, offering prayer, or just being present. This pastor and his church were there for Joyce's family and because of that, it changed their life.

When someone is hurting, offer help. This fulfills the Word of God, which says weep with those who mourn (Romans 12:15). Let's show we care and lighten someone's load of pain. God blesses those who care.

Day 37

Today's Scripture:

"Blessed is the man who walks not in the counsel of the ungodly, nor stands in the path of sinners, nor sits in the seat of the scornful; but his delight is in the law of the Lord, and in His law he meditates day and night. He shall be like a tree planted by the rivers of water, that brings forth its fruit in its season, whose leaf also shall not wither; and whatever he does shall prosper" (Psalm 1:1-3 NKJV).

Today's Testimony:

I believe God didn't save me *from*, but saved me *to* something. I was raised in church. Our family not only attended regularly, but church was the center of our lives. My parents held to the verse in Proverbs 22:6 that says, "Train up a child in the way he [she] should go, and when he is old he will not depart from it" (NKJV). I have always related it to planting a young tree as in Psalm 1, which is planted by rivers of water.

As I grew up, Sunday school teachers, pastors' wives, church leaders, and families were my heroes and the people that I idolized and wanted to grow up to be like. But at the age of eleven in a Vacation Bible School altar time, it all became real and personal to me. I remember kneeling in the altar area. I raised my hand that I wanted to be saved and repeated the simple sinner's prayer the VBS director led us in. I am sure I had done this before, but this time it was different.

At that age I hadn't done too much to be "saved" from; perhaps my worst offenses were a quick temper and watching too much TV. But it was clear that after that prayer I began to think and ask questions about how to live as a Christian. I had a genuine conversion and became a "tree planted by the rivers of water." I began to try and be more like Jesus. I remember asking my mother, "If I am really saved, I should act differently, right?"

I have always been known for my stubbornness, and I believe that has helped me to stay "planted" in my faith. My testimony may seem simple, but salvation is simple. Salvation is not about the bad I have done but what God has done for me - the work of the Cross. It's been over forty years since I prayed to be saved; I certainly have not been perfect and life has not always been easy, but I did choose to stay in church and work for Him.

I did grow up to be like those church leaders, Sunday dchool teachers, VBS directors, and especially the pastors' wives. In fact, I am currently the pastor's wife of the church where I was saved.

—Debbie

Today's Takeaway:

Let this be an encouragement to those working in church and raising children; you *can* be a godly influence and role model to those where you minister. It's definitely easier to plant a young tree than a fully grown tree. Because Debbie was in that nurturing atmosphere seeing all those leaders, she wanted to be like them even as a young girl. I'm so thankful for God's saving power and God's keeping power. God is *faithful*!

Day 38

Today's Scripture:

"And surely I am with you always, to the very end of the age" (Matthew 28:20b NIV).

Today's Testimony:

I began a relationship with God at about seven years of age. I went to Catholic school and was taught about God the Father, Jesus His Son, the Holy Spirit as Comforter, Jesus' mother (Mary), saints, angels, and prophets. There were times as a child that I prayed because of family situations. I would pray, "God, Jesus, Holy Ghost, Mary, Joseph, guardian angels . . . help."

Through the years I have felt confident in calling out to God for help. From the day I got my driver's license and He kept me safe from hitting a child that ran out in front of me in the road, to the day God was with us when our own son was hit by a car and given zero chance to recover. He suffers from total brain injury. Many years later we still take care of him—God is with us. We called on Him when our youngest son was a marine and in danger of being shot, bullets whizzing by his head—God was there. When I got sick from a diseased gallbladder and it resulted in pancreatitis and an eight-week hospital stay—God was with us. When a saw blade broke and hit my husband's neck only two centimeters from his major artery—God was with us. He never leaves us.

I am far from perfect, but I am forgiven and grateful to be His child. When I get hurried and want things to happen, I remind myself: "His will, His way, His time." Our job is to pray and fast, praise and worship, love and forgive, stand strong, resist fear, and follow Jesus' example. I give Him all the glory and honor. I thank Him each day for every breath.

—*Kathleen*

Today's Takeaway:

Kathleen reminds me of going to visit my grandmother. How about you? I love her. She is filled with wisdom and love. The one thing she said that sticks out the most to me is "God is with us!" The Bible says *Emmanuel* means that very thing. If one of the names of our God actually means that He is with us, He *must* want us to remember it.

When we go through things we don't understand, tough things where maybe there's no easy answer, God is with us. Sometimes, just knowing that God is listening when we tell Him all about the problem we're facing is enough. The good thing is, not only is He listening but He works on our behalf. Christian maturity helps us reach a place where even if His answer to our problem is not what we wanted, we can still trust Him that He knows what He's doing. That's hard, isn't it? I sometimes think I have a good plan for how it should all be worked out. The truth is, God has a great plan, not just a good plan. Sometimes we need to let go of our bologna sandwich long enough for Him to replace it with a steak dinner. His plans are always better than ours!

Day 39

Today's Scripture:

"Bless the Lord, Oh my soul, and forget not all His benefits: . . . who redeems your life from destruction, who crowns you with lovingkindness and tender mercies"
(Psalm 103:2, 4 NKJV).

Today's Testimony:

My testimony is that of a God who saves to the uttermost, heals broken hearts and broken lives, transforms minds and redeems lives from destruction.

I grew up in a faith-filled home and my heart was attracted to the light of Christ at a young age. When I was thirteen years old, I got filled with the Holy Spirit at youth camp. I left camp having experienced God so intimately that it would leave a mark on my heart for the rest of my life. From that moment on, I knew without a shadow of a doubt that God was real.

After high school, I made new friends who introduced me to the party life. First Corinthians 15:33 says, "Do not be deceived: 'Bad company corrupts good character'" (NIV). I have heard it said that sin will take us further than we want to go, and for me, that was true. I remember being so convicted that I told the Holy Spirit to leave me alone. I wanted to have fun while I was young, but I knew I would one day come back to Jesus. In doing so, I took the grace of God for granted. My life quickly became a downward spiral into darkness as I pursued drinking and sexual promiscuity. I lived four years apart from Christ, seeking my own selfish ambitions, but it felt like decades because of heartache.

I became so blinded by sin that I found myself involved with a man who was mentally and physically abusive. He would pull me on the floor by my hair and back me against the wall so he could punch me on the sides of my head. One day, the abuse was very bad and he was swinging a metal pole at me. He grabbed my arms and forced me into my own car. While driving, he told me to look in the backseat, to which I saw a rope and duct tape. He said he was going to tape me to a tree and leave me to hang there.

—Dawn
(To Be Continued in Tomorrow's Reading)

Today's Takeaway:

Scary, right? Absolutely! Thankfully, even though Dawn had contemptuously told the Holy Spirit to leave her alone, He never leaves us! God was there. It's sad, isn't it, when her heart was so moved to serve the Lord at a younger age. But God doesn't turn His back on us because we make bad decisions; He continues to deal with our hearts, giving us opportunities to turn to Him, waiting for us to cry out to Him in surrender. Whatever you need, He is able. Don't wait! Cry out to Him today—for you or a friend.

Day 40

Today's Scripture:

*"But in my distress I cried out to the Lord; yes, I prayed to my God for help.
He heard me from his sanctuary; my cry to him reached his ears"*
(Psalm 18:6 NLT).

Today's Testimony *(Continued From Previous Day):*

Having been forced into my own car, now being driven somewhere to apparently be taped to a tree and left, I went into survival mode. I looked for street signs so that I'd be able to find my way home. I remember trying to strategize how I might be able to escape. I didn't once consider that hell would be waiting for me if this man really wanted to take my life. He dragged me into high grass and raised the metal pole to hit me. Something within me cried out to God. I'm so amazed; it wasn't my thought to ask God to save me. In God's great love, He showed up when I wasn't even looking for Him. The next thing I saw were the red tail lights on my car as he drove away. It was 3:00 in the morning; I walked home in the dark and talked to the Lord all night long. I found peace and rededicated my life to Jesus.

My hardships were far from over with this man; he came back and would not leave my house. He was abusive mentally, physically, and sexually. For hours, I would hide out in a room by myself, reading and praying every promise from my old teen study Bible. For the first time in a long time, I noticed myself smiling so hard that my cheeks hurt. Jesus was healing my deep wounds and shame.

I read in Matthew 6:14 that we are to forgive so we too could be forgiven. I knew I needed to forgive that man, but I didn't know how to do that while I was still stuck in the chaos of abuse. One day as I was held against the wall, I felt an overwhelming and resounding urge to tell him that I forgave him. When I said the words "I forgive you" out loud, he hit me faster and harder. Then a look of confusion came across his face and he just walked away. I know now that voice I heard urging me to forgive him was the voice of the Holy Spirit.

During that time, my mother was a missionary in Ethiopia, Africa. Her trip was cut short and she was headed home to stay with me. My mother was not afraid of this man and immediately got help from the authorities. I look back and realize this was God's practical way of saving me from my situation. All glory and honor belongs to Jesus Christ, who redeems my life from destruction.

—Dawn

Today's Takeaway:

Forgiveness is hard, and I can't tell you that it will come easy when it's your turn to do what Dawn had to do. I don't think she could have done what she did in her own strength. That was a God-move! I'm so thankful for a God who brought her mother to do what she could not find within herself to do—get help. Thank God for mothers who operate in wisdom.

Day 41

Today's Scripture:

"And my God shall supply all your need according to His riches in glory by Christ Jesus"
(Philippians 4:19 NKJV).

Today's Testimony:

I have been saved since I was thirteen years old. God has provided so many wonderful things in my life and brought me through many trials.

I was blessed with the Christian husband I prayed for at age thirty-five. When we were ready to start a family, the doctor told us we would not have children due to my age. About four months later, my brother-in-law, who is a pastor, felt led by the Lord to pray for my husband and me. Within thirty days, I found out I was pregnant. Unfortunately, two days later my husband was laid off from his job. I had my daughter at age thirty-eight, and while my husband wound up unemployed for two years, God always provided everything we needed.

Due to his layoff, my husband was able to take care of my daughter for nine months and they have such a special bond from that time together. Just about the time we were getting low on funds, God provided a good job for him. He has been unemployed four times during our relationship, and each time God has provided a better job and taken care of all of our needs. God also blessed us with a second pregnancy and my son was born when I turned forty.

I'm thankful also for the beautiful home and great school district God has given us in which to raise our children. He has also recently fulfilled my dream of being a stay-at-home mom. This timely blessing also allowed me to be available to help my children with virtual schooling due to the Covid-19 pandemic.

I have learned through the years to remain faithful to the Lord and that everything happens in God's timing. God cares about us; He wants to provide for us. He is able to see us through anything—even providing the much coveted and hoarded toilet paper during a pandemic.

—Angie

Today's Takeaway:

I love how positive Angie is in her testimony. We sometimes tend to focus on what we don't have when we don't get it, right? She prayed, like Joseph did, for answers. Some of those did not come for literally years. Her husband that she prayed for didn't come until she was thirty-five! She and her husband prayed for a family and that was delayed as well. Thankfully, this prayer was answered pretty soon, only to be followed by another trial.

That's how life is, isn't it? We walk up mountains and then in valleys. Let us learn to "count it all joy" and be positive, carrying our needs to the Lord. He cares and loves us so much that He provides all that we truly need in His good timing.

Day 42

Today's Scripture:

"For God so loved the world that he gave his one and only Son, that whoever believes in him shall not perish but have eternal life" (John 3:16 NIV).

Today's Testimony:

When I was a child, I accepted Jesus Christ as my Lord and Savior. As I grew into my teenage and young adult years, I walked away from Him. I started doing things that I knew were not pleasing to God, such as cursing, smoking, drinking, and even having unmarried sex. I felt conviction from the Holy Spirit about what I was doing, but I ignored it for a long time.

Later I got married, and immediately we started having marital issues because neither one of us was truly serving God. My husband still loved drinking while I had my own struggles, but eventually, I decided to give my life back to the Lord. I asked God to forgive me for walking away and sinning against Him. I gave up all the sins I had been doing, yet my marriage continued to fall apart. I continued to pray, asking God to help me to grow in Him. My husband, on the other hand, decided it was not for him and we eventually went through a divorce.

I went through a depression for a long time, but God never left me. He put a very faithful, praying woman of God in my life; she was there every time I needed a friend and prayer warrior—never too busy or sick of hearing me cry or asking why. She would always pray with me and give me God's Word.

Day by day, I started growing closer to God and stronger in my faith. Since then, I have had my ups and downs—even another divorce—but somehow, God has always come through for me; He will never leave nor forsake us.

I have had many close calls in my life with heart issues and other sickness, yet God has continued to spare my life. I know God has a reason for why I am still alive—He has work for me to do. I am not perfect by far, but I am forgiven. My desire is to live for God and do His will, not my will.

I have come a long way. I've made many mistakes, but I serve a forgiving God, a loving God, and an all-powerful God. If you fail, ask for God's forgiveness and move forward. Through all the ups and downs, God knows my heart and my desires. He continues to bless me as I grow in my walk with God.

—*Jackie*

Today's Takeaway:

I love Jackie's honesty. She confesses her imperfections, and still she continues to strive to give her all to Christ. He does know her heart, as He does ours. That's all that matters. Let us give all of our inadequacies to Him. He forgives and teaches us to be more pleasing to Him with each passing day.

Day 43

Today's Scripture:

"She [Hagar] gave this name to the Lord who spoke to her: 'You are the God who sees me,' for she said, 'I have now seen the One who sees me'" (Genesis 16:13 NIV).

Today's Testimony:

I was in my late thirties and single. I loved my career; I made good money. I was happy with life. However, I was a heavy drinker, smoker, and recreational drug user. Then I found out I was pregnant. I was in such a state of denial; I had been on birth control pills since the age of fourteen; I took thirteen pregnancy tests because I was sure there was something wrong with each one.

My knowledge of God, at that time, was that He was to be feared, blamed for anything bad, and called on when I was driving drunk, or asked for help coming down from a bad high. My childhood hadn't been easy; I have Tourette's syndrome and my father didn't cope with it well. By the time I was ten, I knew I never wanted to be married or have children—being an aunt was perfect for me.

Two weeks after confirmation that I was pregnant, I had an appointment at Planned Parenthood to have an abortion. I felt no guilt or shame as I walked past the few protesters for my initial consultation. I didn't tell the father, my family, or my friends that I was pregnant. I thought so little of what I was about to do; to me, it was just a matter of a procedure, rest, and back to work.

The evening before my appointment, I was balancing my checkbook when, all of a sudden, God's presence filled the room. I will never forget the voice which told me, "If you have this child, I will take care of you." Terrified, I called my sister, told her I was pregnant and planning to have an abortion, but that I was now scared: if this voice told me not to have the abortion and I did it anyway, what would happen? She told me it was God hitting me over the head because *that* was probably the only way I would listen. I didn't show up for my appointment at Planned Parenthood, but it wasn't because I had a change of heart and wanted a baby. I was just afraid *not* to have the baby. I had a miserable pregnancy, but miraculously my daughter was born in perfect health.

I had a long journey of constant questions about God and the Bible, but thankfully I accepted Christ as my Savior. I was shown such love and patience by my church and pastors. There was a void in my life for many years that I never knew existed. I thank God every day that He gave me a chance, and I see so many times in my life where He was intervening for me without my knowing it.

—*Elaine*

Today's Takeaway:

God is so patient; I am sometimes shocked by it. Are you? But then I read about the children of Israel who failed time and time again, then I look at my own failures and I think, that's who He is. I want to be like Him, do you? *Help us, Lord.*

Day 44

Today's Scripture:

"The Lord is not slow to fulfill his promise as some count slowness, but is patient toward you, not wishing that any should perish, but that all should reach repentance"
(2 Peter 3:9 ESV).

Today's Testimony:

Have you ever thought about where you would be if you hadn't given your life to Jesus? I would probably be dead. God always had His hand on my life. I was raised in church. I can remember singing Christian songs at the top of my lungs as a toddler.

Then we moved to a new town where I began public high school and rode the bus. It was hard to fit in; so, when a cute guy began to walk me to class, I was so taken by his good looks, I was smoking with his friends between classes. Next, I started skipping classes and drinking all day. I would go back to the school, catch the bus and go home. I was one of the "cool kids," or so I thought. I got pregnant the next year, when I was sixteen. I had to tell my parents because I started to show. It didn't go so well.

One night I overheard them talking about the options. When they mentioned abortion, my boyfriend and I decided to run away to California. We got as far as Chicago and lived in the car. The police would move us on until one night we were taken to jail. That night they let everyone go except me because I was a minor. The next day my grandmother and parents came to pick me up. It was a silent ride for hours going home.

A wedding was planned and my boyfriend and I were married. Our parents were very supportive, but my husband soon got mixed up with drugs. My home became a "drug house." I delivered a beautiful baby boy alone because my husband was too busy celebrating becoming a dad. He began to abuse me sexually, mentally, physically, and emotionally; he began to cheat on me. He was in and out of jail. I would leave him and then go back to him. It was a roller coaster, but after four years and another child, I decided to get a divorce. An opportunity came to move and I grabbed at the chance for a new beginning.

One night I turned on the TV, but nothing was on except someone singing, and I began to listen; it was a Billy Graham Crusade. I started to cry and, right there sitting on my floor, I gave my life to Jesus Christ. Soon after, I met a man at my friend's house and after a while he asked me out. One year later we were married. We have been married forty-three years. God has blessed me.

—*Connie*

Today's Takeaway:

God specializes in new beginnings. If you think He only likes "perfect people," take a look at the Bible—it's full of people who needed second, third, and fourth chances. That gives me hope! He doesn't throw people away; He waits for repentance. What a patient, loving Father.

Day 45

Today's Scripture:

"Do you see this woman? I entered your house; you gave me no water for my feet, but she has wet my feet with her tears and wiped them with her hair. . . . Therefore I tell you, her sins, which are many, are forgiven—for she loved much. But he who is forgiven little, loves little" (Luke 7:44-47 ESV).

Today's Testimony:

Going to church was always something I did. I grew up singing along to hymns and old choruses as my mom led the church into worship. I remember playing "restaurant" in the church kitchen and "preaching" sermons from the pulpit as my sister "led" on the piano. My fondest memory of my grandma was sitting in the church pew next to her and she would scratch my back. I loved her gentle touch during Sunday's sermon. I was very comfortable at church; it was like a second home to me.

As I grew into my teen years, I started questioning everything I knew and that quickly grew into rebellion. I had learned all the "don'ts" of Christianity. "We don't smoke, drink, cuss, chew, or run around with those that do," was the mantra I heard over and over in my teen years. Those words alone were not enough to keep me out of trouble. I did most of those things (don't tell my parents, they still don't know).

None of the sins of my early teens had been life-altering, but that was about to change. At the age of sixteen, I found out I was pregnant. My boyfriend and I didn't know what to do. We kept it hidden for five months until we finally decided, with encouragement from a stranger sent by God, to tell our parents. Telling my mother and seeing the reaction from my father is, to this day, the single hardest thing I have ever had to face. The disappointment in his face horrified me. I felt like I had crushed the most important person in my life. The shame I felt was almost unbearable. As I began to show, everyone at school took notice. I would walk the halls knowing what the whispers were about. Parents of friends would make rude comments. It was tough, yet I knew the life that was growing inside of me deserved the best I could offer.

—Tina
(To Be Continued in Tomorrow's Reading)

Today's Takeaway:

I remember the day, as a teenager, I was summing up what I knew about the Christian life. *Is this thing really just about a set of rules?* I thought to myself. Then as quickly as that question formed, I had my answer. *No! It's about love. Everything changes when you factor in love.* The reason many of us struggle so badly with rebellion is that we skip that part sometimes and reduce this thing to the list of "don'ts." Oh, but when you think about the fact that Jesus left Heaven to allow Himself to be born and placed in a cow-slobber-covered manger inside a stable that probably smelled of manure, views change!

Day 46

Today's Scripture:

"Do you see this woman? I entered your house; you gave me no water for my feet, but she has wet my feet with her tears and wiped them with her hair. . . . Therefore I tell you, her sins, which are many, are forgiven—for she loved much. But he who is forgiven little, loves little" (Luke 7:44-47 ESV).

Today's Testimony *(Continued From Previous Day):*

My boyfriend and I decided to get married, and not long after, our baby girl was born. Afterward, we attended church just as I had always done. This time was different though. I wanted to do better and be better for my little family. God began to show me, through my husband and my daughter, what a relationship looked like. He was showing me what love was: Not merely a list of things not to do, but putting others above yourself. Somewhere in the process of learning and growing, praise God, I was wholly committed to Jesus Christ.

I have been married to my boyfriend now for twenty-four years. We have been in ministry for twenty years—seventeen of those as lead pastors. We have been blessed with four more children. Our unplanned baby is now getting ready to be married to an ordained minister and she is actively involved in youth ministry, music ministry, and the pro-life cause.

God has been good to me. I have not earned it or deserved it, and yet, He lavished it upon me. He took a stubborn child and rebellious teenager and created a beautiful love story that began an even greater legacy. I chose the above verses because I am that woman. I am the woman that was not worthy to touch Jesus, yet He allowed me to pour my love on Him like oil upon His feet. I have been forgiven so much, so in return I love much.

—Tina

Today's Takeaway:

I applaud Tina for her determination not to end her baby's life no matter what she went through. She chose well. She put her baby first. For some mothers, that may mean giving their babies up for adoption; I understand that. Bravery comes in many forms. I'm so glad our God is the God of many second chances! He doesn't throw us away when we take a wrong step. We need only read His Word to see that—it's filled with imperfect people—thankfully for me. You too? That's OK. God knows we need His forgiveness. That's why He makes ways for us to turn our hearts back to Him.

If you find yourself needing that today, He's waiting for you. Aren't you thankful that He takes stubborn children and turns them into women of God? Me too; and by the way, so are Mary, Martha, Rahab—and I could go on and on.

Day 47

Today's Scripture:

"I can do all things through Christ who strengthens me" (Philippians 4:13 NKJV).

Today's Testimony:

My name is Crystal and I'm in my mid-thirties. I am a beautiful product of God's love, mercy, and grace; and I'm proud to be able to say that today, because I didn't always believe that.

I was born to a young mother who was addicted to drugs. She was only thirteen years old when she had me. I was born premature and sick. At the age of seven, I was sexually abused by an uncle for several years. Confused about my identity and not knowing if I liked boys or girls caused me to be sexually active at an early age.

I saw my mom get abused almost every day by my stepfather, who would also abuse me physically and emotionally. We were beaten with 4x4 wood posts, sticks, and anything else he could use. By the age of eleven, I was helping my mom's friends deal drugs. I witnessed my mom working as a prostitute, which of course, kept her in and out of jail. Before my twelfth birthday, I decided to run away to live with some friends. I took a job that paid me under the table and was homeless for several weeks for fear of going back home. Looking back, I faced way too many life-threatening experiences.

At seventeen, I had my first child and two years later welcomed my second. Five years later, at the age of twenty-four, I was given a book to read by my aunt, who had been praying for me for so long. I didn't like to read much, but I devoured that book in two days. I don't think I've ever experienced so many emotions. I told my aunt I wanted to visit her church.

—*Crystal*
(To Be Continued in Tomorrow's Reading)

Today's Takeaway:

My heart breaks to read how Crystal and her mother were so abused and battered! I can't imagine her living homeless as an eleven-year-old child and working a job to take care of herself. These things break the heart of our Lord too. He hates abuse. He wants all of His daughters to be treated with the respect and the love that He gives them. Those who don't will stand and give an account of it someday. Tomorrow you will read the rest of Crystal's story and see how God was working in her life. He was watching over her and had a plan for her—just like He has a plan for you. Things may look bleak at times, but let us never forget that our Lord is there and He is a God who takes notice and He will make all things right in His time!

Day 48

Today's Scripture:

"So if the Son sets you free, you are truly free" (John 8:36 NLT).

Today's Testimony *(Continued From Previous Day):*

My heart was so hungry after reading the book my aunt gave me. I wanted to go to her church, and then I felt led to go to the altar. I remember feeling so much shame, fear, and unworthiness to go to the front. But when I did, I met with an amazing woman of God who shared a similar testimony. She prayed over me while I wept. For more than an hour, she stayed with me, crying and praying. I made a decision that has forever changed my life. I accepted Jesus as my Lord and Savior.

If only I could truly put into words what it feels like when you accept Jesus into your life—it was the most beautiful and literally breathtaking experience of my life. At that moment, every bad experience and trauma that I carried for so long was just lifted; I could finally breathe. It was the moment Jesus breathed His breath of life into me—the moment I took my first real breath. I no longer needed to carry my past, the shame, the guilt, and the identity of the world. I am a new creation in Christ Jesus. My identity is found in Him.

After a couple of years I got married and had two more precious children. I continue my amazing journey in the Lord with my family. Through all of this, God has shown me how to love, forgive, show mercy and compassion to others even when they don't deserve it, because I know I didn't. Through this small portion of my testimony, I pray that women can know that there is hope in Jesus. There is redemption from a broken past. You can be set free and healed. All it takes is faith as small as a mustard seed. Today I have courage in knowing that no matter what I've been through or still go through in life, God has got me, and I can do all things through Him.

—Crystal

Today's Takeaway:

The things that have happened to you in the past can be redeemed and in no way have to define your future. You can be set free by the Son—and when He does that through your salvation, it is truly done! Does this mean He waves a magic wand over you and you don't have to do your part by choosing to forgive those who have caused you pain in your past? No, Jesus taught us to forgive those who have wronged us, but once you've been forgiven, it's easier to forgive others.

Crystal asked God's forgiveness, then started the process of forgiving those who had hurt her, and then she forgave herself. Don't forget the last part—the enemy likes to zero in on that one and drag it back up. Remember, you are set free.

Also, shout-out to the godly aunt who prayed for Crystal for so long! And for all the prayer warriors who are calling out names and haven't given up. Praise God! Keep going! There's a "Crystal" coming your way.

Day 49

Today's Scripture:

"We are God's masterpiece. He has created us anew in Christ Jesus, so we can do the good things he planned for us long ago" (Ephesians 2:10 NLT).

Today's Testimony:

My dad died when I was five; I blamed God and my mom and grew up angry. My mom was young in the Lord, but she took us to church and did the best she could, although she didn't understand God or His love for her. She was tough on me and it broke my spirit so much I didn't care about my life: I had no respect for her. I was in a dark place inside and out. My mom eventually got remarried; I had no respect for my stepdad either.

At age seventeen my life spiraled out of control. I moved into a house of chaos with my girlfriend from school. Her older brother and her mom smoked marijuana; that was what I saw as freedom. I dated my friend's older brother and partied at his house. I drank, took drugs, and slept with him. I walked in complete rebellion and total defiance of God. Eventually, the consequences of my decisions began to tumble in on me—I was going to get kicked out for not paying rent. I wondered where I would go. I was getting ready to go into my senior year of high school. I fell on my knees on the bathroom floor and cried out to God for help. At the end of the summer, I got my driver's license and parked my car at my parents' house.

Just before the next school year, I went on a trip to an amusement park in the state below us and I drove. I took my boyfriend, his brother, and his girlfriend who was eight months pregnant. We enjoyed the amusement park for the day and camped out that night. We headed for home the next morning. As a new inexperienced driver, I got lost. I came to a turnaround on a two-lane highway. I didn't pull up close enough to the intersection to see what was approaching; I just went. A semi-truck carrying 80,000 pounds plowed right into our car and pushed us a hundred yards into a bean field. As a result, my boyfriend died, the girl in the backseat lost her baby, and her boyfriend dealt with physical issues. I had a brain injury which took me back to a childlike existence and went through rehab for an entire year learning how to walk, talk, read, write, and function as a person. The total healing of my brain happened over a long period of years.

My spiritual healing came early in my recovery. With a childlike perception of life, my faith led me to experience God easily. He revamped my life over a period of years. He led me down a path to do some amazing things by His grace. I published a book sharing my testimony titled *A Life Redone: My Journey to a Life of Freedom*. I shared Christ with many and led them to Him. The more I plug into Him, the more I can bring Him glory.

—*Laura*

Today's Takeaway:

Thank You, God, for turning a tragedy into a testimony!

Day 50

Today's Scripture:

"And the Lord, He is the One who goes before you. He will be with you, He will not leave you nor forsake you; do not fear nor be dismayed" (Deuteronomy 31:8 NKJV).

Today's Testimony:

Everyone feels lonely sometimes, maybe like you just don't fit in with the crowd. That was me—especially in a large group or even with my family during holidays or special gatherings. Growing up and all through school, I was pretty much the kid that was off by themselves. I was the one that was bullied, teased, and put down because I didn't drink, smoke, do drugs, or wear things like the fashionable miniskirts that some of the other girls wore.

I was raised in church. I don't remember my exact age, but I remember it was in my preteen years. One day I was in church, and I felt something tug at me during the altar call—it was the convicting power of the Holy Spirit. I finally went forward and received the Lord Jesus Christ as my Savior.

After I got saved, the emptiness and loneliness went away. I found I could be comfortable in a large group and even around my family. I suddenly began realizing and feeling that I was not alone even if I felt like I was. The Lord God was with me all the time. I understood then that Jesus had His times of feeling alone and betrayed. He looked to His Father and knew His Father was there for Him. Today we have the Holy Spirit with us; we are not alone. It was just totally amazing how that lonely feeling disappeared after I accepted Jesus as my Savior.

God is faithful; no matter how you feel, no matter if everyone leaves you, no matter how alone you are, He is there. He loves you more than you could ever possibly know or comprehend. It may seem like a Christian cliché, but it's true that your relationship with God can fulfill all of your needs. Seek Him and you will personally experience His love for you.

—Betty

Today's Takeaway:

One of the greatest comforts of all as a Christian is the fact we are never alone. Never. No matter what we face from the time we get saved forward, *He is with us.* Things always feel better when someone is with us, don't they? For one thing, we can talk to them about it. Don't you love that? You may think I'm crazy, but I talk to the Lord about everything that comes up—if I'm happy about it, I talk to Him; if I miss the mark, I talk to Him about it. No, I try not to complain to Him, unless something is really wearing on me. If I do, He can handle my concerns about things and guide me through it.

Try seeking Him out. Talk to Him, and see if you don't begin to feel His presence giving you peace.

Day 51

Today's Scripture:

"I have been crucified with Christ; it is no longer I who live, but Christ lives in me; and the life which I now live in the flesh I live by faith in the Son of God, who loved me and gave Himself for me" (Galatians 2:20 NKJV).

Today's Testimony:

Four generations of my family have attended the Church of God. I was raised in the church and attended all services: Sunday school, church services, revivals, youth meetings. It seemed like I was in church all the time. There was always a lot of activity going on, and a lot of children around.

However, even though I was very involved in the church, I really had not made a personal commitment to accept Christ as *my* Savior. Outside of the church, I was not very active, and did not belong to any school groups. I was far from being popular. When I was around thirteen years old, I attended a Vacation Bible School at a church with a friend of mine. As I listened to the speaker teach an object lesson about tickets to Heaven or hell, it hit me like a lead balloon that I wanted to go to Heaven to live with Jesus. I began crying frantically. They dismissed the kids to go to class, but I could not go. I stayed in the church auditorium and spoke to the speaker and gave my heart to the Lord. My life was changed.

As a pen pal, I began writing to a young lady at a Bible college in town. Every time she wrote to me, she ended with Galatians 2:20. I looked that scripture up and it has stayed with me all these years. "I have been crucified with Christ; it is no longer I who live, but Christ lives in me; and the life which I now live in the flesh I live by faith in the Son of God, who loved me and gave Himself for me" (KJV). That became my testimony and is still one of my favorite scriptures.

I married a pastor at the age of eighteen. God has been with me all these years, and I have tried to let people know that Christ loves us and gave Himself for us. What a difference He can make in our lives!

—*Charla*

Today's Takeaway:

The power of the Holy Spirit to draw us to Christ is so amazing! Charla had been in church her entire life. So many seeds had been sown into her, but it was the perfect moment she heard the Gospel presented that it was harvest time for her soul. Let me encourage you, if you work with children of any age, you never know what moment the children under the sound of your voice may be ready to receive the message of the Gospel. I was seven when suddenly I realized that Jesus died on a cross just for me. Understand, the Holy Spirit draws *all* ages. Be ready to respond—for yourself, or to lead some young person to ask Christ to live in them since the life we live is by faith in the Son of God.

Day 52

Today's Scripture:

"But God, being rich in mercy, because of the great love with which he loved us, even when we were dead in our trespasses, made us alive together with Christ— by grace you have been saved" (Ephesians 2:4-5 ESV).

Today's Testimony:

In the darkest time in my life, I walked away from serving God. My dad passed away and I blamed God for my pain. I went into such a dark place that I became someone I didn't like. I was hurting my children and destroying my marriage.

It became so bad, I thought there was no way I could find my way out of this deep dark place. One night I had a dream where the Lord spoke to me. In the dream I told the Lord I didn't know how to come out of this place I had found myself in. Then I woke up and realized I needed to pray.

I prayed and repented of everything I had done. I gave my hurt and accusations to God; I turned it all over to the Lord. I was saved. Day by day He brought me out of the pain I'd been feeling. He healed my relationships. He saved me when I was my own worst enemy. His great love for me was there and walked with me daily. I'm so thankful that He healed my broken heart and life.

—Karen

Today's Takeaway:

It's part of our human nature to love someone so deeply that we feel like part of us is taken away when they die. Saying goodbye is the number-one thing I hate the most here on earth—in any situation. I hate it when everyone has had a wonderful time together and now they have to get in their car and go home; or when it's been a holiday and the family gathered together to eat and make memories, but now it's time to leave; or especially standing by a casket looking down at a face that is more dear to you than words can express. The sting of goodbye is painful. I *long* for the day when we will never have to leave, never say goodbye again!

That day is coming. There's only one catch: We've got to be ready to meet, not only them, but more importantly Jesus, in Heaven. The Bible says one day Jesus will come to take the "righteous dead" to Heaven, and then we who are alive and remain will be "caught up together" (see 1 Thessalonians 4:16-18). We'll get to go to Heaven together, and be together forever. I like the sound of that, do you? And those "righteous dead"? They won't stay dead any longer. We all will be changed in a moment, in the twinkling of an eye, into our new perfect bodies without sickness or age (1 Corinthians 15:51-52). There we will "know as we are known" (see 13:12). There we will worship the Lord who made it all possible. There is nothing here on earth worth missing out on that great day.

Let's live looking for the place of no goodbyes.

Day 53

Today's Scripture:

*"Then you will call upon Me and go and pray to Me, and I will listen to you.
And you will seek Me and find Me, when you search for Me with all your heart"*
(Jeremiah 29:12-13 NKJV).

Today's Testimony:

I was blessed to grow up in a Christian home. My mom took my sister and me to church every Sunday and Wednesday and taught us about Jesus on a daily basis. My dad joined her in raising us to serve the Lord after he gave his heart to God when I was twelve years old. They have both been a great influence in my life and I am thankful for them.

When I was five years old, I remember getting on my knees, folding my hands, and asking Jesus into my heart while I was playing all alone in a tent in our basement. By the grace of God, I have never fallen away from Him. I've had many Sunday school teachers and youth leaders that have impacted my life as they gave of their time and energy to teach me about the love of God.

Jesus has brought me through some difficult times and has helped me to learn to look to Him for everything. He is my Savior and friend. I would never be able to maneuver this life without Him. Through each day the Lord shows me His faithfulness, and He continues to draw me closer to Him as I seek His face.

—Gina

Today's Takeaway:

Here's one of the testimonies that makes my momma heart glow. All testimonies are wonderful, but it's the ones where children give their heart and follow Him all the days of their lives that make my heart do backflips! That's the ideal. That's the greatest and best hope a mother can have, isn't it.

Whether you are a mother reading this or you influence others like a mother (we all influence others in that way whether you realize it or not), think right this moment of a child Gina's age when she was saved—five years old. Take a moment to pray for that sweet one right now, that the Lord would draw his or her heart to Him so they would give their heart now and avoid so many pitfalls the enemy would love to lead them into. Then be that godly influence like Gina had that helped her to know exactly what to do in her little tent in the basement. Someone had shown her how to pray.

Pray with others so they will learn how to do it. No big words are needed—remember, you're talking to a friend. I've prayed for years according to the acronym *PRAY: Praise, Repent, Ask* for help for others, and ask for help for *Your* needs. Prayer is our lifeline. Thank God, it became Gina's too.

Day 54

Today's Scripture:

"But whenever someone turns to the Lord, the veil is taken away. For the Lord is the Spirit, and wherever the Spirit of the Lord is, there is freedom. So all of us who have had that veil removed can see and reflect the glory of the Lord. And the Lord—who is the Spirit—makes us more and more like him as we are changed into his glorious image"
(2 Corinthians 3:16-18 NLT).

Today's Testimony:

There is a song titled, "I Need You More," by Lyndell Cooley and Bruce Haynes. A line in it says, "I never want to go back to my old life." That sums up my salvation story. I was nineteen when I was saved, and I'm twenty-four now; I can wholeheartedly tell you, I never want to go back to my old life. While I was growing up, even though those around me did it, I never swore, drank alcohol, or smoked. It's pretty mind-blowing to look back and think how easy He made it for me to love Him. When I look back on the timeline of my life, I see that He was with me preparing me for His perfect timing of when I'd give my life to Him.

I started attending church regularly at my best friend's church after I graduated high school. I met some really amazing people and joined their youth group. I was so interested and eager to learn more about my Savior. It was like I couldn't get enough. Our youth group started to grow and we had Bible study twice a week. I remember leaving my house to head to Bible study one night, and as I was walking out the door my grandpa said, "Didn't you already go to Bible study this week?" I just said yes and ran out the door; I just couldn't get enough. I was so happy to have a place where I belonged. God precisely placed me at that church with those amazing people to help lead me to learn more about Him.

One Sunday our pastor gave an altar call and a friend looked at me and asked, "Would you go to the altar with me?" So I went. I remember being at the altar and just stretching my hand out while I covered my face blocking my tears from being seen. I never realized how much hurt I felt in my heart until I turned it over to Jesus. I had pain from battles I'd tried to fight on my own for so long that I had never let go of the pain of past mistakes and regrets. Once I said, "I'm Yours," I knew I was free. It's now five years later and, "I never want to go back to my old life."

—Chelse

Today's Takeaway:

There's nothing like knowing you are free from the past, is there? It's a wonderful feeling to let it all go and embrace the forgiveness that Jesus offers. You don't have to go back to your old life. Seek Him and go forward.

Day 55

Today's Scripture:

"And you must commit yourselves wholeheartedly to these commands that I am giving you today. Repeat them again and again to your children. Talk about them when you are at home and when you are on the road, when you are going to bed and when you are getting up" (Deuteronomy 6:6-7 NLT).

Today's Testimony:

One Sunday night after I had been to church with my family, I began to think about salvation. I remember I was a fourth-grader, and that night most of my brothers and sisters were already in bed. I decided to ask my mom what I should do to be saved. She told me to simply pray and ask Jesus to come into my heart and forgive me for my sins. She said I would then need to try my best to live for Him each day.

I told her that I would like to get saved the next time we went to church. I was so thankful when she explained to me that I didn't have to wait until we went to church. She knelt down right there by the couch with me. I was so thankful I was in my fashionable nightgown since I was going to talk to God. Then my mother prayed with me. After she finished praying, my mom cried; I cried too, and I knew at that moment God is real and I always wanted to live for Him.

From that day on, I knew God could truly see me, and that He cared. He still does. He has proven Himself faithful to me all of these years. He is my Savior, my healer, my strength, my comfort, my hope, my Father, my Creator—my everything. The same God that met me in my living room when I was in fourth grade has been meeting me ever since. I will always give Him praise.

—Wanda

Today's Takeaway:

How sweet. I believe God smiled at His little daughter wanting to be pretty in her "fashionable nightgown" to talk to Him about being saved. It's the greatest possible situation for a child to come to know Christ, because if they continue to be discipled throughout their lives, so many of the enemy's plans to harm them are disarmed. As they learn more about the Word, they learn how to live for God and how to handle life's problems as they come instead of giving in to temptation and fear.

This was true for Wanda. Once she understood that God was real and that He could see her and He cared for her, it naturally led her to trust Him with her problems and needs. Let us follow the childlike faith that matured into a lifelong habit of walking with Him. I want to grow up to be like Wanda—and still wear "fashionable gowns" doing it!

Day 56

Today's Scripture:

"Let all those who seek You rejoice and be glad in You; let such as love Your salvation say continually, 'The Lord be magnified!'" (Psalm 40:16 NKJV).

Today's Testimony:

I was not raised in a Christian home even though my grandparents, on both sides, were faithful church attenders. My parents divorced when I was six years old, and my dad raised me along with my five older siblings by himself. We didn't have a lot of supervision and we would often get into trouble when my dad came home. He didn't have a lot of patience with us, so he was very eager to let us go to church when some folks from a Baptist church invited us and gave us a ride. I remember going to the altar to pray to be saved at that church and later was water-baptized. I don't know how much I understood about Jesus, as a child, but I'm thankful for the foundation that was laid.

Thankfully, when I went to college, my roommate was a Christian. While I was there I went to a Christian concert where I was asked if I would go to Heaven when I died. I realized I couldn't give a definite yes to that question, even though I had accepted Jesus as my Savior as a child and had rededicated my life in high school. I prayed again, that day, to get rid of any doubt.

While still in college I met my now husband. His parents were Church of God pastors. My father-in-law preached a sermon once about how we are all jewels in God's hand. I was tremendously blessed by that message. I found myself at the altar again, but this time it was to worship God for how much He loves us.

—Fannie

Today's Takeaway:

I'm so thankful for people who invite and bring kids to church. I'm not sure they ever realize the impact they are making in the kingdom of God. I was one of those kids; I grew up to be in ministry. Fannie was one of those kids; she also grew up to be in ministry. God bless the people who haul kids that aren't theirs to church—they help lay that sweet foundation of Christ! That was Fannie's first visit to God's altar.

What about you? Have you been to the altar? It's a wonderful place of redemption, assurance, healing, and consecration. If you need salvation or reassurance that you are saved and ready for Heaven, make an altar wherever you are and Jesus will meet you there. I'm so thankful for the altar!

Day 57

Today's Scripture:

"And we know that in all things God works for the good of those who love him, who have been called according to his purpose" (Romans 8:28 NIV).

Today's Testimony:

I facetiously asked my husband, "Did we roll the dice crooked and blow on them sideways?" We aren't gambling people, it was just an odd day full of a series of unfortunate events.

I am a pastor's daughter. I was raised in faith, with faith, by faith. I have always believed He will work all things together for my good. But this particular day was different than any day I had yet encountered. It stretched my faith, that very faith that had been ingrained in me at such a young age. Yet, for the very first time in my personal life, I had a front-row seat to God's love, provision, and protection. I could actually see His mighty hand in every event that unfolded before me, I now thank Him and praise Him through my storms.

While driving home from out of state, our boat-trailer tire passed us in the fast lane. After four hours of sitting on the turnpike, a tow-truck driver (reluctantly) saved the day. When we finally arrived at our home late that evening, we noticed our garage door was cracked. Our initial thoughts were, *You gotta be kidding me, someone broke in?* To our surprise it was much worse.

—*Brittany*
(To Be Continued in Tomorrow's Reading)

Today's Takeaway:

What a day! Poor Brittany. There used to be a funny song on a TV show that went, "If it weren't for bad luck, I'd have no luck at all." This sounds like the beginning of one of those stories. The thing that some Christians would like to do is imagine that coming to Christ means all your difficulties in life melt away after that. It isn't so. The Scriptures don't describe that. Some Christians say if you are in the will of God, then everything will always go smoothly for you. It isn't so. The Scriptures show the life of Jesus as being anything but smooth, and He was certainly in the will of God.

We must understand that when we become a Christian, we know that even through difficulty, God is working on our behalf to help us face anything that comes so we can make it. He also guides us to respond in the correct way to what comes. Our response should be different from the world's response—that's tough, isn't it? But true. We pray to grow in our maturity in Christ to learn the right way to respond to trials and temptations. Tomorrow we'll see what happened in Brittany's life and how she responded.

Day 58

Today's Scripture:

"Dear brothers and sisters, when troubles [of any kind] come your way, consider it an opportunity for great joy" (James 1:2 NLT).

Today's Testimony *(Continued From Previous Day)*:

We were greeted by the sound of rushing water and the realization that our entire house had flooded. We ventured through in disbelief, walking under collapsing ceilings and in ankle-deep water while viewing the leftover fragments from the fruits of our labor. Then we noticed a note on the table that read, "Home owners call the Fire Department for details." That's when our dog walked in with her stomach cut wide open and had to be rushed to the veterinarian hospital.

It's easy to say that the circumstances of this particular day shook our faith; it's also easy to say that the next few months were not a walk in the park, unless that park is Jurassic Park! But it wasn't just a day of unfortunate events, it was also a day of fortunate protection. God knew everything we would encounter. He is Jehovah-Jireh, my provider; Jehovah-Nissi, my protector. He worked all things together for our good.

This is how awesome He is. No accident or injury happened on the turnpike, waiting for the tow-truck driver. That time delay was inconvenient for us, but it created an opportunity for a FedEx man to see the water rushing out of our garage and make a call to the fire department to step in on our behalf. Their efforts not only protected our insurance claim but also allowed minimal damage to our personal belongings, like our son's irreplaceable art work that hung on a wet dilapidated wall, or our cars in the garage not being totaled from the collapsed ceiling. God protected the little things that were important to me.

Things you have worked so hard for can just disappear after a four-day trip, and your whole world can be flipped upside-down. God didn't stop our storm, but He allowed unfortunate, inconvenient things to occur to protect us. I encourage you to look for His mighty hand in all of your endeavors, to have the faith to thank Him and praise Him through your storms, and to have peace knowing He is in control and working all things together for your good even when it looks like they are falling apart. Do not fear an unknown future to a known God. I have learned that He strategically orchestrates the odds on our behalf; that when it seems that your faith can be swiped away in a day, it can actually be increased and multiplied.

—*Brittany*

Today's Takeaway:

Yes! I feel like Jesus, when He met the Roman centurion in Matthew 8:5-13 and said, "I have not found such great faith, not even in Israel!" (v. 10 NKJV). Brittany's faith was increased by all she went through. *I want to be like that.* Let's all be like that. Look for the good in all situations. Count it all joy!

Day 59

Today's Scripture:

"Those who wait on the Lord shall renew their strength; they shall mount up with wings like eagles, they shall run and not be weary, they shall walk and not faint" (Isaiah 40:31 NKJV).

Today's Testimony:

Being a single mom involved with drugs and alcohol causes a life with many hurdles to jump over. The emotional, mental, and spiritual emptiness that way of life can bring is enough when you're single, but so much more miserable as a mother. I can say that God has delivered every promise He said He would when it comes to Isaiah 40:31 in my life. I did have to go through many trials, and I know there will be more, but verse 29 states, "He gives power to the weak, and to those who have no might He increases strength" (NKJV).

I will never forget the day the Lord touched me and gave me the strength to walk down the church aisle to the altar. I was so done with my current life that I might have fallen at the altar instead of kneeling. I can tell you that when I was able to stand back up, I knew without a doubt that God had washed me clean and my life was about to take a different path. I had a deep, deep joy; I had a certainty and love I had never felt before. I can say since that day, I have never had a desire to drink or take drugs. A few months later I was able to give up smoking. God has walked me through this course, and at times He had to carry me. He has given me the faith and knowledge to know, not just hope, that He will never leave me.

God changed my life so drastically that now, when I meet people and share my past, they find it hard to believe. He has given me everything I need to follow a different path. Another scripture I have held close is Philippians 4:19: "And my God shall supply all your need according to His riches in glory by Christ Jesus" (NKJV). Today I can say I depend on God for everything in my life, and He has never let me down. I wouldn't trade a single day with God for one second of my old life.

—Brenda

Today's Takeaway:

I once heard a friend that had been bound by drugs and alcohol describe the experience as getting caught to a giant Velcro ball: Every time you tried to pull yourself free, you got stuck even deeper in the tangle of it than you had ever been before—until you were so exhausted and hopelessly stuck that there was not even a hope of ever pulling loose. How sad and impossible! The good news is that Jesus is the God of the impossible. He does give power to the weak. We don't accomplish these things in our own strength; it's in Him that we get free from any sin! So if you have something you need today, trust the God of the impossible. Lean on His strength to get it done.

Day 60

Today's Scripture:

"And it shall come to pass, that whosoever shall call on the name of the Lord shall be saved" (Acts 2:21 KJV).

Today's Testimony:

I was born the middle child in a family of nine children. Our house was very busy but close-knit. We had a lot of love and many memories of holidays and trips to my grandfather's cabin. Because of the influence of my mom's parents, we always attended church. It was quite a sight, the picture of all of us kids sandwiched between my mom and dad trying not to move an inch. But somehow, every Sunday we survived the chaos of getting everyone ready, piling into the car, and marching in like an army.

While raising nine kids and working a job, my dad somehow completed college with a degree in engineering. But with his degree came job offers from all over the United States. We moved from one coast to the other as each job became a better opportunity. Finally, we settled in a place we called home. At school I met the friend who would eventually change my life. After many invitations, I found myself attending her church. It was quite a culture shock; it was much different than the churches I was used to. Yes, each church worshiped Jesus, but this church did it in high gear. They sang faster songs, the preacher got much louder, and the people reacted to the Holy Spirit in a way I had never seen before.

This was a large church and their youth group consisted of fifty-plus teenagers, but I was slow to become a part of it. After much urging by the youth pastor, I started going to some events and even said a prayer, but it was at a revival that God really got ahold of my life. I got saved and, a few months later, received the baptism in the Holy Spirit. Suddenly, I was all in. I assisted in children's church, was on the bus team, and even went on door-to-door visitations. During this time, I felt the call to serve in the medical field as a nurse, but our youth pastor felt I needed to give Bible college a chance. I decided to trust God and He came through. Everything I needed to go was there in one week.

Through my roommate at college, I met my future husband. We got married the very next September and have now been married thirty-nine years. He was a preacher and suddenly I was a pastor's wife! I had no idea what I was getting into, but God has blessed us with many miracles, and three great sons. From a teenager in the youth group to pastor's wife. God is good.

—*Carla*

Today's Takeaway:

It's a wonderful thing to see how God orders the steps of His girls. Look at the training Carla was getting in her young years that would prepare her to be the pastor's wife she is today. God is preparing you to use the gifts He has placed within you. Get ready! He'll open a door for you. Will you let Him use you?

Day 61

Today's Scripture:

"But you, when you pray, go into your room, and when you have shut your door, pray to your Father who is in the secret place; and your Father who sees in secret will reward you openly" (Matthew 6:6 NKJV).

Today's Testimony:

"Mirror, mirror on the wall, who is the ugliest one of all?" With my head bowed down, tears falling, I stared at the scars on both of my arms. Anxiety arose as I heard the wood creaking from the footsteps walking toward the door. I pulled my sleeves down and wiped my tears away. I left my true self in the privacy of my room and entered into the real world. Yes, the pastor's daughter was suffering from self-harm and other internal issues. Consider this: one of the biggest struggles for some as a "pastor's kid" is that they feel like they have to maintain a level of perfection that God did not intend. For me, years of self-harm and damage were kept hidden due to this struggle.

I grew up and pressed forward; I got married and lived a life that I was convinced was "OK." The feelings of rejection, the feelings of being unwanted always lingered at the forefront of my mind. I went through a divorce. Then one day, I took courage and started to seek God's will for my life.

God began to work with me in such a powerful way. I started singing again, I began to form covenant relationships in my home church, but I became distracted. I entered into a relationship, looking for a person to fill the void of loneliness. Soon I was left looking at myself in the mirror with mascara running down my face from crying. As the water ran and I cleaned my face, I felt God say, *It doesn't have to be this way.* I wiped away my tears and decided, "God, my story will not end in ashes." I fell to my knees, begging God to heal my heart. I prayed and cried there for hours. After my time of prayer I felt the Lord speak to me, *Prepare this room for Me, not to visit but to live.*

It was then that God began to work. I began to pray for Him to expose me, for Him to show me areas where I needed to work. I learned to spiritually confront myself. I needed to do a self-analysis and be OK with the results. Thirty years old, a pastor's kid, and I had never experienced God in such a tangible way. He gave me the ability to understand how much He loves me.

My secret place allowed me to form a stable and continuous friendship with my Father, and that is a journey to be discovered.

—*Jaciris*

Today's Takeaway:

When we get alone with God and pour out our souls to Him, allow Him to show us how to live, and let Him fill us with love and understanding—something wonderful happens! Powerful transformation of our lives becomes possible when we spend time with Him. Commit to this daily.

Day 62

Today's Scripture:

"If God is for us, who can be against us?" (Romans 8:31 NKJV.)

Today's Testimony:

My salvation story begins with pain—the kind of pain that left a hole in my heart with lingering questions about my worth. People say time heals all wounds, but how can you heal when you're shutting God out of your life? Five years after I lost my dad, while I was in college, I finally decided I didn't want to be mad at the world anymore. So I got ready and made the choice to go back to church.

I didn't surrender immediately. It took some time, but I kept going. Months went by, but I didn't give up. Somehow I knew there was help for me that I could receive.

Finally one day, I went to church with my now husband. At the end of service, there was an altar call. The pastor called anyone to come up to pray who had something heavy on their heart; anyone in need of prayer. I decided to go. I bent down at the front pew, alongside my boyfriend and friends. I rested my face in my hands and I let go. I let go of the pain that had been weighing me down for six long years. I let go of the blame I had cast on my late father. I let go of the guilt that had burrowed into my stomach. That day, on that front pew, I gave my full heart and soul to God. Ever since that day, I trust God is bigger than any mountain I may ever face.

—Erin

Today's Takeaway:

I'm a mother and I can't help but feel an overwhelming urge to take Erin in my arms and rock her back and forth. She had lived in grief and pain for so long. Losing her father left her in complete emptiness. She did not deal with it and so she could not move forward. That pain grew bigger and got more tender and hard to live with each day.

All the while, her heavenly Father wanted to soothe her pain and give her peace that passes all understanding. Are you hurting? Is there pain that you're carrying around right now? Understand that it will only grow bigger and bigger, making it harder and harder for you to function in your daily life until you do exactly what Erin did—let it go! It's time to turn it all over to the God who loves to take our burdens and roll them away, replacing them with sweet relief and peace.

If you're dealing with grief today, understand there is no shame in talking with trusted Christian friends or leaders who can walk you through your pain and help you to process it. This is a Scriptural action that God provides for His children. Romans 12:15 tells us to "weep with them that weep" (KJV). We help one another through pain!

Day 63

Today's Scripture:

"Give all your worries and cares to God, for he cares about you" (1 Peter 5:7 NLT).

Today's Testimony:

My story began before I was even born. My mother was told that she would most likely wouldn't have children due to different female problems. However, when she was eighteen years old and dating my dad, she became pregnant with me. I can only imagine the shock she experienced. I am so grateful for this life that I have been given.

Most of my childhood I was raised not going to church. I remember praying and loving Jesus, even though I hadn't been taught anything about Him. Addiction runs on both sides of my family. I was always so fearful I would end up addicted to drugs or alcohol. When I was thirteen years old, my mom rededicated her heart to the Lord and found a church for our family. We immediately began serving in ministry. I was very involved in my youth ministry. I remember the day that I truly got saved like it was yesterday. I was at church and was questioning if the Holy Spirit was real. I prayed for the Lord to show me and instantly I was filled with the Holy Spirit. I felt joy like I have never felt before! I knew that I wanted to spend the rest of my life serving the Lord!

Life with Christ has been filled with many highs and a few lows. I was able to graduate from high school and attend a Christian university for a while. I went away to college, even though I knew in my heart my purpose was to be a wife and mother. I truly believe I was called to be a homemaker. I came home from school and married my very best friend a couple of years later. We had three beautiful children in two and a half years. Our life was crazy, but we were enjoying every second of it. Tragedy hit when I was twenty weeks pregnant with our fourth child and went for our anatomy scan. During the scan we were told the baby had no heartbeat. I was crushed and heartbroken. I was angry with God. I had spent the majority of my life serving Him and I didn't think I deserved to go through this.

The night before I had to have surgery, the Lord covered me with a peace I can't explain. I knew He was with me and took my grief from me. I know that without Him I couldn't have emotionally healed from the miscarriage. Even if God doesn't answer our prayer the way we are hoping He will, He is still sovereign. Even when healing doesn't come, I will still worship Him.

—Chasity

Today's Takeaway:

I'm so thankful that God makes beautiful things from imperfect situations, aren't you? He can make us flourish in the middle of asphalt, just like determined dandelions pushing up no matter what has been done to stamp them out. When God is with us, nothing can overcome us. In the anguish of miscarriage, God reminded Chasity that He was there. He provided peace we cannot possibly understand. The Lord cares about our grief and comforts us. Praise God!

Day 64

Today's Scripture:

"I will be a Father to you, and you shall be My sons and daughters, says the Lord Almighty" (2 Corinthians 6:18 NKJV).

Today's Testimony:

I grew up in the Catholic faith. My parents and their ancestors before them were devout Catholics. I enjoyed going to church every Sunday and catechism classes during the week. Christmas midnight Mass was my favorite service, yet I always had the feeling something was missing. God was tugging at my heart back then; I just didn't know it.

I was four when my father was killed in a tragic car-train accident a mile from picking my two-year-old brother and me up from the babysitter. My sense of identity, security, and unconditional love was taken away from me. I was always told I was a daddy's girl, but I was too young to remember. The hurt was too much for my mother, and she didn't talk about my dad. I remember trying once to ask questions about his life, and she cried. I stopped asking after that. We moved back to my mother's hometown and I rarely saw any relatives from my father's side after that. I don't blame my mother; I know she was doing the best she could to survive.

When I was seven, my mother remarried to a divorced man and we moved to his small town. My stepfather was verbally abusive at times; this reinforced my insecurity. He had a temper and I never wanted to get in trouble, so I became the "good" girl with good grades and did whatever I was told. Later I witnessed my stepfather being abusive to my brother; it broke my heart.

When I met my future husband, he took me to his church. The service was unlike anything I had ever experienced! I was nervous and timid, but the music kept drawing me in. When we married at that little old country church, my stepfather refused to come, as I was not marrying a Catholic, and kept my eleven-year-old stepbrother from coming. I was crushed. I had no father to walk me down the aisle nor for the father-daughter dance. There was no contact (not by my choice) with my mother, stepfather, or stepbrother for over a year after my marriage.

—Kelly
(To Be Continued in Tomorrow's Reading)

Today's Takeaway:

Let's pause here in Kelly's story, because so many times a girl's dreams of walking down the aisle on her wedding day are shattered by some circumstance beyond her control. If this is you, I am so sorry. It hurts. Little girls' dreams are real and valid, but let me say this: beautiful things are in store for you when you commit your way to Jesus. In Heaven, all tears will be wiped away! Your good Father knows all things and He will work things together for your good. People are flawed and sometimes they *think* they are doing right when, in reality, they are in the wrong. Try to forgive and go forward.

Day 65

Today's Scripture:

"When my father and my mother forsake me, then the Lord will take me up"
(Psalm 27:10 KJV).

Today's Testimony *(Continued From Previous Day)*:

There I was, having gotten married without the presence of my immediate family and the heartbreak of going through it without any presence of a father figure. At church, the Word was preached about a holy and loving Father, but I couldn't relate to any description of a loving father since I didn't have the remembrances of my father while I was growing up. I was very insecure with low self-esteem and always feeling like I never belonged anywhere. I couldn't understand it. Why would a holy Father want *me* to be His daughter? I would like to tell you it didn't take me long to realize that His Word is the truth like it says in 2 Corinthians 6:18, "I will be your Father, and you will be my sons and daughters, says the Lord Almighty" (NLT). No, unfortunately, I related more with doubting Thomas.

Praise God, He never gives up on us. It took many years for me to believe He was delighted to have me as His daughter, but I now know I am His! Repeat after me, my sister: "God is my Father and I am His daughter." Believe it! Receive it! Bury that promise and truth so deep in your heart that you never forget. Rise up, straighten that crown, and go forth! Memorize and worship with the beautiful song about our God, "a Good, Good Father."

—*Kelly*

Today's Takeaway:

There's nothing sweeter than to see a little girl with her arms wrapped in a hug around her daddy's neck. I love the term "Girl Dad." I've seen firsthand how the love of an earthly father can calm the world around his daughter; I've known that joy in my own heart. I count myself so incredibly blessed to have experienced it. I'm swallowing down tears just thinking about it.

On the other side of that coin, I've also seen the incredible swell of love and pride that a father receives from the love and attention from his daughter. Dads enjoy seeing their girls blessed, grow, and thrive. When she turns her attention to him, he listens to her completely. Wow! That's how our Father treats His girls. Walk through your day thinking about that wonderful thought!

Day 66

Today's Scripture:

"I will praise you forever, O God, for what you have done. I will trust in your good name in the presence of your faithful people" (Psalm 52:9 NLT).

Today's Testimony:

The Lord has been with me from a young age. I gave my heart to Jesus when I was seven years old. I was baptized with the Holy Spirit at age thirteen, and I enjoyed going to camp meetings and youth camps as a teenager.

I never planned to marry a pastor, but I fell in love with my husband at age eighteen. We married a year later and had three sons quickly. Though my husband felt called to the ministry, he worked several secular jobs until the Lord prompted him for us to move several states away for him to attend Bible college.

The Lord gave me a job while my husband went to school and then he worked as a janitor in the evenings. It was very hectic raising three young sons, but we made wonderful friends. One day, our eight-year-old son was playing in the neighbor's yard on a trampoline when he fell off and broke his leg. After surgery, we were told his growth plate may be affected, causing one leg to be shorter. Our church prayed and wrapped their loving arms around us. They organized a team of volunteers to come and sit with our son so we could go to work and school. They showed their love in practical ways; we will never forget their kindness. Our son's leg grew normally, and he is now 6'4" tall.

We were at the school for less than two years when we were called to pastor a small church in Michigan. We learned many things about ministry there, and we grew into a close-knit church family. After almost seven years, we got the call to go to another church. Since we were in close proximity to our families, it was especially nice that both my parents and in-laws were able to attend our church. My husband's father was an alcoholic, so the greatest miracle was when he finally came to church and accepted Christ. My husband was also able to baptize his father in water, which is an experience we will never forget.

Over the years God has blessed us in so many ways; we have seen miracles performed in our lives and in the lives of people we've pastored. Jesus is coming soon; we must pray for more souls to come into the Kingdom!

—*Cindy*

Today's Takeaway:

Cindy has been faithful to the Lord and He has been faithful to her. She and her wonderful husband have given their lives in continual service to Him, and still do so even into their retirement. Praise God for such calling! The kingdom of Heaven is different because of them. It causes me to examine myself. Is my life pointing others to Him? Will Heaven be different because of me? Let's live faithfully, like Cindy.

Day 67

Today's Scripture:

"If we confess our sins, he is faithful and just to forgive us our sins, and to cleanse us from all unrighteousness" (1 John 1:9 KJV).

Today's Testimony:

For many years I struggled with a secret. There were good days and bad days. On the good days I wouldn't think about it, but on the bad days my heart bled with pain and hurt.

In the '90s, I went through a divorce from a man who abused me verbally and physically. I was a lost, single mom, searching for identity. When I started dating again, I met a man and was in and out of a relationship for several months. This chapter of my life ended with a trip to a local Christian pregnancy center where my suspicions were confirmed. They tried to convince me to take an ultrasound to see the baby, but I stormed out of there with only one mission—to abort my child. Unfortunately that mission was accomplished, and it tore my world apart later in life.

After marrying my second husband, I went into depression because of what I had done. I had never gone through the grieving process; instead I hid the secret that had been killing me on the inside. My husband suggested that I speak to a certain lady who had gone through the same situation. I finally got the courage to speak to her and found out she led a class at that very same clinic I had gone to when I found out I was pregnant. Was this God? I decided to take her class, called "Surrendering the Secret." It taught me to forgive myself, and to ask for forgiveness from my daughter, who never got to meet her brother, to ask forgiveness from my unborn son, and most importantly, to ask forgiveness from God.

I never knew that God could forgive me for this; but once I understood that and asked Him, I knew God had forgiven me. Then, I was finally able to forgive myself. So much was released from me. My heart began to heal through the forgiveness of God. Finally, through this healing process, the salvation of God came through.

Although I still hurt for my son, I know that he is with God, our Father in Heaven. Today, God has blessed me with a loving husband, sweet children, and wonderful grandchildren. I am so thankful for all He has done for me.

—Heather

Today's Takeaway:

The enemy never tells you the whole story about his plans. He only shows one side, the easy fix. He never shows the agony and pain attached to it, but it's always there. Heather is not alone. I've held sisters as they wept through this journey. The good news is the same grace that was made available to Heather is there for us all. It's by grace we're saved, not by works. Our righteousness is like filthy rags. Only Jesus' blood is pure enough to wash away sin. Feeling guilty? Pray. Feeling prideful? Pray! Neither one is OK. Only humbling ourselves before Christ makes the difference with Him.

Day 68

Today's Scripture:

"I am my beloved's, and my beloved is mine" (Song of Solomon 6:3 KJV).

Today's Testimony:

I grew up in an average urban American family and neighborhood. My dad worked in a steel mill, and my mom stayed at home. We went to church on holidays (mostly Easter) because I remember the sunrise service, breakfast out, and getting a great Easter outfit.

My grandmother had a relationship with Jesus and taught me the power of prayer from a young child. When I was twelve, I remember that my grandmother's church did a dramatized sermon about hell and the consequences of not knowing Jesus. I remember getting down on my knees asking Jesus to come into my heart. I know I was saved that night, but I'm not so sure I really understood.

I began to attend church and attend Bible study, but there was not a lot of discipleship that took place. Then, because I was the only person saved in my family, it was really up to me to figure it all out. After that I was hurt in the church—there were some religious people who discouraged me and I began to drift further away from the Lord. My foundation wasn't solid, and I sank into a pit. So at the age of sixteen I walked away from the Lord, but the Lord never left me. Jesus pursued me. When the Bible says Jesus will never leave us nor forsake us, but that He is with us always, He wasn't kidding.

In a few years I had run as far away as I could go. I was sitting at the picnic table at my parents' house, and Jesus called me. I heard the Lord's audible voice as He told me He loved me and wanted my life. It was the most precious day I can remember. Jesus made me a promise. I didn't really know the Word of God, but Jesus spoke His Word to me, "Seek My kingdom first, and My righteousness, and all these things you desire, I will give them to you" (see Matthew 6:33). It's a promise He has kept for forty-three years. I also felt a call into the ministry, but I didn't know what that meant; it was God's secret for a time. I knelt down beside the picnic table and gave my whole heart, my past, my present, and my future to the Lord. I gave Jesus every burden, every weight, and every sin. All of my shame came off that day; Jesus made me brand-new. Jesus called, and I answered, "Yes!" It is a decision that I rejoice in every day.

—*Melody*

Today's Takeaway:

(Melody's words) When I was twelve I prayed because I was afraid and I didn't want to go to hell, but when I was sixteen I prayed because I wanted the full life that Jesus had to offer. I wanted to go to Heaven someday, but I wanted to live for Jesus every day. Jesus became my Lord and Savior, and He has proven His love for me over and over again.

(My words) He pursued Melody and she turned to Him. Doesn't it feel wonderful to be wanted and loved by our Father?

Day 69

Today's Scripture:

"After breakfast Jesus asked Simon Peter, 'Simon son of John, do you love me more than these?' 'Yes, Lord,' Peter replied, 'you know I love you.' 'Then feed my lambs,' Jesus told him. Jesus repeated the question: 'Simon son of John, do you love me?' 'Yes, Lord,' Peter said, 'you know I love you.' 'Then take care of my sheep,' Jesus said. A third time he asked him, 'Simon son of John, do you love me?' Peter was hurt that Jesus asked the question a third time. He said, 'Lord, you know everything. You know that I love you.' Jesus said, 'Then feed my sheep'" (John 21:15-17 NLT).

Today's Testimony:

When I was young, I gave my heart to Jesus, and He has always been faithful to me. He has ordered my steps and has always met all my needs.

As a young wife, I had my first baby; seven years later, I had my fourth baby. One morning, I was praying on my bedroom floor. I told God, "I don't know how I am going to serve You. I am barely making it through the day and I have to take my children everywhere I go." It was then that I looked at my Bible and these words were lit up to me: "Feed my lambs." I went to take care of my kids and later in the evening, I read: "Take care of my sheep."

My children had friends over and some stayed for days. They watched Bible videos as they played. I supplied them with Bible storybooks. I truly loved all the children. After all my children grew up, I helped with the teenagers at church. Then I had surgery for ovarian cancer, but during the surgery I suffered my third heart attack; I was given a 10 percent chance of living—that was nine years ago. The heart attack did weaken me physically and I did not have the stamina to help with the teenagers anymore, but God was not finished with me.

During one of our church services, God told me that my time for caring for children was over. My senior friends needed help and I would visit them in the nursing home. It was there that I would try to lead them to salvation. This is where I saw God make a way for me to minister now.

While I am still weak physically, God spoke to me one more thing He wants me to do—to eagerly wait on Him, knowing He will supply my needs. God has been so good to me!

—*Elizabeth*

Today's Takeaway:

Elizabeth is a friend of God! She loves Him and wants with all her heart to feed His lambs—she started with her own little lambs, then other children, teens at church, and finally people in the nursing home. We are told to love others as we love ourselves. This story is a great picture of that!

Day 70

Today's Scripture:

"For all have sinned and fall short of the glory of God" (Romans 3:23 NKJV).

Today's Testimony:

"Girl, stop all that fidgeting. What is wrong with you?" My grandmother repeated it multiple times, and the evening was just beginning. At seven years old, I struggled sitting still in general. However, that night was a culmination of weeks of anticipation and excitement; sitting still was almost impossible. We had finally arrived at the large arena and taken our seats. That place was massive, and I had never seen anything remotely comparable. My home church was wonderful but would top off at around 100 in attendance. The fact that thousands would gather to hear the Gospel and hundreds would flood the altar was breathtaking. Again, my grandmother leaned over and began to say her speech to be still, but interrupting her mid-sentence, I said, "I know. I really know, but you don't understand how awesome this is!" This amazing woman of God smiled, squeezed me tight, and pointed toward the stage. People were beginning to sing, and the atmosphere was electric.

In retrospect, this night was important in many ways because of the routine developed at my home. Every Saturday night, my sister and I sat on the floor in front of my mother while she curled our hair with pink sponge rollers in preparation for church the next day. Every Sunday morning, I sat in front of the television to watch evangelical services while Mom took those rollers out of my hair. I never missed a service. I'm not sure why I was so mesmerized by preaching at seven years old, but it stirred my heart. Now I know that it was the power of the Holy Spirit welling up inside me.

I don't remember the sermon, but I do remember Romans 3:23. "All" included me, and I began to realize God had bigger plans than simply seeing a preacher; I would truly see Him. Experiencing a supernatural tug at my heart, tears poured down my red cheeks, and I ached for more of Jesus than what I had previously known. My sweet grandmother was aware of what the Spirit was doing at that moment, and hand in hand, she walked me to the altar. As I prayed, I fell deeply in love with Jesus; I was now a new creation. Then with the crowd, I sang, "He touched me and made me whole."

—*Christal*

Today's Takeaway:

It's a powerful thing to feel the Holy Spirit move on your heart. There is nothing comparable to it on the face of the earth or beyond. Little girls are no exception to that rule—I can just see Christal in my mind's eye, tears flowing, little hands lifted, worshiping her Savior! What a beautiful picture! Have you ever experienced that? There's nothing like full surrender to Him—nothing held back. How long has it been since you prayed that way, telling Him again that you love Him with all of your heart, asking Him to cleanse you of any sin that could possibly be found in you, worshiping Him for all He's done for you? Put sponge rollers in if you need to, and worship!

Day 71

Today's Scripture:

"Now unto him that is able to do exceeding abundantly above all that we ask or think, according to the power that worketh in us, unto him be glory in the church by Christ Jesus throughout all ages, world without end" (Ephesians 3:20 KJV).

Today's Testimony:

I asked Jesus into my heart after a Petra concert that I attended with my youth group; I was fifteen years old. But even though I was walking with Him, it didn't necessarily mean I was always listening to what He was trying to teach me on a daily basis.

For me, asking Jesus into my heart was the easy part. I didn't want to suffer the consequences of my sin and I loved Him; I wanted Him in my life every day. Webster's Dictionary defines *salvation* as "preservation or deliverance from harm, ruin, or loss." This was the hard part for me; the work that comes after salvation—the hard work of submitting to God and His Word.

I got married and my husband and I went to the mission field. I found that it can be a lonely place, especially when you don't speak the same language as the people you are serving. So I had a lot of time with God; many hours of reading, praying, and listening; mostly listening. In my spirit I heard my heavenly Father say, "Jamie, wake up. Your marriage is crumbling around you. Let Me help you. Give it to Me. I will make it better than you can even imagine."

You see, Jesus had been pricking my heart for years about submitting to and showing respect to my husband. I would listen and repent—over and over, for years. This was harder for me than asking Jesus into my heart. This would require a lot of pruning by my heavenly Father. One day in prayer, Jesus showed me my heart as if it were laid out on an operating table—and let me tell you, it wasn't pretty; pride never is. However, this new alone time with God broke me to my core. Once again, I listened, and repented. But this time, it stuck. God did a new thing in my marriage, and He started with me. God loves us too much to allow us to keep sabotaging our own lives. He must bring correction in order for us to fulfill His purpose and plan for our lives. The process wasn't easy, and it definitely wasn't comfortable; but it was so necessary, and for that I am forever grateful.

—Jamie

Today's Takeaway:

Getting pruned is uncomfortable! Sometimes it's almost unbearable, and makes you feel "picked on," but the end result is beauty and fruitfulness. Marriage is hard. Showing mutual respect is absolutely necessary, and there are times you just have to choose to show honor because it's right, not because you feel like it. These things take Christian maturity and love.

Day 72

Today's Scripture:

"Choose for yourselves today whom you will serve" (Joshua 24:15 NASB).

Today's Testimony:

In Joshua, the Scripture tells us we must choose whom to serve. Thankfully, I did use my free will to choose Him, but it was not because I was able to follow the examples set by my family. My examples of a mother, father, and a family unit were not good ones; I grew up in a family tormented by mental illness. My mom was trapped by schizophrenia; my dad was undiagnosed with bipolar disorder, and had major control issues. Both parents were much too distressed to even notice their absence of love for me.

My family, as all families, were born into a world of sin. My dad divorced my mom and later remarried. I found myself wounded from the divorce at a young age, neglected by both parents, and emotionally abused. Later, as a teenager, I experienced physical abuse from my dad, until one day, he left large black and blue bruises on my backside. I knew that wasn't normal and found help from my fourth-grade teacher. It was then that the physical abuse stopped. My dad then proclaimed himself to be an evangelist and was even named the pastor of a local, small, country church, but on the inside of the house, the love of God was not in him according to 1 John 4:8.

At the age of seventeen, I decided to step away from the family home and attend a youth group of my choice. I accepted the Lord as my Savior and I chose to find the path that He wanted for my life. After I graduated high school, I felt led to attend a Christian college two hours from home. My family disagreed, but drove me to the college and left me. I felt abandoned and all alone, but I learned in the Bible that for those without a father and mother, God would be there. He is a good God!

—Kari
(To Be Continued in Tomorrow's Reading)

Today's Takeaway:

We live in a world that is filled with imperfect people; sometimes they are dealing with mental illnesses, sometimes with chemical imbalances. All these things can affect the way they deal with the people around them—even people they love. This is a hard subject, but God is a loving Father whom we can turn to in the midst of these difficult issues. We can take our disappointments and pain to Him. He heals hurt—even hurt that has been locked up for years. He's also private. Are you afraid or just unwilling to talk to anyone else about it? He'll listen and help you. Bury your head on His loving shoulder and tell Him all about it; He's always listening and understands when no one else can.

Day 73

Today's Scripture:

"He made the hearts of them all. And He understands whatever they do"
(Psalm 33:15 NLV).

Today's Testimony (Continued From Previous Day):

At the age of nineteen, I wanted to please God and do BIG things. I *thought* I heard His voice, so I married a man twenty-two years older than me. He was wheelchair-bound and said he was an evangelist. After fifteen years of marriage and two children later, I was no better than when I left home. In fact, my husband was bound by pornography and deep in debt. He had control issues, and I was now emotionally and sexually abused. My husband often told me, "You won't ever be good enough." The pain was great and it hurt even physically in my heart. I reached a deep depression, and I lived in fear.

With much counsel and prayer, I divorced my husband. Psalm 119:11 instructs us to store His Word in our hearts so we won't sin; I did my best to follow that guidance. I did my best to teach my children the ways of the Lord. Through the love and support of my pastor and his wife, my church family, and much prayer, I stayed the course. In the past six years, God has healed me. My healing is found in a daily renewal through prayer with my God—who saved me, forgave me, protected me with His mighty righteous right hand, and continues to keep me every day. He is the binder of wounds and the lover of my soul. I vow to stay close to His Word of truth for my life. I owe my life to my God, the Maker and Creator of the heavens and the earth.

—*Kari*

Today's Takeaway:

Nobody said life would always be easy. We wish for Barbie's dream house with no problems, no stress, and no failure; but the reality of our lives sometimes brings pain and disappointment. What matters is how we respond when it comes. Remember, we don't have to handle anything on our own. Sure, we decide who to serve, but it's God who walks us through it.

Are you facing problems today that seem so big you see no possible way through it? Trust the One who is building you a mansion in Heaven right now that will put Barbie's house to shame! He will get you through every situation if you'll only trust Him—no matter if the problem is out of your hands or not. He always leads when you ask. Talk to Him; He understands everything from mental illness to addiction. He's not put off by your asking; He's waiting on you.

Day 74

Today's Scripture:

"For great is your love, reaching to the heavens; your faithfulness reaches to the skies"
(Psalm 57:10 NIV).

Today's Testimony:

I was never abused growing up; I was never addicted to drugs. I never struggled with the major battles that some others faced. When thinking about my testimony of salvation, I wondered what I could say that might testify of God's love when He saved me.

To be perfectly honest, I felt a little guilty for not struggling through the difficult things that some have endured, but then I realized my experience really is something wonderful to testify about.

While praying I was reminded of when I was a child, back to the first time I realized I needed to be "saved." At the time, I was four years old. My mother was being released from the hospital after giving birth to my younger sister. My dad received the call to come pick her up. I was upstairs in my bedroom when I saw my father leaving without me. I was yelling out the window that I wanted to go. I leaned on the bedroom window screen, when it gave way and I fell two stories onto a concrete driveway!

My father ran to my lifeless body. He picked me up and rushed me to the hospital. My grandmother, who was at our house, hit her knees crying out to God to save me. She spoke life and blessings over me. She prayed that I would live and not die. I was diagnosed with a closed head injury with excessive fluid on the brain. Miraculously, I soon recovered completely. The doctors told my parents when I was discharged that it was a miracle I didn't die. I had no serious complications from the fall.

I gave my heart to Jesus when I was nineteen years old, but I feel like my *life* was saved first at four years old. God honored my grandmother's prayers and allowed me to live. He had big plans for me. I have been involved in prison outreach, youth ministry, care and nursing-home ministries. I have also traveled and served the poor in Guatemala and the Dominican Republic, but I feel my greatest mission field is in home missions. I feel like this is the plan He saved me for. I love to testify to others how God saved me and spared my life when I was four years old.

—*Darlene*

Today's Testimony:

God stepped in and spared Darlene's life for His glory. She has used her gifts and talents on foreign mission fields and in home missions. Thank God for a praying grandmother. She knew her God was a healer. Two stories high was nothing to a God who formed Darlene's body and knit her together in her mother's womb.

Do you need healing today? It may be for God's glory that this has come about. Ask and believe God for healing. When it comes, tell someone what God did. Testify about what God has done. Bring Him glory and see what He does from there.

Day 75

Today's Scripture:

"Create in me a clean heart, O God, and renew a steadfast spirit within me. Do not cast me away from Your presence, and do not take Your Holy Spirit from me"
(Psalm 51:10-11 NKJV).

Today's Testimony:

It all started with a godly lady I knew; it was her persistence in inviting me to come to church with her that got me where I am today.

I could not get her off my back, so to speak. I would see this woman of God coming and I would try to hide from her.

I know God used this sister and her dedication to Him as His servant to point me to Him. I am so blessed that God didn't give up on me. That's why, right now, today I am saved.

Thank You, Jesus! Hallelujah! I will never forget this sweet sister, who attended the local church. I'm thankful for her persistence by her continual efforts to invite me until I came. I dedicated my life to Christ, and I'm still serving Him today.

—*Marlene*

Today's Takeaway:

I can just see this picture in my mind's eye. I can see this sweet saint of God on her mission—a general in the army of God. I can see her spot her assignment—Marlene, and she's on the run. She doesn't want to talk to this godly saint because she's heard it before—yes, God is good, He can help her, she should come to hear the Good News. What Marlene may not have known at first was that it wasn't just tenacity or stubbornness that was driving this sweet saint. It was the love of Christ that was driving her. She was not willing to give up on Marlene because God isn't.

Is there a "Marlene" in your life? Tenacious inviting works. I'm living proof. My family finally went to church because someone kept on inviting us until we came. Don't give up! Keep inviting until they come. Why? Because you love them.

Someday, you'll look back and see that your ceaseless invitations resulted in people you loved coming to know Christ and getting established in fellowship with other believers and being discipled. Look around you—there are friends, family, coworkers, all people needing what you have. Be the next "general" and get on your mission.

Day 76

Today's Scripture:

"But if I say, 'I will not mention his word or speak anymore in his name,'
his word is in my heart like a fire, a fire shut up in my bones.
I am weary of holding it in; indeed, I cannot" (Jeremiah 20:9 NIV).

Today's Testimony:

As a small child I always loved the Lord. I was a young Catholic girl who talked to Jesus all the time. I prayed often and said the rosary. I went to confession every week. I was what people would call "a good girl" because I never drank, smoked, or slept with anyone until I married; all I did was dance. I always felt that God and I had a close and special relationship. I even felt there was a time I was thinking about becoming a nun. One day a dancer friend of mine asked me if I was saved. I had never heard that expression before, so I asked her what it meant. She explained that it meant to pray to Jesus to receive salvation. I was eager to pray and receive all that there was for me. That very night I asked Jesus into my heart. As I prayed, the Holy Spirit flooded my soul; I didn't quite know what was happening. All I knew was that I wanted to pray like that constantly. I was shaking with excitement!

Ever since then I decided to read the Bible—actually I felt like I wanted to devour the Bible. I would go into my bedroom and read for hours and hours. I have been reading the Bible ever since, preaching the Word of God to everyone I can. I try to convert as many souls as I can to Christ.

—Diane

Today's Takeaway:

Jeremiah said God's Word burned like fire in his bones and he would get tired if he tried to hold it in (Jeremiah 20:9). Diane is on fire for God like that. She can't keep it inside. She has to share it. Praise God! People are going to know she loves the Lord.

When I was a child in Sunday school, there was a lesson that has always stayed with me: "If you were put on trial for being a Christian, would you be convicted? Would enough people have evidence from your life to see Jesus in you?" When people see our lives, there should be no doubt; not because of our Christian T-shirt, or our bumper stickers, but because of our lives, the evidence of our words and actions, and the way we treat other people—the ones we know and don't know.

What about you? Is there evidence in your life? If someone asked the people that work around you, or go to school with you, or live near you, would they know you're a Christian? How would the people who aren't Christians describe you? Hmm. That's worth talking to the Lord about today—whether good or bad.

Day 77

Today's Scripture:

"His descendants will be mighty on earth; the generation of the upright will be blessed"
(Psalm 112:2 NKJV).

Today's Testimony:

I was raised in church all of my life. I was filled with the Holy Spirit at the age of sixteen. Then I got married and moved away. I came to know a kind of life that was not conducive to a simple country girl; soon I fell away from grace. Through my job, I became a social drinker and social entertainer. Truly involved in the world, Satan had me convinced that I was on the top of my game, but God had other plans for my life.

One night, in 1979, God gave me a dream. There were sounds and a lot of commotion coming from Heaven—beautiful sounds with a lot of activity. My mother was there and also a lady minister I had known from when I was a young girl. There was the most beautiful carriage; it was black and full of diamonds, pulled by black horses. I said to my mother, "What is happening?" She replied, "Jesus is coming." I said, "I want to go." The lady minister replied, "It's too late now." I immediately awakened. What a terrible feeling knowing that it was too late for me to make it.

Later, as I was dressing for work, the Holy Spirit was so strong in my bedroom that I fell to my knees by my bed and rededicated my life to Christ. I have never looked back since then. I believe that after that dream, if I had said no to the Holy Spirit, I would not be alive today. God chased me and overtook me with His Spirit. I will always be grateful to God for His love for me, even in my sins. It is amazing how God can take a life and turn it around.

God had a plan for me. I went on to go to Bible college earning several degrees; worked as a foreign missionary helping many lepers and as a home missionary helping poverty-stricken areas. I served as a chaplain, worked in a safe house helping battered women and children. I served senior adults, and worked in my local church. He had all that in store for me, and who knows what else? I'm following His plans—not mine. He's a great God.

—*Flora*

Today's Takeaway:

Boy, did God *ever* have plans for Flora? She has done some of everything. I'll bet the enemy checks to see if she's awake before he goes outside in the morning. She may have run from God's plans for her at first, but when she surrendered her life to Christ, He poured out favor and blessed her to serve Him.

I want to be like that, don't you? Flora's not His favorite, you know. He loves all of His girls and He has plans for us all. What He's looking for is not so much *ability*, as it is, *availability*. Are you available to Him? Have you told Him you'll do whatever He wants you to do? Be ready! He'll open doors when you say you're available.

Day 78

Today's Scripture:

"I will never leave thee, nor forsake thee" (Hebrews 13:5 KJV).

Today's Testimony:

I grew up in a good home, but not a godly home. My parents were hardworking people who provided excellently for our family. While they were not intentional in their pursuit of God, they were very open to any interest we displayed. They took us to Vacation Bible School and took us to church when they had time off work. I sometimes walked to a church down the road for Sunday school.

One time at church, they explained salvation as the egg shoot in *Willy Wonka*. Down came an egg (a person) and God decided "Heaven or hell." This felt disgusting to hear as an eight-year-old child. I wondered, *Would God really leave my eternal destiny up to chance?* I ran home afterward and asked my mom if it was true. She said, "No way." But she couldn't really explain to me how to be saved.

The next year a different church knocked on my door and invited us kids to a special event. They picked us up on a church bus and I heard my first clear explanation of the Gospel. While I didn't accept Christ then, I wanted to learn more. It seemed crazy to me, even at nine years old, that salvation was a free gift and all I had to do was accept it.

Over the next several years I grew in knowledge about Jesus. I soaked up Sunday school lessons and learned Bible doctrine. At thirteen, I realized Jesus died for me and loved me. I went to the altar, repented of my sins, and asked Christ to save me.

I have had trials since then, but Jesus has never once left me. He promised, "I will never leave thee, nor forsake thee" (Hebrews 13:5). God is a perfect loving Father who always has time for me. As a woman, it's easy to struggle with comparison. My story isn't perfect; no one's is, but it's mine. I learned long ago not to wish for greener grass, but to water where I'm planted, and I will continue to grow in Him.

—*Ashley*

Today's Takeaway:

It's hard for me to hear an eight-year-old was told that getting saved was just a matter of being labeled as a "good egg headed for Heaven, or a bad egg headed to hell." I'm so thankful Ashley got another chance to hear the greatest story ever told. God sets us up to get more chances to hear the truth because He loves us. He wants us to hear the truth, let it take root in our hearts, and "spring up" into an understanding of His sacrifice to save us, and then help us through life, growing where He plants us.

It is very easy to wish for greener grass; I think all of us have known that feeling at some time or another. It's a sign of maturity and wisdom to try watering your grass first before deciding to move on. There are times when moving to another situation is the answer, but the Lord guides us in all decisions when we ask Him. Thanks for that, Ashley.

Day 79

Today's Scripture:

"Christ redeemed us from the curse of the law by becoming a curse for us—
for it is written, 'Cursed is everyone who hangs on a tree'"
(Galatians 3:13 NRSV).

Today's Testimony:

One warm Sunday evening at church, there was a special speaker. We went to the altar to pray, but then I was the last one left praying there. The pastor and special speaker walked by me. I heard the speaker ask the pastor if they should stop and pray with me. The pastor said, "No, we'll leave her, she'll be all right." At first this hurt me, but I continued to pray and I heard Jesus call my name. He said, "Evelyn, if you had been the only one, I would have gone to the Cross for you." I realized I was the one of those He left the ninety-nine for, like the parable in Matthew 18:12-14: "What do you think? If a man owns a hundred sheep, and one of them wanders away, will he not leave the ninety-nine on the hills and go to look for the one that wandered off? And if he finds it, truly I tell you, he is happier about that one sheep than about the ninety-nine that did not wander off. In the same way your Father in heaven is not willing that any of these little ones should perish" (NIV). That is when I knew I was redeemed; Jesus had regained possession of my heart with His blood on the cross.

My life has been anything but easy. Satan has attacked me in every way he knows how. Prior to this encounter with Jesus, I was divorced. I was living in sin, even though I knew better. I had been raised in church. I had been saved when I was younger, but had walked away. I now felt like this world would be better off without me. As a result of this, I attempted to take my own life. Thank God I didn't succeed. I ended up in a hospital for six weeks while I had children at home. It was a dark time in my life.

Thanks to this encounter with Jesus, I now speak life over myself. I declare the following over my life daily, and you can too when you give your heart to Jesus: I am courageous. I am victorious. I am loved. I am blessed. I am gifted. I am anointed. I am healed. I am beautiful. I am whole. I am confident. I am forgiven. I am grateful. I am generous. I am strong. I am powerful. I am fruitful. I am God's masterpiece. I AM REDEEMED.

—Evelyn

Today's Takeaway:

It's a beautiful and powerful thing to be redeemed by the power of Jesus. He doesn't care what we have done, He just wants to wash away the guilt and shame. Live in that glorious victory for yourself. Turn everything over to Him and walk as His masterpiece.

Day 80

Today's Scripture:

"For God so loved the world, that he gave his only begotten Son, that whosoever believeth in him should not perish, but have everlasting life" (John 3:16 KJV).

Today's Testimony:

If you were to have a second chance in life, what would you do with it? I found myself in my thirties and in a downward spiral. Everything around me had fallen apart—I mean everything. I had lost two marriages and four children. A third relationship was on its way out. I lost not only my home, but also my family that I had hurt and used to the bitter end. All the friends I'd ever had didn't know me anymore; I didn't know myself anymore.

When I thought back to my childhood years, I wondered how I got to this place and how I would ever get out. I tried to blame it on my childhood, my parents, my ex-husbands, anyone or anything, but I never seemed to find justice. I would look at myself in the mirror and wonder, *Who are you? Why are you here, and where are you going?*

That's what happens when you turn to drugs, alcohol, and this world for answers. When I would get drunk, I was looking for joy—but it only lasted for a moment. That experience never ended the way it started; it always ended in misery, pain, and regret. When I would get high on drugs, I was trying to find peace, but I never found real true peace. I would gamble and win, which caused a great rush—but, again, only temporary. Even the addiction of nicotine held me captive, just another monster. In relationships I was trying to find love and contentment.

Relationships always ended up wrong without either love or contentment. Before I knew it, addictions would not let me go. No matter how hard I tried, they grew worse and worse until one day I realized they were going to kill me. They didn't love me, give me peace, joy, or contentment. I finally realized I could no longer go on this way. The addictions had no mercy; their mission is to seek, kill, and destroy. I was looking for peace, love, joy, and contentment, but in all the wrong places.

—Kylie
(To Be Continued in Tomorrow's Reading)

Today's Takeaway:

There is only one source of joy, love, and peace, and that is in Christ. The world can offer what they call a "good" time, but there's only pleasure in sin for a season, then there's that HIGH price to pay. The enemy doesn't show you addiction when he shows you that "good" time; he doesn't show you shredded relationships when he shows you the "other man"—that's because he's out to steal your peace and, ultimately, your life. Cling to your God and avoid the enemy's traps.

Day 81

Today's Scripture:

"For God sent not his Son into the world to condemn the world; but that the world through him might be saved. He that believeth on him is not condemned: but he that believeth not is condemned already, because he hath not believed in the name of the only begotten Son of God" (John 3:17-18 KJV).

Today's Testimony *(Continued From Previous Day):*

One morning I was alone at my home after an argument with my boyfriend, and I didn't have any desire to live any longer. I watched him drive out the long driveway and felt nothing but deep, dark despair. I fell to my knees, looked up and cried out these words: "If there is a God in Heaven, please help me now." All of a sudden, every bad thing I had ever done came before my eyes as if a movie were being played. I was convicted, contrite, and broken over all the things I had done. I started saying to God that I was so sorry. Each time I said it, I felt there was a purging going on inside of me. Things were being released as I thought about everything in my entire past. I began feeling very lightweight as I wept bitterly with a sorrow I had never felt before. I got up from the floor and began to walk; my legs were weak as if I was off-balance.

I ran to my car and drove to my brother's home who is a Christian and who, in the past, I very much avoided. He took me in his arms and comforted me and read the Bible with me. Later that evening another brother, who recently had a similar experience with God, came to talk with me. He told me how he and people from the church had been praying for my salvation. He asked me if I would go to church with him. I did just that. I went with my brother and gave my heart and life to the Lord Jesus Christ that very day. The Lord took all of my sins—my addiction to drugs, alcohol, gambling, nicotine, and all the things of this world—and gave me a new life and a chance to follow Him and honor Him, and I took it.

The Lord not only took all my burdens upon Himself and lifted them from me, but in the process He restored to me my children, my family, my career, and brought me out of debt. He paid it all, and now I am forgiven and free. I am alive in God and dead to sin. I no longer have to be a slave to sin, because of the finished work the Lord Jesus Christ did on Calvary. Jesus died on the Cross once for all sin and for all people because He loves us.

—Kylie

Today's Takeaway:

I feel like singing the old song "Victory in Jesus" as loud as I can right now. The very moment Kylie began to turn her life over to Jesus, *He began to work victory for her.* That's the kind of God we serve. He is greater than sin. She ran to Him and He met her there. I feel like shouting, "Hallelujah!"

Day 82

Today's Scripture:

Since God so loved us, we also ought to love one another" (1 John 4:11 NIV).

Today's Testimony:

In many ways, this story starts with my parents. They love the Lord and are fully committed to living for Him. They took my brother and me to church, taught us about God, and set a godly example for us.

When I was five years old, our church was having a huge weeklong children's revival with a guest team who came in and ministered. I quickly noticed that each night ended with a question: Did anyone want Jesus to forgive them for all the bad things they had done, and be their Lord and Savior? The kids who responded would go into a side room for a few minutes, and then all of them would come out with king-size candy bars. I asked, "Well, how come everyone didn't get a candy bar?" They explained to me that, because of the special and important decision those kids made, it was for them.

I just wanted a candy bar and was going to figure out how to get one. On the last night of the crusade, I realized that if I didn't raise my hand and go into that side room, I wouldn't get a candy bar. So I did it, not really understanding what it was all about. I thought they were telling them who Jesus was. I knew that but decided I'd do or say whatever so I could to get a candy bar. However, once I was in the side room with several other kids and workers, they began to speak clearly about what sin was and everything Jesus went through on the Cross. I remember them saying, "If you were the ONLY one on earth, Jesus still would've come from Heaven to let them beat Him and die on the Cross to forgive you so you could go to Heaven with Him."

It was now personalized for me; I was overwhelmed with emotion. I couldn't understand why He would do all that for me, but they explained it was because of His great love. So even though the bait was a candy bar, Jesus' love hooked me. I asked Jesus into my heart that night and asked Him to give me the strength to love Him and tell everyone I could about what He did. He answered my prayer because I remember times that I would wake up in the night, thinking of my family and friends who did not know Jesus yet. I would cry and kneel beside my bed to pray that Jesus would save them. That night started the most wonderful relationship and journey with Jesus. It has not always been easy and life has brought many trials to me, but I wouldn't have been able to make it without His steadfast love, strength, and faithfulness.

—Carrie

Today's Takeaway:

The power of the truth of what Jesus did for us, that's what touched and changed Carrie's life. It's what changes us all. I love the second part of her prayer where she asked Jesus to give her the strength to love Him and tell everyone she could. That's the part we all need. Let's all pray for that! His love "hooked us" too.

Day 83

Today's Scripture:

"'For I know the plans I have for you,'" says the Lord. 'They are plans for good and not for disaster, to give you a future and a hope'" (Jeremiah 29:11 NLT).

Today's Testimony:

If anyone had told me six years ago that I would accept Jesus, be baptized, work in youth ministry, and get married, I would have thought they were crazy. I would have laughed. How can someone as broken, unloved, lonely, and wild as I was, be so blessed, highly favored, and loved? Little did I know, God had already written my story way before I had even accepted Him in my life.

My childhood wasn't bad, but it wasn't great either. Growing up in two separate households wasn't easy. Not only was it hard to adjust to a new environment, but also it was hard hoping my parents' new spouses would love and accept my brother and me. At the age of eight, I experienced my first sexual assault. I was told it was OK to do these things when we play "house," so it went on for a while. When I realized this wasn't OK, I asked to live with my dad because I felt unsafe with my mom.

My father raised my brother and me from the time I was eight until eighteen. At the age of fourteen, I became the victim again. I was sexually assaulted by someone who was supposed to be a family friend; he was fifteen years older than me. After months of abuse, I thought this is how my life was going to be—how men were. I felt as though I was unlovable, that I deserved it and no one cared. Because of this, my first relationship revolved around physical and emotional abuse for three years. I didn't know any other type of love/relationship.

Years later I was invited to attend a church service by a dear friend. Everyone was so welcoming, loving, and eager to help others become closer to Jesus. Within six months of attending, I fully accepted Jesus as my Lord and Savior. I felt so much love, joy, peace, and acceptance! I finally had the knowledge that I truly am enough in Him. I made the decision to be baptized. The feeling I felt coming out of the water was indescribable, knowing that everything from my past—wrong deeds and sins—were gone. I knew I was born again.

I am now honored to be our church's youth leader. It has definitely stretched me, along with making me aware that I am stronger and wiser than I thought by the grace of God. I am also now married to a wonderful man who loves Jesus—proving all men are not the same, and breaking the cycle I had endured.

—Aubrey

Today's Takeaway:

For anyone who feels that it's too late or thinks God couldn't possibly use you for good, think about Aubrey's life. The enemy tried to stop her from God's calling on her life. If He can use her, He can use you.

Day 84

Today's Scripture:

"And I am sure of this, that he who began a good work in you will bring it to completion at the day of Jesus Christ" (Philippians 1:6 ESV).

Today's Testimony:

I grew up going to church with my family every Sunday. I loved going to church and learning about God. Yet, as I got older, I sensed something was missing at our church, but I didn't know what it was. I just knew I needed more of God. Jesus said, "Blessed are those who hunger and thirst for righteousness, for they shall be satisfied" (Matthew 5:6 ESV).

One day while at work as a secretary, I had an experience with God that I would never forget. God spoke to me in an audible voice about my future. I know this sounds crazy, but He said, "You are going to marry a man named Gary." I began to think of men named Gary that I knew. None of them seemed right to me. I dismissed it from my mind; but I told God I was open to His plan for my life. I didn't understand at the time what had just happened to me, but years later I would understand.

God has spoken to me at other times, not usually audibly, but in quiet ways. He spoke to me once as I looked at a puzzle that was laying in pieces strayed on the table; He told me He was making my life fit together into a beautiful picture and to trust Him. In Jeremiah 29:11, we read, "For I know the plans I have for you, declares the Lord, plans for welfare and not for evil, to give you a future and a hope" (ESV). It would be years after I was married when the Lord would remind me of giving me the name of my husband. I rejoiced over the perfection of His plan.

On my twentieth birthday, I met my future husband. He asked me to go on a date with him to church. I thought that was a great idea and I went with him. During the service that night I felt the love of God in such a special and wonderful way. The very atmosphere was electrified with God's love. This love was what I had been looking for, for a long time. A few months later I got born again, baptized, and filled with the Holy Spirit.

I have now served the Lord for over forty years. I love to pray, study the Word of God, and work for the Lord. God has been so good to me.

—Colleen

Today's Takeaway:

I've never heard God speak audibly, but I know He has a purpose when He does. He has perfect plans for us and He reveals them to us at the right time. We can trust Him to work things out for our good and lead us in the path we need to take. He wants to give us a future and a hope.

Day 85

Today's Scripture:

"Believe on the Lord Jesus Christ, and you will be saved, you and your household"
(Acts 16:31 NKJV).

Today's Testimony:

How could a strict Catholic family, let alone a Catholic teenage girl, know Jesus personally? How could God save a family of nine so quickly and perfectly? How could a family who was content and committed to the Catholic church become radical for God? As the wind of the Holy Spirit swept through the Charismatic Movement in the '70s, it changed everything for us. Beginning with my mom, we all repeated a prayer that was so simple, yet the most important prayer ever prayed. We normally recited Catholic prayers, never venturing out of the norm, but this was something new and exciting—talking to Jesus. We invited Him into our hearts according to the scripture above in Acts 16:31.

It seemed like discipleship came quickly as my father taught us the Bible every night. We were all feeling the tug for more. I was fifteen and met my boyfriend, now husband, who grew up in the Pentecostal church. We decided to go to each other's church, starting with mine. I still remember his reaction as he looked around observing Mass. The following week I attended his church. I could not believe what I was seeing. It reminded me of the radical change our family went through, especially when we were baptized in the Holy Spirit. The next week all nine of us showed up at church. For a small church, we were very noticeable and welcomed. This became our new church.

There were some consequences in this newfound freedom in Christ. Friends disowned us, and we even heard we were excommunicated from the Catholic church. However, God began to use our gifts and talents. At age nineteen, I began playing the piano in the church, not knowing someday my husband would be a pastor and worship leader and I would play for him.

We saw many miracles through the years, but the one I cherish most is the night my husband prayed for twins; then we had identical twin boys. Today they are married and very involved in ministry along with their wives. One of my greatest joys is seeing my grandchildren at church. How life would have been so different if someone had not shared Jesus with our family long ago.

—Julie

Today's Takeaway:

You don't realize what impact you have, not only on the person you talk to about the Lord, but their entire family. Just telling about what God has done in your life can cause someone to stop and think and possibly ask for prayer. Then, don't wait—pray right then. It could make the difference in an entire generation or, like in Julie's case, several generations. Be the one God uses today!

Day 86

Today's Scripture:

"He comforts us in all our troubles so that we can comfort others. When they are troubled, we will be able to give them the same comfort God has given us"
(2 Corinthians 1:4 NLT).

Today's Testimony:

I remember the day of my salvation clearly. I was nine years old; I was at a church summer camp. I was kneeling at the altar and I looked up to vividly see the feet of Jesus on the cross; to this day I still clearly remember it. After that, everything changed—the colors were more vivid; I saw everything differently. It was a profound experience for a young girl.

My parents divorced when I was twelve, and I dealt with my mother who was cruel. I grew up in a very rigid and strict home; I felt I could never measure up. My grandfather was the patriarch of our family and he played a huge role in my life.

Later in my thirties, I was diagnosed with bipolar 1 disorder after many years of intense struggling and confusion. Life was not easy. It was around this time that I had an abortion. Professionals would ask if I wanted to hurt myself. No, I didn't want to hurt myself—I wanted the pain to stop.

At this point in my life with all my pain, I didn't see God as being any help for me after all my sin. I was lost—deeply and utterly lost. I had no hope of Heaven and peace. I see now I had to rediscover my own relationship with Jesus. That is when His love broke through the hard shell that was around me. He gave me peace and acceptance about my parents' divorce, and an understanding and love for my grandfather. They were doing the best they could with what they had. God has also been healing the devastated place in my soul from my abortion.

I began to know God's healing on so many levels in my life. I learned of His grace. Legalism left me hopeless, knowing that I could never measure up or be good enough. Works never gave me peace, no matter how intensely I tried. But today, the mighty love of God washes over me every step of the way and I am powerfully saved and free to live life in victory. He has somehow turned all the pain of my past into precious opportunities to reach out to others as I walk in His footsteps.

—*Deb*

Today's Takeaway:

How sweet to know that relief that comes when the love of God washes over our soul and washes out all the grit and grime of our past sins and hurt. There is no peace apart from Christ. If you are busy working to try to be good enough or do enough to merit your place at the "table," forget it. It can't be done. Sure, He wants you to serve others—but *because* you're saved, not to get there. Remember that, and be at peace.

Day 87

Today's Scripture:

"I love you, Lord, my strength. The Lord is my rock, my fortress and deliverer; my God is my rock, in whom I take refuge, my shield and the horn of my salvation, my stronghold" (Psalm 18:1-2 NIV).

Today's Testimony:

I grew up in a non-denominational church; in that setting I grew up thinking I believed in God. Then I married, but that marriage failed due to going the ways of the world. Later I married again; I now had two daughters and my husband.

One morning, I woke up and realized I needed a fresh start. It was an unexplainable and unshakable urge to attend church. My husband and I got up and got our daughters ready, ate a quick breakfast, and headed to church. There was a guest speaker that day who is also an incredible sheriff and medic in a nearby county. Little did I know, the sermon I was about to hear was going to change my mind, my heart, my soul, and the way I lived the rest of my life.

I was struggling with anxiety, had a short fuse often becoming angry, was cursing too much, and drinking more than I should at night. I was secretly lusting over a new coworker at the medical office I worked in at the time. I was falling deep in a rabbit hole and not living a Christian life, even though I claimed to believe in Jesus Christ. A stranger would not have had the slightest clue I believed in Jesus based on watching my behavior and attitude.

The sermon I heard rocked my world. It was about "CBA" or "RBA"—"Commitment/Recommitment, Behavior, and Attitude." It was like hearing God for the first time with my heart—that I need Him and I can't live this life without Him.

—*Emily*
(To Be Continued in Tomorrow's Reading)

Today's Takeaway:

Not everyone is called to preach, but they say everyone preaches a sermon to those around them by the life they live. *Gulp!* It's true, isn't it? Emily said a stranger around her wouldn't have the slightest clue that she believed in Jesus by watching her life. I applaud her incredible honesty. It's only when we are gut-level honest with ourselves that we can begin to see ourselves as Christ sees us. He knows all—even the thoughts we think to ourselves. *Commitment, behavior* and *attitude*—we read the rest of Emily's story tomorrow to see how these words rocked her world.

How's your world? Is it time for some honesty? Let's all do like David did in Psalm 139:23 and ask God to search our hearts and try our thoughts.

Day 88

Today's Scripture:

"My little children, these things I write to you, so that you may not sin. And if anyone sins, we have an Advocate with the Father, Jesus Christ the righteous"
(1 John 2:1 NKJV).

Today's Testimony *(Continued From Previous Day):*

Something inside my soul was so shaken by the words and passion from this guest speaker. He spoke about making a *commitment* to Jesus Christ by confessing with your mouth and believing in your heart that Jesus died for our sins and asking Him to come into your heart and be your Lord and Savior; or maybe you're committed but you need to recommit. Maybe your Christian walk is in a rut and you're just sort of lost and going through the motions.

He spoke of having a *behavioral* change; to be transformed out of the world, not conformed to the world. Be the same person you are in church as you are on the street. If you've made a commitment, then you need to behave like it.

Lastly, he spoke of *attitude*. People should wonder why you're so fired up and wonder what's different about you. Be the one that people are drawn to, not because it's you, but because you're filled with the Holy Spirit. Obedience to being a faithful wife and a merciful, loving mother is not weakness. Obedience is strength.

I confessed to my husband my secret lust as soon as we got home from church. We both cried and prayed to God right there in his old Tahoe in the driveway. I begged God to take away these lustful feelings. Being a Christian means if we sin, we confess it and ask forgiveness. My husband was incredibly shocked yet grateful for my sincere honesty, and forgave me. To this day we have a rock-solid marriage because Jesus Christ is our firm foundation. Whether it comes to our marriage, raising our little girls, finances, life decisions, self-conduct in public, while driving, giving thanks for our meals—every area of life no matter how big or small, good or bad, there is no rock like our God. Grace found me. His mercy and grace saved my life and my soul.

—Emily

Today's Takeaway:

Hallelujah! Grace did find Emily! You can sense it just reading her story. She heard the truth preached and she responded by confessing her sin—not just to her husband but to God in prayer. Then from that day forward, she made a conscious effort to do things differently. She acted in a different way because the Difference-maker had moved in her heart. It touched every area of her life—marriage, family, finances, conduct—ALL!

When He moves in, changes happen. If they don't, check-up. Pray again. The Scripture says you'll be transformed by the renewing of your mind, not conformed to the world (Romans 12:2). You'll be different.

Day 89

Today's Scripture:

"'For I know the plans I have for you,' declares the Lord, 'plans to prosper you and not to harm you, plans to give you hope and a future'" (Jeremiah 29:11 NIV).

Today's Testimony:

I was blessed with two loving Christian parents whose devotion was directed to the well-being of their two daughters. Our home was a prayerful and loving place. But both of my parents died when I was in my late twenties. I called our time "short but sweet."

Quite the opposite was my first marriage. I called that time "long and sour." In my naïve heart as an eighteen-year-old girl, I had the desire to have the home my parents raised us in. But our home was nothing like it.

My husband was nine years older than me, and just back from Vietnam. Our first daughter was born after a year of marriage and the next child, nine years later. My husband's PTSD turned into regular physical abuse. I hid this well from others due to the heaviness and shame. We no longer went to church; my time was spent caring for the girls and getting my degree in medical administration.

Hurt, scared, depressed, and confused, I finally filed for divorce. I never thought my heart would mend or that my tears would dry. One day I went over to a friend's house seeking some comforting words. But she wasn't home, so I sat on her patio in the back of her house and cried. I had forgotten so much of what was taught to me. But I wasn't forgotten; my God was there with me.

Suddenly, the Holy Spirit reminded me, "I will not leave you or forsake you." Bible verses started pouring into my conscience. I wiped away the tears and began to seek my God and His plan for my life. Through it all, He's been there. He's been merciful, forgiving, and healing—always directing me toward my real home.

Since my patio encounter, the Holy Spirit has continued to lead me. He is the One who gives us faith and perseverance. We can trust God. His promises *are* our eternal hope. Proverbs 22:6 says, "Train up a child in the way he should go, and when he is old, he will not depart from it" (KJV). This life is difficult and can be full of disappointments, but in-between, there is so much joy, happiness, and the blessings of God.

—*Suzanne*

Today's Takeaway:

Suzanne didn't realize it, but those seeds her parents had placed down inside her were there and ready to spring forth just when she needed them the most. Godly raising never goes to waste. It may look like it for a time, but it's there. Whether you're raising kids today, or you've been raised to love Jesus, know this: that Word is worth the time. It teaches, trains, and directs you to righteousness—just when you need it. It helps you get the "sweet" out of life.

Day 90

Today's Scripture:

"Let your roots grow down into him, and let your lives be built on him. Then your faith will grow strong in the truth you were taught, and you will overflow with thankfulness" (Colossians 2:7 NLT).

Today's Testimony:

I can't remember a time in my life when I wasn't at church. I'm a PK (preacher's kid), so I was always at church. We were there *before* the doors opened, and we were typically the ones who shut and locked them when the day was done. My life was filled with Wednesday nights, prayer nights, youth events, potlucks, revivals, mission trips, drama practices, music practice, and Sunday school. You name it; we did it. And I loved it!

I loved the rhythm and life that seemed to flow from church and all its activities. The problem for me lay in the fact that I was more in love with church than I was with Jesus. I knew Bible stories, worship songs, and Scriptures. I knew a lot of *stuff*, but I didn't really know a lot about Jesus.

I was a modern-day, preteen Pharisee. I followed all the rules—I was afraid not to. I was terrified of being left behind, going to hell, and being in darkness for eternity. These thoughts plagued me, especially at night. So, I made sure to do all the *things* necessary to make it to Heaven.

I lived like this until I was sixteen years old. Around this time, the love for the rhythm and flow of church life began to fade. I began to wonder why Christianity felt mostly boring and powerless. I imagined God as this far-off Being who was watching over me to be sure I didn't mess up. I thought I was in church to get a "get-out-of-hell-free" card from God.

That's when the Holy Spirit really started to work in my heart, and I realized I really didn't want to be *that* person. God began drawing me out of relationship with church and into a real relationship with Jesus. That decision changed everything. I found a Father who genuinely cared about me and the things I cared about. I found a Friend who cheered me on in new adventures. I found a Comforter who held me when I fell apart. I found so much more than a Dictator and a Judge who only sought justice and punishment.

I found so much more than I could ever imagine or list on these pages. And the great news is, I am not done. There is an eternity of God left for me to discover, and that's what I love about the rhythm and life of a relationship with Jesus.

—*Danielle*

Today's Takeaway:

What a beautiful journey—and it's not over. How short we sell God when we only see Him with a giant fly swatter or far away and uninterested in our lives. Neither picture is accurate at all. He is a Friend that wants to stick closer than a brother. Open yourself up to the real I AM.

Day 91

Today's Scripture:

"Train up a child in the way he should go: and when he is old, he will not depart from it"
(Proverbs 22:6 KJV).

Today's Testimony:

I am so grateful for my parents who raised me in church and in the way of the Lord. My parents took my brothers, sisters, and me to church as often as they could. At home, every evening they would have a family devotional time, which we all had to participate in. As the years passed and I became a teen, I didn't want to go to church anymore; I wanted to do as the other kids did and go where they went. But, as long as I was living at home with my mom and dad, when they went to church, I had to go as well.

When I finally got married, my husband and I didn't go to church. We lived in a small town away from my family and friends, not too far, but it seemed like it to me, because I didn't get to see them but once a week, and that wasn't enough for me. I was so lonesome for my family and needed to be closer to them again. I remember asking and praying to God about moving closer to them and my friends. It wasn't long before we got to move closer to them in the same town.

I had made God a promise, that if He would help us to move closer, I would go back to church. Well, I didn't keep my promise. Then I got very sick; I was afraid if I went to sleep at night I might die. I was in a bad state. I knew what I had to do. There was a church only four blocks from where we lived, so the next Sunday morning service, I had decided it was time to go and give my heart to the Lord. By this time, I had two beautiful little girls; one was small enough to carry, and the other held my hand. We walked to church, as I didn't drive at that time. God knew what I needed and what it would take to get me there. I did give my heart to the Lord that day; that was about fifty years ago.

It hasn't always been easy, but with the help of the Lord, the church, and friends and family, it has been worth it. I praise God for His plans for our lives: "plans to prosper [us] and not to harm [us], plans to give [us] hope and a future" (Jeremiah 29:11 NIV). I am no longer afraid of going to sleep or of dying. God is faithful; and I believe that since I raised my daughters in church, they will be saved and with me in Heaven, and stand on God's promises.

—*Linda*

Today's Takeaway:

Linda was "trained up in the way she should go." That's why she had such a hard time getting away from it when she got older. She knew the right way to go, and the Lord kept nudging her. Have you ever felt that? It's actually a good thing. It means God is guiding you to do what's right. Follow the Spirit's leading.

Day 92

Today's Scripture:

"Then I heard the voice of the Lord saying, 'Whom shall I send? And who will go for us?' And I said, 'Here am I. Send me!'" (Isaiah 6:8 NIV).

Today's Testimony:

My story starts before I was even born. When my mother was seven months pregnant with me, my father was on his way home from work when he got into a car accident that took his life. All my life I've been told how much I look like my dad and have his personality. Growing up I tried to not let any of this affect me, but I know it is part of what defines me.

When I was two, my mom married my stepdad, and a few years later had my sister. I don't really remember how we got into church, but my parents were youth pastors and music ministers for most of my childhood; however, they got hurt in church and we moved all over. I jumped from school to school. We finally settled down and I started middle school. I met a pastor's daughter and started going to church with her. That was when I really started retaining information about the Lord and how much He can do. The one thing that stuck out to me during this season of my life was when people would share their testimonies. I thought I didn't really have a "testimony."

As I got into high school, I started hanging out with the "cool kids" and getting invited to parties. Meanwhile at home, my stepdad started to get a hardened heart, putting me down every day, chipping away at my self-esteem with every word that he said to me. I turned to drinking, then cigarettes, then marijuana; that even led me into cocaine at one point in my life! I wasn't trying to make a testimony, it just happened with the season of life I was in and trying to cope with everything that was happening to me. This whole time I would think, *What would my life be like if my real dad was still alive?* I was still going to church with that pastor's daughter this whole time, and she knew everything I was doing. I finally realized what I was doing to myself, and one Wednesday night I recommitted my life to the Lord! That was my most defining moment!

A few years later, at camp, I was called to be a missionary. I quit college and started an internship for missions' work that took me to France, Ireland, Scotland, and Haiti. I got to see amazing miracles and things happening all over the world, but the Lord had more for me. That's when I started getting into youth ministry and really realizing that we need to see the miracles and amazing things happening here too!

—*Megan*

Today's Takeaway:

(Megan's words) Not all defining moments are good, and some might hurt to talk about. But as we go through life, we need to remember that our life is not our own and we have the choice to share or to keep those moments to ourselves. (My words) Our testimony gives strength to others!

Day 93

Today's Scripture:

"I will never leave you nor forsake you" (Hebrews 13:5 NKJV).

Today's Testimony:

I was not raised in a Christian home, although my grandmother was a minister. From an early age, I had the desire to go to church. I would go to different churches of different religions but could never quite find the church I was looking for. I would always go to the altar and ask for salvation. But when I left the church, I would not feel any different or stop living how I was living; I knew I wasn't truly changed.

Finally, when I was twenty-five years old, I visited a church in Florida where I knew I truly received the salvation of God. I knew because I turned from my ways and started relying on Him. This was the change I had been looking for.

Throughout the years, I have experienced loss, but my God never left me. I lost my son when he was only thirty-one years old, but in this trying time, I realized God was never going to leave me because of His promise in Hebrews 13:5. After that, I lost my mother, sister, and brother all within a year of each other. I knew He was with me even then. When my husband passed away and later I was diagnosed with breast cancer, I continued standing on my salvation and faith. I began to believe God's Word in 1 Peter 2:24, which tells us by Jesus' stripes we are healed; I am cancer-free for ten years now. No matter what has come in my life, God has brought me through, even through the heartache of my daughter being killed in an accident and my other son dying from a heart attack. Through all of this, GOD has stayed by my side, He has given me the peace that passes all understanding, and each day I wake up is a gift.

—*Betty*

Today's Takeaway:

Betty is a *warrior*. Let's take a close look at her amazing life so far. She longed for God—she wouldn't settle for anything less than the real, life-changing transformation she knew she could have in Him. Then when tragedy came, she held onto the Word of God that assured her she wasn't alone. No matter what came in her life, she faced it with the Word and stood strong. What a powerhouse! We are made strong in Him. It's not our own strength; we are like a pine needle that gets duct-taped to a steel post—the strength isn't coming from us.

Could you use some of that strength today? Betty didn't use it all up. It's all waiting for you too. Open up the Word and let it infuse you with power. Pray it, quote it, write it down, and tape it up so you can see it to remind yourself what God says about you and your situations. Add God to your life and you become Superwoman!

Day 94

Today's Scripture:

"Now may the God of hope fill you with all joy and peace in believing, that you may abound in hope by the power of the Holy Spirit" (Romans 15:13 NKJV).

Today's Testimony:

I spent over half my life separated from God. It was the kind of separation that I didn't consciously know; I just knew everything inside me wasn't at peace. Consequently, my teen and young adult years were very shallow. I was easily influenced by what the world made look glamorous; I tried to look and act the part of whatever situation I was in. I did whatever my heart desired, so I should've been happy, right? Actually, I looked happy on the outside, but on the inside I was struggling.

Praise God, that all changed one day when I attended a church service where my brother was a youth pastor. I remember my soul felt at peace as I heard the salvation message; however, all the outside factors—like hearing other people praying out loud and praying all around me—sent my flesh into flight mode. It took me a while to go back to church, but I decided to surrender no matter what, because I believed with all my heart, soul, and mind that Jesus Christ was my Lord and Savior. Hallelujah! I asked Jesus Christ into my heart, and from that day forward He saved, sanctified, and set me apart so I may do His work.

I have now found that nothing is more fulfilling than sharing my best friend, Jesus, with others. Through Him, my life has purpose, and even through trials I see the Lord's hand working all things together for good. He has blessed me beyond. The Lord's love is everlasting, and I take great comfort in knowing I will take that love with me into eternity.

—*Thereasa*

Today's Takeaway:

Its hard work to look "happy" like the world wants us to, isn't it? Use just the right camera angle, then just the right filter, go to the right places to take the picture, and even post it at the right time of day to get the most "likes." You've got to show the world how "popular" and "successful" your life is. If you make one mistake in the process of posting on social media, then the facade or false appearance is ruined. It's exhausting to keep up a fake life making yourself appear to be something you're not. The sad thing is that Jesus gave His life so we wouldn't have to fake ours to have real peace and joy, but some *still* try to do it all themselves.

How about this: Since our Lord loves us so much that He wants us to have life and have it more abundantly, let's trust Him with our hearts and forget trying to "look and act" the part. Live with joy because you really *have* joy. Let's try worrying a little less about our social media too. We need all the freedom we can get!

Day 95

Today's Scripture:

"He lifted me out of the slimy pit, out of the mud and mire; he set my feet on a rock and gave me a firm place to stand" (Psalm 40:2 NIV).

Today's Testimony:

I *was* in a slimy pit. As I sat in jail, I looked around and asked myself, "How did you get here?" I knew how I had *physically* gotten there, but *what* had led me to the decisions that earned me my final set of handcuffs? I thought back to the last time I was really happy. Then I realized I'd walked away from God.

I was a young mother once. I had keys to the church to get the altar ready for Sunday morning. I did *not* want to mess up; it was an honor to be chosen for such a job. I would often find myself looking to God for answers, talking to Him all throughout the day. That is when the enemy came for me.

He started with little whispers about how this drug or that drug would give me more energy. "You can still be you, just better," he said. And I believed him. I started finding comfort in drugs and alcohol. At first, it was fun; but little by little, things started to fall away from me—the money, the house, the keys, the family. Days turned into weeks, weeks into months, and months into years. It was everything *but* fun. I did more drugs just to stay numb; it was way easier than feeling despair. If I had drugs, I had friends. And they didn't tell me I was wrong; they didn't encourage me to get better. We didn't talk about how much we missed our kids. We didn't cry. We just took the devil's hand and agreed: We weren't good enough for a career and kids; we weren't strong enough to fight him, not smart enough to succeed, everyone was better off without us. I didn't think I wanted to die, but I had forgotten how to live. That went on for eight whole years. Eight lonely Christmases. Eight lonely birthdays. Eight years of my life.

That is when God stepped in. And it is my firm belief that He let it go on for so long, so I would remember how it felt. I was a hopeless dope-fiend. And that day, I looked around my cell and I saw ten other hopeless faces. That's when I heard keys jingling and the guard opened the door and said, "Who wants to go to church?" I remember the light that came on in my eyes. When nobody moved, somehow, I stood up.

—*Jennifer*
(To Be Continued in Tomorrow's Reading)

Today's Takeaway:

How can He love us when He knows our failures? I don't know. We love our kids no matter what, right? We loved them instantly when they were born, and they hadn't done a thing to deserve it. Well, we're His kids and He just loves us, and there's nothing you can ever do to stop it. If you're in a place where you feel like you're a failure, understand this, God is God of "do-overs." He gives new mercies, new chances. Start now by talking to Him and believing He is able.

Day 96

Today's Scripture:

"A man's days are numbered. You know the number of his months. He cannot live longer than the time You have set" (Job 14:5 NLV).

Today's Testimony *(Continued From Previous Day):*

When the guard asked who wanted to go to church, I looked around that jail cell and decided it was time. I got upstairs to "the church" and a member of the ministry team asked me, "How much time do you have?" I really didn't know how much time I had left on this earth. I knew she meant how much time in jail, but I didn't know that either. I just broke down and cried. She asked me if I wanted to change my life. I did. I told her every ugly detail of the past eight years. She told me to go back to my cell and pray for God to deliver me from the addiction. I didn't want the other girls to know I was crying or praying. So, I stepped into the cold shower and prayed, and I cried some more. I was not the same person when I stepped out of that shower.

God *did* deliver me. He *did* restore me. He *did* love me. He *did* forgive me. He *did* guide me. It was all true. God saved my life that day. I live for Him because He died for me. Today I walk along a narrow road and I am never, ever lonely.

—*Jennifer*

Today's Takeaway:

How much time do you have? Just imagine someone asking you that question. We don't ever know and can't know; but one thing we can know is our Father thinks we *are* good enough, strong enough, and smart enough—because He created us Himself. He also knows that people are better off with us around, for He made us to be with them. Sure, we get things wrong sometimes, but we must never believe the lies the enemy whispers to us. His goal is to steal, kill, and destroy—first your joy and witness, but ultimately, your life.

Hold on to your Father's hand. No one ever walked away from God while down on their knees submitting to Him. Walk with Jennifer on that narrow road. She learned the hard way. Oh, how I wanted to wrap my arms around her when I read that she broke down and cried—but then that's just what her Father did, and His hugs are the best!

Day 97

Today's Scripture:

"And I am sure of this, that he who began a good work in you will bring it to completion at the day of Jesus Christ" (Philippians 1:6 ESV).

Today's Testimony:

The choir was practicing the Sunday song during a Wednesday night rehearsal while I slid under church pews—trying to stay hidden from the other children who were seeking to find me. Parents would glare from the choir loft, trying to get our attention so we would stop our game of hide-and-seek, but we avoided eye contact. This is just one of the great memories I have of growing up in church.

My parents were involved in choir, church council, Sunday school, and anything else planned. I learned at a young age that I wanted to be involved and participate in whatever I could to share the Gospel. I joined the choir, attended the youth group, taught Sunday school, organized Vacation Bible School, and helped wherever I could.

It wasn't until a retreat with our youth group that I completely understood what it meant to truly trust Jesus with my life and accept Him as Savior. This certainly didn't mean I was exempt from teenager trials—I made many wrong choices, rebelled in many ways—but I knew in my heart these were disappointments in my heavenly Father's eyes (as well as my earthly parents' eyes). God used these experiences to constantly point me to Him.

I'm so grateful for the Lord's guidance and love that has carried me into adulthood and continues to direct me as a wife, mother, and soon-to-be grandmother. I know I must turn to my heavenly Father first, to always talk to Him in every situation. Sometimes this is harder to do than other times, but Christ has to be a constant.

Thank You, Jesus, for Your blood on the cross, for saving me from eternal separation from my heavenly Father. Lord, help me to remember to put You first in my thoughts, my words, my actions. Help me to teach Your ways and Your Word to my children and grandchildren, to allow You to guide me in every way. Forgive me, Father, when I sin against You after all you have done for me. Help me to turn from sin. I know Your grace is enough. In Your holy name I pray, Amen.

—*Kimberly*

Today's Takeaway:

What a beautiful prayer! This testimony thrills my heart. I love to hear of someone who grew up enjoying the house of God. It's what I imagine Jesus would want. I can see Him smiling as children enjoy His house, can't you? Yes, I want to teach reverence, but gently and with love. His house is to be a happy one for children—and adults too. Smile and enjoy your time there.

Day 98

Today's Scripture:

"Trust in the Lord with all your heart, and lean not on your own understanding; in all your ways acknowledge Him, and He shall direct your paths"
(Proverbs 3:5-6 NKJV).

Today's Testimony:

I have always been a person who sees "the glass half-empty." A few years ago, the glass became very empty for me. I quit my job of over twenty-three years. It seemed like life was in full dump mode. I am a pastor's wife and our church of several years was not growing. My husband was trying to deal with that and with my health issues while working a secular job and doing ministry. My mind was constantly on what I could have done to cause this and how we were going to make it without my income.

I began filling my days by reading a devotional and the Bible more than usual. Instead of leaning on my understanding, I began to really live by Proverbs 3:5-6. I determined in my heart to trust the Lord.

Since then, every bill has been paid and the church has grown by five people. I lost my mother, but even through that, I know God has been with me. I know He has everything in control even when I don't. I just praise Him for all His goodness and mercy.

—*Denise*

Today's Takeaway:

The cares of life can begin to pile up and feel overwhelming to us at times. It makes perfect sense—we try so hard to do our best, don't we? When we work so hard, shouldn't things work out? In a perfect world, they should. The problem is, we live in a far-from-perfect world. We live in a world flawed and stained with sin. The enemy of our soul targets especially those set apart to serve the Lord. He wants to steal, kill, and destroy. He accuses us, blames us, and lies to us to make us think things that happen are a result of our laziness and lack of intelligence or talent. He loves to make us feel LESS.

Denise realized how to combat the enemy and his lies—with the Word. She began to fill her days with the Word and trust in the One who could see her through every difficult trial. She began to find victory over her enemy. So can you! Don't listen to the enemy's accusations. Remember, the Bible says he is a liar. Battle him with the Word of God.

Day 99

Today's Scripture:

"And they overcame him by the blood of the Lamb and by the word of their testimony, and they did not love their lives to the death" (Revelation 12:11 NKJV).

Today's Testimony:

I didn't dream of being a junkie. I don't think anyone does. As a little girl, I had hopes and dreams. But by the time I was thirty-four years old, I was a junkie. I was *lost* in every sense of the word. All my hopes, all of my dreams, all of my plans, had been drawn up into a needle and shot or pressed into a pill and swallowed until the only thing I had left to look forward to was oblivion. I was sick. I felt like there was no hope.

I didn't start out that way. I had a mom and dad who loved me. But my mom struggled with alcohol and drugs, and her life was spiraling out of control. My father tried to stand beside her. She went through treatment several times, but eventually my dad had had enough. My parents divorced and my father remarried. My dad and my stepmom did the best they could to shield my brothers and me from my mom's addiction, but they couldn't shield us from the pain of her absence. I was an outwardly happy child, but inwardly struggling with feelings of rejection and low self-worth. I took my mom's addiction personally and blamed myself for being unlovable.

If my own mom wouldn't stick around to love me, who would? This was a thought I carried into my teenage years. So while she was battling with her addictions, I created some of my own. I started smoking cigarettes and dabbled with alcohol and pot between the ages of twelve and fourteen. I also experimented with boys and I ended up getting pregnant at fifteen. After I had my son I thought, *I'll be the mother I never had.* And for a while, I was. I worked on the weekends, successfully completed twelfth grade, and graduated high school.

But then, ten days after I graduated I lost my mother to her addiction. I was only seventeen, and the last time I had spoken to her, we argued. I blamed myself. And this time, it was my life that spiraled out of control. I began to run. I ran from my past and from my pain, but mostly from myself. So the irony was, I ran to what killed her. I started small again—alcohol, weed, sex, cigarettes. Then I quickly graduated to ecstasy, cocaine, LSD, crystal meth . . . I didn't care what it was. I just didn't want to feel.

—Shelley
(To Be Continued in Tomorrow's Reading)

Today's Takeaway:

The enemy has a lot of nerve. How could he possibly pull this on the daughter of a woman he completely destroyed? But he did, and what's worse, it worked. Shelley, instead of seeing what happened to her mother and taking the opposite path, took the same path. Let's learn better.

Day 100

Today's Scripture:

"'For I know the plans I have for you,' declares the Lord, 'plans to prosper you and not to harm you, plans to give you hope and a future'"
(Jeremiah 29:11 NIV).

Today's Testimony *(Continued From Previous Day):*

I went from being a seventeen-year-old girl, who just graduated high school, to a twenty-year-old woman who was addicted to drugs and secretly broken. So when I was given an opportunity to move away, with a family friend, I did.

I got pregnant again, and after I had my daughter, I was introduced to pain pills. I became addicted to them almost instantly. The men in my life, even my children, became "second" to the relief that I thought opiates provided from my pain.

I tried to get clean, but I couldn't do it. I failed, so I continued to use. I got arrested for DUI's, domestic violence, and shoplifting. Still, I continued to get high. All of the drugs I took to make me feel OK with being alive were killing me.

I had another child whom I immediately had to give up. So by the time I hit my early thirties, I was so tired. I was tired of the loss, the emptiness, the suicidal thoughts, the toxic relationships, and the pain pills that I couldn't afford and couldn't shake. By that point, all my children were with other people and my family had washed their hands of me.

While attempting to shake the pain pills, I started using IV meth. My world became a dark and sadistic place. I lost my mind. Literally. Paranoia took over and everyone became my enemy. I just wanted to die. *I was dying.* I couldn't see my children, and my family was through with me.

In the course of my addiction, I had tried three different treatment centers that taught me I would *always* be a drug addict—that my addiction was a disease. I felt doomed. I would always be this way. But that's where I was wrong. "For I know the plans I have for you. . . ."

—Shelley
(To Be Continued in Tomorrow's Reading)

Today's Takeaway:

Does Shelley have a target on her back that the enemy has placed there, or what? He constantly lies to her and now tells her that she will always be addicted. He is a liar and the father of all lies (John 8:44). We need to believe God's Word, not the lies the enemy tries to tell us.

Day 101

Today's Scripture:

"Jesus looked at them and said, 'With man this is impossible, but with God all things are possible'" (Matthew 19:26 NIV)

Today's Testimony (Continued From Previous Day):

I reached out to my stepmom expressing my desire for help. She stepped in and pointed me in the direction of a ministry called "Beautiful Deliverance," run by Lisa Kapp. I remember calling, and the lady who answered responded with warmth. Not only did they find me a faith-based treatment center, the Mission of Hope, but they gave me a ride across state lines to get there. In my old life I could barely get a ride to the grocery store. I was stunned.

When I met Lisa, I admired her jacket, and she literally gave me the jacket off her back. I will never forget that. So I went to treatment. I went in the program thinking this was my last ditch effort to find myself—and I found God instead; not that He was ever lost.

A few days after I entered the program, I surrendered my life to Christ and began my journey in recovery. It has been the hardest, most wonderful, blessed, and uncomfortable period of growth I've ever experienced. I graduated from the program and chose to stay with the ministry. I didn't go back to the same destructive relationships or places. I started a new life. In the course of five and a half years, I have paid off all my fines, and God has completely restored relationships with two out of three of my children. I have the privilege of being a leader in Celebrate Recovery and have had the opportunity to speak at different rehabs and churches. I've remarried and have been active in jail ministry, recovery ministry, and basically anywhere God can use me. God has turned my *mess* into a *message*—and He wants to do the same for you.

It's important for you to understand, you are not what you have done; you are who God says you are.

—*Shelley*

Today's Takeaway:

That's my God! That's what He does! I'm crying and trying to contain myself right now because I'm so thankful about what He did for Shelley. And I know He does for all who come to Him. That's why John 3:16 says "whosoever." Praise God—He means anybody!

No, you don't have to be bound by crystal meth to need deliverance; He delivers from lying, from jealousy, from anything that has you bound and miserable. The point is He's able and He cares. Just ask!

Day 102

Today's Scripture:

"There is therefore now no condemnation to them which are in Christ Jesus, who walk not after the flesh, but after the Spirit" (Romans 8:1 KJV).

Today's Testimony:

I was just twelve years of age at youth camp and expecting something good from God. One evening in the altar service, they called for anyone who wanted to accept Jesus as their Lord and Savior to come up to the front and make a pledge to follow Him. It was then that I realized I had never prayed the sinner's prayer—I had never been saved. With my counselor that night, I stood up and made a commitment to follow God. That same week at church camp I was filled with the Holy Spirit, and I was so excited to get back home to share my testimony with everyone at my church.

Like most kids coming home from camp, I was on a spiritual high. I knew if I wasn't careful I would find myself right back where I was before. I was able to keep that flame burning for a couple of years with the help of our youth leaders and a few elders in the church, but eventually I let the flame burn out by growing cold and walking away from God. Soon I found myself in sin.

By the age of sixteen, I had become a mother to a little boy. I wasn't expecting my sin to catch up to me, but it did. Broken and not sure what to do, I knew at that time the only right thing I could do was to raise my son in church. I picked myself up, brushed off the shame, repented, and brought my baby to church. I knew I needed God then more than I ever needed Him before.

A couple of years later I met my husband, got married, and had two more beautiful babies. We have worked for the last eight years in youth ministry and have loved every minute of it. God took everything the enemy meant for evil and turned it for good. My son, who is now thirteen, is a constant reminder of God's grace. Though we may walk away from God, He never walks away from us.

—Alicia

Today's Takeaway:

I'm so proud of Alicia for making up her mind to do what was best for her baby—not for herself. She could have hidden at home in shame, but she pushed through, not only to repentance for herself, but also to commit to raising her little boy in the house of God. Bravo, Alicia! God saw that obedience and blessed her with a new plan—a family. He's so good. That's our Father!

Day 103

Today's Scripture:

"Here I am! I stand at the door and knock. If anyone hears my voice and opens the door, I will come in and eat with that person, and they with me" (Revelation 3:20 NIV).

Today's Testimony:

At fourteen years old, I had a vision. I had never seen one before. I saw God in the sky. The picture was like a popular painting. It is the painting of God walking to a door. He was dressed just like that picture, and He walked up to the door, looked at me, and then walked through that door. I was young and did not understand any of that. I just thought that was so cool.

As years went on, I messed my life up terribly. I got pregnant before I got married. I drank alcohol and I was horrific to people. My husband said I could cut people with my words like a knife and smile as I turned the knife. When I married my wonderful husband, it was not that way. In the early part of our marriage things had been better, but now my family was torn completely apart.

This is how I know you can be anywhere and ask God to save you. I bent down in my bedroom closet one day and told my Savior if He would put my family back together, I would serve Him for the rest of my life. At that moment I asked for forgiveness, and from that day I have served my God. I have slipped and not done things right always, but that is the beauty of God. He picks you up and brushes you off and says it's OK. Just repent and keep walking toward Him. We will do it together. My God is absolutely good!

—*Marcia*

Today's Takeaway:

I'm so thankful Marcia allowed Jesus to come in. He made a radical change in her life! He changed her words and treatment of other people. When Jesus is on our inside, others should be able to tell by our treatment of people on the outside. If we find ourselves treating others badly, it's time for a checkup. Something is wrong.

When we fail, does it mean we're headed for hell? It means we need to repent of the wrong we've done. We also need to find out what happened. What caused the problem in the first place? Have we neglected our time in prayer? Is there some "sore" spot that we need to take to God for counsel? If you find that you have missed the mark, talk to God and investigate. Maybe there's a reason. If you stumbled on a dip in the rug, maybe you should look under the rug to check the problem—there could be a rotting floor under there. If there is a problem, God can help you find the solution.

Marcia is right; God is absolutely good!

Day 104

Today's Scripture:

"God's law was given so that all people could see how sinful they were. But as people sinned more and more, God's wonderful grace became more abundant"
(Romans 5:20 NLT).

Today's Testimony:

I grew up in church; my parents took us every time the doors opened. My father was involved with many roles; he worked with the Royal Rangers, he was on the board, and cleaned the church every week. My mother similarly worked in multiple areas such as the Joybelles group, the worship team, and in the nursery.

I have three siblings, and my parents would say I was the most stubborn. My father and I would butt heads a lot. Unfortunately, the godly man everyone got to see at church was not always the side of him I saw at home. My father had anger issues which he didn't know how to control. There were times he would beat me to the point where I would have bruises and marks. I would go to school with long sleeves and pants even in the warmer months to hide the abuse. The older I got, the worse the beatings became, and at times I would walk away bloody. This caused me to hate my dad and feel hate toward the church. I felt they couldn't see my dad for who he really was, so they must be fake.

I was incredibly angry at the world in my teenage years. When I was sixteen, I started dating a guy from work. He was my hero, because he promised me that he would protect me from my dad. I believed him so much that I would do anything for him. I loved him and he became my world. The main problem was he didn't go to church, so I eventually stopped going to church myself. I was with him for five years before he broke my heart by being with my younger cousin/best friend at the time. I was so caught up with him that I continued to date him for two more years. One would think I would've been strong enough to walk away, but I wasn't. We bought a house and a dog together because I was sure he was the man I would marry. Then after two years, he cheated on me again, but this time with his coworker. A man who promised to protect me and love me ended up hurting me worse than my father ever did.

—*Kristina*
(To Be Continued in Tomorrow's Reading)

Today's Takeaway:

Kristina was fighting for love; she just didn't realize at the time that she didn't have to fight. We'll hear more about her story tomorrow; but for now, let's just say, looking for "love" in a man who doesn't understand that God is our true source of love will never be a good idea.

If you are hurting, beware of where you turn to feel better. It's a dangerous idea for a person with an open wound to go to a disease-ridden person for treatment, yet that's the idea many use. Go to God; He's the Healer!

Day 105

Today's Scripture:

"He is so rich in kindness and grace that he purchased our freedom with the blood of his Son and forgave our sins" (Ephesians 1:7 NLT).

Today's Testimony (Continued From Previous Day):

I was so lost and broken that I turned to drinking and smoking. At first, it was just on the weekends, but then it became every day except Sundays. Even though I wasn't serving God, I knew I must respect Him. The lifestyle I was living brought me to many parties. At one of these parties, I'd had way too much to drink. So, I went to lie down in my "friend's" bed where I thought it was safe. I passed out and shortly after, she sent a guy into the room. I couldn't do anything because I was so drunk. All I remember was repeatedly saying NO, but he did not listen. It felt like a bad dream, but when I woke up the next morning, I quickly realized it was a reality. It wasn't until two months after being raped that I went to the hospital in pain. I was diagnosed with STD (sexually transmitted disease). I was devastated. They also told me there was damage to my uterus and I would not be able to have children.

Meanwhile, my brother started serving in the church; he prayed for me daily. He wrote scriptures on index cards and put them in my room or taped them around the house. He never gave up on me and I eventually went to church with him. There I received complete healing from the STD. This changed my heart. I gave my heart to Jesus and started working in youth ministry with my brother. I wanted my life story to be a testimony by helping the youth to not make the same mistakes that I did.

It has been eight years now working in youth ministry since God turned my life around. I am now happily married to a godly man with a beautiful baby girl. I was told I wouldn't be able to have children, but I did, and we are even believing He will bless us with another child in His timing.

God has even brought healing to my relationship with my father. We are both serving in God's kingdom after both stepping away from the church, and have found forgiveness and healing. Our extraordinarily strong bond and love for each other is all due to God.

—Kristina

Today's Takeaway:

(Kristina's words) Keep your eyes on the Lord and know that He has your best interest at heart. He will never leave you nor forsake you. You may even feel at times that your situation is hopeless, but God has a bigger plan. Stay strong and keep your heart chasing after what God has promised for your life.

Day 106

Today's Scripture:

"God is our refuge and strength, an ever-present help in trouble" (Psalm 46:1 NIV).

Today's Testimony:

Generation after generation, in my family, we were baptized as babies. We were taught many rules by priests, through their perspective. We were churchgoers, but not Bible-reading Christ-followers.

I was the "woman at the well." Once I started reading and applying God's Word to my life, His truth and love flowed in and through me and I gave my heart to Christ. That created a life lived in hope. But life lived in obedience, now that's a tough one! I am forever grateful for the Cross. Knowing Christ has given me freedom from fear and condemnation, and I am thankful for every moment. Yes, even the heartbreaking ones. Several years ago, I sat in the hospital praying for my granddaughter to be healed. But when I saw her nurse run to the elevator, I knew she was going to get my daughter and son-in-law, and it wasn't good. Just the day before, I had sat in the ICU with my granddaughter, hugged her and whispered in her ear that Jesus loved her. Now, in that same ICU bed, she died. She left this world for a better one. I felt many feelings: shock, sadness, despair . . . and yet deep inside, there was peace.

Years later, my son passed away, and I had been in prayer for him that very morning. The pain was heart-wrenching. Now, you may be asking, "What do these stories have to do with salvation?" And the answer to that question is *Jesus.*

He was with me and never left my side. And He was with *them.* He was right beside them in their moments of temporary pain, and into eternal freedom. *Salvation* is being rescued and knowing that Jesus is your Rescuer and Redeemer. He is our ever-present help in times of trouble.

—Sharyn

Today's Takeaway:

Being thankful for the cross is almost a hard thing to think of, isn't it? To be thankful for such a terrible thing that happened to our Lord is an awful thing to say. Except that's not the meaning of the sentiment at all. When Sharyn and I and other Christians say we're thankful or grateful for the cross, we aren't meaning we are glad of the fact Jesus suffered, but that He was *willing* to suffer. We aren't glad His hands and feet were nailed through, but that He allowed it. We aren't thankful the soldier pushed a crown of thorns so far on His head that it pierced veins and caused blood to matt His eyelashes, but that He didn't call down armies of angels to stop it. He endured the cross so our sins could be atoned for and a way could be paid for us to go be with God in Heaven. For that, we are forever grateful!

Day 107

Today's Scripture:

"Jesus said, 'Father, forgive them, for they do not know what they are doing'"
(Luke 23:34 NIV).

Today's Testimony:

My salvation experience began when I walked into my first Alcoholics Anonymous meeting. At the age of forty, I crossed into the threshold of the AA room, and when I did, I felt I was entering a new life and leaving an old one behind; little did I know how true that was.

In AA's twelve-step program, step #2 is to turn your life over to a higher power. I was not willing to do that. I was raised as a Jehovah's Witness and thought that was the only way to be in God's favor. I didn't understand what Jesus did for us or what it all meant. I continued to resist for over a month. I was stubborn, and fought with God, not wanting to give in. After struggling and fighting with God, I reluctantly surrendered. That's when everything changed. I started reading the Bible and attending a small Christian church.

On an Easter Sunday morning, I walked into a church where the pastor was telling the story of Jesus and His crucifixion. As I listened, in my mind's eye I was able to visualize everything that was happening; when Jesus was nailed to the cross, I became Him on the cross. As the pastor relayed the words of Jesus when He said "Father, forgive them, for they know not what they do," I felt the love of Jesus that it took for Him to go through the torture. Then I asked the Father to forgive me. I felt His love so strong that I wept like a baby. I now know why Jesus did what He did. What love!

Since that time, I have had Jesus as a friend that I can trust. He brought me through alcoholism, smoking, incurable cancer, the death of my only child, the death of my parents, and the death of my husband. In each of these experiences I have learned how the love of God works in our lives. It was different with each tragic event, but oh, so very real. I wouldn't be here today without Him. God will never leave us nor forsake us. That's why I shout and praise Jesus in church and every chance I have. Our God will meet us where we are.

—*Sally*

Today's Takeaway:

Aren't you glad He meets us where we are? There's no pretense with Him. He doesn't dangle anything out of our reach. He just loves us and genuinely wants our love back. He's waiting to forgive and help us with everything we struggle with, help us deal with every tragedy that's coming, and hold our hand when we need a friend. That's who He is. Why, then, is it hard to spend time with Him sometimes? It is because the enemy works hard to hinder that time. Do whatever it takes to keep it intact—it's your lifeline to the Cross!

Day 108

Today's Scripture:

"I eagerly expect and hope that I will in no way be ashamed, but will have sufficient courage so that now as always Christ will be exalted in my body, whether by life or by death" (Philippians 1:20 NIV).

Today's Testimony:

As a small child I remember always attending church with my mom and dad. At the age of twelve I followed all the "rules" and asked God to save me. However, it was later clear to me that I didn't truly get saved until I was fifteen.

Shortly after giving my heart to Jesus as a teenager, I was diagnosed with a tumor in my spine. I was told I would probably never walk again. My hair was waist-length, and this fifteen-year-old girl was proud of it. It was my "crowning glory." The radiation procedure I had to undergo was going to take that away from me. I remember my pastor's wife coming to me and saying, "God is asking if you're willing to give up your hair." I had to trust God. I was all in, and determined that everything was His. I surrendered my pride and gave it to God. But God was (and still is) so gracious. After surrendering everything to Him, the doctors ended up only having to shave a quarter-size circle in the back of my head . . . not even seen, and I was not paralyzed.

In my early twenties I began searching for something more. I somehow knew there had to be more than rules and regulations on how to live for Jesus. I had a friend who was Spirit-filled. I went with her to a women's retreat, and that's when I found the "more" that I was looking for. I was filled with the Spirit and learned this walk with Jesus was a relationship, not a book of rules.

I am now fifty and still holding on to Jesus. The medical effect of full-body radiation from so long ago is now very prevalent. Over the last several years I have endured thyroid cancer, peritonitis that placed my body in a state of high toxicity, a neurogenic bladder that destroyed both kidneys, and PD dialysis that has failed so I'm currently receiving "HEMO" dialysis. More recently I've lost my sight in both eyes and learned that I need heart surgery. Nevertheless, my God is still faithful. I am taking one day at a time, trusting Him with every minute. Yes, I am still blind. Yes, I still need heart surgery. Yes, I still have to have dialysis. And yes, I am still diabetic. But God is still faithful. I will continue to trust Him. I will hold fast to His hand. I will say today, my "crowning glory" is I am His and He is mine. I will continue to hold fast to His hand.

—*Cherylynn*

Today's Takeaway:

If you ever wanted to see a girl version of modern-day Paul that says, "For to me to live is Christ" (Philippians 1:21)—here she is! This lady has made up her mind to give glory to God and trust Him no matter the outcome, no matter the cost, no matter the inconvenience. She lives for Christ and exalts Him in her body.

Day 109

Today's Scripture:

"Consider it pure joy, my brothers and sisters, whenever you face trials of many kinds"
(James 1:2 NIV).

Today's Testimony:

Even as a child, I had close communion with God. I prayed a lot. My parents were never churchgoers growing up, so I attended various denominations and churches with neighbors and siblings. I was even sent to a Catholic grade school for five years.

I was twenty years old when I accepted Christ. In a tiny little church with probably thirty people in attendance, I heard the salvation message, which planted that right, final seed for me. A young and handsome preacher spoke about the salvation message and I heard testimonies.

I went home and prayed for Christ to save me. Before that, I could never understand a word of the Bible, but I began attending church. Soon, I was reading my Bible and understanding what I was reading, and I felt a change. It was as if scales on my eyes were peeled away. With each day that followed, I slowly understood more and more about God and the salvation of Jesus. Shortly after, I married and had three children. I raised them to believe in the truth of Jesus.

—*Dolly*

Today's Takeaway:

Dolly heard the message and it took root in her heart. She prayed, and she said it was like scales were removed from her eyes. This is like the story of Ananias praying for Saul in Acts 9; when the scales fell from Paul's eyes he could physically see and his spirit could see as well. Dolly could see spiritually. Suddenly, she understood reading the Word when she could not before.

Have you had trouble understanding the Word of God? Pray for the Lord to open up your eyes to "see" the meaning. He can! The Holy Spirit can guide you. Talk to your pastor. Do your part and the Lord will do the rest. When you hunger and thirst for righteousness, you will be filled (Matthew 5:6).

Use a Bible with a trusted commentary on the side, or look up related scriptures that go with the words in your Scripture passage. Also, taking notes during a sermon can open up your understanding of the Word as well. Bible studies and trusted podcasts are good sources for learning too. Soon you'll find that you're hungry for more and getting stronger in your faith.

Day 110

Today's Scripture:

"Casting all your care upon him; for he careth for you" (1 Peter 5:7 KJV).

Today's Testimony:

I was brought up in church. When I was about nine years old, I went to church camp and one of the lessons was on Heaven and hell. The lesson burned into my mind; my life changed that very moment. I know now that the Holy Spirit was touching me. From that moment on, I tried to live the best I could. I tried to pray every night. All through my teen years I tried to be the best person I could be. I could feel Him drawing me; that never went away.

When I got married to my teenage love right after I graduated, I continued going to church on and off, but he didn't go. I still felt the Holy Spirit drawing me constantly; I just didn't commit to anything. I thought it was easier that way with my husband not being saved.

Soon I began to experience loss in my immediate family, including my twin sister at the age of twenty-two. I found it harder and harder to handle things. Then a few years later, I really went down a dark, deep, sad place when my mom died; she was only fifty-one. We were so close. I had nightmares and cried all the time. Then one night after waking up screaming for her, I decided I had to have more of the Lord—there had to be more!

The kids and I started looking for a church; we visited so many and none of them felt right. In the meantime, we moved and decided to try a church down the hill. The kids and I walked in and I knew it as soon as I sat down. I went to the altar the next week and gave myself completely to the Lord. Then I was filled with the Spirit. Suddenly I could see and feel what I had been missing all those years that I was not submitting to Him. He even worked it out for me to serve as clerk of the church. He always has a plan.

Later my husband left me with three children—two were ours and we were raising my twin sister's daughter. My world fell apart again, but this time I had the Lord's strength to lean on. I remember going to church that night. We were having special services, and I went right to the altar and He wrapped His arms around me so tightly. The love He and my church family showed me was like nothing I ever felt. The Lord knew another trial was coming after my mom died, and He knew I would need Him even more than I ever did then. He is so good, and I am so thankful for His love, mercy, grace, patience, and most of all, the fact that He never leaves or forsakes us.

—*Deborah*

Today's Takeaway:

God always knows what's coming. He has strength and mercy waiting for us when we need it. If we'll hold His hand, He'll guide us through every difficult path, showing us which way to step to avoid pitfalls.

Day 111

Today's Scripture:

"In your book were written, every one of them, the days that were formed for me, when as yet there was none of them" (Psalm 139:16 ESV).

Today's Testimony:

I accepted Jesus while attending Vacation Bible School at the age of six. Throughout the years, I followed and unfollowed Jesus. I had not yet learned the importance of trusting someone else to shape me into a decent human being.

I'm an adopted child, given to an alcoholic father and a mother who struggled with mental illness. I became someone who sought love in all the wrong places—I tried drinking and smoking; I barhopped; I dated the wrong men; I cheated. But the worst offense of mine was believing the lie from the enemy that I was responsible for cleaning up my disaster before I could allow God back into my life. I discovered this was not the case at all.

I was married at twenty-two, and had two children by the age of twenty-four. I had God on standby, in case I needed Him. Eighteen years later, I found myself in a hospital emergency room watching my husband fighting for his next breath after a day of drug abuse and an attempt to commit suicide. I realized I had arrived in this scenario by my own choices. I had struggled during the entire marriage to get my husband sober. I thought I could bring him to Jesus. But instead, here I was staring fate in the face and too afraid to ask God for help.

As I sat there looking at my life in pieces, I heard the Lord speak directly to my disaster, "I have something better for your life, but you have to choose to believe." I ignored it the first time. The second time, I knew He was serious. As soon as I accepted, God moved on my behalf. He supplied every need. He directed me to a church that took me in and loved me back together. I began to believe He was my rescuer no matter how deeply I was lost.

As I look back over the shattered pieces of my life, I can see God has stood beside me even in the times when I chose to unfollow Him. He never wavered. He never left. He never took His eyes off of me. Today I know, no matter what trouble I am in, God will reach down, pick me up, tell me He loves me, and redirect my path. I know now His plans have always been good for me. I know He loves me because I am His beautiful creation. He loves me unconditionally.

—Brenda

Today's Takeaway:

No matter how far, no matter how deep, no matter how wide—His love covers a multitude of sins. And at the end of the day, when we surrender to Him, we are daughters of the Most High King. God is right beside us asking us to accept Him and His love.

Day 112

Today's Scripture:

"What do you think? If a man owns a hundred sheep, and one of them wanders away, will he not leave the ninety-nine on the hills and go to look for the one that wandered off?" (Matthew 18:12 NIV).

Today's Testimony:

Years ago, I had a great life. I had a husband and four kids with a home, car, and lots of friends who loved me. One day I went astray and lost it all. I lost respect from all my family, friends, and for myself. I turned to drugs and alcohol to ease the pain I felt. I was lost and thought God had given up on me.

I lived on the streets homeless for a long time, eating out of dumpsters, living in abandoned buildings with rats and roaches. I had no money and no place to clean up. It was horrible. There were no rooms available in the shelter; I was scared to sleep for fear that I wouldn't wake up—I had seen too many people on the street who didn't wake up. Many freeze or get shot or stabbed to death or even worse. I was in a building once where a girl who was in the room above me was found beheaded.

The next day I went down to the river and sat thinking about what to do. I kept hearing something that sounded like someone whispering to me. When I looked around, no one was there except a man by the edge of the river about half a block from me. The voice said, "You are better than this. Don't give up; take my hand. The man you see needs you to help him." I found myself going over to that man. We started talking; he told me he was there to end his life by jumping in the river. I talked him out of it and told me things couldn't be that bad. Then I heard the rest of his story. We decided to try and work out our problems together. It's been twenty-four years now and we are still together.

Later we saw a friend working in a church yard and started talking. This renewal of friendship helped to change the direction of our lives. We decided enough was enough, and with God's help we gave up alcohol and decided to get in church. We got saved, regained our family and friends, and respect. God has even blessed us now to have our own home and a ministry to the homeless and the needy. By His amazing grace and love, I am healed. Thank You, Jesus!

—*Darleen*

Today's Takeaway:

His amazing love never ceases to amaze and astound me. He covered Darleen and kept her. Now He uses her to minister to others in a way that many could not possibly understand. God never wastes pain! She went through a lot, but *all* of it is being used to serve others and help them find their way now. Hallelujah! Whatever you're going through, remember He'll use it for His glory.

Day 113

Today's Scripture:

"I will give you a new heart and put a new spirit within you; I will take the heart of stone out of your flesh and give you a heart of flesh" (Ezekiel 36:26 NKJV).

Today's Testimony:

I was born into a Christian family and attended church regularly while growing up. Our church and denomination believed in holiness, but it was to a large degree an outward holiness. The women were required to dress a certain way and keep their hair long. We weren't supposed to wear jewelry or makeup or go to the movies. I don't remember hearing much about the love of God. Salvation seemed to be all about rules.

When I was a teenager, I was invited to go to a winter retreat with some friends from a church in another community. The youth group from their church was invited to a church at a ski resort in a mountain town, and would participate in the services that were going to be held each evening.

One evening I wasn't feeling well and didn't go to the service, but I stayed in the room where all the girls slept. This room was right next to the sanctuary and I could hear the testimonies by these young people.

I knew I needed what they had. I had never surrendered to the Lord because I really didn't know He was a loving God. In my mind He was someone to be afraid of and not someone you could have a relationship with, but I longed to know the Savior in a personal way. As I was lying there in my sleeping bag, listening to the service and the wonderful testimonies by the youth group, it was like I had a vision: I saw myself standing on top of a cliff high above the ground, and I knew I had a choice to make. I could either remain the way I was, miserable and afraid, or I could take a step forward. That meant stepping off the cliff, and I knew one of two things would happen when I did—I would either fall to the ground and be destroyed, or someone would catch me. In this vision I took that step off the cliff and I didn't fall! It was as if I stepped onto a big hand that held me up *and wouldn't let me fall!* Then I went to sleep and slept all night.

When I got up the next morning, I didn't even think about the night before, until I went outside. When I stepped outside and saw the pure white snow all around, with the sun shining on it and making it sparkle, all of a sudden I remembered, and my heart felt just like that beautiful clean snow! I felt such peace in my heart, and there was no turmoil or fear—I just felt brand-new!

—Maud

Today's Takeaway:

(Maud's words) It's amazing what God can do if you just trust Him! That was many years ago, but He has been faithful and I still have that peace He gave me when I trusted Him for salvation. I took a step of faith, and He gave me a brand-new heart!

Day 114

Today's Scripture:

"Who shall separate us from the love of Christ? Shall trouble or hardship or persecution or famine or nakedness or danger or sword?" (Romans 8:35 NIV).

Today's Testimony:

Have you ever just needed to be loved? You know, that unconditional type of love: love me just as I am; love me with all my inconsistencies; love my kinky hair, brown eyes, skinny body, and average abilities. Can you just love me?

I was born into a family of ten children to a young couple. I was the fourth oldest child—smack in the middle of two older sisters and two younger sisters. With no real position in the family, I got lost in the crowd. I felt the need to be appreciated, loved, acknowledged, but I was lost in the middle.

I was bullied in school all the way through the seventh grade. I would fight back but I didn't want to fight; I just wanted to have a good childhood. I received Christ at a young age, so I trusted Him to help me through my teenage years. I didn't know I was going to need Him for everything—even being loved by family.

My mother died and left ten children behind, ranging from the age of three to sixteen; I was only twelve. My father was placed in a mental hospital because he had a mental breakdown. We were all separated and placed in different homes. I lived most of my teenage years in several girl facilities. I felt unloved, unwanted, undesired, and alone. I didn't know how to pursue God, how to trust Him, or how to love Him. I was searching for someone to mother me; a mentor or anybody that would want to be with me. Due to this intense search, I ended up in a lot of bad situations. I was pursuing love in all the wrong places, but God protected me. He watched over me; He led me out of a lot of dangerous situations.

Nothing I did could separate me from the love He had for me. Even getting pregnant at the age of sixteen could not separate me from His love. Although I was encouraged to have an abortion, I refused. I would end up leaving the girls' facility to live with my sister. I had my baby and left school; I would resume my education later. I graduated from high school and pursued my degree in applied science. I later had two other children, but God loved me so, He provided for me. He was with me every step of the way. I have learned that nothing can separate me from His love.

—*Janice*

Today's Takeaway:

God showed His incredible love to Janice. He was with her in the girls' facilities, even when she didn't realize it. He had a great plan for her life. She went on to become a minister of the gospel of Christ. She shares the good news of His redeeming power. No matter our circumstances, God has the final say!

Day 115

Today's Scripture:

"We will not hide them from their children, showing to the generation to come the praises of the Lord, and his strength, and his wonderful works that he hath done" (Psalm 78:4 KJV).

Today's Testimony:

The Lord spoke to me one day through His Word and told me, "Before you were born, I knew you." I thought, *Me, You knew me?* He spoke to me again and said, "I have loved you with an everlasting love." I thought to myself, *Surely, that can't be me.*

At nineteen, so much is coming at you—the pressure to pick a career; work to pay for college; perform, perform, perform. Then, one day, a "nobody" like me met a King and realized she was a princess. I gave my heart to God and became His daughter—a real-life daughter of a King!

Each day is now an adventure; some adventures I would rather not go on, and some I look forward to—laughing, crying, talking, giving and taking—but always learning to listen to my Father. The days we live aren't always about us, even when you're a princess; they are about what our Father needs us to do for those He puts in our lives.

One day as I read in Psalm 78:4—"We will not hide them from their children, showing to the generation to come the praises of the Lord, and his strength, and his wonderful works that he hath done" (KJV)—the Lord spoke something special to me.

I'm not a mother, but there are still children—my Father's children—in my world, and I want to show them the praises of the Lord, His strength, and His wonderful works. That is my mission—to share with the next generation what wonderful things our God has done.

Now as you go through your day, allow me to pass something on to you: May the Lord lift up His countenance upon you, and give you peace (Numbers 6:26).

—*Georgina*

Today's Takeaway:

You didn't realize you'd be reading a testimony written by a princess, did you? What's better is that if you're a girl that has given your heart to the King, then it's also a princess reading the testimony too. The Lord loves all His daughters and has a plan for all of them. His plans don't involve being served like "normal" princesses; instead, He wants His girls to serve others, share His blessings, and praise Him. In return, He pours out His love and guides through every trial. Straighten your crown, girl! You've got a great "work" to do for the King!

Day 116

Today's Scripture:

"And if [we are His] children, [then we are His] heirs also: heirs of God and fellow heirs with Christ [sharing His spiritual blessing and inheritance], if indeed we share in His suffering so that we may also share in His glory" (Romans 8:17 AMP.).

Today's Testimony:

I grew up in a home where my father was not saved, but my mother loved God. At some point in my teenage years, we went from being Catholic to being Pentecostal, although we didn't go regularly. I had a rough home life. I was always a little overweight. My father battled many addictions, and was abusive to my mother. My siblings would get mad at me and call me all kinds of names; kids in school did this as well. These labels stuck to me like glue through high school and into my adult years.

I met my husband shortly after I graduated, and we were married within a year. We soon had our children and I stayed home with them. A friend invited us to her church and we went. We enjoyed it, and eventually got stable in our attendance and tithing, and became very involved in the ministry.

The closer I became to God, the more I loved Him. Then I realized something was not quite right with my thinking—I still carried all those labels people placed on me into my marriage. People spoke negative words to me so much that I believed them. I knew my husband loved me, and he thought I was beautiful, but I still felt insecure.

When my children were in high school, I decided to go back to college. I joined an online Christian college; this is where God grew me. Through some classes, I realized God created me the way I was for a reason. Things I used to think were wrong with me were my strengths. I was an emotional person, not because something was wrong with me, but because empathy is a strength God gave me. It was so freeing to know who I was, and I stand confident in that. Now I try not to take negative things people say about me to heart.

—Melody

Today's Takeaway:

Your worth and identity are only found in Christ. You have to receive it, believe it, and then walk in it daily. You are a conqueror and co-heir with Christ. Put on your armor and walk boldly in the gifts God has bestowed upon you! If you think God skipped over you, think again. He has a plan for you.

Day 117

Today's Scripture:

"Count it all joy, my brothers, when you meet trials of various kinds, for you know the testing of your faith produces steadfastness. And let steadfastness have its full effect, that you may be perfect and complete, lacking nothing" (James 1:2-4 ESV).

Today's Testimony:

It's never been lost on me that I was born into a family that loves and serves the Lord, and what a true blessing that has been. I came to know Jesus Christ in a personal way in the basement of a Church of God church at the age of five. My father was upstairs in the main sanctuary preaching a message. After some children's church songs and a lesson centered on John 3:16, I clearly remember a desire in my heart to draw close to Him. Shortly after that experience, I was baptized in water and, from that age on, I have had a burning fire in my heart to dwell in God's house.

As many Christians will know and understand, giving your life to Jesus doesn't mean you are destined to live a life free of trials and difficult circumstances. A few years ago after two years of infertility, my husband and I experienced a devastating fourteen-week pregnancy loss. We certainly walked through the darkest of seasons, but that entire time I felt Jesus walking right beside us. We prayed and remained faithful, then soon we saw our reward a couple of years later when we welcomed our beautiful daughter into this world.

I share my story as a testimony that when you come to know Jesus and faithfully hold His hand, you will come out on the other side of every trial victorious in the precious name of Jesus.

—*Chelsea*

Today's Takeaway:

Chelsea points out Christians shouldn't expect to walk through fields of daisies the rest of their lives after they give their hearts to Jesus. The Scriptures clearly tell us that in this life we *will* have trials and tribulations but not to be afraid because He has overcome the world (John 16:33). He will help us to overcome whatever we face when we trust the situation to Him.

Are you able to trust your problems to Him? Follow Chelsea's example. Pray and be faithful while you wait for Him to work out your problem. Worship Him for the answer He will provide—whatever that may be. It may not be what you expect. Then watch Him work. When He delivers, do what Chelsea did and testify about it. Praise God! He is good! He does deliver. And that is why we can count it all joy, because we remember how He delivered us the last time we called on Him and how He delivered our friends, and those in the Word of God. He is the same God now.

Day 118

Today's Scripture:

"For what the law could not do in that it was weak through the flesh,
God did by sending His own Son" (Romans 8:3 NKJV).

Today's Testimony:

Life was literally worthless. My marriage and relationship of seventeen years was destroyed by alcoholism and infidelity. I had done everything to help the man I loved get free from alcohol. We had been through in-patient and out-patient rehab, one-on-one counseling, and couples counseling. I had even tried working for the physician that directed the local chemistry-dependence hospital. It had all succeeded for one year, but then the infidelity beast arose once again.

I was afraid of the anger outbursts and jealousy. I remember two sleepless nights having an open ear listening for the garage door as I paced up and down the hallway. I couldn't deal with losing it all and felt I had no way out. I had been carrying two jobs, raising a teenager, and I was hopeless.

My family was not that far, but the phone call was long-distance and the money barely stretched far enough to cover the basics. I was ashamed and devastated and I didn't want my family to be in pain for me. If I talked about it I would break down, and I had to keep myself going for my daughter. I was in sales and in the medical field; it was important to be who I needed to be to keep my jobs.

My heart was torn apart and I didn't know what to do. I got a piece of mail from a local ministry with writing on the envelope. I briefly looked at it and threw it aside. I didn't have time for junk mail. I don't know how many of these I had thrown away, but today this one didn't get thrown away. God had something else in mind.

—*Dianne*
(To Be Continued in Tomorrow's Reading)

Today's Takeaway:

Just when we feel hopeless, God steps in and causes the plan that He's been working all along to come together for our good. We'll see tomorrow that He pulls in things from everywhere to help His daughters. Sure, He could work things out in the way we want them to be done, in the time frame we want them done, but he is God and His ways are higher and better than ours. You and I have to trust His plan; He is working for our good. Wait on Him and worship while you wait, because it will make you stronger and increase your faith.

Day 119

Today's Scripture:

"Therefore, if anyone is in Christ, the new creation has come: The old has gone, the new is here!" (2 Corinthians 5:17 NIV).

Today's Testimony *(Continued From Previous Day):*

Even though I always threw out the envelopes from this local ministry as junk mail, here this one was, sitting on my kitchen table. Why didn't this one get thrown out like the rest? I sat down.

Out of desperation and boredom, I grabbed the envelope. On the outside it said, "Someone wanted us to send this to you." I opened it and there I read the "Roman road to salvation" scriptures. Romans 8:3—"For what the law could not do in that it was weak through the flesh, God did by sending His own Son" (NKJV)— was one of the scriptures I read.

I couldn't do this myself. I knew I was trying to do everything on my own, and I could not fix it. I went into my bedroom, and fell on my knees sobbing, "God, if You are out there, please help me; I want to die! I cannot live without my husband." Then I prayed the sinner's prayer that was written on the envelope, and fell asleep on the floor. My husband didn't change, but one night, after about two weeks had passed, I realized I was still alive and I had changed! I had been ready to die, but I didn't feel dead! I didn't know how it happened. I took a bath and started to cry and thanked God. I said, "I want to sing with the angels in Heaven to You, God." Somehow I know I began singing with the heavenly hosts! My tears were flowing and I could hear Heaven; it was beyond anything in the natural! I was so overwhelmed that I asked God to stop because I felt as if my heart was so full that it would burst! I could not believe what had happened; it was the beginning of a new life!

—Dianne

Today's Takeaway:

"Therefore, if anyone is in Christ, the new creation has come: The old has gone, the new is here!" (2 Corinthians 5:17 NIV) is what happened to Dianne. The old things passed away and new life came! I have a feeling that if we could talk to her right now, she would tell us that it wasn't how she thought it would happen but God moved in her life. Sometimes the other person doesn't change first, even though we want them to, and they might need to. The person that can change is *us*. Let's give ourselves to the Master to let Him craft us into what we need to be and see what effect that might have on our situation.

Day 120

Today's Scripture:

"I will exalt you, Lord, for you lifted me out of the depths and did not let my enemies gloat over me. Lord my God, I called to you for help, and you healed me. You, Lord, brought me up from the realm of the dead; you spared me from going down to the pit" (Psalm 30:1-3 NIV).

Today's Testimony:

I can't remember a time without the presence of God. My mom took me to church as an infant, and every night we prayed together—especially for my dad to know Jesus. She taught me to love God. My mom and dad fought a lot when I was small; it was in those hard nights I felt the Father's nearness as I would sing worship songs Mom taught me. When I was five, I asked Jesus into my heart. I asked my mom to pray with me and immediately I felt the joy that comes when the Holy Spirit moves into a person's heart.

When I was twelve, my mom and dad got a divorce. I was devastated; I never imagined that would happen to *me*. It was hard to see my mom heartbroken. I struggled too. We had recently moved, and we didn't have a church home; I was in a new school, and I was bullied. I felt alone and broken.

Finally, my parents put me in a different school, and God blessed me with more friends than I could imagine. One of them invited me to her church; that simple invitation was life-changing. The following summer on a mission trip to Colorado, I was filled with the Holy Spirit, and God did a major healing in my heart. I remember telling Him all the things I missed out on. He said to me: "I am the fulfillment. I fill the empty parts of your life from past to present . . . if you let Me. You are whole; you will walk as though you've never been broken." What a promise to hold onto, and I did hold onto that! Every time I felt broken, I would remember God's promise.

After the divorce, my dad gave his heart to God, and our relationship was restored. My mom remarried and is now healed and happy. I eventually went to college and met the love of my life. I've learned a lifetime of lessons about unconditional love and healthy conflict from my husband. Most importantly, conflict doesn't mean a terminated relationship.

—*Christina*

Today's Takeaway:

There are fewer things that rock a person's world more than finding out their parents are getting a divorce. The very best thing anyone can have to prepare them for it is to have Jesus in their heart. The Lord not only comforts us but heals us. Divorce isn't the only thing that can cause you pain or brokenness; life is filled with situations that can leave you feeling broken, but our God can make all things new. Somehow He makes a way when there seems to be no way. It's not always how we originally planned it, but His plans are always for our good. Trust Him today; He's working for your good.

Day 121

Today's Scripture:

"But you are a chosen generation, a royal priesthood, a holy nation, His own special people, that you may proclaim the praises of Him who called you out of darkness into His marvelous light" (1 Peter 2: 9 NKJV).

Today's Testimony:

My salvation story began in my mid-twenties. I was working in a hair salon with some women who were Christians. They invited me to their church, and off I went to my first women's event.

That evening I encountered a heart-piercing message, and saw women weeping at the altar. I witnessed women dancing in the Spirit, speaking in other tongues, and I heard praises going up. I thought, *If God is real, He is surely among these people and they really love Him.*

I was immediately drawn to God and His moving in my life. My husband and I began attending services, going to discipleship classes, and forming relationships with others. We were active in the church and growing. One specific night, however, life's weights had begun to compile and become too heavy for me. Then God gave me a vision of myself on the living room floor accepting Him as my Savior. I hesitated for a brief moment and then thrust myself on my knees and began crying out to Him that I needed Him.

My husband sang "Amazing Grace" over me while I was being saved. I asked the Lord to take over my life and my heart that night, and He did. The next day while praying, He revealed to me that although I had been attending church for a couple of years, it was just the night before that I had truly accepted His proposal. Yes, I'd been gleaning from the Word, attending church, worshiping, and falling in love with Him, but it was in that one moment that it all culminated.

He had pursued me and I had finally accepted. For each person He has a plan and purpose, and mine came to fullness one night on my living room floor. I am and will always be a sought-after daughter who was created, chosen, and kept by the King of the world, and so are you.

—*Danielle*

Today's Takeaway:

It all started with an invitation. She was invited, wanted, included. There was something in those friends that Danielle worked with that made her want to see what made them different. Then when she went, she saw worship to our Lord and it touched her heart. She wanted to come back. She came again and again until her heart was ready to accept Him. Have you truly accepted Him? Just coming to church isn't total surrender to Him; you can't experience His full plan for you until you surrender. But oh the joy that comes when you do!

Is there someone watching your life? Invite them in and see what happens.

Day 122

Today's Scripture:

"He saved us, not because of works done by us in righteousness, but according to his own mercy, by the washing of regeneration and renewal of the Holy Spirit" (Titus 3:5 ESV).

Today's Testimony:

I was raised in a faithful, God-filled home. I grew up serving in the church; I became a worship leader when I was thirteen. I come from a long lineage of pastors, worship leaders, and teachers of the Word. I was simply walking in my family's footsteps, getting molded into what the Lord had planned for me, and I was enjoying it. But, as I've come to understand, it's a vulnerable position to be in to get hurt, to question, or go through denial. Getting hurt in church is one of the worst hurts a Christian can go through; it causes a person to feel rejected and displaced by their own people, or family, and that is what happened to me.

I felt traumatized, hurt, and angry; I felt rejection from my own leaders and didn't know what to do except run away. I questioned if God was even real—how could His own people hurt their "brothers and sisters"? As a result, I turned away to the wrong influences, and threw away my God-filled identity.

I started to run away from my problems; I began to drown my hurt in vaping and using a broken razor blade to inflict pain on myself. I felt broken on the inside, so why not break myself on the outside? It got worse until I put myself into an incident that almost took my own life. That was when I realized I needed help or I would kill myself. So I told God if He was really there to move inside me, or I would just quit!

That Sunday, I went to church. They had an altar call, and just out of spite I went up there. I knelt before God—something I hadn't done in so long—and I just wept. I yelled at Him; I asked Him *why*: "Why do this to me; why put me through this? Are You even real?" That's when a girl came down to the altar and started praying for me. I began to shake and to lift my voice; then my prayers changed to another language. I didn't know what was happening; I just kept weeping and praying!

That's when I realized, there was no way on earth that God wasn't real! I also realized, sometimes God leads us to "slay lions and bears to prepare us for our Goliath." Yes, the Bible promises trials and tribulations, but it is only to prepare us for the biggest things we'll face and for the divine plans He has for us!

—*Jadyn*

Today's Takeaway:

I wish I could tell you everyone in church is perfect, but they're not. Christians make mistakes. Sometimes they hurt others and need to ask forgiveness. Learn to ask quickly. Learn to forgive quickly. Both are essential!

Day 123

Today's Scripture:

"I sought the Lord and He heard me, and delivered me from all my fears"
(Psalm 34:4 NKJV).

Today's Testimony:

As a child, I was extremely shy and hid from people. I dealt with ongoing night terrors. Not only did I battle with insecurities and inadequacies, but also with harsh and often abusive treatment. I was full of fear.

I was regularly taken to church, first by my mom and then by my aunt when my mom stopped attending. I was always so excited about being in the Lord's house. I wanted to attend every service or event that would take place. I felt safe, joyous, and free. I felt shelter and peace. At age thirteen, during a three-week winter revival, I accepted Christ into my heart. There was a powerful move of God taking place. Then on Valentine's Day, I was filled with the Holy Spirit. That night changed the course of my life.

My life's blessing is not one of being pain- or trouble-free. I have faced three battles with cancer. The first and second I faced simultaneously. In the '90s, I was caregiver not only to my mother, who was diagnosed with ovarian cancer, but also my then two-year-old daughter, who was attacked with leukemia. I say "attacked" because I was shown in a dream, while she was still a newborn, that the enemy sought to kill and destroy her.

My mother succumbed to cancer after a four-year battle. But through those years, she came back to Christ. Thankfully we were able to have a healing in our relationship that I had longed and prayed for all through my childhood. I know she is with the Lord, and I will see her again.

As for my daughter, the enemy threatened her life on three separate occasions during her treatments. We came so close to losing her, but God intervened and miraculously kept her. Praise God. She is now a healthy wife, mother, and career woman. I wish I had the space to lay out how God moved in and through our lives. He is amazing.

—*Teresa*
(To Be Continued in Tomorrow's Reading)

Today's Takeaway:

Years ago I heard a song by C. T. and Becky Townsend that says, "He'll be enough for me." You haven't even heard all of Teresa's story yet, and you can already see that this is true for her. She has faced the darkest of nights and seen the face of God deliver her. She knows beyond a shadow of a doubt that He's able. But her story's not over yet. Neither is yours. Are you convinced that He's able? Let Teresa tell you, He is. He's with you now, whatever you're facing.

Day 124

Today's Scripture:

"Those who live in the shelter of the Most High will find rest in the shadow of the Almighty. This I declare about the Lord: He alone is my refuge, my place of safety; he is my God, and I trust him" (Psalm 91:1-2 NLT).

Today's Testimony *(Continued From Previous Day)*:

After facing ovarian cancer with my mom, then going through my two-year-old daughter's leukemia, I thought my battles with cancer were through, but I was wrong. The third battle was just recently, but this time not as a caregiver—I faced breast cancer. I am now celebrating one year post-breast-cancer treatment. The Holy Spirit warned me, prepared me, and kept me through it all—that made the journey so much easier; well . . . *easier* isn't the correct word. I am still dealing with some things as my body continues to heal, but as I said before, the Holy Spirit has been with me every step of the way. I never felt alone or abandoned. He has gone before me in all things. I have never doubted His love or tender mercies in my life. So, for me, blessing has not been pain-free, but it *has* been fear-free.

Blessing has shown forth in my life through the constant presence of the Holy Spirit. He has led, guided, and directed my path. He has provided me with the close family I prayed for as a young girl.

These precious gifts I hold close as they are answers to prayer. We are covered with the anointing of the Lord, and are truly blessed in all our comings and goings. Why should I fear? I leave with you Psalm 27:1: "The Lord is my light and my salvation—whom shall I fear [or dread]? The Lord is the [refuge and] stronghold of my life—of whom shall I be afraid?" (NIV). And Psalm 34:4: "I sought the Lord, and He heard me, and delivered me from all my fears" (NKJV).

—Teresa

Today's Takeaway:

Teresa trusted in the Lord and He prepared her and equipped her to face every situation that was coming her way. I love that! If we will stay in tune with Him, He'll make us ready for battle. He knows full well what's around our corner. If we can prepare, we won't be so easily knocked flat by the unexpected.

Prepare on your knees, girl! Prepare with the Word of God as a sword and shield. When you do, you will have weapons at your ready when the tough times come. Also, if you're standing near Him, you'll be able to hear when He whispers instructions to you. He spoke to Teresa, and because she was *near* Him, she heard. Make it a point to live near your Lord at all times.

Day 125

Today's Scripture:

"And we know that all things work together for good to them that love God, to them who are the called according to his purpose" (Romans 8:28 KJV).

Today's Testimony:

I grew up in a loving family, and was raised Catholic. However, I was never taught what it meant to have a relationship with Jesus Christ. As a result, I always sensed something was missing. My life was devastated when my parents got divorced, but it was from that point I began to seek a relationship with Jesus.

Some friends invited me to go to church with them. I was so blessed; it was nothing like the Catholic services I had attended. Afterward, they explained what it meant to be saved and to have a relationship with Jesus. It was on this night that I accepted Jesus as my Lord and Savior. Again, all things worked together for good.

I now understood, in a personal way, what it meant to have Jesus in my life. He became my faithful friend who would never leave nor forsake me. I experienced true love, joy, and peace. He became my all in all.

It was at this church I met my husband. We were both in youth group together, but were just friends. He wanted to date me, but I didn't want to date him yet. After all, I was eighteen and in college; he was sixteen and still in high school. Besides, he knew God had called him into the ministry and that he was going to become a pastor. At that time, I did not want to be a pastor's wife, but thankfully, we remained friends even though our lives took different paths.

I went on to nursing school and became a registered nurse. He went on to a Bible college to become a minister. Little did I know then, that nine years later, we'd begin dating and the following year, get married. I thank God for the loving relationship we have and that our lives together have been so richly blessed. I'm also thankful for the call on my life to be a pastor's wife.

We wanted to start a family, but were devastated when we found out we couldn't have children. Still, we held onto God and His Word, "With God all things are possible" (Matthew 19:26 KJV). Our prayers were answered when God blessed us with a son we adopted from South Korea; and again, when we adopted another son. They both bring great joy to our lives. I am truly assured that all things work together for good.

—*Susie*

Today's Takeaway:

Isn't it wonderful how God orchestrates our lives? He knew when Susie would be ready to accept His plan for her to serve Him as a pastor's wife. Now she's one of the very best. He'll open doors for you too. Be ready to answer His call for your life. He'll guide you if you are open to Him.

Day 126

Today's Scripture:

"This I declare about the Lord: He alone is my refuge, my place of safety; he is my God, and I trust him" (Psalm 91:2 NLT).

Today's Testimony:

One summer, I started experiencing sciatica problems with my right leg. Because I had experienced this before, I wasn't very concerned; it had always gotten better after a couple visits with my chiropractor. This time was different. I found no relief. After several visits with my family doctor, physical therapy, and then spending most of my time in bed, I finally went to the emergency room and asked for an MRI.

My diagnosis was: cancer in both lungs with metastasis to the spine—stage IV, inoperable, incurable, terminal. I was handed a death sentence. I could not process all that she had told me. I was numb; I had no symptoms. How could this be cancer when all my doctors and my therapist had agreed it was just my sciatic nerve? I was then transferred to a bigger hospital with more doctors, and more tests. I got the same diagnosis. I had never been so scared in my life.

You would think that after a diagnosis of cancer, I would have fallen to my knees and pleaded with God to heal me; but I didn't (I am so ashamed to admit this). I was so numb, it took everything in me to just breathe. Satan had found me in a weakened state and tormented me. He tried to convince me I didn't deserve to be healed because I hadn't attended church in a long time. I had no prayer life, I wasn't reading my Bible; and my faith . . . well, that made a mustard seed seem like Mount Everest. Not only did I have cancer, but I was a big ol' dying mess. But God knew what I needed and placed people in my life who prayed for me.

—*Terri*
(To Be Continued in Tomorrow's Reading)

Today's Takeaway:

This is every person's nightmare, isn't it? There's just one thing that makes this so much worse—Terri didn't have the Lord to lean on. Sure, He was there waiting for her to turn to Him, but she didn't have the comfort that only He can supply when we are holding on to His strong hand. The great thing she did have were godly friends who were there and prayed for her *to know* Christ.

Are you in a position like this? Are you the godly friend? Pray and lead your friend to the feet of Jesus. He is able to see us through *anything we face*! Are you the one living in the nightmare? Trust your heart to Jesus. He's there with you. He'll walk you through every scary step and give you peace that you won't even understand or comprehend.

Day 127

Today's Scripture:

"And the peace of God, which surpasses all understanding, will guard your hearts and your minds in Christ Jesus" (Philippians 4:7 ESV).

Today's Testimony *(Continued From Previous Day):*

It would seem it couldn't get much worse than having stage IV lung cancer, but let me tell you about my *spiritual* cancer. You see, my spiritual cancer was far more advanced and more terminal than my physical cancer. My spiritual cancer, like my physical cancer, had no symptoms at first. I had stopped reading my Bible—no symptoms. I had stopped praying daily—no symptoms. I had stopped attending church—no symptoms. I had no symptoms until it had "metastasized" throughout my whole spirit. I carried bitterness and unforgiveness in my heart; I had created the perfect breeding ground for spiritual cancer to grow. I finally knew what I needed to do to "fight" this battle:

1. I rededicated my life/heart to God (John 3:16).
2. I decided to accept what *I* couldn't change (Proverbs 3:5).
3. I changed my attitude; I chose to be happy in spite of my diagnosis (Romans 12:2).
4. I counted it all joy (James 1:2).
5. I trusted God (Psalm 91:2).

Cancer has changed me more spiritually than physical; the "worst" thing that has ever happened to me has made me a better person. I am more kind; I love more and I do not take one minute for granted.

As of today, my original tumors are gone. I am so thankful for all that God has done and is doing in my life. I am thankful for His grace, mercy, and His love and kindness for me. I am so very thankful for a healing I did not deserve.

—Terri

Today's Takeaway:

Terri has overcome much more than lung-cancer tumors. She has beaten "spiritual cancer" completely—and that is the one that can kill the soul. I praise God for what He is doing in her physical body too. Apparently, God is not finished with Terri yet.

She understood her "fight." Do you? We may not be facing a visit with an oncologist, but we daily face the enemy of our souls. The same one that had convinced Terri to stop reading the Word of God will try that on you. The same enemy that told her she didn't need the house of God will supply you with excuses. The same enemy will distract you from a regular prayer life until you won't remember the last time you prayed. Beware, "spiritual cancer" can be contagious. Hold on to Jesus. Remember, no one and nothing can pull you away from Him. Keep holding on to that powerful hand!

Day 128

Today's Scripture:

"Yet you, Lord, are our Father. We are the clay, you are the potter;
we are all the work of your hand" (Isaiah 64:8 NIV).

Today's Testimony:

I was blessed with a praying, believing mother who loved the Lord with all her heart. She showed day in and day out, through trials and pain, through need and want, through good times and not so good times, that God was the most important thing in her life. She took us to church every time the doors were open, she shared nightly devotions with us, she prayed fire down from Heaven when it was needed, and she was a constant reminder that faith and love for God was our foundation.

When we lost my father two weeks before I turned sixteen years old, she lost the love of her life. I remember seeing her broken before the casket and wondered if she would blame God. Yet, through her pain and brokenness, she allowed God to comfort her and hold her in His arms to strengthen her. Her faith increased more and more. She was always into the Scriptures, singing songs of Jesus all day, journaling her thoughts and prayers to the Father, and loving others with a love that could only come from God.

There is no doubt in my mind that I am a product of a praying, believing mother who modeled God's love. Through her ministry to me, I was born again at the age of eleven, set on the path that God ordained for me. I was drawn into a life of chaplain ministry, and now that I am retired, I look forward to new ministries. My desire is to be *all* that I can be for my Father, as I yield myself daily to His call and direction. Without the woman that God placed in my life as an example and testimony of Him, I would not be who I am today.

If you don't know your true identity, you too can become a vessel of honor. I urge you to get into the Word, find a new life in Jesus by accepting His salvation, and develop a personal relationship with the Father, allowing Him to show you His plan for your life.

—*Anna*

Today's Takeaway:

As a mother, reading Anna's account of her exceptional mother makes me want to get out paper and take notes! What a beautiful testimony of how a mother shaped her child's life by living as a godly example in front of her day after day, in good times and bad. The love of God touched Anna's soul at a young age; she opened her heart to the Lord, and we see how her life has been lived out glorifying Him. What an example to follow—in mother and in daughter! Praise God for a real-life Proverbs 31 example lived out in modern-day life for all us girls to see!

Day 129

Today's Scripture:

"Jesus saith unto him, I am the way, the truth, and the life: no man cometh unto the Father, but by me" (John 14:6 KJV).

Today's Testimony:

I was a rebellious preacher's kid. I grew up in the church. I felt like it was church every day, twenty-four hours a day, seven days a week. At that time, the preachers' kids were set aside and treated differently than the other children in the church. There were so many rules and not much grace; this began my journey to leave God, the church, and anything to do with it behind.

I remember when I was five years old, my brother and I were walking to the candy shop to spend our weekly allowance. My mom had purchased a little white Bermuda shorts set with socks and a sweater to match for me to wear. Some people from our local congregation called and complained; my dad said my outfit had to go back. This was the beginning of my anger. From that day on, every time a "no" was given to me I filed another slice of anger toward the church and God. When I hit my teenage years, I decided I was leaving home and the ministry. That is when things really went south in my Christian life. I chose a route of alcohol, partying, drugs, witchcraft, shamanism, and anything else I could find that was the opposite of the Christian life. I used the excuse that these people didn't judge me; they accepted me as I was, and I felt more welcome with them than I was in the church.

In all of this, I had a mom and dad who never stopped praying. I was a fighter and mean; I stirred up trouble. I can't tell you how many times I had someone's life in my hands ready to take it and something in the back of my mind would say, *You can't do this,* and I would stop. Then one night I went to help sing at a revival; a minister had requested my brothers and me to sing. I was sitting in the back of that church, feeling very uncomfortable during the altar time. Suddenly I felt a tap on my shoulder and heard a voice say, *You need to go.* I looked at my husband and told him to leave me alone, but he said, "It wasn't me." The voice again said, *You need to go; you know the right way.* I stood there and thought, *No, this is not for me.* Then the voice said, *Evelyn, I have called you. You know the way; if you don't go tonight, I will harden your heart.* I ran to the altar and gave my heart to the Lord. Since that night I have tried to serve God, and all the things in my past are gone. My life's motto is, "If God can reach me, He can reach anyone." Someday I want to hear, "Well done, My good and faithful servant."

—*Evelyn*

Today's Takeaway:

Preachers' kids are very special to the Lord. They serve Him sometimes before they even know Him. Unfortunately, sometimes they are scrutinized unfairly and they carry some scars they were never meant to bear. Instead of scars, God means for there to be blessing; let this be your trade day!

Day 130

Today's Scripture:

"I shall not die, but live, and declare the works of the Lord" (Psalm 118:17 KJV).

Today's Testimony:

I accepted the Lord Jesus Christ at the age of twenty-four because of a sweet friend who talked to me about Jesus. This was very new to me as I was not raised in a faith-based home but more like an atheist home. My parents had nothing to do with church or its activities.

Soon there was a Billy Graham Crusade near me; I made a lifelong commitment and jumped into studying the Bible daily. It was a momentous shift in my life. God has led me and blessed me many times over in my forty-five years of serving the Lord. I eventually found a Spirit-filled church where I continued to grow and get involved in church leadership and all types of ministry. God has allowed me to do everything from teaching Sunday school to leading children's Christmas pageants.

It has also been a privilege to serve on numerous committees within local churches, be involved in outreach ministry at a retirement facility, and serve as vice president and also president of local Christian women's organizations. God is so good! He equipped and enabled me to serve others.

Years ago, I was diagnosed with systemic lupus and given ten years to live. This was a severe blow to me. The next seven years were filled with good times but challenging times in and out of hospitals. Our pastor and his wife prayed earnestly for a breakthrough and healing. Finally, there came a significant shift in my health. A very dear friend began quoting Psalm 118:17 over my life daily: "You shall live and not die!" Another Christian friend sent cards and letters weekly with the phrase "This too shall pass." Upon seeing the doctor for blood work periodically, there came what we hoped for—remission, seven years after the diagnosis. Although there have been flare-ups from time to time, my remission is in its twenty-seventh year. All praise to a healing Jesus!

—*Marcy*

Today's Takeaway:

What wonderful friends Marcy has. I want to have friends like that. I want to *be* a friend like that, don't you? She was led to Jesus by her friend; two of her other friends quoted the Word of God over her and sent cards/letters to her with the Word in it. She was healed.

The Word says that to have friends we must show ourselves friendly (Proverbs 18:24). If we want a friend like that, we have to be a friend like that. Let's do our best to follow Marcy and her friends' example. Let's show care because that's how Jesus lived His life.

Day 131

Today's Scripture:

"So let us come boldly to the throne of our gracious God. There we will receive his mercy, and we will find grace to help us when we need it most" (Hebrews 4:16 NLT).

Today's Testimony:

I was raised in a Christian home. My earliest memories are of church, Bible stories, and bedtime prayers. My parents told me about Jesus, who He is, and all He has done. They made talking about Jesus and to Jesus very natural and a normal way of life. They were not perfect parents or perfect Christians, but they were intentional. They purposefully laid a solid foundation of truth in my life as they made Jesus the center of our home.

So, it's easy to see how I asked Jesus into my heart at a very early age. So early that I can't tell you when it happened. At least not the first time. I see now that my struggle was with perfection. I wasn't following Jesus perfectly. I messed up, a lot. I had an attitude, was mean, got angry, lied, or listened to something I shouldn't have. The list is endless. And each time, I knew I did something I shouldn't have. In my young perfectionist mind, I viewed myself as straddling the fence.

I was fourteen when I decided this merry-go-round needed to stop. So, I knelt at the altar at the end of a Sunday night service and decided I was all in. There would be no more wishy-washy stuff. I was going to follow Jesus wholeheartedly. This is when I became *religious*. It fits perfectly into a perfectionist's hardwiring. I worked so hard to follow all the rules and be good all the time. I had to maintain my footing and stay on the path. But, by the time I hit my early twenties, I was exhausted. And I had failed miserably at doing it all perfectly.

That's when I was perfectly positioned for the revelation of grace and mercy. It came to me as I watched my husband work out his salvation with fear and trembling. He was a newly saved addict with a sordid and shameful past. He didn't know any rules. He just knew Jesus. He wasn't trying to do it perfectly; he was just trying to be with the One who set him free. It was messy. It was intense. And it was beautiful. As I watched him sort through it all, I witnessed God's love being poured into his life. I realized God never expected perfection from anyone. He wants to be our Father, Friend, and Guide, empowering us to live in holiness. He wanted me to have what my parents had been so intentional in teaching me—Jesus at the center of my life.

—*Kim*

Today's Takeaway:

From the first moment we ask Jesus into our hearts, He moves in and begins to work. He never stops. He continues to teach us more about Himself as we open ourselves up to Him. All He wants is to be the center of our lives.

Day 132

Today's Scripture:

"Our Father which art in heaven, Hallowed be thy name. Thy kingdom come Thy will be done in earth, as it is in heaven. Give us this day our daily bread. And forgive us our debts, as we forgive our debtors. And lead us not into temptation, but deliver us from evil: For thine is the kingdom, and the power, and the glory, for ever. Amen" (Matthew 6:9-13 KJV).

Today's Testimony:

For ninety days straight, seven days a week, I said the above prayer at the end of every Alcoholics Anonymous meeting I attended. We would say this prayer as a group holding hands. I grew up in church and heard this prayer throughout my childhood, but I never understood it until I was in AA. *Why*, I wondered, *after all these years of going to church, did it not sink in?* I believe it was because I had not been *ready* to hear this prayer until I got to a place in my life where I would listen.

A few years ago I finally got to that place. I didn't realize it at the time, but I'd become an alcoholic. I wasn't faithful in church, and one night, my life took a turn for the worse. I went out with some coworkers I had just met, and we went to a bar. I told myself I would just have one drink. *What could that hurt?* I reasoned with myself. One drink led to many, and then I decided to *drive* home.

At a red light, I looked to see if anyone was coming and didn't see anyone; as I was just about to go, a cop passed and he swerved his car a bit. I waited and then drove. I ended up getting pulled over because he thought I was going to hit him. They arrested me and I spent the night in jail.

The next day I was released; it was cold and snowy out. I had to walk from the jail to my car since it was left where I was pulled over. I had no coat, and my phone was dead. I was wearing steel-toed shoes, and I realized I had no one's phone number memorized.

—Mel
(To Be Continued in Tomorrow's Reading)

Today's Takeaway:

In the Lord's Prayer, we ask God to "lead us not into temptation." I know Mel wishes she had prayed that prayer before this horrible night. What an awful trap the enemy led her into. Tomorrow we'll hear the rest of her story and see her response to her situation. What do you do when you find yourself tricked by the enemy? Do you quit? Lay down in the dirt and give up? No! It's at that moment that we cry out to God and He comes to our rescue. The enemy wants us to think that God turns His back, too ashamed of us, to come when we call, but He is the opposite of that. He *always comes* when we call. So call Him; He's listening.

Day 133

Today's Scripture:

*"Our Father which art in heaven, Hallowed be thy name. Thy kingdom come
Thy will be done in earth, as it is in heaven. Give us this day our daily bread.
And forgive us our debts, as we forgive our debtors. And lead us not into temptation,
but deliver us from evil: For thine is the kingdom, and the power, and the glory,
for ever. Amen"* (Matthew 6:9-13 KJV).

Today's Testimony *(Continued From Previous Day):*

Walking through the cold wind and snow after the shame of spending the night in jail for being drunk and driving was horrible. I had no coat, awful shoes, and a long walk ahead of me.

I left the jail and started heading to the car. At this time I had already been awake for more than twenty-four hours. Halfway through the walk I started talking to God. I said "God, why me? Why am I going through this? I know I put myself in this position. I just want to get to my car. Please Lord, if you get me there, I swear, I will never have another drink." I talked to Him and yelled at myself all the way to my car—which ended up taking me three hours. In the midst of my walking, I felt like I was going to die. I wanted to just lie on the side of the road and die. I kept hearing, "keep going". So I did. When I got to my car, I started crying and I sat inside. I cried, "Lord, I am so sorry. Please help me. I can't do this anymore without You."

From that day, I have faithfully been in church and have not had alcohol! I may not attend AA anymore, but I do say the Lord's Prayer to remind me God can keep me from temptations and to remind me of what God did for me that day.

—Mel

Today's Takeaway:

I believe the Lord was telling Mel to keep going to get to her car, but I believe He also wanted her to keep going beyond that. He urged her along toward salvation. He knew she was ready to surrender her will to His. His will for us is infinitely better than ours. Ours gets us jail time; His gets us Heaven-time!

Today, you need to keep going. Don't give up! The Lord is with you, and He sees all the frustration you are dealing with. He sees when you've been wronged and overlooked. Know this, He is not overlooking you. You are the apple of His eye and He delights in you. Take time today to talk to Him, tell Him all about it, then praise Him because He is working on your behalf. Keep going!

Day 134

Today's Scripture:

"Be still, and know that I am God" (Psalm 46:10 KJV).

Today's Testimony:

I was raised in a godly home from day one. My father was my pastor. All I knew and saw from the beginning was how much the Lord loves me. I loved Him too. I was in church every time the doors were open, sitting on the front row listening to my dad preach about how much the Lord wants us to trust Him with everything and give Him our whole hearts. I always thought I did; I felt pretty confident in that.

A few years ago, though, my world started falling apart, little by little. When my dad passed away, it left a hole in my heart. I struggled understanding why my dad had to leave when he loved so many people and the Lord so much. I continued to go to church like I was taught. I went through the motions of it all. I mean, I loved the Lord.

Several years later, I went to have a minor out-patient surgery that shouldn't have taken over an hour, but instead I woke up having been admitted to the hospital for a few days. I started feeling pretty good and was sent home to finish recovering. I was home for a couple of hours when the worst pain I have ever felt hit me. I couldn't breathe. I was rushed to the ER where they found a pulmonary embolism in my left lung. I don't remember the first couple of days being there. Depression was at an all-time high for me. My hospital room was dark and cold. Even though I had family around me, I felt alone. Fear overtook me in such a bad way I thought I might die. The doctors found I had a blood-clotting disorder. They found there had been numerous clots in both legs previously that I knew nothing about. I needed to be on blood thinners for the rest of my life along with plenty of other medications. I came home with nurses to make sure I was OK.

I remembered what I had been taught since I was a child by my parents. I closed my eyes and decided that day to let go and let God handle it. Trust Him always, and be still and know that He is God. Right then, at thirty-six years old, I truly gave Him all of me.

—*Sandra*

Today's Takeaway:

Depression is real and it is powerful. Sometimes it sneaks in like a slow leak under a floor and it's doing damage that we don't even detect. It weakens our foundation until we get under a heavy attack and then we crack when we least expect it. There's no shame in dealing with it. Everyone has hurt and needs help sometimes. Jesus said to bear one another's burdens and fulfill the law of Christ. It helps to talk things out with someone, especially when we've gone through life-altering events like losing the bedrock of our life, or a major illness.

Day 135

Today's Scripture:

"But Jesus beheld them, and said unto them, 'With men this is impossible; but with God all things are possible'" (Matthew 19:26 KJV).

Today's Testimony:

When my brothers and I were little, my mother took us to church, but my father didn't go with us. Sunday school was fun, and I learned the Bible stories.

As a young bride, I talked to God and said that I didn't know Him. So I started to read the Bible to get to know Jesus, the Son of God. Salvation through Jesus was revealed to me, and I had no doubt in my heart or mind that Jesus was my only way to Heaven, so I knelt by my bed and accepted Jesus as my Savior.

I began to talk to others about how Jesus died on the cross and His blood paid the price for our sins so we could go to Heaven. It wasn't until we started attending church that I had anyone to disciple me, or help me grow in my Christian walk. Soon after we started attending church, my father joined us. I was praying for him constantly. He was not saved and he had a very dangerous job. But one evening, my father walked to the front of the church to accept Jesus. I was amazed. God answered my prayer. My daddy was saved.

That night, when my husband and daughter were asleep, I knelt by the coffee table in the living room and prayed. "Oh God, You saved my daddy. You answered my prayers. If You want me to do anything for You, just let me know." I heard God say, "I want all of you." For some reason I was not at all surprised to hear God, and I replied, "Of course! You have all of me." Again I heard, "All of you." *Wham!* It was like my eyes were opened and I understood. At that moment, I totally committed my whole life to God. I became sanctified—everything I say, everywhere I go, everything I do, I know Jesus is with me. He is my Savior and my Lord.

Many years later I sat with my father, holding his hand when we knew he was dying. He comforted me by saying, "We love each other. We love Jesus. We'll be together again." I have no doubt in my heart that this is true.

—*Marie*

Today's Takeaway:

I believe Marie was her "daddy's girl," do you? I know something else: it's going to be a sweet reunion in glory, isn't it? Yes! First, we'll see Jesus, the One who gave Himself for us on the cross. There's no telling how long we'll spend in His presence. Then we'll be reunited with all our loved ones. Then I believe I'll know all of your family and you'll know all of mine. I can't wait for that. The best part is that we never have to leave each other again. What a happy day that will be! Are we ready to go today?

Day 136

Today's Scripture:

"Before I formed you in the womb I knew you [and approved of you as My chosen instrument], and before you were born I consecrated you [to Myself as My own]; I have appointed you as a prophet to the nations" (Jeremiah 1:5 AMP.).

Today's Testimony:

When I was five months old, my parents gave their heart to the Lord. That started a journey of a family that loved Jesus and going to church. At eight years old I came to the knowledge that I was a sinner and needed a Savior. During a revival I gave my heart to Jesus and was filled with the Holy Spirit. I decided to be baptized to declare my salvation. I always knew God had His hand on my life; I felt His presence with me.

My dad was called into the ministry, and years later he became a pastor. I always worked and served alongside my parents. I grew up singing and sharing the love of Christ, and serving the Lord and people at every opportunity I could.

When I turned sixteen years old, I felt a call from God to preach the Gospel. I had a burning desire to be a pastor's wife. God saw fit to bless me with the desire of my heart and sent me a mighty man of God who was also called to pastoring and ministry. Together my husband and I served for forty-eight years as pastors. I loved every moment that I worked alongside my husband in the work of the Lord.

We retired from pastoring a few years ago, but we serve in ministry at our local church. The calling of God will always be there. God is so good and faithful!

—*Jeannie*

Today's Takeaway:

God is so good! He began to deal with Jeannie at eight years old—leading her to be saved and baptized. Some are not sure, but I know children can definitely experience God's touch. I remember that wonderful feeling of being baptized in water. On a cold Sunday morning, I was baptized in (what I still believe to this day to be) the coldest water I've ever felt. Still, it made no difference to me, other than the chills it caused for a while. Decades later, I can still feel the power I experienced coming up out of that water. Tears sting my eyes even now when I think about how God can touch a child. I've never gotten over it.

Do you work with children, have children, or know any? Pray that the same power of God that touched Jeannie will begin to touch their lives even now and call them to serve the Lord. What a high honor—to be chosen to serve Him.

Day 137

Today's Scripture:

"But ye are a chosen generation, a royal priesthood, an holy nation, a peculiar people; that ye should shew forth the praises of him who hath called you out of darkness into his marvelous light" (1 Peter 2:9 KJV).

Today's Testimony:

When I was a little girl, the first person who ever told me the story of Jesus was my mother. She told me how He loved me, and gave His life for me. I didn't really understand it then, but I knew that Jesus was someone wonderful and that was enough for me.

Later, when I was seven years old, we were invited by my uncle to go to church. Since my family didn't go to church, I was so excited. At his church, I heard Bible stories and watched them come to life with pictures on a flannel board. The teacher explained how the Bible was truth and if God could help the people in the Bible with their problems, He could help us today. Then after the class, it was time for children's church.

I loved children's church. There were songs, stories, games, and then a Bible message. The man asked if anyone wanted to pray and ask Jesus to save them and forgive them of their sins. I sat in my seat and thought about his question. *Have I ever asked Jesus to save me?* I wondered. I couldn't remember ever having prayed such a prayer. I deliberated whether I should go to the altar to pray. Then the prayer time was over and it was time to leave.

Later that night, when I got in bed, I thought about the question, *Have I ever asked Jesus to save me?* As I lay there, I realized I'd never prayed to be saved, but I knew then that I wanted to more than anything. I wanted to be ready for Heaven. In my seven-year-old mind, I didn't realize I could pray right then. I thought I *had* to go back to church to pray. Every night of that week, I was so afraid that something would happen to me before I could go back to church and ask Jesus to save me. I told no one. I just lived in fear, all week long.

The next Sunday, I practically begged my parents to take me back to church. I was so ready when that children's pastor gave his message and asked if anyone wanted to pray to be saved. I immediately went to the altar and gave my heart to Jesus. I will never forget the feeling of peace that flooded my soul. Soon after I was baptized. I never got over it. I had no idea at the time how desperately I would need the Lord to get me through what was about to happen in my life.

—*Tammie*
(To Be Continued in Tomorrow's Reading)

Today's Takeaway:

Since this is my own testimony, I'll tell you, I didn't know what was coming, but God did—He always does. Salvation is the greatest weapon we can have to fortify us for the coming trials we face. It was the same God that saved me when I was a little girl, that carried me through every horrific battle—and that is the same for you!

Day 138

Today's Scripture:

"I will say concerning the Lord, who is my refuge and my fortress, my God in whom I trust" (Psalm 91:2 CSB).

Today's Testimony *(Continued From Previous Day):*

Soon after I was saved, life got difficult fast. My parents divorced; we moved away from my dad, whom I adored, and my little brother and I rarely got to see him after that. Money was a scarcity and we lived all over, eating little and barely getting by, until we finally settled into a used trailer that was parked beside my new stepfather's mother's house. I personally liked the government project house where we had just lived better, but I had no say in the matter.

It had been a whirlwind. My parents each met someone after the divorce and re-married. Suddenly within three years, I went from having one brother to having five brothers and sisters. There was much bitterness concerning the divorce and my life was miserable for lots of reasons. I prayed and God strengthened me. When I did get to see my dad, he would tell me to do the best I could, and try to be good—and I was trying.

One night I woke to a raging fire in the trailer. My mother handed me the one-year-old baby and said she was going back to look for the two-year-old. I was barely conscious from smoke inhalation, but I got out the back door carrying the baby. My seven-year-old brother never woke up from the smoke; neither did the two-year-old my mother was searching for. They both died in the fire together. My face was severely burned. My stepfather's lungs were badly damaged as he tried to get to them; my mother's hands were burned. We lost everything and had no insurance. We were devastated, heartbroken, and didn't think we could go on. My poor mother almost didn't make it, but she gave her heart to Jesus and somehow He gave her a measure of grace to take a step at a time. God slowly, painfully at times, healed my face completely. There's so much to tell, but I'll say that God Almighty walked with me through every step—He was there through each grueling part of the nightmare.

On the other side of it, I can say He caused me to rise with the ashes and go forward to do what He has called me to do. I thought after I'd made it through that trial, surely there would never be really tough places again. I was wrong, but God is still just as faithful now as He was then. He never changes!

—*Tammie*

Today's Takeaway:

Looking at my face now, I know God is a healer. Not only did He heal me on the outside, but He also healed my inside. We never went to counseling about the fire; I refused to bring it up around my mother because I was afraid of her tears, so we never spoke about it, ever. I thought I'd explode with grief. God touched me; I cried out to Him in the night and screamed into my pillow. He comforted me and healed my pain.

Day 139

Today's Scripture:

"Don't let anyone look down on you because you are young, but set an example for the believers in speech, in conduct, in love, in faith, and in purity" (1 Timothy 4:12 NIV).

Today's Testimony:

"My name is Catherine. I'm fifteen years old, in high school, and proud of being a Christian. I invite friends to church when I get a chance. My faith is very important to me and people know it. I always try to put Jesus first in all I do, and I love my church."

Kelly: Reading this, you may say that was short and sweet . . . and it is. It's sweeter than you will ever know. Catherine has been in my girls' class since she was eight years old and now she is a member of our youth group. I am her pastor's wife.

Watching Catherine grow into the beautiful young woman that she is has been an honor for me. I have watched her grow from a quiet young girl into a leader. She invites others to church and is not afraid to share her faith. Watching her grow into confidence as she stands in front of the church on the praise and worship team fills my heart with wonder. The skits or dramas that are performed are all done for the glory of the Lord. God has been so good to Catherine and her family, and our church has been blessed to call them members. Not only does Catherine serve in church, but she also serves the community by helping out at the Feeding America truck each month at the church.

The scripture above says it all. We are not to look down on our youth. They are the church of today! I have seen Catherine and our youth being examples in speech, in conduct, in love, in faith, and in purity. This is a wake-up call to the church. They are watching us, listening to us, hearing us; and what they watch, listen, hear, and see us do will impact how they conduct themselves. We need to embrace, teach, pray, guide, encourage, and love our young ones or the world will do it for us. Blessings to you, Catherine, and every single young person out there!

—*Catherine and Kelly*

Today's Takeaway:

Scripture says to give honor to whom honor is due (Romans 13:7). I love it that this time it happens to be a pastor's wife noticing one of her own young ladies in her church! We honor your life, Catherine. Keep up your stand for Jesus. He will bless you beyond measure. We often talk about how our young people are watching the lives of those older than them, but this goes the other way too. Older people's faith is boosted and encouraged by the young people around them as well. Paul encouraged Timothy in 2 Timothy 1:6 to fan into flame the gift of God that was in him—that faith first lived in his grandmother and then in his mother. Stand up and be a witness—for those older and younger than you.

Day 140

Today's Scripture:

"You didn't choose me. I chose you. I appointed you to go and produce lasting fruit, so that the Father will give you whatever you ask for, using my name" (John 15:16 NLT).

Today's Testimony:

My earliest memories of learning about Jesus were when I attended a local church with my family. We were happy and all together, but for some reason we stopped attending church when I was seven. A few years later, my parents divorced and we dropped out of church.

When I was fourteen years old, I was invited by a friend to a new youth group for young girls to gather after school once a week. Our youth group director was twenty-four years old, married, and the mother of two. She was just starting out on her journey with Jesus and was eager to share her newfound love with others. She wanted to begin by sharing this new love with a group of teen girls. Looking back now, I'm thankful that group included me. We were each challenged to read one of the first five books of the Bible, summarize it, and report back to her. I was assigned the Book of Numbers and my, oh my, I thought it was the most boring book ever. I couldn't understand why it was added to the Bible. Now I appreciate how detailed the Lord is, and that's probably what He was trying to teach me then.

It didn't take long for the leader's contagious love of Jesus to spark curiosity in me. I had so many questions about Jesus and the Bible. I looked forward to meeting with her, and preferred alone time outside of group gatherings so she and her husband could answer more of my questions in depth. I was so eager to be around her that I was at her home and her mother's home practically daily. Wherever she was, that's where I wanted to be, and I was always following right behind her. She made me feel part of her family. One Sunday evening she invited me to attend church with her and her family. They were so eager to answer all the questions I had about Jesus, salvation, and more. After the service, I had an opportunity to ask even more questions to her pastor. I was just so hungry and they were so gracious to answer as much as they knew—all the while still pointing me to the answer-giver, Jesus. The night ended with me officially committing my life to the Lord and being baptized. It was a day and a feeling that I will never forget.

—*Melissa*

Today's Takeaway:

Melissa was hungry and thirsty for the Lord. This came about because of the youth group started by a young new Christian. How wonderful! One new Christian brought about the birth of another new Christian. She welcomed her questions and answered them by studying the Word and pointing her to Jesus. That's what we do. We shine a light and it draws others to Him.

Day 141

Today's Scripture:

"I will give thanks to You, because I am awesomely and wonderfully made; wonderful are Your works, and my soul knows it very well" (Psalm 139:14 NASB).

Today's Testimony:

I grew up going to church. We were the family that if something was happening at church we were there. I accepted Christ at a young age during a Vacation Bible School at our church.

As a child I was diagnosed with a skin disorder, *neurofibromatosis*. This condition causes tumors to grow all over my body. As a person gets older, the condition generally gets worse. This is my case. Due to my condition, it left me struggling with my self-esteem. This led to bouts of depression, particularly during my teen years. I was made fun of in school. I was constantly tormented in my head with feelings of unworthiness and shame. Fear had a stronghold on me.

During my teen years, thoughts of wanting to die engulfed me. When I was twelve I had brain surgery. During this season I was taking catechism class at my church. The Lord sent some amazing teachers my way who showed me love—despite the stinky attitude I had developed. It was a turning point in my life because they started to crack my outer hardened shell.

It would still be years before I found freedom in my mind. It would take years for me to truly understand that I was loved by Christ. God even called me to speak His word despite a terrible fear of public speaking. I thank the Lord for the journey. I'm so blessed that I am a daughter of the one true King.

—Danielle

Today's Takeaway:

Jesus told Paul His grace was sufficient for him when Paul asked for a certain difficulty to be removed from him. This is sometimes a hard thing for me to swallow. I want things I don't like to be taken away—the sooner the better. The answer is that sometimes God does things differently. I don't pretend to know or understand God's ways, but I do see the results. I see a mighty woman of God in Danielle. She has learned to stand strong in the presence of hardship. She is able to live a life of joy and speak words of life in the face of struggle. I imagine God bragging about her to the enemy and making him skulk off defeated, and I smile.

God knows what He's doing. He does all things well, whether I understand it or not. Can we trust Him? Oh yes, you better believe it. He can handle your situation and dilemma perfectly. Give it to Him and stand strong like Danielle.

Day 142

Today's Scripture:

"I can do all [things] through [Christ] who gives me strength" (Philippians 4:13 NIV).

Today's Testimony:

I grew up in a house with my mom, dad, and three older brothers, with lots of laughs, love, hard work, and dedication. We went to church every Sunday. As a family we were very active in volunteering. It looked good on paper. However, we never learned that there is a relationship to be had with a heavenly Father. The only thing I learned was that loving people and doing good acts was all you needed to get to Heaven. Something was missing. No fault of anyone; you can't teach something if you don't know it.

Years later, I got invited to a different type of church, and from there I started to see things differently. A dear friend invited my son and me to a fun day at their church. We were hooked. The carnival was good, but the message was amazing—you can have a relationship with God if you know Jesus. I knew there had to be more than being born, doing good things, and dying. I remember that day as if it were yesterday. The worship team was playing "Above All," a song about a forgotten rose that was trampled on the ground and God saw it. I heard that and said, "That's me." I felt like the forgotten rose in the song. I gave my whole heart, soul, and spirit to God that day; I invited Jesus in and started to connect in a way I never knew possible. I felt complete.

Now today I'm able to mentor, not only my own children, but I've had the honor and privilege of counseling hundreds of people from many different age groups, all while allowing God to fill me up to overflowing. I'm in awe of where I was to where I am now. With His strength I've been able to walk, crawl, climb, and run through so many things. Philippians 4:13 has been (and will continue to be) my life verse. I hold it near and dear to my heart as the truth, and I will stand on it till the day I am called home to my heavenly Father.

—*Mindy*

Today's Takeaway:

It is a common myth that the way to Heaven hinges on a scale of how much good we do versus how much bad we do. If the good outweighs the bad, then we go to Heaven; if not, then to hell. It's a simple matter according to this fallacy. The truth is that it's way more than a scale—actually, everything hinges on *love*. The Lord who loves us gave His life for us so we could have a way to Heaven. It's amazing how many of us don't know or understand that major truth, but, oh what a blessing when we do grasp it! Then we can soar on that love. Believe that He loves you so much that He knows how many hairs are on your head right now; He knows your thoughts, your cares, and your tears. He also knows how to get you through absolutely anything.

Day 143

Today's Scripture:

"The Lord is good, a refuge in times of trouble. He cares for those who trust in him" (Nahum 1:7 NIV).

Today's Testimony:

I grew up attending a mainline denomination. I enjoyed Sunday school, learning Bible stories, and making crafts, but I never remember hearing the plan of salvation. I believed in the Bible stories, like David and Goliath and Noah. I even believed in Jesus, but I never heard of being born again or a plan of salvation.

School was difficult for me. I barely passed sixth grade. I was an underachieving, unpopular, overweight girl. I dreaded going to junior high. The one bright spot was when I got in seventh grade art class. I had a passion for art. It was the only thing I knew I could excel in, but even better than art class was finding a best friend there. We were a lot alike. We were both "artists" and unpopular but she was different from me in a special way. She was a Spirit-filled Christian. Little did I know how important her friendship would become to me.

I made it through middle school unscathed, but high school was a different story. It was a turning point for me—new friends, new ideas, new opportunities, and gradually a new way of life. I wanted to hang out with my older brother and have fun. I wanted to be "cool". The world can be pretty exciting for a fifteen-year-old. It didn't take long before I was "in the world" way over my head.

My best friend and I were still close; she hung out with me and my new friends but she didn't participate in what we were doing. I knew her parents would never approve of her being with us. Her mom and dad caught wind of some of the things that I was involved in; they were about to forbid her to associate with me, but God was working all things out.

—*Dianna*
(To Be Continued in Tomorrow's Reading)

Today's Takeaway:

No matter what age you are, you never escape the feeling of wanting to be included, of being wanted in the group, of being accepted; that's human nature. It hurts to be rejected. That's why a best friend feels like finding a golden treasure. In Dianna's case, she found a true treasure—a friend who would point her to Christ. Are you a true friend? Do you offer to pray for your friends? Do you tell them when you receive a blessing or an answer to prayer so they can know that God is good in your life? Tomorrow we'll find out the rest of Dianna's story, and you'll see how the coin flipped in this relationship. Sometimes the blessing becomes the blessed.

Day 144

Today's Scripture:

"Praise be to the God and Father of our Lord Jesus Christ, who has blessed us in the heavenly realms with every spiritual blessing in Christ" (Ephesians 1:3 NIV).

Today's Testimony *(Continued From Previous Day):*

Although my best friend and I still hung out with all my new friends, I knew her parents would never approve if they found out she was with us. She didn't approve or participate, but still I knew they would soon end our friendship because of what I was doing.

In the early spring, my best friend's mother stepped outside one bitter cold morning. It had snowed a couple of inches overnight and had almost completely covered the crocuses that were in bloom. She thought to herself that the poor beautiful flowers were going to die in the cold. The Lord spoke to her heart at that moment and said, "Dianna will die too if you leave her alone." Right then, she had a change of heart. Thank God! The friendship was allowed to stay intact under the close watch of her parents.

About six months later, the conviction of God got ahold of me in a dramatic way. I felt as though I had committed an unpardonable sin. At that time there were church services being held during the week in a barn that someone had told me about. I was under such conviction that I called my best friend and asked her to go there with me. I'm sure she couldn't believe her ears. I had never experienced God like that in my life. He was so real. I was saved and filled with the Holy Spirit that night. What a glorious experience! I asked my friend why she had never told me about Jesus' salvation before. Well, of course she had, but I wasn't ready. God has perfect timing. I thank God that my friend and her parents didn't give up on me. By the time we graduated high school, a lot of the kids we hung out with had gotten saved. Never give up on the ones you're praying for. God has a plan and His timing is perfect.

—Dianna

Today's Takeaway:

I believe the beautiful convicting power of the Holy Spirit came to Dianna through the prayers of her best friend's mother. I think God rewarded that praying mother for her obedience to the voice of God to keep their influence over Dianna and allowing the friendship but under close supervision. I love what happened next. It was Dianna who invited her friend to church. This time it was the friend who was blessed to see all that time spent on her friend come to fruition—she was able to see her get saved. How wonderful!

Don't give up on your lost friend or loved one. Keep praying and being there. God is still working His plan.

Day 145

Today's Scripture:

"'Though the mountains be shaken and the hills be removed, yet my unfailing love for you will not be shaken nor my covenant of peace be removed,' says the Lord, who has compassion on you" (Isaiah 54:10 NIV).

Today's Testimony:

One morning I was dying inside as I went on my bike down to the Mississippi River out in a cove. I went out there to end my life. I saw a boat with a diver by the bridge looking for a person that had jumped off the bridge that day. Because of the current of the water, they didn't find the body. I thought to myself, *I really don't want that happening to me.* I just sat at the river and started to realize how powerful the current of the river was!

All I could remember staring at that water was that God created the earth; I had been taught that as a child. Now I had dug my hole so deep that I thought God couldn't help me. I was so angry at God. I thought He hated me because of my mom and my husband's deaths.

I broke down at the river and cried out to God. "You made this Mississippi River; will You please help me?" I believe He heard me. At that time, I backed away from the deep bank of the river. That was my wake-up call! I knew I needed God again in my life. Right then I knew I had an encounter with God. His peace came over me—a peace I had not known before. He saved me!

Last summer as I was traveling, I stopped at that very place at the Mississippi River. I began *praising God,* for now I am a follower of Jesus. I was remembering all He has done for me, putting the enemy in his place—under my feet. I give glory to God only, for His mercy and grace. I have had the opportunity to share the love of God to those that He has put in my path. I will continue to show the love of God in reaching out to the wounded. I stand in the gap and pray for those who are wounded and hurting as they read this. I pray that God will meet you right where you are, in Jesus' name.

—*Barbara*

Today's Takeaway:

I'm so thankful that God *does* meet us right where we are. He doesn't insist that we clean up and put on clean robes like Pharaoh demanded before he would see Joseph (Genesis 41). God comes to us! Jesus even met the thief right on the cross, bloody and guilty (Luke 23). Praise God! He saw Barbara on the riverbank and came to her rescue. She cried out to Him and He answered. He's just waiting on us to call.

If you need Him, call. He's listening. He will answer. The answer may not be to give you what you want, but that's OK. He's a good Father who will supply your need—not your want.

Day 146

Today's Scripture:

"And I will pray the Father, and he shall give you another Comforter, that he may abide with you for ever; even the Spirit of truth; whom the world cannot receive, because it seeth him not, neither knoweth him: but ye know him; for he dwelleth with you, and shall be in you" (John 14:16-17 KJV).

Today's Testimony:

I grew up in church. I remember being saved as a teenager. However, like so many these days, I fell away from the church and my walk with God.

It started mostly in my senior year of high school and into my first few years of college. It began mostly with alcohol and partying, then turned into sexual immorality. I knew it wasn't how I should be living as a Christian. I would ask forgiveness, but never truly repent. Then one day I found myself sobbing in the middle of my bedroom floor. I thought I had found "the one." He was charming, cute, and popular. I was head over heels, but then he betrayed me. I took him back. He promised he loved me and that he had made a mistake. I was afraid of losing him; I forfeited my purity. Our relationship became a cycle of guilt and shame. I know the Holy Spirit was trying to pull me, but I allowed the pull of sin to be a stronger influence in my life. At that time I felt farther away from God than I ever have!

Then the day came when I discovered that this "love of my life" had been betraying me for some time. I was heartbroken! There I was, with a tear-stained face, crying for the pain to go away, when an unexpected answer came. I remember, like it was yesterday, the first time I heard God's voice. He said, "He is not the one." I know it's not profound, but at that moment, it was exactly what I needed to hear. He spoke comfort into my broken heart. I had heard the voice of *the One* who loved me—even in all my sin!

I kept these words close to my heart; and when I met the man God had picked for me, I knew right away in my spirit that he was the one. God ended up being the light in my darkness. He helped me to find my way back to righteousness. I rededicated my life to the Lord. I remember when I prayed at the altar that day—I felt as if God reached down and lifted me out of the dark pit I had been living in and brought me back into His light. He reminded me that He had never left me, and He never would.

—Jennifer

Today's Takeaway:

God understands broken hearts. He's also a loving Father who wants all of His girls to *talk* to Him about who they spend their time and especially their lives with. It's a big decision. Be careful not to leave Him out of the loop.

Day 147

Today's Scripture:

"Prove by the way you live that you have repented of your sins and turned to God"
(Luke 3:8 NLT).

Today's Testimony:

Growing up, I had a godly mother but I chose a different path. I never felt "pretty" or "special", so I turned to drugs and alcohol to stop the pain I felt. It quickly became a habit. After that, every time I felt hurt, I used alcohol or drugs, but especially marijuana.

My mother, who was my rock, was always there when I needed someone to come to my rescue. She would call just to tell me she was praying for me. However, one day she went into the hospital for a routine hernia operation and due to complications that no one saw coming, passed away. Even though I was an adult, I felt so scared and alone without her.

My mother watched Christian television often and one day, when I was feeling alone and depressed, I followed her example and turned it on instead of using drugs. I heard the message of Christ and it touched my bruised, broken, and wayward heart. I finally realized I couldn't possibly manage my own life, smoking pot, and getting drunk. I knew something was missing and I had just found what it was. It was Him. So right there alone at home in my living room, I asked God to forgive me and save me from myself, this world, and the emptiness that was engulfing me. I told God I believed that Jesus, His Son, had died for me and that God had raised Him from the dead. Then I asked God to forgive me for all of my sins and to be the Lord of my life.

I instantly felt a great weight taken off me and felt peace. A love engulfed me that could only come from God. I knew He was there and forgave me. I have never felt loneliness or deep sadness again.

—Lucinda

Today's Takeaway:

We don't realize how everyday habits—listening to Christian messages, tuning our radio to uplifting music, tuning in to a godly podcast—can influence the people around us. You may not know it, but you're an influencer. Be careful that you're influencing in a good way. Be sure you're pointing someone to Christ in what you do—knowingly or unknowingly. People are always watching whether you like it or not. Live for Christ, then even your small Christian habits will come naturally.

Lucinda's mother ultimately helped lead her daughter to the Lord by just establishing a routine of watching godly programming. How wonderful is that? Her prayers were answered. In our cars (maybe especially there), in the grocery store, on social media, on our jobs—let's live like we do when we're in God's house. It's called being genuine!

Day 148

Today's Scripture:

"You did not choose me but I chose you. And I appointed you to go and bear fruit, fruit that will last, so that the Father will give you whatever you ask him in my name" (John 15:16 NRSV).

Today's Testimony:

As I sit here pondering the day my life changed so very drastically, I am reminded it happened a very long time ago. I was seventeen years old and of course, thought I knew everything there was to know. I had just started college and on my second day, I met the man who would later become my husband.

I was raised Catholic and thought I had my life totally figured out. The day we met, he asked me out; I declined, thinking he was rather arrogant. He continued to be persistent, and I soon decided I would try one date. That night we went to dinner; it was awesome and I realized I was wrong about him. I remember getting into his car and on his glove box he had a little plaque; it read "I LIVE FOR JESUS." I remember thinking, *That takes guts.* I loved Jesus but didn't really *know Him.* On our second date he took me to see a movie called *The Omen.* To say the movie scared me would be a great understatement—I was terrified! We talked about the movie, the Antichrist, and the last days. As he was taking me home, he invited me to come to church with him. He said his pastor had asked him to speak. I responded that I had my own church; I had no desire to go to his.

He dropped me off, walked me to the door, and said good night. I went in, got ready for bed, and that night . . . I wrestled with God. All night the Lord kept telling me I was going to go; I argued I would not. I distinctly remember finally sitting up in my bed and yelling out, "Fine, I will go."

I will never forget that day. People were raising their hands and speaking in tongues. I sat in the last pew by myself. I can't remember what he preached. What I do remember is when he finished, the pastor took the microphone and asked, "Is there anyone who would like to give their heart to Jesus?" I don't know how I found myself kneeling at the altar, but there I was. As we prayed, I felt the power of the Holy Spirit in such a powerful way. I can still remember how completely different I felt.

Walking out of church after praying, I thought, *Wow, the sky is so blue and the grass is so green!* I was delivered that day from drinking and smoking. It was one of the most incredible days of my life.

—*Debra*

Today's Takeaway:

Deliverance changes everything. Giving our heart to Jesus and letting Him wash away every hindrance in our hearts makes our entire outlook different, doesn't it? Praying each day reopens that same channel of communication with our Lord. His mercies are new every morning!

Day 149

Today's Scripture:

"Jesus said, 'Let the little children come to me, and do not hinder them, for the kingdom of heaven belongs to such as these'" (Matthew 19:14 NIV).

Today's Testimony:

I grew up in a Christian home where I didn't have a choice about going to church. I was just your average farm girl, hardworking, tough as nails, and a little sassy; but I knew we were supposed to help others, and go to church. My parents made sure of that. Our church had a children's program called "Kids-to-Kids," led by our awesome children's pastors. They made church fun! For example, we got to throw whipped-cream pies at them when we memorized all the books of the Bible. To me, it was just a fun place to go and learn how to be a good person. However, I questioned if Jesus was real or if He was just a made-up story to teach us lessons.

One day when I was about eight years old, they were talking about the Holy Spirit. They taught that God sent the Holy Spirit to always be with us after Jesus died and rose again. I listened to every word that was said, and after the lesson, we went to another room to pray together. My children's pastor asked me if I would like to have Jesus in my heart. I told her I had prayed that before, and asked for forgiveness for my sins, but that since then, I had made mistakes at school and was mean to my friend. She assured me that God would forgive me, and asked if I would like to invite the Holy Spirit into my life. I said, "Yes." I figured I would give it a try.

As we began to pray, I felt the presence of God. I began to cry and became overwhelmed by the joy that was suddenly inside of me. In that moment, I realized the Bible we learned about was more than just another book full of stories—it is true. And Jesus really does care about me. From that day on, I have always known the Holy Spirit is in me and always with me. Even when I make mistakes, even when I don't feel Him there, He is beside me, helping me, and loving me through it all.

—*Cassie*

Today's Takeaway:

Cassie became the girl with a smile that could light up a room, because she knew that Jesus was inside her, and nothing could take away her joy. Give Him your life like Cassie did. Jesus will never let you down. He is always there! He answers prayer, not always the way you want, or when you want, but His timing is best. Trust Him and know that His Word is real!

Day 150

Today's Scripture:

"Nothing in all creation will ever be able to separate us from the love of God that is revealed in Christ Jesus our Lord" (Romans 8:39 NLT).

Today's Testimony:

I struggled with fear most of my childhood. Even though I was raised in a loving home with attentive parents, I feared being rejected and unloved. Often, my first waking thoughts were wondering if I would be rejected that day. I remember feeling choked by thoughts that my mom, dad, siblings, or friends would suddenly stop loving me.

Because of this fear, I never let anyone see the real me. I always wore a "mask" and pretended to be what I thought everyone wanted me to be. I thought if people really knew me and saw what was happening deep inside, they would not accept or love me. All this pretending and repression led to struggles with pornography, a fascination with Wicca, anger toward God, and thoughts of ending my life. Looking in the mirror, I saw how deeply insecure I was and hated myself for being such a mess, but I never shared with anyone because I was afraid of rejection.

I remember the day the breakthrough started to dawn. In a pinch, my dad used my laptop and it didn't take long for him to discover some of my secrets. He called to ask me about them, and I lied, blaming someone else. He seemed to believe me, and we ended the conversation with each other, but the conversation with the Holy Spirit was just beginning. I remember feeling His deep conviction in a way that I had not in a very long time. At the same time, He whispered to my dad to dig deeper because there was more to the story.

—Gabrielle
(To Be Continued in Tomorrow's Reading)

Today's Takeaway:

Fear is paralyzing. Since the Word says God did not give us a spirit of fear, but of power, of love, and a sound mind (2 Timothy 1:7), we know fear comes from the enemy. God had a great and wonderful plan for Gabrielle's life. Fear got it off track from an early start. How the enemy tormented her! I get angry when I think of it.

What about you? Is there an area of your life that you are letting the enemy push you around and bully you? If so, you're like Gabrielle—you're due a breakthrough. Do you need to repent? If so, do it, then call on the One who is powerful enough to push the enemy out of your life. Picture Him like the big brother you call to take care of the bully on the playground. Our God is great enough to deliver us from our enemy. Read tomorrow to see what God did for Gabrielle. He wants to see you through, as well. God is greater than all fear.

Day 151

Today's Scripture:

"There is no fear in love; but perfect love casts out fear, because fear involves torment. But he who fears has not been made perfect in love" (1 John 4:18 NKJV).

Today's Testimony (Continued From Previous Day):

I was at a friend's house and could not sleep that night. After wrestling with myself and the truth all night, I spent the next day trying to ignore it all. But, when I came home that afternoon, my dad asked me about my computer again. As he probed, the dam broke, and I told him everything. All night long I had imagined him being angry, yelling, and rejecting me, but instead he wrapped his arms around me and cried with me. My dad showed me the heart of God as he held me in his arms and assured me of his love, promising to help me through this.

My heart was pounding as all my secrets came to the surface and I asked him not to tell Mom. I was ashamed, full of regret, and certain she would not love me anymore if she knew. Choking on fear, I laid on my floor and wept. As I laid there, pleading with God to take my life, I looked up to see her standing in my doorway, fist clenched, tears streaming down her face. Feeling ashamed and embarrassed, I threw my hands over my head hoping to cover my face and body, begging her not to look at me. In an instant, she sprawled herself across my body and wept with me saying over and over, "I love you, Gabrielle . . . I love you, Gabrielle! Nothing you could ever do would ever make me stop loving you."

As she held me, I saw a picture of me on the floor weeping and my mother laying over me; but then, instead of seeing my mother, I saw Jesus laying on top of me covered in my sin, shame, and regret. Instead of hearing my mother's declaration of love, I heard Jesus saying how He loved me. In that moment, I realized how deeply Jesus loves me as He willingly laid in my mess and wept with me.

The fear that had choked me was suddenly unraveling and I could breathe. I began to see that I was accepted and loved by God, and I began to repent. All the sin, hurt, and shame came pouring out. It was like vomit, purifying my body from poison and toxins. With its release, came freedom, and I felt weightless and clean. And, I knew I was loved and accepted completely.

—*Gabrielle*

Today's Takeaway:

This is a picture of Jesus and us. There we are waiting for judgment and deserving it, but instead, we receive grace and mercy. There we are in our shame, but we get wrapped up in His love. He covers us with His blanket of shed blood and we are washed clean and given a white robe, all because we cried out in surrender to Him. No fear here. Only pure love.

Day 152

Today's Scripture:

"I will praise You, for I am fearfully and wonderfully made; marvelous are Your works, and that my soul knows very well" (Psalm 139:14 NKJV).

Today's Testimony:

It has taken me five decades to begin to understand how much God loves me. Until recently, dark scales covered my eyes from seeing the depth of His love.

I was abused as a child—physically, emotionally, and sexually. Believing my existence on earth was only to suffer, I hated everything about myself. Rarely did I hear anything different than I was worthless, ugly, stupid, dirty, unwanted, and a burden. I craved kindness. I longed for acceptance. I just wanted someone to love me. At eighteen years of age, I married the first man who said he loved me. We were married for thirty years. We had some wonderful times, but also some of the most damaging times of my life. I thought I'd married someone very different from my father, but it turns out, he treated me the same.

Both as a child and an adult, I was not believed; I was even blamed for the abuse. I have always felt alone, even when I was surrounded by loved ones. Later, I received a diagnosis of post-traumatic stress disorder (PTSD). I suffered nightmares, flashbacks, and paranoia. I could not see my life improving. I had two different counselors try to refer me, saying they could not help me. I found myself alone, homeless, and extremely physically ill. I was void of any hope and certain that my death was the solution to bring peace to my family. At the last moment I cried out, "Jesus, help me!" He did!

My PTSD didn't vanish overnight. Satan bombarded my brain with lies. It took the Word of God to chase those lies out of my mind and fill it with the truth. I have scriptures written on sticky notes everywhere; they remind me of God's truth. I copy things like "I am wonderfully made," and "If God cares so wonderfully for the flowers, won't He more surely care for you?"

I now have great peace and am so happy, I cannot contain my joy! I'm constantly seeing God's blessings. I never dreamed my life could be this good! Every day I awake with excitement and thanksgiving for what the day holds. All this is possible only because of God's goodness and love.

—*Debbie*

Today's Takeaway:

God is the God of the IMPOSSIBLE! You may think there is no way for you to overcome the years of abuse or pain you endured, but I'm telling you, God can. Debbie is telling you, God can. It won't be in your own strength. It will be through the power of the Word of God. It is the truth that is like a two-edged sword—it will cut out scar tissue from your soul like a skilled surgeon. Grab the sticky notes, girl; follow Debbie's lead! Wallpaper your space with the Word!

Day 153

Today's Scripture:

"The Lord is my light and my salvation; whom shall I fear? The Lord is the strength of my life; of whom shall I be afraid?" (Psalm 27:1 NKJV).

Today's Testimony:

I remember . . .

Many, many years ago (over 70 now), I was a little girl who was being raised in church. As a child, I gave my heart to Jesus. I know, looking back, that the commitment to live for Jesus my entire life was not fully understood then. And even though the exact date is no longer remembered, the joy of being saved is still alive in me.

I can't recall feeling different or seeing a big change in my life at that young age; but as the years have passed, I have felt the Lord many times teaching me, protecting me, guiding me, and encouraging me to grow in His love and presence.

Thinking over all these years of life, as they happened to me, I know how good and necessary it was for me to have been saved at such a young age. What great strength the Lord provided for me that I needed growing up. What guidance there was for me all through the years. What pitfalls I avoided because I followed His plan for me instead of another plan.

That is why I love the passage in Psalm 27:1: "The Lord is my light and my salvation; whom shall I fear? The Lord is the strength of my life; of whom shall I be afraid?"

I'm so glad I asked the Lord to save me as a child, but that is not the *most* important thing. My prayer is that all who read this will know—it's not how young or how old you are when you ask Jesus to save you . . . it's that you do.

—*Shirley*

Today's Takeaway:

You don't know Shirley . . . yet. In Heaven, you will, if you accept Christ. We'll all be together there, you know. Shirley is a joy. She has served her Lord with joy and gladness, with determination and steadfastness. She means that part of Psalm 27:1 that says, "Whom shall I fear?" No one! She has lived long enough to see that there is absolutely nothing and no one too big for her God. She knows beyond any shadow of a doubt that He's able.

Does that mean she's always had *yes*'s to her prayers? No. Has she always gotten the outcomes she wanted in trials? No. It means she knows God is able to see her through anything. And He'll do the same for you too—just make Him your Lord!

Day 154

Today's Scripture:

"Be strong and courageous. Do not be afraid or terrified because of them,
for the Lord your God goes with you; he will never leave you nor forsake you"
(Deuteronomy 31:6 NIV).

Today's Testimony:

Both of my parents abandoned me at an early age. My grandparents adopted me at the age of three and raised me until the age of thirteen. I had ten wonderful years with my grandparents. My grandfather was a preacher and I went everywhere with him. He taught me how to care for others, how to put their needs ahead of ours, and the most important thing—how to depend on and love God! My grandfather was my rock. Little did I know my world was about to be changed.

My grandfather died of an aortic aneurysm. I remember being picked up from school and going to the hospital. I was devastated. For two weeks after his death, I did not recall anything. At the age of thirteen, I didn't know how to process this major loss. I sunk into a deep depression. At the age of fourteen, I had to go live with my dad, who had another family. I could only pack a few of my belongings because they didn't have room. I was hurt, angry, and felt like I was being thrown away.

I attempted suicide. I came home from church after telling one of the youth there that this would be the last time they would see me. She informed the youth pastor. They sent an ambulance to my door when I had just finished swallowing hundreds of sleeping pills. In the hospital I overheard my father tell the doctor that I didn't have issues with my mental health and didn't need any help. I realized then I was on my own. I was lost, hurt, and I had forgotten God.

When I was eighteen, I was asked to come to church by my coworker. I came to church and it was different than I was used to. The pastor made sure to explain things to me. I remembered my grandfather talking about the Holy Spirit, but I had never witnessed His power like this! After a few months of going to church, I read my Bible more, prayed more, had more peace, and knew I needed Jesus in my heart. I was not where I needed to be. I went down to the altar and gave my heart to Jesus. I had a lot of issues, but Jesus took them and delivered me! Now I have a wonderful husband, son, and a life that I would have missed. God had a plan. He always does!

—*Leigh Ann*

Today's Takeaway:

The enemy had plans to take Leigh Ann out, but God had different plans! She needed to be able to talk through some very difficult life tragedies and changes with someone she could trust. Have you been there? Yes, she could talk them over with Jesus and He is always there, but sometimes when those mountains are really high, take someone's helping hand and talk it over.

Day 155

Today's Scripture:

"Give, and it will be given to you: good measure, pressed down, shaken together, and running over will be put into your bosom. For with the same measure that you use, it will be measured back to you" (Luke 6:38 NKJV).

Today's Testimony:

I had the privilege of being brought up in the church from a young age. From my earliest memories, I have always known the Lord and He has always walked with me and talked with me. But I also remember when I accepted Jesus in my heart. I was six years old, and the actor who played Nicodemus in a radio show called *Gospel Bill* came to our church. He shared the familiar Gospel story and asked all of us children if we loved Jesus with all our heart. He gathered us all around the stage and I prayed a prayer of salvation. I was so excited to have Jesus in my heart. It made it even more special that my favorite radio character from *Gospel Bill* was there. His real name was Ken Blount. It was a life-changing experience.

The year 2020 was a year of great pain and suffering for many families. My family of seven also knew pain and loss during this time. We had been in the ten-year process of buying the home we were financing from the owner, when all of a sudden the owners of the house wanted to have us refinance or move out. We were not in the financial position to refinance, so we had ninety days to move out.

I became angry and bitter, not at God, but at the fact that what we had worked so hard for was being taken away. So, we began to hunt for a new home. With our large family, I kept praying, "Lord, it doesn't have to be beautiful, but it needs to fit us all." So, we viewed a few homes that were very small and I said, "Lord, we will praise You for anything." One day we came across a homeless man behind a local restaurant, and the Lord kept telling me to bring him food and money. So, we followed His directions and did as we were told. I believe God rewarded us for giving to that man. A few days later, God blessed us with a beautiful home that gave us all the room we needed. We are thankful every day and have nothing but peace and joy in this new home because God gave it to us.

—*Melissa*

Today's Takeaway:

Not everyone can say that a celebrity led them to the Lord! You may not have heard of Gospel Bill, but he was quite well known back in the day. What a great memory for Melissa and every child that he led to Christ. The truth is, although Gospel Bill was the celebrity, Jesus was the star of the story. He's the One who helped Melissa and her family in the crisis they faced about their home. His Word guides our response to the hurting world around us.

Day 156

Today's Scripture:

"The Lord is my rock and my fortress and my deliverer; my God, my strength, in whom I trust; my shield and the horn of my salvation, my stronghold" (Psalm 18:2 NKJV).

Today's Testimony:

My salvation story is not like most. I was fortunate enough to be born into a Christian family. I was always told about Jesus and God. We were at the church every time the doors were open. I was six years old when I accepted Jesus as my Lord and Savior.

I remember my grandma was the Sunday school teacher, and she asked if anyone wanted to ask Jesus into their heart. I remember how proud I was and excited to be His. I told everyone! Sure, in life I've had to ask for forgiveness and rededicate my life to God. However, I'll always remember that six-year-old, excited, giddy girl and her love for Jesus.

I have had to endure a lot of medical issues and family issues in my life; but from infertility to other health scares, one constant remains—my love for God has not changed. My strong faith, and love for Jesus, has always gotten me through the healing of many things. Jesus is truly my rock. My salvation is everything. Be encouraged that no matter what your salvation story is—even though you may think it's not special compared to others—*every* salvation story is special.

—*Krista*

Today's Takeaway:

Were you raised in church? Be proud of that. Were you raised outside of church and came to Christ later? Be proud you're serving Him now. No matter your road to arriving in your walk with Jesus, what really matters is what you are doing now. I'd love to look back and say I was raised from my birth to now in God's house—but I can't. What I can do is decide what to do *now*!

I *love* the fact that Krista was proud to be His, and still is. That's what we are as His girls. We are proud to make the decision from this day forward to do what's right for ourselves and our families or those around us. We may not be able to change what's behind us, but we *can* choose what we do from here going forward. That's the most important thing.

Grab your shield and horn of salvation; run to His tower when you need a refuge or stronghold. He's our *Rock*! There may be times that you're going to want to hide, but be assured, He is a strong tower. You're always safe with Him. Go to Him and pray. He'll help you!

Day 157

Today's Scripture:

"The Lord is my strength and song, and He has become my salvation; He is my God, and I will praise Him; my father's God, and I will exalt Him" (Exodus 15:2 NKJV).

Today's Testimony:

God has always been a big part of my life. I received Jesus at seven years old and was baptized when I was twelve. When I came up out of the water, I was filled with the Spirit. When I hit my early twenties, I came to realize just how important God truly was in my life. He protected me through many things growing up and saw me through difficult trials. Without Him, I have no idea where I would be today.

Even though I had trials in my life, I was truly blessed. I had a husband and two great kids. We were all doing great, until I felt a lump. My doctor didn't catch it or feel it until it was too late. I got it removed, and finally, I was in remission and ready for reconstruction. However, during the surgery, the doctor had to stop because the cancer was back. While in the hospital, reading the Word of God and feeling all alone, a nurse I had never seen before came and encouraged me with Scripture. No one knows who she was, but I knew God sent me an angel in the form of a nurse. God was with me through it all.

A few years into remission, and my healing from cancer, I was visiting my sister in Florida. While there, I fell and broke my heel severely. I had to have surgery and the doctor made the incision diagonally instead of horizontally, and casted it so I could come home. I remained in a cast for almost two years. The incision would not stay closed; every time I walked, it would tear open. The enemy really tried to hinder me. This was very painful, but it did not stop me from going to church and worshiping my Savior and healer, Jesus Christ.

Soon after, we had a revival at our church and the minister called me over as I was hobbling off the stage. He had the church to pray for me and the wound closed. Praise God! My doctor was in shock and asked how it happened. I told him that God completely healed me. He asked me why I didn't do that sooner. I asked him if he believed God healed it, and he said, "Yes." So I asked him why he didn't pray for me. God is an awesome God, who still brings healing today. Doctors can't change the facts, but God can. We must learn to walk by faith and to trust Him with everything in our lives. Nothing is impossible with our God!

—*Brenda*

Today's Takeaway:

You can't keep a godly woman down! She's armed with the Word of God, great faith, worship, and a sense of humor. I love her asking the doctor why he didn't pray for her. Ha! God is our healer. Not even a cast for two years can stop us when we *know* that our God is able. Sisters, trust your Healer!

Day 158

Today's Scripture:

"But he was wounded for our transgressions, he was bruised for our iniquities: the chastisement of our peace was upon him; and with his stripes we are healed"
(Isaiah 53:5 KJV).

Today's Testimony:

Throughout my life even as a child, I had a desire to serve and know God but wasn't raised in a Christian home. I knew about God but did not know Him in a relationship. We didn't go to church, so I really didn't know how to have a relationship with Him; but even as a child, He brought me through many trials. As He did this for me, it made my life stronger and caused me to be sensitive to the needs of others. I've always had the desire to help others because of how God helped me.

I grew up in a very dysfunctional family with an alcoholic father who was verbally abusive. My father suffered a stroke when he was in his forties, adding to the stress of our home. There were a total of eight kids including me, and we all had to deal with this circumstance on a daily basis. In spite of this, I was able to overcome it and use it as a lesson in life of how I wanted to live my life both as a spouse and as a parent.

At age twenty-three, I got married and a year later, our son was born. When he was a few months old, we realized he had breathing problems, so we took him to the hospital. They tested him and we were told he had cystic fibrosis, an incurable lung disease, and that he had a life expectancy of two years. We were devastated by the news! My mother-in-law was a Christian and she had us bring him to her church for prayer.

—Ellen
(To Be Continued in Tomorrow's Reading)

Today's Takeaway:

When we get handed news that comes as a death sentence, we have a decision to make—whether to accept it and walk on, or to take it to Jesus and ask Him for healing. Isaiah 53:5 says Jesus paid for our healing. I understand some Christians receive their healing on the other side, but some receive healing *now*. All receive healing, but I'm in favor of that *now* kind, are you?

Now, when you factor in the momma of a two-year-old, stand back! She's definitely in favor of the *now* kind of healing. Ellen wanted her son healed and it done yesterday! Fortunately, she had a mother-in-law who believed and got her church to pray over him too. Would you and your church do that? If not, start it! You'll see tomorrow, it's worth the trouble to pray for the sick.

Day 159

Today's Scripture:

"And we know that all things work together for good to those who love God, to those who are the called according to His purpose" (Romans 8:28 NKJV).

Today's Testimony *(Continued From Previous Day):*

God performed a miracle and our son was healed of cystic fibrosis. We recognized God's power and grace which was extended to us, and both my husband and I committed our lives to Jesus. We joined the church and became actively involved and helped disciple others. God then blessed our family with another son and daughter; they eventually grew up to be successful people. God helped both of them to overcome hurdles in their lives. To God be the glory! Though we experienced many trials especially in health and finances, God always made a way where there was no way, even allowing my husband to get his education to become a project manager.

At age seventeen, our first son woke up one morning with a severe headache and was very sick to his stomach. My husband came home from work and took him to the doctor, where he passed out. On the way to the hospital in the ambulance, his heart stopped. At the hospital, the neurosurgeon came out and told us that our son would not live through the night, but if he did, he would be a vegetable with no hope of a future. I quickly told the neurosurgeon that although what he said might be true, he as the doctor did not have the final say about whether our son lived or not, nor would he as the doctor determine his future—that was God's decision. Every time I walked in the room, they would tell us more bad news, but I would not accept it. I continued to speak healing scriptures over my son. They ended up performing brain surgery, placing a shunt in his brain to relieve the pressure and to remove the fluid that was there. Miraculously, God healed not just his brain but his heart too, which according to the heart specialist had suffered irreparable damage as well. Our son left the hospital three weeks later and was able to graduate high school on time. He went on to Bible college, and after graduation he became a minister and an ordained bishop in the Church of God.

—*Ellen*

Today's Takeaway:

Thank God for a mother who knew that God was in control and no one else. Ellen completely trusted Him and even reminded doctors who is in control. Don't you think they remembered her and her great faith after that case was closed? Her great faith built the faith of everyone around her. God continued His work even past what He started in the hospital. He continued on into Ellen's son's future, calling him to ministry. Who would know better what God could do than the one He did it for? If God has done something for you, tell about it. No one can tell it like you can!

Day 160

Today's Scripture:

"Whenever I bring clouds over the earth and the rainbow appears in the clouds, I will remember my covenant between me and you and all living creatures of every kind. Never again will the waters become a flood to destroy all life" (Genesis 9:14-15 NIV).

Today's Testimony:

I remember my mom putting me and my little brother on the Sunday school bus to go to church. My teacher had a contest going for us to memorize the Lord's Prayer. The prize was a little New Testament Bible with beautiful colored pictures of Jesus. I worked to memorize the prayer and I received my Bible. I loved my little Bible. I was only seven years old when I asked Jesus into my heart, to forgive my sins, and be my Lord and Savior. One of my favorite memories from back then was of singing my Sunday school songs to Jesus by my house chimney when I'd get home.

Over the years I have gone through difficult days, like losing my dad; I loved him very much and he loved me, but God comforted me. I have fought the enemy with the strength God gave me through His Word and His presence. I've shared my stories of victories with the world. Jesus has never left me, and continues to allow me to know and see His unfailing love and mercy. He's my mighty warrior and the keeper of my soul. All glory and honor belongs to my triumphant King of kings and Lord of lords. His loving-kindness is better than life to me. I know His promises are forever true unto a thousand generations.

—Robin

Today's Takeaway:

Robin is like a beautiful breath of spring air that flows over you and refreshes you as you spend time in her presence; the reason is because she has been in His presence! She refreshes those around her. She is a pastor's wife that started out loving Jesus as a child. No, her life hasn't been smooth sailing, so she has learned to fight like a spiritual "Ninja". She is sweet but tough!

That's a great plan, isn't it? Let's be sweet girls when it comes to treating others with kindness, but tough girls when it comes to putting "Satan underneath our feet" (see Romans 16:20) and wielding our swords of the Spirit!

Let's also not forget how wonderful it is that the Sunday school teacher took the initiative to have a contest to encourage the kids to memorize the Lord's Prayer. How wonderful! Teachers, thank you for going the extra mile, for the crafts, the snacks, the games, the "plays," the cards, the hugs, the prayers, the preparation to study your lesson so you can answer questions accurately. Thank you for making a difference in the kingdom of Heaven!

Day 161

Today's Scripture:

"Look at the birds. They don't plant or harvest or store food in barns, for your heavenly Father feeds them. And aren't you far more valuable to him than they are?" (Matthew 6:26 NLT).

Today's Testimony:

God sent a bee. OK, stick with me on this. This is a story about my daughter coming to understand why Jesus came to die for us.

One hot summer day we were swimming at a family member's house. A bee accidentally landed in the pool and our two kids noticed it. I fished it out of the water with a toy basket and put it on the ground waiting for it to recover and fly away. Well, it didn't recover right away and we thought it was dead. It had really just passed out. This upset our youngest child. She didn't want the bee to die. This turned into a series of questions from her:

"Why did the bee have to get hurt?"
"Can Jesus save the bee?"
"Why do people get hurt?"
"Why do people die?"

Recognizing where her brain was going, my husband realized she was ready to have a deeper talk. He told her about the Gospel. He told her that because of sin, God needed to come up with a way to save us. He told her that Jesus was the way and because of Him, we could be forgiven of our sins. Our seven-year-old daughter gave her heart to Jesus right there in the swimming pool.

Some might say she was too young to understand, but I bet she will never forget that conversation with her daddy in the pool. We've had conversations about accepting Jesus to live in her heart before, but she would always say, "Maybe later." We think God knew what a dying bee would do to the fragile heart of our girl and He sent it at just the right moment.

—Erin

Today's Takeaway:

God uses all things for His glory; I have no problem believing He could use a bee. How sweet to think of a dad leading his daughter to know Jesus right there in a swimming pool. I wonder if he baptized her too? Ha! This is exactly the tender relationship that our heavenly Father wants to have with His girls. Is something bothering you? Go to your Father. Ask Him about it. He can handle your questions. If you will listen (be still and open to His speaking to you in prayer) and you will be open (read the Word, waiting for Him to lead you), then He will answer your questions just like this dad did.

Talk to your Father about everything on your heart. He wants to celebrate with you, comfort you, teach you, guide you, and sometimes, when you need it, correct you. It's OK, He does everything with love and care. He's a good Father!

Day 162

Today's Scripture:

"The name of the Lord is a strong tower; the righteous man runs into it and is safe"
(Proverbs 18:10 ESV).

Today's Testimony:

As a young girl, I remember being asked to go to Sunday school with a neighbor friend. The only problem was I went without permission from my parents. They didn't know where I was and were looking everywhere for me. They eventually found me and took me home. After that though, our family started to go to church. And I am happy to say, this experience led my mother and her husband to salvation.

I was then raised in this church from about five years old when we started going. I don't remember the exact age I gave my heart to Him, but I have always loved Jesus. I do remember getting filled with the Holy Spirit at thirteen years of age.

I was married at the age of sixteen, pregnant by seventeen, and had another baby fifteen months later. I was just a kid. But God was with me. And He helped us along.

We moved closer to my husband's family. His mother was so good to me, but still, I was homesick. My husband's sister came into town and offered to drive us back home for a visit. I was so excited to see my family; I missed them very much. My mom wired us the money for the trip, and I couldn't wait to go. However, at the last minute my husband changed his mind; I was devastated. So I took the kids, got a ride into town, and caught the next bus for home. I was scared, but God was with me.

My mom picked us up at the bus station; it was so good to see her. And guess who showed up the next day—my husband! We decided to make our home there in my home state. We've been there for thirty-seven years, and raised five children. My husband got saved and we raised our children in my home church. We were very active with the youth and in the bus ministry. Wonderful years!

We have now been married for sixty-one years. We have many grandchildren and great-grandchildren. Praise God, we are blessed!

—*Sandra*

Today's Takeaway:

It's amazing how God takes what seems like small events to us at the time and they become pivotal events in our lives. Sandra's family was saved, all because she was invited to Sunday school! The small invitation from a child was all it took to turn an entire generation in God's direction. How marvelous!

Day 163

Today's Scripture:

"O Lord my God, you have performed many wonders for us. Your plans for us are too numerous to list. You have no equal. If I tried to recite all your wonderful deeds, I would never come to the end of them" (Psalm 40:5 NLT).

Today's Testimony:

I was raised in a church home and was saved as a young girl. My uncle was a minister in the Church of God. He pastored and preached from the time he was sixteen until he was eighty-one.

When I got married, my husband and I moved to another state. My husband wasn't saved. We had a child and I decided I wanted to attend a church like where I was raised. I found one and decided to go. I got my son ready and we went to the church. Soon they had a revival, and on Saturday night my husband said he wanted to go with me. During the service he went to the altar and got saved. Not long after that, God called him to preach.

After a while, God called our pastor to another ministry. Our state overseer asked my husband to fill in temporarily as pastor until they got a full-time pastor for our church. I believe God had something else in mind for my husband and for me because that was forty-one years ago. Since then we have seen many people saved, healed, baptized, and discipled. God is so good.

—*Barbara*

Today's Takeaway:

God doesn't usually tell us His plans for us ahead of time. I think He does that because it might scare us to death if we could see what He sees. The truth is, His ways are higher than our ways and His thoughts are higher than our thoughts (Isaiah 55:9). He knows what's better for us than we do. That's the bottom line! I'm so glad He does what is best for us. He knew that Barbara and her husband were a perfect fit for their church—even if they didn't know it at the time. Now decades later, they have generations following Jesus because of their willingness to serve.

Barbara was absolutely right! God is so good—and He'll do good in your life too; just be willing to follow His plan.

Day 164

Today's Scripture:

"Once I was young, and now I am old. Yet I have never seen the godly abandoned or their children begging for bread" (Psalm 37:25 NLT).

Today's Testimony:

I am thankful for the opportunity to share my salvation testimony. I was not raised in church. My mom would send me to church when I was a child if there was a church close by. Maybe in my case, that was enough for the seeds of the Gospel to be planted in my spirit because I have always had a desire to go to church, even when I didn't have the encouragement to go. I just always wanted to go to the house of God.

In junior high a friend invited me to her church, and my stepdad would take me and pick me up every Wednesday and Sunday; but it wasn't until I was in high school that I had a genuine encounter with God and gave my heart to the Lord Jesus. It changed my life forever. I was seventeen years old at the time; I am now seventy-four. I can testify that through all fifty-seven years of living, God has been faithful to me.

I would encourage anyone who has not experienced the love, mercy, forgiveness, and faithfulness of the Lord Jesus, to pray and surrender your life to Him. Along with salvation comes joy, peace, and contentment that cannot be found anywhere else. I know because I experience it on a daily basis.

—Connie

Today's Takeaway:

Lawyers say there's no better witness than an "eyewitness." Well, here you have it from an eyewitness—the faithfulness of God. All her life, Connie has experienced love, mercy, forgiveness, joy, peace, and contentment. You mean, it's been "smooth sailing" for her all these years? No, God didn't promise that, did He? He promised He would be there to see us through it. That's what He has done for Connie, and that's what He'll do for you.

If He were an up-and-down, here then not here, undependable kind of God, would David have testified about Him, "I have never seen the righteous/godly abandoned"? Would Connie testify "all fifty-seven years . . . God has been faithful"? Consider these eyewitness testimonies and decide for yourself "whom you will serve," like Joshua asked the Israelites in the wilderness (Joshua 24:15 NKJV). Choose well. *Your* victory depends on it!

Day 165

Today's Scripture:

"But Jesus said, 'Let the little children come to Me, and do not forbid them; for of such is the kingdom of heaven'" (Matthew 19:14 NKJV).

Today's Testimony:

I had a difficult childhood. My dad was abusive and spent all his money on junk, while we slept on the floor. Through it all, I still loved the Lord and gave my heart to Him. Mercifully, the Lord helped me forget most of the painful memories so that I could move forward—only remembering them as I got older and better able and more equipped to deal with them.

I married at seventeen and have been married now for forty years. God blessed my husband and me with several sons, though I endured the loss of one. We've seen a lot of good times through the years, and God has helped us through many hard times and difficult medical trials.

Fourteen years ago, my husband and I were called into the ministry. We each had good jobs and were working at our local church. Church was our life, but God was calling us deeper. We both felt that call and we obeyed, although at times it meant sacrifice. We see that God has seen us through and sustained us in all circumstances we have faced.

That is why I feel we have a different type of church. Our congregation has been blessed over the past years. We have a benevolent ministry and love helping people in all walks of life. God sends people to the church to join in to help in ministry right when they are needed. It's a beautiful, diverse group of people who love to minister to others. I think it's what the kingdom of Heaven will look like.

I'm so thankful God counted us worthy to call us into ministry and we haven't had a moment to look back. We are doing our best for the Kingdom until God tells us we are done.

—*Paulette*

Today's Takeaway:

When we live for our Lord, doing our best for the kingdom of God, there is no better existence under Heaven. The pain of your past, the heartaches of this world, can't weigh you too far down when you have your eyes fixed on your Lord and on His kingdom.

After all, we are only strangers passing through this world. Heaven is our real home; let's not get too caught up in the "rat race" here trying to have the biggest house, the coolest and most expensive car, and so on. At any moment, Jesus could come back, and the real things that matter should be first. Forget the car. Let's fish for men and women!

Day 166

Today's Scripture:

"Therefore, if anyone is in Christ, he is a new creation; old things have passed away; behold, all things have become new" (2 Corinthians 5:17 NKJV).

Today's Testimony:

Growing up I always had a "mask" on—the mask that was smiling and laughing. On the surface I wanted everybody to see me as reliable and happy, but deep down I was upset and frustrated. These feelings initially stemmed from leaving a culture of Buddhism and my mom when I was just four years old and moving to the U.S. with my dad. He had remarried and suddenly I was thrust into a culture and language I didn't understand. As a young child, I desperately wanted to blend in and be a part of the people around me. I tried my best to not speak my native language and instead learn the teachings of the Jehovah's Witnesses with my new blended family.

At eight years old, I gained a sibling; I was excited and wanted to help; somehow this led to conflict and arguments within the family. I would hide, but the next day all would be well. This cycle taught me to keep everything inside; just put on a mask. That's what I did during my school years when I got picked on for how I looked different or how funny my name sounded. I would just laugh it off, so the bullies wouldn't get the satisfaction that they hurt my feelings. It was my way of blending in.

When I became a young adult, I got mixed up with people who drank and did drugs. I hung out with them for a while in this lifestyle, but deep down I was tired and fed up with the person I was. When I met my soon-to-be husband, he introduced me to a different kind of church. My whole thought process changed the night we went to see a "Heaven's Gate, Hell's Flames" production while in Florida. I'm a visual person and the way that show was performed spoke volumes to me. Afterward, I knew what I was missing in my life. When they asked for people to come down to the altar who wanted to accept Jesus into their heart, I couldn't get down there fast enough; I was bawling my eyes out. Then and there I decided never to look back at my old lifestyle and only move forward toward Him.

My change didn't happen overnight: He's still continuously working in me and through me. I'm thankful for His grace, that even someone as unqualified as me can be welcomed into His embrace. That smiling mask I used to have has been replaced with a genuine smile.

—*Sareeya*

Today's Takeaway:

I can't imagine how strong Sareeya must be to have been able to leave behind her mother and entire way of life at four years old and move to America, and learn a new language, family, and *everything*. She is an amazing woman of God today! God had a great plan for her life. Believe me, she needs no mask. Her smile lights up a room. It's because of Jesus inside of her. Ditch the mask! Show *you*!

Day 167

Today's Scripture:

*"The master was full of praise. 'Well done, my good and faithful servant.
You have been faithful in handling this small amount, so now I will give you
many more responsibilities. Let's celebrate together!'"* (Matthew 25:21 NLT).

Today's Testimony:

I accepted Jesus Christ at the age of twelve during an altar call at a Sunday morning church service. I had been attending church since I was two weeks old. I had not committed any "big" sins but knew I needed to ask God to forgive me and come into my heart. Even though I had gone to church all those years, I wanted to make sure that if I were to die I would go to meet Jesus.

If you lived in our household, you were required to attend church. So that Sunday morning I made the decision that I would serve God because He loved me and I loved Him. Throughout the years I have gone through many mountaintop and valley experiences, but I never let go of God. I always knew He would make a way. I may not have known how or when He would do it; I just knew that He would. In Hebrews 13:5 God said, "I will never leave thee, nor forsake thee" (KJV). I take great comfort in knowing God will never leave me.

My mother was God-fearing and a woman of great faith. She taught me to read the Word and seek God for decisions I needed to make in my life. As a child growing up, she taught me to stop and think and ask myself if I would take Jesus there, or would I do this or that if Jesus were there. All of the decisions I've made and experiences I've encountered have made me the person I am today. As I grow older I think more about Heaven and what it will be like when I get there. When I have gone the last mile of the way, I want to make sure I am ready to meet God and hear Him say, "Well done, thou good and faithful servant."

—*Emily*

Today's Takeaway:

Years ago, it was popular to wear "WWJD" or ("What Would Jesus Do?") bracelets. There was a lot of discussion about them, but one thing is for sure: If you think about each decision like Emily's mother taught her, it *will* impact your decisions. God knows your mind, your thoughts, and intentions. Be honest with yourself because He already knows.

Stop to think: Would Jesus go here? Would He post this? Would He act this way? Would He react this way? It's a tough, tough word, I know. I'm looking at myself in the mirror to receive this one, but we all want to hear Him say, "Well done," don't we? Then we must *do well* to hear it.

Day 168

Today's Scripture:

"Therefore, if anyone is in Christ, he is a new creation; old things have passed away; behold, all things have become new" (2 Corinthians 5:17 NKJV).

Today's Testimony:

I was nine years old and living in a broken home. I loved my dad . . . but he was abusive, a weekend drunk, a hard man no one wanted to mess with. You see, broken boys grow into broken men and create broken homes.

But then one day, my dad's cousin invited him to church and he actually agreed to go. I went with him. It was a little scary—people were acting "crazy." The pastor was preaching and a woman jumped up and shouted praises while waving her hanky. I had never seen anything like that before. I didn't know what was going on. But then I saw something that really threw me for a loop. As that preacher stood preaching by the altar, my dad got up out of his seat and walked down front. *What in the world is happening?* I wondered.

I looked up at the altar and it looked like people were ganging up on him. When he stood up and walked back to the pew, my dad was wiping tears away. I'd never seen my dad cry before that day.

So for two weeks, I watched him like a hawk. I wanted to know what had happened to him. He talked differently and acted differently. This man was unfamiliar to me, but I knew it was for the good. I liked this "new man."

After two weeks of "hawk duty," I decided there was something to this God . . . He must be real to make a man act as differently as that. So I waited patiently for the preacher to end his sermon, and when he did, I walked down and bowed at the altar. I didn't know how to pray; I really didn't know who God was; I just knew I needed Him. I wanted to be changed too. I don't remember the words; I just remember the tears. Two weeks later, I was filled with the Holy Spirit. Praise God!

That's my salvation story. I watched God change my dad; and from that point on, no one could have convinced me He wasn't real. And then He changed me too.

—*Melissa*

Today's Takeaway:

This is a "two for one" deal where a father got saved and it caused his daughter to get saved; but in reality, there's no telling how many people went on "hawk duty" to see what could have caused such a change in this man. More people are watching us than we can possibly know. I have a feeling there were more who came to know Christ from seeing this "new man." That's what it's all about!

Day 169

Today's Scripture:

"Jesus said unto him, Thou shalt love the Lord thy God with all thy heart, and with all thy soul, and with all thy mind" (Matthew 22:37 KJV).

Today's Testimony:

A beautiful, clear night sky is full of countless stars. We know there are billions more that we can't see. Psalm 147:4 tells us God not only knows how many there are, but knows them each by name. Is that not beyond amazing? And of all the billions of humans He placed here, He sees me. He cares about me.

I was blessed with parents who knew God, and who made certain that my sister and I not only learned *about* Him, but learned to *know* Him. We watched my father take the ups and downs of life as either God bringing them about, or allowing them. He was never shaken up, never without hope. He taught us God has a purpose for each life, and that we should ask Him to show us what He wants us to do and to be.

I'd like to say I learned long ago to be like my dad, but I can't. It has taken many years to learn the steady trust he had in God. In life we experience many things and we learn something from all of them. You can't really know how to be happy if you've never known sadness. You don't appreciate companionship and friendship if you've never been alone. In all the things we face, we see how much we need God—how much we need His guiding hand, His protection, His strength.

There were times I didn't listen to God's voice. He didn't pull away; I did. Looking back, I see those were the hardest times, the seemingly hopeless times. I see now that He was still watching me, waiting for me to learn and come back to Him. How wonderful and marvelous that the One who controls all of creation would care so much about me; and He only asks one thing—that I love Him.

When you love someone, you want to be near them, to have an intimate relationship with them. How different my life might have been if I had always loved God whole-heartedly. But through it all, the good and bad, He has been there leading, teaching, protecting, and drawing me closer to Him. How could I not love Him?

—*Ruth*

Today's Takeaway:

The beautiful, matchless Creator of everything takes time to know us—each of us. That is mind-boggling! It's also beautiful. I'll never get over the fact that He knows me, yet still loves and cares for me. How about you? Do you realize He watches you and waits to hear your voice?

Day 170

Today's Scripture:

"And because we are his children, God has sent the Spirit of his Son into our hearts, prompting us to call out, 'Abba, Father'" (Galatians 4:6 NLT).

Today's Testimony:

I was twelve years old sitting in a little church in West Virginia when I felt the Lord deal with my heart.

A gospel group was up at the front of the church singing about Heaven, and I thought, *I want to go to that place they are singing about.*

My parents took us to church when we were very small; but at this time, I went to church with my best friend and her family. I am thankful that someone stepped up to take me to church.

The day I accepted Christ as my Savior was on a Father's Day. I remember going home that day after the service and I told my dad I had one more gift to give him for Father's Day. I explained I had given my heart to Jesus and I thought that was the best gift ever. I will never forget that day, and I play it over in my mind as I am older now. I wouldn't trade my decision to follow Christ for any reason. I plan to make it to Heaven someday. As they say, I've come too far to turn back now.

Little did I know then, but God had special plans for me. He led me to the little church to hear the singing that day. After I grew up, I would eventually marry one of the young men who sang in that gospel group that led me to the Lord. You may never realize the plans the Lord has for you, but if you trust Him, He will lead and direct all areas of your life.

Now I'm a pastor's wife and that young man is still singing. The best part is, the Father's Day gift that I told my dad was for him turned out to be the best gift I ever got. Thank You, Jesus, for saving my soul.

—*Terri*

Today's Takeaway:

Our heavenly Father loves to plan great things for the lives of His girls. He puts gifts and talents in each of us that are unique and plans for these talents to be used to bless others. I love the fact that not everybody's gifts are the same. God makes us so diverse. There is room for everyone to work for Him. Terri works for the Lord in different ways than you or I do. Her ways aren't better, or worse, just different. I love that. There's a lot to do. He needs us all. It feels so good to work for Him. Want to help? Talk to your pastor. He'll be thrilled to hear from you—and you'll make your Father smile too.

Day 171

Today's Scripture:

"Choose you this day whom ye will serve" (Joshua 24:15 KJV).

Today's Testimony:

When I was seven years old, I vividly remember going with a friend to a summer Christian gathering. I was asked if I wanted to accept Jesus as my Savior and I said yes; we bowed our heads and prayed a simple prayer. Little did I know that memory would be a beautiful anchor and reminder that God had a plan for me from an early age.

I grew up and went to church on Sundays but really didn't understand what having a personal relationship with Jesus meant. I knew I was saved and would go to Heaven, but I didn't know He wanted to talk to me every day, that He wanted to help me make good decisions. I didn't know He wanted to guide me from fear to faith and from defeat to victory on a daily basis. It was a process that I am still working on today.

I went away to college. It was the first time I was independent, away from my parents and the rules I grew up with. I felt excited and scared all at the same time. I soon got caught up in the college lifestyle. It was a small campus, so there wasn't much to do.

I was persuaded by some of the girls in my dorm to join a sorority. At the time, I wanted to make friends and fit in, so I agreed. My roommate and I were soon swept into sorority life. At this time, you had to pledge to the sorority. It was a three-month process and it involved a lot of hazing and humiliation. I continued, eager to please and follow the crowd. As I got further into the sorority, I began to get curious about some of the "fun" they were having—the drinking, smoking, and drugs. It started off slowly, but soon I was in the middle of it all. By the end of the first year, I was drinking every weekend. I was smoking a pack of cigarettes a day and I was regularly smoking pot. I had also gained the understanding that if I dressed scantily, I could gain power over men and get all the attention I wanted. It was a very slippery slope, and I had no idea that with this life came some serious side effects.

—Haley
(To Be Continued in Tomorrow's Reading)

Today's Takeaway:

So if you're just tuning in from the world's view, you might be thinking, *She's just having a little college fun; what's the big deal?* The problem is, this is not just the world's view, it's the enemy's view too. Let's not forget his reasons for his view—it's not so you'll have fun. His plan is to steal (your safety), kill (your friends, your dreams, you), and destroy (your brain, your finances, your good name). No one ever sets out to do these things, yet they happen often in these "fun" settings. If you're in this, think, *whom* are you choosing?

Day 172

Today's Scripture:

*"But if you refuse to serve the Lord, then choose today whom you will serve. . . .
But as for me and my family, we will serve the Lord"* (Joshua 24:15 NLT).

Today's Testimony *(Continued from Previous Day):*

As my second year began, I eagerly returned to college, ready for another year of partying. My grades weren't really important anymore. I could get by without too much effort, but I was definitely more interested in my new lifestyle than my education. By late fall, I began to get sick. It started off as a cough but quickly turned into pneumonia. I went home over Christmas break and went to the doctor for antibiotics. While at home, I started to have panic attacks. I started to struggle with anxiety. I began to develop obsessive thoughts and couldn't sleep. It was frightening. My parents took me back to the doctors. They prescribed me antidepressants. I knew that was not all that needed to change. I could sense the Holy Spirit calling me. I didn't understand it, but I knew I was being asked to choose. One late night, I couldn't sleep; I laid on the couch, tossing and turning. I was filled with anxiety. I grabbed my mom's Bible off of the side table. I lifted it in the air and I said out loud, "I choose Jesus." I knew that it was a turning point. Over the next months, God led me to leave that college, that sorority, and transfer to another university.

That next fall, I started at a large university. Through a series of events, God led me to meet some girls who attended a local church. I started attending the college group, which led me to start attending the church regularly. This church family helped me understand that knowing God, having a personal relationship with Him, seeking God in His Word, and worshiping Him with my voice and my life was how I was supposed to live.

Twenty-three years later, I still attend that church. I found my husband there; we were married by the pastor, and now all four of our children have been dedicated by those godly men and women in that body of Christ. God is faithful. What He says, He will do when you trust Him and allow Him.

—*Haley*

Today's Takeaway:

Thank God! Haley decided she would choose Jesus. It turned her life around. It turned her from sickness to healing, from anxiety to peace, from panic to calm. When she made her decision, action followed. She didn't go right back to the group that had led her to that place of chaos. She made a change.

Sometimes, we need a fresh start, away from past negative situations. Pray and seek the Lord for direction. He'll guide you in the right path.

Day 173

Today's Scripture:

"Put on the full armor of God, so that you can take your stand against the devil's schemes. . . . Stand firm then, with the belt of truth buckled around your waist, with the breastplate of righteousness in place" (Ephesians 6:11, 14 NIV).

Today's Testimony:

When I reached my teen years, I discovered a world I never knew existed. Until then, I had attended a small, private, Christian elementary school that reinforced what I was being taught at home. But, in junior high I transferred to a public school, and everything changed. This new environment was a hard transition for me, but more than anything, this change made me very aware of the cultural differences between my new school and my Christian home.

It didn't take long for me to realize just how different I was compared to my peers. I didn't wear the clothes they did, say the words they said, listen to what they did, or spend my free time outside of school the way they did.

The enemy used this change as an opportunity to deceive me. Not long into my first year, I began to eat the lies the enemy was feeding me. I became more and more insecure in what I knew was truth; I allowed their choices to influence me, and as a result, I eventually laid my "belt of truth" down. I developed a skewed perspective on what I thought about followers of Jesus and the purpose of living. I began engaging in activities that didn't keep me pure and in right standing with God. The enemy piled shame on me for the sin I was welcoming into my life. It wasn't long before I found myself broken, deeply wounded, and desperately in need of Jesus.

After several years of struggling, my parents sent me to stay with a couple on their farm as a last attempt to help me find my way back to the Lord. I arrived angry, bitter, hurt, and clouded with lies, but I was so lost I didn't know how to get back. One day, as I was working in the horse barn, worship music was playing, and I suddenly heard the words in my heart to this spontaneous prophetic song: "You are My love, you're worth pursuing" (Trudy Den Hoed). As those words washed over my wounded soul, I fell to my knees and instantly felt Jesus there with me, singing that song right to me. At that moment, I knew it wasn't too late. There I found the truth and strapped that "belt" back on.

—Lydia

Today's Takeaway:

The Lord sees us where we are and He knows our hearts. He does pursue us. He wants us to be close to Him. Let's run to Him, not from Him.

Day 174

Today's Scripture:

"I will rejoice and be glad in Your faithfulness, because You have seen my misery;
You have known the troubles of my soul" (Psalm 31:7 NASB).

Today's Testimony:

I was nine years old when I asked Jesus into my heart. At church one Sunday, I responded to an altar call. There were four of us—my sister and I and two friends from the neighborhood. I would love to say from that day forward I've lived for Christ every day. But the truth is, after several years of going to church, I walked away from the church and toward the world. I still knew deep inside He was with me, and I needed Him, but I bought into the lie that I could do life on my own.

It was in my forties when I knew I could no longer do life on my own. I slowly started to give things over to God; not everything, but enough to feel His presence, to feel I was living the Christian life, but I really wasn't. Then in my fifties my life "fell apart," again. And when I say fell apart, I mean an implosion that took me completely by surprise; I never saw it coming, not like that. Everything—marriage, kids, finances—completely changed in the blink of an eye.

I fell to my knees one day in my kitchen and gave everything to the Lord. I asked Him to tear down the walls I had built that kept me from Him. I knew they were there—I could feel them when I prayed, when I was at church, when I would read His Word. I knew at that point Jesus was all I needed and all I wanted. He is so faithful!

My marriage has been restored. He provides for us every day. My kids are still a work in progress, but the Lord hears our prayers for them. I know one day they will also be restored. I thank God often for the amazing testimony they will one day have for His glory. The walls have come down and now I'm living a life I only once dreamed of, not because I have stuff or lots of money, but because I have freedom in Christ.

—*Lisa*

Today's Takeaway:

Living life on our own means living it outside the blessing of God—I don't want life that way. Lisa knows the results of that now. She's seen both sides and absolutely wants ⁀ live God's way now. Life's too short to live it with regret. Wherever you are now, give ⁀thing to God, holding nothing back and live inside the blessing. It's not so great ⁀ings your own way with no guidance from the God who knows it all. He's the

Day 175

Today's Scripture:

"She is clothed with strength and dignity, and she laughs without fear of the future"
(Proverbs 31:25 NLT).

Today's Testimony:

Worry. Anxiety. Inadequacy. Disappointment. Failure. Disapproval. Every day of my life was lived under these dark clouds. There were times of happiness and love as well, but these feelings were *always* in the background. These things defined every aspect of my life. On the surface, I looked put together, content, and hardworking. As much as I knew that's what others saw, I didn't feel that way. Sure, I worked hard and did the best I could, but the clouds were always there and would, at times, come pouring down on me. These feelings overtook me when my closest "friends" and coworkers weren't there and I wasn't able to do the things they wanted. When I would look around my house after a long day and see laundry and dishes that still needed to be done, or when someone would ask me to help with something and I bent over backward to make it happen for them. Over time, these feelings added up more and more and began to overtake my life. I was finding my worth in the approval of others.

I grew up in church my whole life. I knew the Bible verses. I knew the songs. I knew God loved me. I was saved through faith in the death and resurrection of Jesus Christ, but I was missing something. (And, if you are feeling these feelings, you are too.) There is so much more to this life and walk with Christ than just believing and going to church. *He* needs to be what defines us.

God finally broke through to me when my husband became terminally ill with cancer and I had two young boys at home. Through his treatments, sickness, and ultimately death, I could no longer be the person that others depended on. I could no longer take care of everyone else and take on more. Instead, I was humbled to a place of needing others to take care of me and my family as I took care of my husband. Everything that I had put my self-worth in was gone.

—Kim
(To Be Continued in Tomorrow's Reading)

Today's Takeaway:

Are you a people-pleaser? Its OK, I'm holding up my hand too. I want everyone to be happy—is that so bad? No, not in itself. The problem is, we're not called to make everyone happy, are we? We're called to please the Lord, our God. It's exhausting to try to please everybody, not to mention it's also impossible. Let all that go; you don't need that job! Jesus said His burden is light. He loves us and gave Himself for us. Read Kim's story tomorrow; until then, understand that your heavenly Father is the One who defines you—with nothing but love!

Day 176

Today's Scripture:

"Take My yoke upon you and learn from Me [following Me as My disciple], for I am gentle and humble in heart, and you will find rest [renewal, blessed quiet] for your souls. For My yoke is easy [to bear] and My burden is light" (Matthew 11:29-30 Amp.).

Today's Testimony *(Continued From Previous Day):*

My faith in God had grown exponentially, but after my husband's death, I felt worthless, even though I had a strong faith. It was in that place God reached me and I saw that my worth comes from Him and not in what I can do for others, and He approves of me, always.

The only thing He requires of me and you is that we put our full faith in Him. Sometimes we have to be taken to our knees and humbled for us to give all of ourselves to Him. Maybe you feel completely shattered and unsure of how to put yourself back together, as I was. That's OK. As you allow God to put your life back together, He will continually show His approval and take care of you as He did me, over and over again.

Friend, those dark clouds of worry and anxiety and fear didn't go away overnight. They still aren't always gone. But, when they start to come back and take over, we have to lay them *back* at Jesus' feet, and God is so good and so patient. He knows our innermost being and knows exactly what we need. Once I take those feelings captive and give them to God, He always replaces that anxiety, worry, and fear with peace, joy, and comfort.

As I walk this road and continue to allow God (instead of others) to define me, God has transformed me. I can truly say I am "clothed with strength and dignity" and can "laugh without fear of the future" (Proverbs 31:25 NLT). Jesus continues to make beauty from ashes in my life. I am remarried now and we have four beautiful children together. By allowing God to define you, He will transform you from the inside out and bless you as well.

—Kim

Today's Takeaway:

Kim found peace; she was transformed. No longer does she live with dark clouds of worry and fear over her life—she lives knowing she has laid all those burdens down at Jesus' feet. I love how she lets us know that sometimes those feelings may try to come back; we lay them down again. Just because feelings come back doesn't mean we have to carry them around again. No! Give them to Jesus again . . . and again until they no longer come back. Only accept what Jesus gives—peace, joy, and comfort.

Only spend energy pleasing God, and everything else will line up after Him. He's the One who defines us, and He's the One we serve.

Day 177

Today's Scripture:

"Therefore, if anyone is in Christ, he is a new creation; old things have passed away; behold, all things have become new" (2 Corinthians 5:17 NKJV).

Today's Testimony:

I was raised in church and saved as a child. During my teenage years, my family stopped going to church. Although I attended church occasionally, I didn't attend regularly again for many years.

By not being in fellowship with other believers, I began to stray from God. First, I started swearing; it became easier and easier. Then, I began to make a lot of poor choices, one after another.

Eventually, I moved in with a man and we lived together for about four years. He was verbally abusive, which was hard enough to bear, but then, he cheated on me. I was hurt and very angry, so I decided to get even by cheating on him. Afterward, I began to feel worthless and began allowing people to treat me accordingly. This only made me feel even more miserable. But in that misery I finally cried out to God and asked Him to help me.

A few days after that prayer, I met a wonderful man of God. On our first date, I committed my life back to Christ. Suddenly I felt like a large weight had been lifted off of my shoulders. I was so happy. I began to see the positive things in life instead of just the negative. I also began to understand people and was able to love and accept them for who they are, instead of judging and criticizing them.

One of the things I remember the most that first month after I came back to Christ was that I cried a lot. Later, I learned that all those tears were a part of my healing process—those tears were necessary. After getting all of that pain out, God restored my heart.

I'm now married to a pastor, teaching junior church, and working in the nursery. I am also blessed to be the director of our ladies' group. One of the things I struggled with the most, after recommitting to Christ, was the fact I had made so many bad choices even though "I knew better." But then, God gave me what I call my "light-bulb moment." He reminded me: "Therefore, if anyone is in Christ, he is a new creation; old things have passed away; behold, all things have become new" (2 Corinthians 5:17 NKJV). Praise God!

—*Shelly*

Today's Takeaway:

Regret is a normal human reaction to our choices, but when we come to Christ, He forgives and He restores. We then have to forgive ourselves and realize we become new. It is time to move forward. If He forgives us, who are we to refuse to forgive ourselves? Pray, cry, then move on.

Day 178

Today's Scripture:

"Teaching them to observe all things whatsoever I have commanded you: and, lo, I am with you alway, even unto the end of the world. Amen" (Matthew 28:20 KJV).

Today's Testimony:

My parents didn't go to church. But one Sunday my uncle asked my parents to come to church so he could win a prize. My parents and us kids went to church for them. That Sunday there was a lady minister dressed in all white. Her face shined like a light was on it. I remember she was very pretty and had a beautiful smile.

All of us kids—sisters, brothers, and cousins—were sitting in the front row. The lady minister came up to me and said, "Come here, honey." She asked who my parents were, and my parents came up front. She told my parents about my heart problems and how I would wake up every night screaming from nightmares. My dad started crying, and she laid hands on me and I felt a warm feeling go through me. She also told my parents I was going to do great things for the Lord. My dad gave his heart to the Lord that night!

A few days later I went to bed and started to say my prayers, but for some reason I didn't want to stop praying. I kept thanking Jesus for saving me and told Him how much I loved Him over and over. I looked up and next to my bed were my two sisters and my two brothers. They were all crying and praying with me. I don't remember them all coming next to my bed because I couldn't stop thanking Jesus.

When my parents came home, my mother heard me crying upstairs and she was scared. My father opened the upstairs door and he told my mother everything was OK. He felt the Spirit of the Lord. I ended up praying in the Spirit all night. That's the night I gave my heart to the Lord.

—Judy

Today's Takeaway:

How powerful! God healed Judy, saved her, and touched her family—all because they were invited to help her uncle win a prize! I love it! Let's get some more prizes ready. Wow! God works in details. He knows about every detail of your life—down to the number of hairs on your head right now! Are you feeling like He doesn't really care, or that He doesn't really know you? You're wrong. He does know and care. Pull away and get alone with Him; pull out your Word, go to church, and on the way ask Him to specifically speak to you through the message from the pastor and then open up and see what happens. You'll see; God knows you. Get ready for what He may say.

Day 179

Today's Scripture:

"For the grace of God has appeared that offers salvation to all people. It teaches us to say 'No' to ungodliness and worldly passions, and to live self-controlled, upright and godly lives in this present age" (Titus 2:11-12 NIV).

Today's Testimony:

My drug addiction started when I was twenty, when I had my gallbladder removed. That was the first time I got a prescription for pain pills. I remember taking the first one; it was a feeling I'd never felt before. My depression and anxiety were gone. I started to take pain pills a few times a week, but it quickly turned into taking them daily, then more and more as time went on. This went on for years. I had to take them before I could even get out of bed to start my day. A few hours later, a few more, and then a few more. They were my lifeline. My days and mood were determined by if and how many pain pills I had that day. I would go to the doctors and tell them whatever I needed to get more. When I couldn't get them from the doctor, I would go buy more. I got to the point of taking them because I needed them so I wouldn't get sick. I would rather stay addicted than to go through withdrawal. I thought there was no way out. I had been on them for so long, I was scared of the person I would be without them.

My husband started to go to church. At first, I went with him just to make him happy. As I continued to go, I began to feel God. Then one day God told me to "stop and follow Him." I came home from church that day and told myself, *This is it; I am done taking these pain pills.* I had forty left; I was going to wean myself off them. Five more, four, three, two, then one more left . . . I thought, *I can do this.* But no . . . I got more! A few months went on, and I kept taking them. But I also kept going to church. I started reading the Bible with my husband and really listening to God.

One night in my bedroom, God told me if I made the first step, He would be right there with me the whole way. This was it; I didn't want to live like this anymore. I told my husband my secret. The first thing he did was hug me. He told me it was OK, we would get through it. He had been praying for me for a long time; he just didn't know why. The next few weeks were the hardest days of my life. My muscles ached; I was sweating, shivering, throwing up. I picked up the Bible. I was yelling to God, "I thought You said You would be here helping me!" The withdrawal was so bad, I wanted to die. The next day I picked up the Bible and started to read it. God told me He never left my side the whole time; I just needed to call upon Him. I prayed day and night for God's help. With His grace, I got through it and am clean now.

—Jennifer

Today's Takeaway:

Praise God! He is our healer, deliver, and our Savior.

Day 180

Today's Scripture:

"You are a hiding place for me; you preserve me from trouble; you surround me with shouts of deliverance" (Psalm 32:7 ESV).

Today's Testimony:

When I was a child, our home was filled with domestic violence, alcoholism, and dysfunction. One night, in the midst of an evening of my father abusing my mother, I hid behind my bed. While I was there, I saw the image of three large men dressed in white. Their presence brought peace and I was no longer afraid. As quickly as the three men came, they left.

A few years later, my parents were going through a terrible divorce. A family friend took me to her church. The ladies in Sunday school prayed over me and showed me such love. Then, while in the sanctuary, I felt that same presence of peace and love I had felt behind my bed that night many years before. I remember closing my eyes and just feeling God all around me.

My life continued in its dysfunctional pattern until I turned eighteen. My mom had remarried and she and my stepfather became Christians. They took me to church. I was immediately nervous around the preacher and knew that God was once again about to move. The preacher called me out from the congregation and told me that God had seen the jail cell I was living in and that the Lord was breaking me free from this cell.

He literally called me out from darkness and I stepped into God's presence. My life made a 180-degree turnaround that night. God saved and redeemed me and set my life on a different path.

The path of the Lord has not always been easy, but I know He has never left me. He was with me as a frightened child hiding behind a bed, as a confused middle-school girl, and then as a broken eighteen-year-old. He will continue to call me to follow Him until my last breath. I am so thankful for God's grace on a girl that never even knew to ask for it.

—*Jenn*

Today's Takeaway:

Have you ever wanted to run and hide? I have. Sometimes when life feels over-whelming, it seems like the best option. Don't worry if you think you can't always go hide when you want to—the Scriptures say God can be our hiding place. In today's scripture we see it, also in Psalms 17:8 and 27:5 as well as many other places, our Lord says He'll hide us under His wings, or in His sanctuary. Jesus has been there. While you're hiding in His safe place, tell Him what's weighing on you, because He cares about your needs. His Word is literally filled with instruction on giving our needs to Him. Do that, and trust that He's big enough to handle your problems, even when you don't know a solution. He's pretty good at having the answers and supplying peace. He's God!

Day 181

Today's Scripture:

"He has delivered us from such a deadly peril, and he will deliver us again. On him we have set our hope that he will continue to deliver us" (2 Corinthians 1:10 NIV).

Today's Testimony:

I was born a "small-town girl." My family was faithful to church. It was there I learned about Jesus and developed a deep love for Him. Although I don't remember the specific day I accepted Him into my heart, I do know that the more I learned about Him, the more I grew to love Him.

As a teen, I attended church youth camp and rode the church bus to camp meetings. Those events were the highlights of my summers. As a senior, I heard about our church's Bible college, and purposed in my heart to attend. No one in my family had ever attended college, and I was not encouraged to go. But with this big idea and God's help, I went. The summer before moving to college my mother became very ill and was hospitalized; she was unable to help me prepare for this huge transition. Despite her current state, the hospital allowed her to be unhooked from her IV long enough to travel with me and my dad. Not long after arriving, I was left to face this new adventure alone. With grants, savings from my job, and strong determination, I pushed through what many would deem impossible. It would be an understatement to say God miraculously provided everything I needed while at school the next few years.

It was during my junior year that I met my soon-to-be husband. He had accepted a call from God to be in ministry. We were married the following summer and together answered the call God had placed on both of our lives. After we married, we moved and began serving as youth pastors. We have now pastored several churches in several states for decades of ministry. Through it all, in every twist, God has continued to prove His faithfulness.

At times I have failed God tremendously. Nevertheless, I know He pursued me with His everlasting love. I am thankful that God is still working in my life today. He has brought me through so much, and I have set my hope on this truth—He will continue to do so for this small-town girl.

—*Julie*

Today's Takeaway:

That small-town girl had a made-up mind to do something with her life. I love that. Arm a girl with a love for Jesus and some determination and grit, and watch her change the world. Way to go, Julie! God saw a faithful handmaiden, like Mary, that He could use. He's still using her to bless people to this very day. Are you allowing Him to use you? All it takes is being willing.

Day 182

Today's Scripture:

"God is not man, that he should lie, or a son of man, that he should change his mind. Has he said, and will he not do it? Or has he spoken, and will he not fulfill it?"
(Numbers 23:19 ESV).

Today's Testimony:

I didn't grow up in a church-going household. I really didn't have an idea of "God" as a little girl. My parents divorced when I was about seven years old; after that, my younger brothers and I moved away to live with my mom.

My mother soon met a guy who was a bad influence, and they ended up becoming alcoholics and using prescription drugs. That situation made for a less-than-optimal childhood. Things at home were often chaotic, and I assumed the role of "protector" for my younger siblings.

At night, the moonlight shined through my bedroom window and made a "square of light" on my floor. When everyone was asleep, I would go sit in that square and look out of the window at the night sky. As I did that, I imagined what life would be like if I were far away from that place. One night, as I was doing that, I heard a voice say to me, "There's a reason you're alive." I immediately felt this deep sense of purpose come alive in me, like something in me instantly responded to that voice. I had no idea what it was, but I immediately thought, *My purpose must be to make sure my siblings have a good life and are safe.*

Years later, my siblings and I were taken away from my mom and went to live with my dad. I was convinced that my purpose for living was complete because my siblings were now "safe." I felt like I had nothing to live for anymore; that was a devastating feeling. Moreover, the years of turmoil I had just walked through had hardened me so much that I often found it difficult to cry, even if I wanted to. At this time, I was beginning high school at a new school.

—Lauren
(To Be Continued in Tomorrow's Reading)

Today's Takeaway:

Our purpose is to glorify God and serve Him. Poor Lauren had been carrying a much heavier weight—the well-being of all her siblings. No child was meant to carry that load; the mental strain of it had taken a toll on her. If you find yourself loaded down with care, check your load! You may be carrying things you were never meant to carry. Remember *your* purpose. Fulfill that and it's enough.

Day 183

Today's Scripture:

"Unfailing love surrounds those who trust the Lord. So rejoice in the Lord and be glad, all you who obey him! Shout for joy, all you whose hearts are pure!" (Psalm 32:10-11 NLT).

Today's Testimony *(Continued From Previous Day)*:

During my junior year, a friend practically forced me to go to a youth-group service with her because she didn't want to go alone. The first night I went with her, I cried during worship, and I was perplexed at the "melting" feeling I experienced in my heart (later I learned that I was feeling God's presence). During the sermon, my heart raced, tears flowed down my face—it felt like someone saw deep inside of me, and no matter how hard I tried, I could not hide. The word *void* also came to my mind repeatedly during the preaching. I felt like a deer in headlights. I went to this youth group consistently for several months; I kept experiencing the same things each week.

Over time, I became incredibly convicted about the relationship I was in at the time. I convinced my boyfriend to come to the youth-group service with me, but it did not alleviate the conviction I felt. I often tried to break up with him after the service but failed miserably every time.

Finally, after weeks of failed attempts to break up with this guy, I decided to try praying once I got home. I lay in my bed and began to pray, "God, please make us break up. Please just *make* it happen." I prayed this over and over, and suddenly I heard the same voice I'd heard as a child say to me, "It's your choice." That was the first time I realized the voice I'd heard as a little girl was God's voice.

Months later, I was still in that relationship, and the conviction and pulling of the Holy Spirit grew more and more irresistible. One Wednesday night, as I sat in my bedroom before leaving for the youth-group service, I called my boyfriend to see if he wanted to come to church. He said no, and in that moment, I prayed to God for strength, and finally broke up with him. The moment I did, I felt something in me break open, and it felt as though all of Heaven rushed to me and filled me. Immediately, I felt genuine, deep joy for the first time in my life. That "void" in me was totally and completely filled in that moment. Since then, it has been a wild, amazing adventure with my Best Friend and Savior—Jesus.

—Lauren

Today's Takeaway:

Lauren was finally able to let go of one burden only to pick up another—a relationship that weighed her down. Now what? Yes, prayer. Ask for help. When you don't know what to do, ask. Then stand strong and watch.

Day 184

Today's Scripture:

*"But when you fast, comb your hair and wash your face. Then no one will notice
that you are fasting, except your Father, who knows what you do in private.
And your Father, who sees everything, will reward you"* (Matthew 6:17-18 NLT).

Today's Testimony:

When I was young, probably about thirteen years old, I made a decision that I was
going to visit my grandma. She was my best friend. I knew that if I was going to visit
her, I would need to fly there. I would bother my parents night and day, nonstop, to get
them to let me go. This wasn't long after September 11, 2001, so my parents didn't love
the idea of letting me fly alone at this time.

However, I was determined. I prayed continuously about it; I wrote every day in a
journal, and even tried selling bracelets to make enough money for a plane ticket. I also
made the decision to fast. I tried to think logically about the most reasonable "treat" to
give up. I chewed gum every day, because I loved the flavor. It was also the "in" thing to
do among middle-school girls. I decided I would fast gum; so until I was at my grandparents' house, I would not chew a piece of gum. I guess that was fortunate for anyone
in close quarters to me.

To make a long story short, I didn't get to fly to my grandparents' house, but I continued to pray. A couple of years later, I was riding in the backseat of my grandparents'
car; they were coming to live near me. My grandma offered me a piece of gum; I took it
from her, unwrapped it, and realized I had experienced the faithfulness of God.

Everyone's story is different. I was blessed to grow up in a Christian home with parents and grandparents that truly loved God. I don't even remember when I prayed to be
saved. My grandpa is a preacher and my dad is a worship leader. I started singing when
I was about three years old and I haven't stopped since. My mom taught me to pray. I
had no choice but to fall in love with Jesus in such an atmosphere.

I have experienced physical healing for myself and witnessed it in other family
members. I have seen God's goodness all of these years. Months before my grandma
passed away, she left me with this note, for my eighteenth birthday: "Stay as close as you
can. Never, never, let anyone rob you of the promises we have in Him. He loves us no
matter what. We are blessed."

—Mariah

Today's Takeaway:

God saw Mariah's sincerity as a child, and He took care of her. The faith of a child
is a powerful thing! Ask children to pray for your needs. I have seen healings and miracles happen when children begin to pray for adults. They simply have no boundaries
to believing God can do what He says He can do in His Word. Let's follow their good
example.

Day 185

Today's Scripture:

"Trust in the Lord with all your heart and lean not on your own understanding; in all your ways submit to him, and he will make your paths straight" (Proverbs 3:5-6 NIV).

Today's Testimony:

I grew up going to church with different family members or friends. I prayed the salvation prayer many times, but never really understood it. Later, when I was in seventh grade, I met a new friend. We became close instantly. Her grandma invited me to go to church with them. I loved it. I felt at home there and started learning more about the Lord. One evening they had an altar call at church and we prayed the salvation prayer. I felt so different praying this time. I felt a change. I was about thirteen years old. A few years later my friend moved away. I didn't let that stop me from going to church. I continued going with her grandma. It was one of the best decisions I ever made. I am now thirty-nine years old and still going to church and living for the Lord.

Over the years my faith was tested a lot. I was always told that I wasn't skinny or pretty enough and would never get married. I began to believe it. I started praying if it were God's will that He would lead me to the man I would marry. I wrote down what I was looking for in a husband and gave it to God. Later, I met a man that I liked. We talked often and he was everything I prayed for, except that he drank alcohol. We stopped talking for a while due to this. I began to pray that if he was the one for me, God would show me. He did; after his problem with alcohol was over, we started talking again and eventually got married.

We knew we wanted a family. A few years later, we found out we were expecting a baby. We thanked God and were filled with joy. However, it was short-lived, when a few weeks later my husband took me to the ER with intense pains. I went into early labor, and the nurse handed me our baby girl as she took her last breath in my arms. I looked at the ceiling and said, "God, I know You have a plan for us." We continued to pray and waited. Almost four years later, my husband and I felt led to be baptized again. As I went under water, I felt the anger and hurt from losing our daughter wash away. A few months later, I found out I was pregnant. We had a miracle baby. He's healthy and doing great.

—*Kathy*

Today's Takeaway:

Kathy reminds me of what Jesus said about Mary: "She has made the right choice" (see Luke 10:42), and that's what Kathy did. She chose well—she chose to give her heart to Jesus, to stay in church, to take her hope for a husband to God, to wait on Him to help that man get delivered from alcohol *before* she agreed to marry him; and when her heart was shredded with pain, she trusted God with His plan. We need her as a role model, don't we? Let's follow her example today!

Day 186

Today's Scripture:

"And we know that all things work together for good to those who love God, to those who are called according to His purpose" (Romans 8:28 NKJV).

Today's Testimony:

Stand! That is what God kept saying, and it wasn't what I wanted to do. I would cry and tell God how hard it was, because things were not like they used to be. My church was dry, and it seemed like it was dying. My pastor was sick and unable to minister; as a result many had left the church. It felt as though God's Spirit had left as well. In those days it was so sad to walk into an empty sanctuary.

As often as I could, I would drive to the other side of the state to visit with my daughter and grandchildren. I would visit her church and ask her pastor to pray with me. He would remind me God is working and wants me to stand. He would encourage me to trust God and trust His plan. This was not exactly what I wanted to hear. I wanted him to tell me to move on to another house of worship. As my pastor's health declined, he decided it was time to retire. God led a young pastor and his family to come lead our church and restore it. That was seven years ago.

I praise God for all His blessings, beginning with the pastor who was there for me during those difficult years. I thank God for *my* pastor who feeds our church and for the beautiful spirit that flows in our services. Romans 8:28 is a scripture that I stand on daily. Like the song says: "If you can't see His plan, trust His heart."

Father, I ask that You bring this scripture alive in our hearts and remind us that Your promise doesn't have our timeline on it. Remind us that whatever comes, You are already there working it out for our good. Thank You, Father. Amen.

—Carolyn

Today's Takeaway:

When we get saved, we begin a journey of learning to stand strong during difficult times. Sometimes our path leads us through dry valleys, but during those times, we have access to the Living Water that can refresh our souls. It's not the ideal for our own sweet house of worship to go through hard times, but it is reality. The man of God is subject to sickness and growing old just like we are. God watches how we treat His anointed; be careful to show honor and respect even in difficulty. Remember how even David honored Saul (1 Samuel 24). Pray for your pastor and your church. God honors those prayers. He took care of Carolyn and her church. He'll do the same for you.

Day 187

Today's Scripture:

"You have hedged me behind and before, and laid Your hand upon me. Such knowledge is too wonderful for me; it is high, I cannot attain it" (Psalm 139:5-6 NKJV).

Today's Testimony:

My parents began attending a Pentecostal church shortly after my younger brother was born; I was about four years old. My family was raised in the church. I have two older siblings and a younger brother. One thing that was constant for us was church. We went every Sunday and Wednesday—it was just normal for us to be there. As I got older, I continued to be involved in the church, because that is what my family did. I was involved in the children's choir, went to youth camps in the summers, and youth festivals as I got older.

When I was a teenager, school was particularly hard for me. I was bullied for the clothes I wore and the way I looked. I was kind of quiet and shy, so I was a bit of an easy target I suppose. I became depressed. I struggled silently because my parents had three other kids with their own things going on. I wrongly felt I was just another burden to them at the time. On one particularly hard day the bullying was so bad, I thought about ending my life while staring at the knife drawer. I can't explain it other than to say God spoke to me, and wouldn't let me do it.

I went to my youth group that Friday night and the message was about God's love. I felt God's Spirit during worship—my favorite part of every service—and then the message spoke to me. I gave my heart to Jesus that night; I cried because I finally knew my place as a child of God.

Times were still tough at school, but I had a newfound hope after that night—I had fully committed to God. He went on to use me through my love of music—I joined the worship team at church. I had friends that welcomed me with open arms. I know I cannot escape God's love; I am His.

—*Melissa*

Today's Takeaway:

It's so hard to look different and be singled out from everyone else. The very last thing a young teenager wants is to look different and be made fun of. My heart breaks for Melissa; I remember this pain. The thing about being a Christian is, ultimately, we are different, aren't we? There are going to be times when even after you pass your teen years, you may have to be singled out because you *are always* going to be different from the world. You will act, think, speak, and look different from the world—or you should. This may earn you some questions, or even some snide remarks—can you handle it? Are you as tough as Melissa? Know your place as a child of God. Be tough, stand up, and give an answer for the hope that lies within you! Just do it with love.

Day 188

Today's Scripture:

"For forty days, being tempted by the devil. And He ate nothing during those days, and when they had ended, He was hungry and the devil said to Him, 'If You are the Son of God, tell this stone to become bread.' And Jesus answered him, 'It is written . . .'"
(Luke 4:2-4 NASB).

Today's Testimony:

I am a child of unwed parents. They broke up before I was even born. Neither of my parents went to church or even talked to me about God.

As a teenager, my aunts began to take me to church. I remember asking the Lord into my heart, and I thought I really understood what it meant to allow Christ to be my Savior; but after a few years I backslid on the Lord, but He never let me go far. He was constantly drawing me back to Him.

Later I started going back to church, but I was lukewarm. Eventually I fell into the trap of temptation. I was going to church and even served there, but I realize now I had never had a true salvation experience. I had never allowed Christ to become the center of my life.

One day in my basement as I was doing laundry, I was talking with the Lord, and I had a vision of a road that split. To the right was God and all that He promised me; as I looked to the left, the road was dark and empty. As I stood there, again facing temptation in my life, God asked me to choose. That day I chose the Lord. That day God began a transformation in my life which only He provides. I thank God that just like in Matthew 18:12, He did the same for me: "If a man has a hundred sheep and one of them wanders away, what will he do? Won't he leave the ninety-nine others on the hills and go out to search for the one that is lost?" (NLT). God left the ninety-nine and chased after me that day.

—Debbie

Today's Takeaway:

How powerful! God spoke directly to Debbie. He showed her a vision and asked her to choose. She doesn't say what her "temptation" was, and she doesn't have to. We're all tempted at times, aren't we? Tempted to lie, be rude, refuse to help when we know we're needed. The important thing is what we do with temptation. What did Jesus do? He dealt with it with the Word. He gave a straight answer from Scripture for every temptation sent His way. That's our guide.

How will you know what scripture to use? Open the Bible, look up keywords in the concordance; search topics for key scriptures that address exactly what you're dealing with; the internet can be a great tool to search for key scriptures as well. Then quote the Word about your situation. The enemy will not stay around for much of the Word of God—it's not his thing. That's why it has to be our thing. It's our sword of the Spirit! Use it regularly. Become a "Scripture Ninja."

Day 189

Today's Scripture:

"Knowing this, that our old man is crucified with him, that the body of sin might be destroyed, that henceforth we should not serve sin" (Romans 6:6 KJV).

Today's Testimony:

I grew up in church. I was a typical church kid in every sense of the word. I knew all of the stories and read my children's Bible all the way through, many times. I loved God. At age twelve, I was baptized, but nothing really changed for me. I still loved God, but nothing changing was the problem. I didn't fully understand what I was doing when I got baptized.

When I was fifteen, I agreed to go on a youth-group trip at the church. In the midst of each and every one of those services, my heart started to understand what the baptism of my childhood meant. With every musician and preacher, I felt God prick my heart. At some point during that weekend, I knew He had marked my life, He had protected me from so much, and He had so much more to do in me. I gave in and let God, the Creator of all things, have me. I surrendered to Him. The "old man" began to die and the "new creation" began to live in Christ. Through the years God has shown me who He is and who I am in Him. He still shows me when I am holding on to something of the flesh and demands that I let it go. My walk with Christ started when I was a little girl in church, and He caused it to blossom into something incredibly radiant.

There was a time in my life when I thought for your testimony to matter, you had to have a "I hit rock bottom, and then God saved me" story. Don't misunderstand, those testimonies are beautiful and wonderful, but I have also come to the realization that what is equally beautiful and wonderful are testimonies like mine. The story of a little girl who loved God, and that love continued to grow her whole life.

—*Kathryn*

Today's Takeaway:

The things Kathryn read and heard taught when she was a child were planted like seeds in her heart. They began to spring up into that new creation when she understood the Cross and Jesus' love. Plant seeds in others around you. One day, there'll be a harvest of their soul.

Day 190

Today's Scripture:

"Be still, and know that I am God" (Psalm 46:10 KJV).

Today's Testimony:

It all began around the age of fourteen when I accepted Jesus as my Savior and into my heart. Growing up, I was a typical moody teenager. My parents would always chalk up my "shortness" or my passive-aggressive attitude as "it's the age" and never take it personally.

In my first year of college, I had it all. I had new friends, a new boyfriend and "the world in the palm of my hands," so to speak. What followed was the ultimate test of faith and the journey of where I truly began leaning on God. My relationship looked more like a daily roller-coaster; it was only a matter of time before each of us went our separate ways. When the emotional waves became more "dangerous," God knew the relationship wasn't healthy and broke it off. At the age of twenty-one, I encountered my first major emotional breakdown. It seemed like everyone and everything was walking out of my life because I was viewed as an "illness" instead of who I really was.

It was determined with the help of medical science that I'd been battling untreated depression, ADHD, borderline personality disorder, and high-functioning autism. The doctor said it was a chemical imbalance within the brain and I needed to be placed on medication to keep me stable throughout the rest of my life. For me, that was a lot to take in at twenty-one. I felt like others would call me "crazy" and nobody would want to associate themselves with someone who is completely "psychotic." I felt like I was unworthy of being loved because of the stigma of mental illness.

At the age of twenty-four, I got my first supervisory position at a local retail store. I climbed my way to the top, set a few district records, and was highly respected. I loved that job and my team. One night, I had a strange phone call from someone saying they were from the corporate office. Long story short, I lost my job due to a social-engineering scam! I fell for it because I was so emotionally invested in my team; it devastated me so much that I threatened suicide. At that moment, I felt I was not only losing my job, but losing a family.

—Madison-Lee
(To Be Continued in Tomorrow's Reading)

Today's Takeaway:

There are so many things about the human brain that we don't understand—and don't need to judge. Just like we don't judge diabetics for using insulin, let us not judge other patients who take their medication as they should. Let us practice compassion and love like Jesus always does. He's the model to follow.

Day 191

Today's Scripture:

"Be still, and know that I am God" (Psalm 46:10 KJV).

Today's Testimony *(Continued From Previous Day)*:

Those thoughts of inadequacy came back stronger than ever and the threats were becoming reality. As I walked out the doors, I had it in my mind that suicide was the only way I'd be loved and missed. I sent a text to a group of my colleagues that day saying, "I will see you on the other side"; before I knew it, the police showed up at my car in the parking lot saying they had received a call that I was threatening my own life and needed to be evaluated immediately. I arrived at the hospital and was asked a series of questions that I don't remember much of. The next morning, I was transported to a mental-health hospital for a week of intensive therapy and observation of behavior.

At the start of the week, I was given a notebook and a pencil by the hospital staff. I was told it might help to record my thoughts to look back on each day during my healing to measure progress and even help motivate others. I threw it to the side and continued to dwell in the depressed state I was in. Two days after being admitted, I heard a voice that said, "Your story isn't over; it's just beginning." About two hours later, I heard the same voice again. I prayed later that night, and God spoke to me. He said, "Take the pencil, write your heart out, and trust the outcome."

As hard as it was in the beginning, I was obedient, and I wrote whatever was on my heart and on my mind. About the middle of the week, I noticed I was talking more at therapy sessions. I was eating more than I did when I first got there. Some said it couldn't be done or that I was doomed to live a life in a psychiatric hospital, but God touched me. His love and persistence of never giving up on me at a time where I felt judged and that my life didn't matter at all, was the very thing that medicine couldn't fix. This is my story, and I'm unashamed to say faith is what really healed me in the end.

—*Madison-Lee*

Today's Takeaway:

I thank God for the healing that He makes possible to all of His girls as they trust Him. Healing is sometimes a long difficult road, sometimes it's instant. Our job isn't to decide how it has to be but to trust Him with the outcome. We pray for ourselves when we need healing and for others when they need it. God's Word is filled with scriptures to encourage us and guide us while we wait.

Remember, God uses many different avenues to heal—His virtue to flow into us like the woman with the issue of blood, doctors, medication, prayer, counselors, time, and possibly things we don't even know about. The point is to trust whatever means He provides us. He is able; He's our Healer.

Day 192

Today's Scripture:

"For by grace you have been saved through faith, and that not of yourselves; it is the gift of God, not of works, lest anyone should boast" (Ephesians 2:8-9 NKJV).

Today's Testimony:

I grew up Catholic, attended religious schools most of my life, and (for as long as I can remember) went to church every weekend. I would go through the motions just to keep my parents happy. My whole life I was taught about church rules and not about God's love and mercy. I was so fearful that if I didn't follow them, God would always be mad at me.

I was taught to memorize prayers and give things up for Lent. I was told to pray to Mary and the saints, and to go to confession and do good things to have my sins forgiven. This always made me feel I was never good enough. On top of that, I could never really know for sure if I was going to Heaven and would have to go to purgatory first to fully get rid of my sins.

My first three years of college I continued to attend Mass. Deep inside I was longing to know God better. When I prayed, I just felt like I was talking to the wall. I couldn't feel God's presence with me. My last year of college I began to question all these things I had been taught.

I made friends with some people who were really trying to follow Jesus. They showed me the Bible and I kept asking questions. One of the first passages I read was Ephesians 2:8-9: "For it is by grace you have been saved, through faith—and this is not from yourselves, it is the gift of God—not by works, so that no one can boast" (NIV). Those verses stuck with me and I began to think how it didn't line up with what I had been taught about salvation. I remember praying and praying to God; I was so confused, telling Him, "Your Word says this, but I was taught something else."

One of my friends invited me to church. The first time I walked in, I felt uncomfortable since I wasn't used to church like that. That Sunday, I was sitting in the service and the message spoke to me; I began to cry and, during the altar call, the pastor's wife prayed over me. Without knowing my background or anything about me, she said, "God wanted me to tell you that you don't need to be confused, He will show you who He is." At that moment, I realized my prayers were being answered—God was listening! For the first time in my life I felt God was with me. Everything changed; I gave my life to Him. I have continued to seek and know Him more and more. Since that moment, I understand it is God's grace that saves us.

—*Julia*

Today's Takeaway:

God is waiting for you with open, loving arms and wants you to come to Him just as you are. He will show you who He is.

Day 193

Today's Scripture:

"But the fruit of the Spirit is love, joy, peace, longsuffering, kindness, goodness, faithfulness, gentleness, self-control. Against such there is no law" (Galatians 5:22-23 NKJV).

Today's Testimony:

I used to think I didn't have much of a testimony. I would listen to others tell about how they were saved from lives of addiction or deep sin and think how boring my story was. I was raised in a Christian home with two parents that loved the Lord. My father taught Sunday school and drove the bus on Sunday mornings.

That was the first twelve years of my life; then my father "fell off the wagon" and started drinking again. He dropped out of church, I think because of the shame of backsliding. My parents made sure my brothers and I went to church; they just didn't go with us. Five years later my father came back to the Lord.

At the age of sixteen, I met a boy who wasn't a Christian, but before we were married, he was saved and baptized. Life happened and we fell away from regular church attendance. Our lukewarm way of life hit us hard when our daughter was born. She was healthy at 11 a.m. that morning, but that night at 10 p.m. her lungs collapsed and she was rushed to the NICU. Thankfully, I knew who to turn to for help. It took me a little longer to realize it, but I needed a church for my children to have the same foundation my parents gave me. I promised God I would work for Him in any position that He needed me. God brought us through.

Now I think maybe my testimony isn't so boring—look at all the heartache I was saved from. That foundation of those first twelve years has made me a strong Christian woman and kept me through times of sadness, happiness, and pain. Always knowing God is there by my side has been a constant source of strength.

—Linda

Today's Takeaway:

The greatest story of a Christian's life is that they gave their heart to Jesus as a child and served Him all their life. The perfect plan of Jesus is to save us, lead us throughout all our lives, helping us avoid pitfalls and traps set by the enemy in order to steal our joy and later kill us. The most wonderful thing a parent can do is lead their children and teach by example, and then the greatest thing the children can do is to receive that instruction. This is the ideal plan. Of course, when it doesn't work out like this, God steps in and gives us second and third chances, and more.

The great thing about our Lord is that even though He does have a perfect plan, He works with imperfect people.

Day 194

Today's Scripture:

"Every time I think of you, I give thanks to my God" (Philippians 1:3 NLT).

Today's Testimony:

One summer day I moved in with a man whom I had found on a couples' dating site. The day I moved in, I knew it was wrong. I didn't know what I was going to do. I wasn't walking with Jesus; I knew of Him, I just didn't *know* Him. But God had a plan!

The Lord had positioned me across the street from a woman of God. She was lovely and vibrant. She went to a weekly prayer gathering at a local church and was a member at another church. One day, she invited me to come with her for prayer, and I went. Seven women laid hands on me and prayed in the Spirit for me.

We know God uses all things for our good. That is what He did for me. Soon after going to the prayer meeting, I began getting sick. I got so sick that I couldn't hold down my job. My sister came to take me back to stay with her for a while. On the trip, we stopped for a rest, and I blacked out, breaking one of my ribs. I was so ill; I didn't know until much later that it was broken. I went to doctor after doctor to find out what was wrong. They couldn't find anything.

I became so sick that I had created a list of pallbearers for my funeral. One day as I lay there, I began to think of my friend. She called me five minutes later. She said, "Don't be afraid in the storm; read these Bible verses I'm about to give you." My sister and my mom read the Bible verses to me; I began to get better. Soon I was able to walk around; suddenly, I knew I needed to return home.

I reconnected with my friend and stayed with her for a period of time. It was so special to me. She taught me a lot about the Lord, and I was saved. She even prayed for me to be filled with the Spirit. She called the church to arrange a water baptism, and five days later I was baptized in the local lake. Soon after my baptism, she went home to Jesus. I am so thankful for her life and how God used her mightily and the family I gained along the way.

—*Janis*

Today's Takeaway:

Janis' friend reminds me of Tabitha in the New Testament. She was a follower of Jesus. Paul encouraged others to follow him as he followed Christ; Janis was able to follow her friend to the Savior. Oh, I want to be like that, don't you?

Other people should be able to follow us to Jesus because we are headed in that direction ourselves. Look around; is there someone in your close vicinity that you could take on your journey? Maybe they're just waiting for an invitation!

Day 195

Today's Scripture:

"I can do all things through Christ who strengthens me" (Philippians 4:13 NKJV).

Today's Testimony:

My salvation story started about fifty years ago, when I started going to church with my husband and children. I was raised a Catholic, so I was surprised at what this church felt like. It was very active and busy and loving. I still attend every time I'm able even today.

I was saved and baptized, and through the years we raised our three boys in the church; the youngest started going to church when he was four days old. My husband was an evangelist and the family would go with him when possible. I have been blessed to teach every age group in the church through the years, and I am currently teaching a small group of older ladies at this time.

God has blessed me in my life with many friends and family living for the Lord, and I still pray the family will *all* be saved before the coming of the Lord. There have been many blessings from God—my son's eyes were healed, my own heart was successfully fixed with a quintuple bypass surgery, and my husband's ability to work and take care of our family. Even years later when my husband suffered a stroke, God helped him. He was down, but not out. When he became disabled, he missed very little church until God carried him home. Today, the Lord continues to bless our family. Praise the Lord!

—*Lael*

Today's Takeaway:

Paul said in Ephesians 1:1, "To the saints (God's people) who are at Ephesus and are faithful and loyal and steadfast in Christ Jesus" (AMP.). I believe he was talking about people like Lael. For the last fifty years, she has been as steadfast as a rock, teaching, caring, praying, and working for Christ in her church. I believe that is what she'll be found doing when her Lord returns. Then she's going to hear those words that we all long to hear one day: "Well done, good and faithful servant; thou hast been faithful over a few things, I will make thee ruler over many things: enter thou into the joy of thy Lord" (Matthew 25:23 KJV).

It's all going to be worth it, child of God. Keep pressing on. Don't quit now. Jesus is coming! Live like Lael. Be faithful and true. He sends blessings and strength to those in His care.

Day 196

Today's Scripture:

"The Lord is like a father to his children, tender and compassionate to those who fear him" (Psalm 103:13 NLT).

Today's Testimony:

I don't ever remember a time not being in church as a little girl. My parents dedicated me to the Lord the first week of my life. I have always belonged to Jesus—it just took me a little while to realize it. My teen years were rough. Life began to change quickly and my parents started to have marital issues that ended their marriage after almost twenty-three years.

At that point in my life, *love* made absolutely no sense to me; I turned to anything for "love" other than Jesus—drugs, alcohol, sex. Anything that would feed my flesh quickly became my new normal. Looking back, I know it was Jesus and the prayers of my grandmothers that kept me alive during that time.

My behavior quickly led into depression and even some suicidal thoughts. I got married at nineteen but ended it just thirteen months later. I just wanted to be loved. It seemed like every male that "claimed" to love me left me. I even struggled feeling loved and good enough for my Dad. I grew up hearing that Jesus loved me, but I couldn't grasp it; how could the heavenly Father love someone like me, and how could I feel loved by Him?

At the age of twenty-one I found out I was pregnant. I ended up having a miscarriage, but just a few weeks later I found out I was pregnant again. The miscarriage was emotional, but this second pregnancy felt different—my life was about to change. The father quickly left after the first pregnancy ended and was long gone before I knew the next was on the way, but God had a plan. About six weeks after I started accepting that I was going to be a single mom, God brought my high school friend back into my life. We fell in love and will be celebrating thirteen years of marriage next month. He has been by my side every day since God reunited us. Together we welcomed a healthy baby girl into the world. I thought my troubles were over; I was wrong.

—Marci
(To Be Continued in Tomorrow's Reading)

Today's Takeaway:

There is no real comparison of love here on earth to the love of the Father for His girls. *Would he lay down his very life for yours?* Few men would; some dads might, but Jesus did. When considering a relationship with a boy/man, God's girls need to consider that tough question and think, *Would I be treated with that level of value?* If not, move on. Never be tolerated, be celebrated!

Day 197

Today's Scripture:

"I have placed my rainbow in the clouds. It is the sign of my covenant with you and with all the earth" (Genesis 9:13 NLT).

Today's Testimony (Continued From Previous Day):

Later we found out we were pregnant again. The sound of hearing we were going to have a son sent excitement through the roof. When it came time to deliver, we heard the most gut-wrenching words any parent could ever hear. "There is no heartbeat, I'm so sorry." The pain at that moment felt like my life was over. All the heartache I had gone through in my life didn't compare. God still had a plan. After the anger settled, I crawled into the lap of Jesus. I knew I had a precious little token in Heaven that I needed to get to see. I wanted something different for my life. A couple months later we found out we were pregnant again, and later welcomed another healthy baby girl into the world. This was followed by another miscarriage, and then finally our last healthy baby girl.

After we had managed to get through the loss of our son, my husband and I decided if we could get through that, we could get through anything. We truly devoted our life together as a couple for Jesus. We decided that Satan would no longer have any hold over our marriage. The generational destruction of the enemy was done. We promised to demonstrate to our daughters what a godly marriage looks like. It wasn't instantly perfect but it was instantly God's.

I learned about the term "rainbow baby" through my journey. A rainbow baby is a baby you have after the loss of a baby. It's God's little promise after a storm. He blessed us with three. There is a God-given purpose for each of our girls. It would be nice if I could end this with a "she lived happily ever after," but in reality life is not a fairy tale. There has been pain and sorrow, but there has also been joy in my life. God always seems to show me something good from pain. Sometimes it takes me a little longer than I would like. but even when God should have given up on me, He never has.

—*Marci*

Today's Takeaway:

For those of you who are waiting on Heaven to see your children again, I believe God gives you a special measure of grace that no one else receives; I think mothers like you need that. His Word says, "He supplies *all* your need" (see Philippians 4:19). After watching my own mother long for Heaven to see her children, I feel certain it's that grace given by God that allows mothers to keep walking forward, while looking backward. Walk on, then, with the full assurance that the measure of grace you've been given will carry you *all the way* until you reach their arms in that heavenly city where they're happy and waiting for you to join them.

Day 198

Today's Scripture:

"What do you think? If a man owns a hundred sheep, and one of them wanders away, will he not leave the ninety-nine on the hills and go to look for the one that wandered off? And if he finds it, truly I tell you, he is happier about that one sheep than about the ninety-nine that did not wander off. In the same way your Father in heaven is not willing that any of these little ones should perish" (Matthew 18:12-14 NIV).

Today's Testimony:

My father was a pastor and I was raised in church. I loved the church and I loved Jesus. I would feel conviction in my heart and always wanted to make sure I was in right standing with Christ. My father had to tell me that I didn't have to come down for every salvation altar call, but I always wanted to make sure. As a child, I would sign up for church wide prayer chains and go into my parents' bedroom and pray for an hour. Bible reading was a part of my daily routine. There was a sensitivity to the Spirit of God in my life.

With all the positives, there were also some views of God I had developed that were unbalanced. I had formulated God as this all-powerful presence in Heaven who was waiting for me to sin, blow it, and then His judgment would be poured out. If I was going through something difficult, I would begin to think I had done something wrong. I was worried about making sure I stayed in line and wouldn't face His wrath.

In my later teenage years, I came into a season where I faltered in my relationship with God. I prayed, read my Bible, and was involved in church, but I felt like a failure. This is where God revealed to me a whole other side of who He is. I discovered a gentle, loving Shepherd who stayed right with me, comforted me, and began to show me the plans He had for my life; the loving Father who offered compassion, mercy, and grace. This blew me away. How could this be?

During this season, He sent women into my life to prophesy about my ministry. I am fulfilling that ministry today. One of them prophesied about my future husband. God began to give me glimpses, in my failure, of what could be if I stayed connected to Him. This transformed my view of my heavenly Father. I felt love and intimacy with God like I'd never felt before. He was my safe place. He would chase me down and love me even when I failed.

—Amy

Today's Takeaway:

(Amy's words) What a blessed opportunity we have to serve an amazing God. He sent His Son so we could have life, and life more abundantly. He offers an overwhelming, never-ending love that we can freely accept. We don't earn this love and don't deserve it, but we can walk in it each day. Remind yourself of the times you received His love when you feel like you didn't deserve it. Let His love wash over you. Let Him be *your* Shepherd.

Day 199

Today's Scripture:

"The thief does not come except to steal, and to kill, and to destroy. I have come that they may have life, and that they may have it more abundantly" (John 10:10 NKJV).

Today's Testimony:

When my brother came home from the Navy, he shared Jesus with my mom, who gave her heart to the Lord right away. He had gotten saved while he was away, but I didn't want to hear about it.

About six years later, I was in a marriage I should've never been in and was so miserable I wanted to die. I think I might've killed myself if I hadn't believed I would end up in hell, and I didn't want that. So, I found myself wishing that a semitruck would just run a red light and put me out of my misery so I could get out of this life I was living. One morning as I was on my way to work, about 6:00, I was coming up to a traffic light that was about to turn green. I slowed down a little and as the light turned green, I sped up and there was a semitruck with a flatbed that ran the red light. I didn't realize what was happening at that exact moment. The front end of my car went UNDER the flatbed and the tires rolled OVER the front of my car and turned my car into the direction the truck was traveling. I looked and saw the semi run up a telephone pole. In the moment I wondered what he was doing or what caused him to do that.

Well, to make a long story short, I was fine—not one thing happened to me. I called my mom and told her about the accident, and she started crying, telling me that she knew I was going to be in an accident. I told her I was fine and didn't get hurt. Then she asked me if I would go to church with her the next Sunday, and I told her I would go with her.

Sitting there in the church service as they gave the altar call, I realized I didn't have a life, so I might as well try Jesus. I went to the altar and gave my heart to Jesus that day.

—*Diane*

Today's Takeaway:

Do you have any guesses whose idea it was for Diane to kill herself or want to get hit and killed by a semitruck? You've got it—the enemy of our soul! He wants to kill, steal, and destroy you. The thing is, God has another plan. He even proved to Diane that He was big enough to see her through a semitruck hitting her and keep her from getting killed. How ironic is that? God knew just how to get through to her.

He's got His eye on you too. He'll show you things that only you could know He's speaking to you. There are times that God will show you little things just for you. When He does, remember to thank Him. It's like your own private text from God. He knows you better than anyone—and still loves you.

Day 200

Today's Scripture:

"For I determined not to know any thing among you, save Jesus Christ, and him crucified" (1 Corinthians 2:2 KJV).

Today's Testimony:

I started going to church when I was five years old. I was invited by a friend to see a puppet show. I memorized all the books of the Bible and received a Bible as a prize. I was so excited to go to church from the age of five to twelve, but my life wasn't changed; I only came for the puppet show.

When I was twelve I was invited to another church, and the preacher made salvation seem so hard that for the next four years I lived in fear of going to hell. Later I went to a Bible camp as a teenager with some friends and heard that all you had to do to get saved was to pray and believe. So while I was by myself one night, I prayed, "Lord, if You are real, I need You in my life and I ask You to come in." The Holy Spirit brought back a scripture to my mind that I must have learned some time during my years of going to church: "For sin shall not have dominion over you: for ye are not under the law, but under grace" (Romans 6:14 KJV).

But when I told my parents what had happened, they got angry and didn't want me to go to church anymore. This made my home life difficult; it felt like my life turned upside-down.

Finally I moved out at seventeen and I worked two jobs while going to high school. I thought this was the best way to fix the problem; but after falling asleep behind the wheel and having a serious car accident, I had to move back home. This made me totally dependent not only on my parents but also on God.

As I grew closer to God, I longed for a deeper experience with Him. Years later while attending church, I learned about the baptism in the Holy Spirit. I prayed and received that filling. I finally felt that my life had turned right-side-up.

—*Melinda*

Today's Takeaway:

Talk about determination—Melinda was determined to move out of her own home if that's what it took to serve God. The problem was, she just needed to trust God with His plan, maybe not hers. (Raise your hand if you've done that. Yes, me too!) God still loves you when you plow forward with maybe a big idea, just not His. He is so patient with His impetuous girls; in fact, He uses that awesome planning ability for His glory. We just have to plan with Him. Lean on God—He has big plans for you. He wants to use *all* that stuff He put in you for great things to bless others and you. Just do things His way!

Day 201

Today's Scripture:

"For it is by grace you have been saved, through faith—and this is not from yourselves, it is the gift of God—not by works, so that no one can boast" (Ephesians 2:8-9 NIV).

Today's Testimony:

I was born into a religion that seemed more about pomp and circumstance than about actual faith. I was taught about the stories of the Bible and what they mean, and memorizing Bible verses was an important part of every child's experience. We were shown how to blend in with the group, and to make sure that no one stood out. Everything was to be done in sync with everyone around you.

When I was a teenager, I was quite rebellious and made some very bad choices, which led the leaders of the church to come to my house often to tell me that I was going to go to hell for how I was living. I asked if they could help me to change my situation and they told me they wouldn't help me, but I was still going to hell.

My father had left this same church when I was young, when my mother left him. He got remarried to a wonderful woman, and together they decided they needed to find a new church. Eventually, they found one and they tried to get me to go with them, pleading with me to just try it once. They told me I could drive myself and if I didn't like it, I could just get up and leave, no questions asked, and never go back. Eventually, I decided to go, just to get them off my back. But something unexpected happened when I walked into their church, something that had never happened when I walked into the church of my youth—I felt right at home. Everyone was so welcoming and warm. The things that were taught at this church were things I had never been taught about the Bible before. They showed me how to have a personal relationship with God the Father, Jesus Christ, and the Holy Spirit.

During this time period, I was engaged in an internal battle. I was still trying to live a life that was fun and exciting, but went against everything I knew to be spiritually right. I was drinking and partying with my friends, and then going to church on Sunday morning. When I would get to church, I'd feel terrible about the decisions I was making, but I felt too weak to stop.

—Heather
(To Be Continued in Tomorrow's Reading)

Today's Takeaway:

When we reduce the Word of God to nothing but a list of rules of what not to do, with a punishment of hell for breaking them, we throw everything Jesus did on the cross into the trash. He hung on the cross to die for our sins because He loves us. This is not about a list of rules. He died so we could have a way to be with Him. He wants *us there*—it's a relationship He's after! His plan is to bless us because He truly loves us.

Day 202

Today's Scripture:

*"Jesus replied, 'I tell you the truth, unless you are born again,
you cannot see the Kingdom of God'"* (John 3:3 NLT).

Today's Testimony *(Continued From Previous Day):*

One Saturday night, I had drunk way too much and was too hungover to go to church the next morning. My stepmom told me I needed to listen to the sermon, that it was very powerful. I told her I would, but kept brushing off actually doing it. Eventually, she tracked me down at her son's house, where I was hanging out with my sister-in-law. She came in and told us, in a very firm "Mom voice," that we needed to sit down and get some tissues, because we were going to listen to this sermon and we would not be getting up. What happened next changed my life forever.

The sermon was on "The Realities of Hell." I knew hell was "fire and brimstone" and people would "burn there for eternity." That night, I went out to the bar, but it took me all night to drink a beer and a half, and it tasted like death in my mouth. I decided that was it for me. I was done. I went to church the next morning, ready to make a change, but I was terrified about how to do it. As I was standing there praying, I heard the voice of God in my spirit. He said, "It's all or nothing!" The battle was over for me. I knew what had to be done. I dedicated my life to Christ and accepted His salvation. I have not had a single drop of alcohol since that day!

That was my born-again moment. I celebrate the anniversary of this day every year as my "re-birthday."

—*Heather*

Today's Takeaway:

Well, "Happy Re-Birthday, Heather!" It's the best thing ever. Truthfully, hell is a real place. Jesus spoke about a rich man being tormented in its flames. My heart breaks for the people who choose it instead of turning to the One who can change it all for them.

That's why it's so important to make sure everyone understands Jesus came so everyone could call on Him and be saved. How sad to know who Jesus is and refuse to ask Him to save you! Let's do everything we can to make sure our friends and family understand who He is—not the list-maker, but the Cross-bearer. The One who willingly hung there for you and for me so we could forever be in Heaven with Him.

Day 203

Today's Scripture:

"Brethren, I count not myself to have apprehended: but this one thing I do, forgetting those things which are behind, and reaching forth unto those t hings which are before, I press toward the mark for the prize of the high calling of God in Christ Jesus" (Philippians 3:13-14 KJV).

Today's Testimony:

I was saved and baptized when I was thirteen years old. As I grew up though, I did not live my life like I knew who God was. I always said I was a Christian, but those were only words. My life didn't look any different than anyone else in the world. I got married, for the first time, when I was seventeen. We had two children together, a boy and a girl, then divorced four years later. A couple of years after that, I became involved with another man who was very abusive. We stayed together, on and off, for about eight years. Within that time, we got married, had a son, and got divorced.

So there I was, in my mid-twenties, already a two-time divorcee with three children. Throughout that time, I would go to church once in a while, here and there, but was never committed. Then tragedy struck, and my world fell apart. My middle son got really sick. I took him to the hospital, and he died the next day. He was only five years old, one month shy of turning six. I was already not living a godly life, but now, I decided I would drink my problems away—I blamed God for taking my son. I was very mad at Him and was not afraid to tell Him so (especially when I was drunk).

I drank for about six years, almost daily. But even then, God, in His goodness, was unfolding His plan. About two months after my son passed away, God brought a good man into my life. I didn't know at the time, though, that he would later become my husband. I was too busy drinking and being angry. However, this man stood by my side. He never left me, he was always there for me, and we eventually got married. With neither one of us saved though, it got rocky and at one point we divorced. Thankfully, later we remarried. Then something wonderful happened.

God is so good! We both rededicated our lives to Jesus and decided to put God first. We attend a great church now and have a wonderful church family. We are involved and maturing Christians. We still have a long way to go, but it's an ongoing process until Jesus comes back to get us. And so, I keep pressing forward.

—*Shelly*

Today's Takeaway:

This is a picture of redemption. Jesus just doesn't give up; He also presses on. He keeps on knocking on our heart's door. Open up, let Him in, and then keep on pressing forward to maturity. Inspire the ones behind you.

Day 204

Today's Scripture:

"Before I formed thee in the belly I knew thee" (Jeremiah 1:5 KJV).

Today's Testimony:

When I was four years old, my mother gave me to my grandparents. I wanted my mom so badly that I grew up bitter and hard-hearted because I continuously thought I wasn't good enough or she would have kept me.

By the time I was a teenager, I learned to escape my pain by using drugs and alcohol; they worked to ease the pain until the "high" wore off then I was back where I started from. So I found myself staying high as often as possible. Before I realized it, I had developed a full-blown addiction to alcohol and Valium.

One summer I was introduced to a lady who would later become my mother-in-law. I had left home at that time and had nowhere to stay. She gave me a place to sleep, fed me, bought me clothes, and took care of me like I was her daughter. After a short courtship I married her son. I watched my mother-in-law exhibit love and peace. I had never heard of Jesus, but she was showing Him to me. He knew me! She would do her household chores while singing hymns and was happy all the time. There was something different about her . . . she had a peace that I knew nothing about. She had what I needed.

I would find myself feeling so guilty for getting high, especially when I was around her. But, she never ridiculed me. Instead, she'd say things like, "You should go to church with me."

She invited me to go to a church revival with her. I had drunk quite a bit of alcohol and had taken Valium that day. Despite that, I agreed to go with her. During the preaching I began to feel a desire to change. I didn't want to get high anymore, I didn't want to be bitter, and I didn't know what to do about it. I'd never heard of praying. The minister's wife asked me if I wanted to pray with her. I told her that I didn't know how and she explained in the simplest terms: "Just say you are sorry for your sins and be sorry and He'll forgive you." As soon as I said the words "I'm sorry," I was immediately released from a five-year addiction and was finally free. For the first time I felt peace, love, and joy.

That was thirty-six years ago and I still serve Him. I know Him and He knows me.

—Glenda

Today's Takeaway:

After all the pain, hurt, and rejection Glenda had experienced, forgiveness was simple. I love how the minister's wife explained it: "Just say you're sorry . . . and be sorry!" God was waiting to forgive her. He was waiting to set her free from addiction and pain. It all started with someone "showing Jesus."

Day 205

Today's Scripture:

"I have seen you in the sanctuary and beheld your power and your glory. Because your love is better than life, my lips will glorify you" (Psalm 63:2-3 NIV).

Today's Testimony:

I was three years old when my parents moved us from our hometown. All of my grandparents, aunts, uncles, and cousins lived in that area. My father took a position as a youth pastor. Two years later, we moved again when my dad was given his first lead pastor position. I grew up visiting family a few times a year, but I never quite had the relationships my cousins had with each other or with our other relatives. My siblings and I (I was the eldest of four at the time) were homeschooled. We moved often, going where the Spirit led, so I never truly felt like I had a home in the traditional sense. I didn't have close family ties, neighbors, or classmates. My home was the church.

When I was seven, my dad pastored a church with maybe a dozen congregants. The church people were my friends. They came to my birthday parties, taught me to play volleyball, and told me Nigerian folktales. I would be at the church almost daily as my parents attended to church business. In the meantime, my siblings and I kept ourselves busy. We played make-believe. I drew, danced, and ran. I climbed the tree behind the white church-house. The church is where I grew up and where I accepted Jesus as my Savior.

We moved from that city when I was around middle-school age. I met a myriad of loving grandparent figures. We were doted on and well taken care of. I grew closer to God. I started going to public high school. We moved again, and I entered a new public high school. I became an adult and went to college. I got my first full-time job and got married. There has been a lot of change in my life. The one constant has been God. In the ups and downs, He has been there. The change doesn't scare me. I met Him as a child and He offered me everything my circumstances could not. As an adult, I cried out to Him and He showed up for me. I get to enjoy the freedom that knowing Him as my Father offers me. His love is more real than I could have imagined.

—*Erica*

Today's Takeaway:

(Erica's words) I'm a young adult, but I have more experience than I did when I accepted Jesus in that white church-house. Now I know that the church building feels too sacred to touch for many. Some feel they have to have it all together before they reach out to God. For me, I associate God's house with my house. I see Him coming to my birthday parties, watching over me as I played for long hours, delighting in my puppet shows and art displays. God's house was a place of stability, family, and fun. It's sacred, yes. But it's also *your* Father's house which, in turn, makes it *your* home too. That is awesome!

Day 206

Today's Scripture:

"For I can do everything through Christ, who gives me strength" (Philippians 4:13 NLT).

Today's Testimony:

I was three years old when my twenty-one year-old mom fled from Puerto Rico to New York City with me in her arms. She was leaving an abusive marriage. She left my two older brothers (ages six and five) behind with my grandmother, until she could find a place for us all. Soon after, both my brothers and my grandmother came to live with us. A couple years passed, and my mom had another baby boy. At this tender age of five, I would help my grandma with house chores and take care of my baby brother while my mom worked.

When I was around eleven years old, my mom started getting sick, suffering from migraine headaches. One evening, she was rushed to the hospital only to be sent back home with a neck brace. That same night, she returned to the ER with uncontrollable headaches only to find she had suffered a stroke. That first stroke hospitalized her, and shortly after the first stroke she had repeated ones. Doctors operated on her several times to stop the bleeds, but to no avail. My mom became paralyzed from the neck down and was left in a vegetative state. During the surgery, they found several bumps on her head and asked my grandmother about them. She told them they were a result of numerous blows to the head that my father had given her. I later learned that he would repeatedly beat her over her head with the back of a machete.

The doctors told my grandmother that the cause of my mother's stroke was secondary to those blows that were issued by my father. He was both a very jealous man and an alcoholic. There were evenings where my father would lie in wait for my mother to return home with my grandmother after a long day at work just to beat her. I can remember as a little girl hiding under my grandparents' bed just to escape from both the horrific scene and sounds.

My mom was in the hospital for eleven months before she passed away. It was during this time, and through my mom's sickness, that I came to know Jesus Christ as my Lord and Savior. I was in the nineth grade. I found it difficult to concentrate and I cried all the time.

—*Rosa*
(To Be Continued in Tomorrow's Reading)

Today's Takeaway:

Poor Rosa, to find that her mother's strokes were caused by her father's repeated beatings had to be more than she thought she could bear. They could have been, except that she was not alone. Thank God! We are not alone. We have a Father who sees and knows our pain. If you feel overwhelmed today, call out to One who sees and knows what you're going through.

Day 207

Today's Scripture:

"Even if my father and mother abandon me, the Lord will hold me close"
(Psalm 27:10 NLT).

Today's Testimony *(Continued From Previous Day):*

I had been very close to my mom. With her confined to the hospital, I was in a grave and distressed state. There was a girl in my class who took notice of my condition and befriended me. She would invite me to have lunch with her every day. Her dad would pick us up and make lunch for us.

One day, during lunch, I was watching the birds fly as I looked out of her kitchen window. As I gazed, I found myself wishing that I could fly away, just like the birds could. Both my home and life were in chaos. My brothers didn't know how to cope with our dreaded circumstance, and turned to a life of drugs and gangs. I had no peace, just a broken heart. Watching those birds fly gave me a sense of peace. As I stared through that kitchen window, my friend looked at me and asked me what I was thinking about. It was then that I shared my heart with her. After I poured out my soul, she uttered the most beautiful words I have ever heard in my life: "Rosa, Jesus loves you!"

This young girl, who was my age, began to witness to me. She told me that if I accepted the Lord, one day I would be able to fly like those birds on the day of the Rapture. I didn't understand anything at the time, but I loved the idea of flying like those birds to escape the pain and sorrow I was feeling.

She invited me to church and I went. The pastor was preaching and he made an altar call. He shared Philippians 4:13 and Psalm 27:10 with me, and I made Jesus Lord of my life that day. During those months my mom was in the hospital, I prayed for her healing, but it never happened. An evangelist came with me to visit her one day and prayed for her. She couldn't speak, but she understood what was being said. She would communicate with a "yes" or "no" by batting her eyelashes. That day, she accepted Jesus Christ as her Savior.

Although my mom never recovered, she gained access to forgiveness and Heaven through prayer. As the years progressed, my grandmother and my brothers also came to know the Lord as their Savior. A year after my mom's death, I met the man who today is my husband of forty years. We have been pastoring for thirty-five years. A fuller and more beautiful life, I could not have ever expected or asked for. To God be the glory!

—*Rosa*

Today's Takeaway:

I'm so thankful for Rosa's brave mother who sacrificed to get herself and her family to safety; there is now peace after the storm. God healed Rosa's mother in Heaven and took care of Rosa—she now has many children and grandchildren. She is blessed. God saw them through it all.

Day 208

Today's Scripture:

"Never will I leave you; never will I forsake you" (Hebrews 13:5 NIV).

Today's Testimony:

My testimony began when I was twelve years old. Growing up, my family didn't attend church. As a matter of fact, I didn't know anyone who did go to church. However, a local church had a bus ministry which was going door-to-door, and they stopped by our house one Saturday morning. They asked if my brother or I wanted to be picked up for Sunday school. Of course, I did!

From that moment on, I was a bus-ministry kid. After going for several months, during a Sunday morning service I remember the pastor giving an altar call, and I was drawn to go down front to give my heart to Jesus.

Later through my junior and high school years, I started to drift away from Jesus. Of course, He never left me, but I left Him. I was doing my own thing. Oh, I would still say a prayer sometimes, but I kept Him at a distance.

I met my husband in my early twenties and we got married; two years later we had our first daughter. We had an up-and-down marriage for several years. I would call out to God during those down times, but still live my "own life" during the good times. Seven years later our second daughter was born. We were in the process of moving back to our home state, to be closer to family. Three years after we moved back home, depression had really taken hold of me, so much so that I had actually contemplated taking my own life.

I was desperate; and that's when I began to see God work in our lives. He began to place Christian people in my life and in my husband's life. I remember thinking, *Something is changing in our lives.* Still, I wasn't quite sure what that "something" was.

My husband had a friend who invited us to his church. We decided that he would go first to check it out, then I would go the next time with him. The second night I went, we realized that we were attending a full-Gospel camp meeting. We were two wide-eyed young adults attending that service. We'd been out of church for at least a decade, but I can tell you that we both felt the presence of God there. During that time, I recommitted my life back to Jesus, this time selling out to Him, giving Him my whole self, my whole heart. And I haven't looked back.

—Rhonda

Today's Takeaway:

Rhonda found out a great truth—it's hard to go your own way and go God's way at the same time! It leads to a constant pulling against God's leading. There's no joy in going opposite to Jesus. Rhonda had heard about the Lord, she'd felt His love enough to recognize the absence of it in her life. Once you know that peace, nothing but His presence will suffice after that.

Day 209

Today's Scripture:

"That if you confess with your mouth the Lord Jesus and believe in your heart that God has raised Him from the dead, you will be saved" (Romans 10:9 NKJV).

Today's Testimony:

My father took our family to church all of my life, which had a great impact on my life. During those years, I was shown and taught the way of salvation and accepted it. I loved God and had a deep desire to serve Him.

After I graduated from high school, I started attending a church that was growing with many being saved. We had a revival and had such a move of the Holy Spirit that while the choir would be singing, people would come out of their seats, get saved, and filled with the Spirit. During that revival, I completely surrendered my life to God to do whatever He chose for me to do.

I met a dedicated young man while attending the church. We started dating and later got married. The pastor and his wife became our mentors and we spent many hours of training under their leadership. They were a real blessing and influence. My husband felt a call on his life and shared this with the pastor, who told him the good parts and tough parts of ministry. He told him to come back if he knew for sure he was called. He gave valuable instruction that would come to bless him greatly in the years to follow.

He *knew* he was called, and we went on to evangelize and pastor churches for many years; I had the privilege to partner in ministry with a praying and anointed pastor and preacher. God has always blessed us everywhere we went. Many souls have been saved, healed, and changed.

The year 2020 was very difficult. I lost my sister with whom I was very close; two weeks later, we lost our precious son at age forty-seven. I am still grieving over these losses, but God is helping me. I know they are in Heaven, and I will see them again someday.

I don't know how anyone goes through losing loved ones without the help of God. If you are not saved, you don't have the promise of seeing your loved ones in Heaven again, but Romans 10:9-13 tells us how to be saved and be ready for Heaven. Living for Jesus is the best life ever. Get saved and make Him a part of your life.

—*Eunice*

Today's Takeaway:

I am so thankful for Eunice's life of service to the Lord. She has served faithfully by her husband's side as a pastor's wife and ministered to so many. Now she is grieving over the loss of her sister and son. She has the arms of her heavenly Father around her and she is receiving comfort and peace. We can be assured of that care when we serve a God like Eunice's. Then we'll know we can see our loved ones again one day if they died in the Lord. What a friend we have in Jesus! He takes care of us *and* them until we're reunited. Hold on, Eunice, happy days are ahead!

Day 210

Today's Scripture:

"Enter through the narrow gate. For wide is the gate and broad is the road that leads to destruction, and many enter through it. But small is the gate and narrow the road that leads to life, and only a few find it" (Matthew 7:13-14 NIV).

Today's Testimony:

It's easy to be considered a "Christian" by popular standards. To some, faith is nothing more than a collection of vague and friendly sentiments. If we see a Jesus fish on a bumper, or a Bible quote on Facebook, so many of us say, "There's a Christian." This was how I thought for years! Here is my story.

Several years ago, I had an ATV accident. I broke all my ribs, broke my pelvis in half, had two brain bleeds, and a chipped shoulder. I also crushed my left leg. I don't remember much right after the accident other than I was in a lot of pain. I was in ICU for forty-eight hours, then was transferred to the critical care unit. I'd never been hurt like this before. My pastor and his wife, along with my brother and sister-in-law, who pastor a church, came to the ICU and had prayer with me.

That evening the doctors told my husband that the brain bleeds had stopped. They were amazed. Normally, someone with two brain bleeds needs surgery to stop the bleeding. I believe, God stopped the bleeding. Sometimes, He needs to get our attention for us to get closer to Him.

I had a lot of time to think while I was healing, along with a lot of prayers asking God to take away the pain I was having. During the five months it took me to heal, I was talking to God every day, twenty times a day. Always the same thing, "God, please take this pain away."

I always believed in God, but never had a relationship with Him. Now I do. I started reading the Bible every day. It took time for me to totally understand our life is not about us, it's about Jesus. I have asked God to forgive me of my sins and to help me have a heart like Jesus. I've asked God to help me forgive and to love.

Our world is changing, and changing fast. To be a Christian in this world of ours, it is not easy. Jesus tells us in the Bible to enter through the narrow gate.

—Tonya

Today's Takeaway:

God speaks through pain like a megaphone! If we couldn't hear Him before, we often can then. There's no tricking God with a T-shirt or a bumper sticker—He sees our hearts and wants a real relationship with us. When we hit tough times like Tonya did, nothing fake will help. It'll take a solid foundation to get you through that.

Are you wondering how? Start by trusting Him with everything you've ever done, believe in everything He's ever done. Read His Word daily. Pray. You'll see the narrow gate.

Day 211

Today's Scripture:

"Therefore, if anyone is in Christ, he is a new creation; old things have passed away; behold, all things have become new" (2 Corinthians 5:17 NKJV).

Today's Testimony:

I was raised in church and saved as a child. During my teenage years, my family stopped going to church. Although I attended occasionally, I didn't attend regularly again for many years.

By not being in fellowship with other believers, I began to stray from God. First, I started swearing; soon it became easier and easier. Then I began to make a lot of poor choices.

I moved in with a man and we lived together for about four years. He was verbally abusive and then he cheated on me. I was hurt and very angry, so I decided to get even by cheating on him. Afterward, I began to feel worthless and started allowing people to treat me accordingly. This made me feel even more miserable. Through that misery, I finally cried out to God and asked for Him to help me. A few days after that prayer I met a wonderful man of God, and on our first date I committed my life back to Christ.

When I turned my life over to Christ, I felt like a large weight had been lifted off of my shoulders. I was so happy; I began to see the positive things in life instead of just the negative. I also began to understand people, and I found I was able to love and accept them for who they are instead of judging and criticizing them. One of the things I remember the most about the first month after I rededicated my life to Christ was that I cried a lot. Later, I learned that is part of the healing process. After starting to get all my hurts out, God was able to start to restore my heart.

I am now married to a pastor. I teach the junior children's church, work in the nursery, and I'm the director of our ladies' group. One of the things I struggled with the most after recommitting my life to Christ was the fact that I'd made so many bad choices. Being raised in church, my thought was, *I knew better.* I'm so thankful that God gave me what I call my "light-bulb moment"; He showed me that I was a new creation and all my "bad choices" were no longer remembered because they were forgiven.

—Neoma

Today's Takeaway:

Jesus remembers your past sins no more. Once you've repented, they're gone! Isn't that wonderful? I'm human, and sometimes I'm apt to remember a wrong done to me the next time I see someone, but not God. He wipes us clean. *God, help us to follow Your example and not only forgive, but forget past sins. Help us practice forgiveness in its purest and kindest form.*

Day 212

Today's Scripture:

"He alone is my rock and my salvation, my fortress; I shall not be greatly shaken"
(Psalm 62:2 ESV).

Today's Testimony:

I felt horrible all week. You see, I had lied to my mom about welcoming the new girl at school. I'm not saying I was outright mean, but I had not done what my heart *knew* was right. At the ripe old age of six, I understood if I befriended the unkempt and odd, new-to-us first grader, after all the social lines had been perfectly placed, then I too would become an outcast. The solution to my inner struggle was to go home and *pretend* that I followed my heart. That's right; I made my mom believe I befriended the shy and lonely girl when no one else would, by telling her some long story of how I welcomed her.

Well, that backfired terribly. Her pride over all of my "kindness" cast a dark cloud of shame over my heart. Then she had to go and tell my dad and grandma about how their little girl made friends with the new student when no one else would. At that point, I wondered if I even *had* a heart anymore. How would I undo this mess I'd made?

Well, good ole Sunday morning rolled around, and I sat next to my mom in our usual second-to-the-last back pew. Dad was in the worship band helping as the service wrapped up, and my brother and sister were in the preschool class. The pastor gave a call for salvation. It's the first time I remember hearing the invitation to accept Jesus as Savior. And oh, did I have sin and need a Savior! As I look back, I'm *certain* I had heard that salvation invitation plenty of times, but it became paramount at that moment because my sin had become apparent and the separation from God was thick. I raised my hand. I needed Jesus to forgive me from my sin and cleanse my heart from the cloud that had camped over it.

—*Monique*
(To Be Continued in Tomorrow's Reading)

Today's Takeaway:

Poor Monique, she wanted to do what was right for the "new girl." She knew what to do; she was afraid of being singled out for doing it. She didn't want to speak out and get singled out for it. Have you been in a position like this? Well, just go ahead and make a reputation for being "that girl"! You know, the one who always sits by the new person, the one who won't laugh at the "dirty jokes," the one who won't go to the drinking parties after work—go ahead and be her! You'll find that you'll get some friends that join *you*. Head up the "different from the world" club. Be proud of that; Jesus is your president. The benefits are out of this world!

Day 213

Today's Scripture:

"Train up a child in the way he should go, even when he grows older he will not abandon it" (Proverbs 22:6 NASB).

Today's Testimony *(Continued From Previous Day)*:

Realizing for the first time that I wasn't saved after having lived an agonizing week of condemnation, I slipped my hand up during the altar call.

My mother must have noticed my little raised hand because she quietly asked me if I wanted to go up to the altar to pray. I was terrified and remember thinking, *Forget it; I'll just deal with the darkness in my heart.* My eyes must have revealed my fear because she said we could pray the salvation prayer *right there*, and together we knelt and prayed. I remember feeling like I could fly that afternoon. The cloud lifted and Jesus now lived in my heart. We had a family gathering to attend that afternoon, and my parents encouraged me to share with them the decision I had made for Jesus. Looking back, I'm thankful for their encouragement to make a public statement of faith and also to be baptized. Sadly, my parents didn't have the opportunity to grow up in a Christian home. They came to Jesus as broken and addicted adults whom God had miraculously set free. I didn't know it at the time, but they were bestowing the "train up a child in the way he/she should go" gift that they didn't receive.

How grateful I am that God rescued them and that I could know Jesus at such an early age. Like so many, I've walked through difficult trials as I grew older, including my parents' divorce and the tragic passing of my sister. It's the love I found through Jesus, even as a little girl, and the hope He offers each day that gives my life meaning, that has seen me through many dark hours, and which makes me an overcomer. The Lord is the Rock of my salvation and the firm foundation of my life. I pray He is yours too.

—Monique

Today's Takeaway:

Monique's momma knew her little girl's heart so well, didn't she? I love the fact that she read her face and told her they could pray right there at their seats. Sweet momma! Jesus was just as real *there* as He was at the front. The point was the repentance and the genuine belief in Jesus. This experience has carried Monique all through her life and now strengthens her as a pastor's wife praying with others to give their own hearts to Christ.

It's this same Christ who strengthened Monique through the divorce of her parents, the raising of her children, the loss of her sister—God never leaves! He continues to be faithful throughout our lives, guiding us and steadying us with a firm foundation. That's why we can say He is our Rock! By the way, Monique and the new little girl at school became great friends the next day.

Day 214

Today's Scripture:

"Let us hold firmly to the hope we claim to have. The God who promised is faithful"
(Hebrews 10:23 NIRV).

Today's Testimony:

God will use all of us who are open to receive His amazing grace. I was born and raised in the Catholic church. I was sprinkled when I was a few months old, received all the sacraments of the church, and went to church every Sunday for thirty-four years; but God had His hand on this Catholic woman all those years.

Back in the '70s, my sister invited me to attend a Billy Graham Crusade. When the invitation was made, I went forward and one of the helpers led me through a salvation prayer. I really didn't feel much that night, but in the coming days, I began to notice that I was not using the little "cuss word" I used to say; I just felt different. I had been changed.

The next year, I was invited to attend a prayer meeting held at a Catholic church. One night when I was praying to receive the baptism in the Holy Spirit, all of a sudden I was filled with the Holy Spirit. I was so excited all night long and was filled with such joy and peace and kept praying in that heavenly language. My life has never been the same since. God uses me now as an intercessory prayer warrior to pray for others when they have a need. I am truly blessed of God.

The Lord brought my husband and me together—he is a minister and we have served the church for many years now. It's such a privilege to serve others.

—Sandy

Today's Takeaway:

It is a great privilege of mine to know and love Sister Sandy. She is pure love and joy and takes great delight in serving others and praying for needs. Though she is a tiny lady, she is mighty in the sight of God. Her prayers are strong and powerful because they are filled with love, joy, and His Spirit.

You may feel because you don't teach, sing, or lead the women's group, you don't really have a ministry. Don't believe that lie from the enemy! He may be trying to silence you because he knows you have a heart for others to pray over their needs—there is no other ministry of the church more vital than this one. I challenge you, if you feel the slightest leading in this area, contact your leaders today and get involved. Prayer turns everything around—it grows churches, it brings healing, it helps the pastor, it brings back visitors, it calls back prodigals, it calms anxiety—*it moves mountains*!

Day 215

Today's Scripture:

"But now, thus says the Lord, who created you, O Jacob, and He who formed you, O Israel: 'Fear not, for I have redeemed you; I have called you by your name; you are Mine'" (Isaiah 43:1 NKJV).

Today's Testimony:

Growing up in a Christian home with parents who taught me how to worship, how to study, how to live for God, and so much more, I was still not prepared for the trials I would face. Throughout my life I have had many trials and "Why, God?" moments, but through each event my faith and my relationships have become stronger.

When I was a young teenager, one night during an altar call, the Lord spoke to me. He said that I would marry a minister, lead people into worship, and, through my worship, chains would be broken, and lives would be changed. He began to pour into me so many things He would do through me and through my worship. I was fearful; I began to think I could never be used like that.

Each day after that, I allowed the enemy to tell me I wasn't good enough, or talented enough, and that no minister would marry me or love me. My fear grew until I was in my early twenties; I became so gripped with fear that it began to spread throughout my daily life. Yet despite this, God continued to work His plan for me, even through my fear of what that held in store for me. Matthew 19:26 says with man things can be impossible, but with God nothing is impossible. This was true for me. No matter what I believed about myself, God continued to surround me. He led me to my husband, who is a minister, and we fell in love and got married. God was working.

During the pregnancy of my first daughter, I was given horrible news that something was wrong with the baby. The first doctor wanted me to terminate the pregnancy. This was never an option as I knew God would heal her or even equip me to care for her if she was handicapped. In our situation, God had other plans for our daughter. He gave me a beautiful and healthy baby girl. Later, when our daughter was one, just as I was falling asleep one night, the enemy said she was his and that I should have let her die like I was told. But my God stepped in and a holy boldness came over me as I began to quote the Word of God over my child, her life, and the life of my household. The enemy fled, and at that very moment, the fear that had gripped me so long was gone. God received all the glory for that—then and even to this day.

—*Stephanie*

Today's Takeaway:

Satan doesn't know who he's messing with when he crosses a saved momma. She didn't take that lying down. And we shouldn't either! We have all the power of His Word to use. Quote it, woman of God!

Day 216

Today's Scripture:

"*We love Him because He first loved us*" (1 John 4:19 NKJV).

Today's Testimony:

Every day we would make our way across the road to have chapel in the church where I attended school. Inside the sanctuary, we'd sit in the pews by grade; I was in the first grade. I remember looking up to see a picture above the platform. It was an outdoor scene of a mountain with a stream. We would sing the song that says God "can do what no other power can do." I knew it was true.

I heard the minister's call to repent: "What would happen if you crossed the street out there, and a car struck you . . . where would you go if you should die?" Even as a little girl, I knew I was a sinner. I knew, if I should die that day, I wouldn't go to Heaven. I knew I needed to repent and ask Jesus into my heart. I raised my hand in response that I wanted to give my heart to Jesus.

Those of us who raised our hand were asked to go into a separate room, with a teacher, who would then pray with us. The teacher asked us a question and said if we answered it right, we could get saved. I couldn't remember the question, but the second girl gave the right answer. I knew if I could remember her answer, I could get saved, but by the time it was my turn I had forgotten the answer. The teacher said those who could not answer the question would have to leave the room and wait for another time to receive Christ because we didn't fully understand what was being said. My heart was crushed because I knew the weight of the situation, the burden of my sin, and the call of my Savior.

I left the room and went outside to sit beside the church on a cement slab. As the other students continued on with recess, the Holy Spirit reminded me, as I had heard, that if I asked Jesus to forgive me of my sins, He would, and He would come to live in me. There with the help of the Holy Spirit, I repented and asked Jesus to come into my heart, and instant peace came over me. He heard me and forgave me of my sins. I was His and He was mine.

—*Rhonda*

Today's Takeaway:

It's sad but people are human, aren't they? This teacher had good intentions but went about her job the wrong way and hindered some children's salvation along the way. The good news is, once the Holy Spirit draws us, nothing can stand in His way. He drew Rhonda and she understood His truth. She called and He answered. Once she repented, peace came flooding in. It really is that simple. Praise God! Knowing your ABC's really is all it takes: **A**–*admit* you've sinned! **B**–*believe* that Jesus died and rose again! **C**–*confess* your sins and ask Him to live in your heart forever!

Day 217

Today's Scripture:

"He heals the brokenhearted and bandages their wounds" (Psalm 147:3 NLT).

Today's Testimony:

My testimony starts around the age of fourteen. Drinking alcohol became a regular habit. It was mainly on the weekends but became more frequent during the summer when school was out. Throughout high school, each year, it seemed, I was doing more and more of it. I made A's and B's without trying and was a good student, nonetheless. I graduated with my class and got a full scholarship to the college in town.

My first year attending college, I lost my scholarship, due to partying. I was having severe anxiety at this point, and got prescribed medication for it, which I abused. Then, I discovered Adderall. I soon found, along with the appetite suppressant, this drug was giving me great physical and mental energy. Over the years, my doctor upped my dosage to the highest they could prescribe.

I was taking Adderall to get up in the morning and keep me going, then drinking and popping anxiety meds in the evening, and doing it all over again day after day. This vicious cycle kept up for nine years. I was taking my own prescriptions, as well as buying more and more off the street. I literally could not function without the "speed." I kept a pill beside my bed at night so I could take it as soon as my alarm clock went off in the morning.

Amphetamines replace a person's brain's dopamine with the chemicals in the drug. So, in order for that person's brain to be "happy" about anything, or even to physically get out of bed, it's dependent on that drug. (The brain will naturally start making its own dopamine again once someone stops taking the medicine.)

—Cecilia
(To Be Continued in Tomorrow's Reading)

Today's Takeaway:

This sounds like a runaway freight train to me. I can't imagine how awful Cecilia feels in the "in-between" places of drugs. I also wonder what all these chemicals are doing to her body. I do know who is behind it all, though. The enemy who wants to drag her down and destroy her. How he must have laughed when she lost her scholarship. Who is he trying to fool with a pill to make you feel "happy"? Don't fall for these cheap tricks, sister! God is our only source of joy.

Day 218

Today's Scripture:

"So if the Son sets you free, you will be free indeed" (John 8:36 NIV).

Today's Testimony *(Continued From Previous Day):*

At age twenty-nine, I tried methamphetamine for the first time. I'd stayed away from it previously, because I knew it would be my ultimate downfall. It was! For the first couple of weeks, I smoked it; then I used intravenously. I was out of control. Nothing else mattered except that next fix. I was selling my prescription of Adderall to keep the supply I needed. During this time, I neglected my bills and responsibilities. I stayed awake for days, even weeks at a time. I didn't eat or sleep. I just went full-force, going, going, going. Nothing I was doing was worth anything. I thought I was being productive, but I wasn't. I ended up quitting my job and quitting school—again. Family members were taking care of my pets. My family, most of all my mother, was brokenhearted, watching me deteriorate. My boyfriend and I were living together, both of us doing the same things. We got kicked out of where we were staying and lived in his vehicle for a while. My mom allowed me to move back in with her, but he was not welcome.

Something finally told me to stop. Two weeks later I found out I was pregnant. I had never felt more in love with anything in my life. I was living back home. I completely changed my world around, for the good of me and my unborn child. I was eating healthy, got a steady job, and slept well every night. Everything was looking up. Then, around the tenth week, I miscarried. Just as I had felt the greatest love of my life, now I felt the greatest heartbreak. I felt every negative emotion, including anger at God. I thought since I was doing "right" now, nothing terrible could happen. In anger I went on what would be my last drug binge full-force for a couple of months, but I didn't enjoy it. I was just trying my best to cover up all the pain I felt! It didn't work. I finally knew I had to make the decision to either die the way I was going, or change my life to live for God.

I repented, and now I owe everything to the One who gave His life for mine. Praise God that we can never go too far to come back to Him.

—*Cecilia*

Today's Takeaway:

(Cecilia's words) There is a saying, "Once an addict, always an addict." But this is a lie. I have been delivered from drugs and that life. Those chains were broken and thrown away. I am brand-new in Christ!

(My words) She's right! It *is* a lie. God makes ALL things new when you come to Him. I love that. You don't have to be an addict to need to be made new.

Day 219

Today's Scripture:

"And he arose and came to his father. But when he was still a great way off, his father saw him and had compassion, and ran and fell on his neck and kissed him"
(Luke 15:20 NKJV).

Today's Testimony:

Growing up in a pastor's home, hearing about Jesus was the norm. I was seven when I received the Lord as my personal Savior. It wasn't much longer after that I was filled with the Spirit. I loved the Lord. I remember always having a desire to do His will. I understood God's love for me. I knew what the Word said was true, but I struggled seeing that the words and His love were true for me. It was hard being a PK (pastor's kid). I felt pressure to be perfect, and like I was all alone. Loneliness was such a familiar friend. This led me to finding "love" in other places, feeling like there was acceptance in guys. This was the beginning of the downward spiral of choices I would make.

When I was thirteen, I was "date-raped." This event pivoted me into rebellion, and an on-and-off relationship with God. I began going from guy to guy to fill the void, but it only resulted in heartbreak. This became the pattern I would live by. The up-and-down relationship with God withered into no relationship with God. The depression became unbearable. Suicidal thoughts set in. It was hard to see hope. But, there *was* hope.

I was twenty-six when I heard God call me to a true relationship with Jesus. God saw me where I was, and He said come on home, just like the Prodigal Son (Luke 15:11-32). It didn't matter my mistakes, or what people thought of me. The Lord showed me who I was in that instant, and the endless love He has for me. He showed me how faithful He was even when I had not been. He revealed to me that He is my source. He is the freedom from my bondage. I gave my heart back to Him.

I am happy to report that my relationship with God isn't a roller-coaster anymore. He truly seems to always amaze me with His blessings and opportunities to glorify His name.

—*Karri*

Today's Takeaway:

My heart breaks to think of the pain and confusion that Karri went through being raped as a thirteen-year-old girl. No one should ever have to endure such treatment. Without taking that abuse to God and counselors, it's no wonder that depression and suicidal thoughts were exactly what the enemy had next on Karri's agenda. God wants us to run to Him with hurt like that. We can't expect "cancer" like that to heal up by itself. Even if somehow you're tough enough to get a "surface look" of normalcy on the outside, your inside needs attention. Bring it to God; don't leave it to "spread" to your heart!

Day 220

Today's Scripture:

"When the Spirit of truth comes, he will guide you into all truth. He will not speak on his own but will tell you what he has heard" (John 16:13 NLT).

Today's Testimony:

I grew up in church and went to a Christian school from kindergarten through eighth grade. Part of the curriculum included chapel every morning, and we also went to church every Sunday. However, during the summers we stayed at our cottage, so we only attended church about once a month. This schedule continued until my mid-to-late teens. During this time, I believed in God, but was not serving Him. I was taught all you had to do was believe and you would be saved, so I tested this way of thinking. I believed I could do whatever I wanted. I knew there might be consequences, but I also believed I was saved and would go to Heaven.

I was twenty-one when I got married; years later we had our first son. Since we lived just down the road from that same church, we started attending there again. It was there that our son was baptized.

In the meantime, my parents started going to a nondenominational charismatic church. They would talk to us about what they were learning; they attended classes to understand the foundational beliefs of the church. My mom invited us to come to a service. At one point in the service I remember looking down at our three-year-old with his hands raised high. Somehow he was feeling something that I didn't feel or even understand. We took the classes to learn what the church was about, and we were committed to Christ, baptized, and received the Holy Spirit. From that moment on, my life has never been the same. God is so faithful! Everything was now different. We went to church every Sunday morning, Sunday night, and Wednesday. We became very involved with children's church, Vacation Bible School, and classes.

We love our church family where we are involved in many ministries. God has truly worked in my heart. We have been blessed. Thinking back, I can see God's hand in all of my life and I thank Him every day for the journey that He brought me through.

—Nancy

Today's Takeaway:

There's nothing like enjoying your local church and being involved there. It makes your walk with God so enjoyable. When you're involved, your whole world changes. Everyone in your world will know it. You want to be there and you want to invite people to come to what's going on.

If your local church is struggling right now, pray for the leaders, volunteer to do one of the things that you see it needs, and encourage those around you that have gifts to volunteer to fill needs. Bless your pastor and see what God does!

Day 221

Today's Scripture:

"But God demonstrates his own love for us in this: While we were still sinners, Christ died for us" (Romans 5:8 NIV).

Today's Testimony:

I wasn't raised in church. I knew *of* God, but I didn't really know Him. I was sure there was something or someone out there, but I had no idea who God was and wasn't really too interested in finding out.

In my senior year of high school, God found me—or I should say, I found Him. I was the girl who wanted to fit in any way I could; I'd do anything to be "cool." I would show up to school late and high, always skipping classes. During that time, I found myself in an abusive relationship; I lost all self-worth and confidence. I would starve myself to lose weight. I had no sense of who I was, or that I mattered. But everything was about to change.

It was my senior-year homecoming and I had no idea I was about to find my two forever loves: my future husband and Jesus Christ. I ran into a guy that I knew from middle school. He went to a different high school, but was there with some of his friends. From that day on, my life was changed. God sent this man into my life to help me find true freedom in Christ. We started dating, and he invited me to a youth-group service at his church. I was hooked. I went to youth services, worship nights, prayer nights—you name it, I was there.

About six months into going to church, I was in my parents' kitchen, and my now-husband asked me if I had given my heart to Jesus and made Him the Lord of my life. Right there, teary-eyed in my parents' kitchen, I made the best decision of my life. I said "yes" to God, who found me in my mess and still loved me.

I want to encourage you with this: God knows who you are; He sees you where you are. You matter! If you have never had the opportunity to know Him; now is your chance. He knows and loves you and He wants you to know Him. You do *not* have to wait for an altar call at a church; you can call out to God right now. Jesus died for your sins and was resurrected so you could find freedom and spend eternity with Him. Tell God you believe this *now*. Don't wait. It will be the best decision you ever make.

—*Nicole*

Today's Takeaway:

I feel there's someone reading this now who needs to pray. Maybe you've already prayed to be saved before now, but you need to pray again. Maybe the enemy has been battling you and you need God to save you, or you need Him to strengthen you because of the battle you're in. Either way, pray where you are right now. *Father, touch my sister as she prays to You.*

Day 222

Today's Scripture:

"Praise be to the God and Father of our Lord Jesus Christ, who has blessed us in the heavenly realms with every spiritual blessing in Christ. For he chose us in him before the creation of the world to be holy and blameless in his sight. In love he predestined us for adoption to sonship through Jesus Christ, in accordance with his pleasure and will—to the praise of his glorious grace, which he has freely given us in the One he loves" (Ephesians 1:3-6 NIV).

Today's Testimony:

My parents would send me to the church down the road, as a child, just so they could have some time alone. We never went as a family. It was a scary thing to do—go to church all by yourself as a ten-year-old. That being said, it's no surprise I didn't have any great feelings about God when I was little. But God chose me anyway. He had great feelings about me.

He placed people in my path who spoke life into me. I had a boyfriend whose family was what I envisioned as "the perfect family." They loved each other and they loved God. I realized this was missing in my family. This was missing in me. From then on, there was a spark inside me to seek out how to get that feeling about God. I wanted what they had.

One day as a teen, I attended a Nicky Cruz crusade with a girlfriend (another friend whom God deliberately put in my path), and I was blown away by his testimony. Something stirred in my soul that night, and when the salvation call was made, I nearly ran to the altar. Forty-eight years later, the Lord is still the center of my universe. Praise God!

Thank You, Lord, that You can take lost children and adopt them as Your own. I haven't always lived according to Your will, but Your grace and mercy bring me back to You every time. Thank you, Holy Spirit, for Your conviction that keeps me on course. And thank You, Father, for putting the right people in my path to introduce me to You.

God knows you and desires *you* as a member of His family.

—*Kathy*

Today's Takeaway:

I know how Kathy feels. I saw a "perfect family" too when I was young. I wanted to be part of that family so badly. The great thing is that God makes us part of His family when we come to Him. We don't have to miss out anymore—He always wants us; He always includes us. Forever, we are His—He adopts us into His family because He loves us and we show Him we love Him by following His Word. His grace and mercy guide us and draw us to Him all along our way. We stay on course by listening to His voice.

Day 223

Today's Scripture:

"To appoint unto them that mourn in Zion, to give unto them beauty for ashes, the oil of joy for mourning, the garment of praise for the spirit of heaviness; that they might be called trees of righteousness, the planting of the Lord, that he might be glorified"
(Isaiah 61:3 KJV).

Today's Testimony:

I live in the country and we live the country life. We take our paper trash to the "burn pit" and set fire to it. Once it's done, there is nothing but ashes. But with God, beauty arises out of ashes.

My whole life felt like a pile of ashes. I was born with a facial defect that doctors couldn't explain. I was born with my right jaw much bigger than my left. They originally thought it was a tumor that would go away with age. I went in for my first surgery at age five to find out that I had no tumor, just extra fat that you would find anywhere else on your body. I've had nine surgeries now, from liposuctions to facelifts.

I thought I had my life figured out as a middle-school student. I was tired of being made fun of and bashed for my looks. Mentally I was worn out. I questioned God all the time. I knew better because I was raised in a church and had a family that taught me better, but I was human. I finally went in for a surgery that I thought was going to change me forever. I was to have a facelift, and my face would be perfect. But God was working on something greater. I got that facelift, but a few days later an infection busted my facelift loose. How does that happen? God was working when I didn't understand or see Him. It made me bitter. It broke me. My hope was shattered.

I went through high school miserable because I couldn't understand why I was dealing with it when nobody else was. *Why me, God? Why would You do that to me? I'm a good person. I go to church. I do good things. Why?* It wasn't until the week before my senior year started at a church lock-in that I finally had my eyes opened. That night God saved my soul as I gave my heart to Him. He changed everything in one moment!

—*Morgan*
(To Be Continued in Tomorrow's Reading)

Today's Takeaway:

God uses people in great and awesome ways that I can't pretend to understand. He saw something in Morgan that He could use for His glory, and He knew her strength would touch hearts and minister to them. Praise God for His hand on her life! I can't wait for you to hear the rest of her story tomorrow. Do you feel like you can't be used for His glory? Think again!

Day 224

Today's Scripture:

"I pray that God, the source of hope, will fill you completely with joy and peace because you trust in him. Then you will overflow with confident hope through the power of the Holy Spirit" (Romans 15:13 NLT).

Today's Testimony *(Continued From Previous Day):*

Right before I started college, I went to see the plastic surgeon. We had a plan to fix my face again. I would start college without *my* face anymore. The doctor's office said it would be around December before the surgery and they'd call me, but they never called. We tried to call; they never answered! The surgery didn't happen physically, but *I* had a surgery spiritually and mentally.

God began to show me He was going to use my face to change lives. While I was trying to change my outward appearance, God was preparing my heart to use the anointing He'd put in me since I was in my mother's womb. I didn't know that my face would take me all over the United States for medical programs and I'd get to be a witness for Him. I didn't know my face would save me from a party lifestyle. I didn't know really what a blessing He had prepared for me all along. I finally accepted who He called me to be as a woman and knew it was greater than what I was settling for.

I spent years saying I'd never have someone special. I despised men. I wanted to live for me and the Lord, but at the same time I was hurting because I was alone. I spent many nights crying, but my tears weren't wasted. One day, a woman of God had a vision of me standing in church with my arms spread out worshiping and a man walked in and said, "That's her." That very thing happened. God sent a man of God to church *for me.* While I was spending nights crying, God was spending nights saving this man from an overdose. He received deliverance from those drugs before he ever came to our church. God was in every detail—so much so that this man never noticed my face. Tell me that ain't God!

Now we have a beautiful family and we work and worship in the house of God together. What was once ashes of my life and his became beauty that no one can deny. Your ashes are no different. God will bring beauty from things you never thought could be brought to life again.

—Morgan

Today's Takeaway:

God did a mighty work *in* Morgan, *for* her, and *through* her. This may be a difficult thing for some. Yes, He could heal her face, but sometimes, He chooses a different plan. He's God and we must trust Him. Give Him your situation. Let Him decide how it should work out. He changes ashes!

Day 225

Today's Scripture:

"Therefore I say to you, her sins, which are many, are forgiven, for she loved much. But to whom little is forgiven, the same loves little" (Luke 7:47 NKJV).

Today's Testimony:

As a teenager, I began a life of promiscuity and looking for love in the wrong places. I became pregnant at the age of sixteen. I've always been a very independent person, and used to taking care of my own problems, so I chose to have an abortion. Without even thinking twice, I just chose what I thought was the best and easiest solution. There were very few people I told about my decision, and I actually went by myself to get it done.

I remember waking up in a holding room feeling drugged. They came in asking if I felt good enough to leave; I told them I did. When I left their office, I felt so sick. I went to the restroom and threw up. I then got in my car and started the journey home. I caught myself nodding off several times while driving. Just before I got home, I had to stop and throw up again. It was *only* by the grace of God that I made it home.

About a year later, I began dating a guy from our church and, sadly, we had a sexual relationship. So once again, I got pregnant, and once again, I chose to have an abortion—even though we had been dating for a couple of years and had a stable relationship. Again, I wasn't thinking of anyone else but myself and what I thought was best and easiest for me.

During all of this, I was going to church. I was even teaching a children's Sunday school class, and attending youth camps. I knew my sin. I would ask God to forgive me—time and time again. I wanted to do right and to serve Him, but I just kept failing. I know now I wasn't right with God, and that was the problem; but by His grace, He helped me get back up and keep trying. He wasn't giving up on me.

Then I met my husband. This was an answer to prayer and was exactly what I needed. I got my life right with God and began a long road of restoration.

God then called us into ministry. We now have been pastoring for over twenty-six years. And I recently accepted a job with a crisis pregnancy center. God is using *me* to help women choose LIFE for their babies. Talk about restoration!

—*Paula*

Today's Takeaway:

Sin grieves the heart of God; it separates us from Him. That's why He sent His Son to die for us, so our sin could be washed away and we could be restored to a right relationship to God. It is wonderful to experience the grace that comes after repentance. Paula struggled until she finally got her life right by giving her heart to God—*then* she was changed!

Day 226

Today's Scripture:

"But to all who believed him and accepted him, he gave the right to become children of God" (John 1:12 NLT).

Today's Testimony:

My earliest memories include sleepovers at Grandma's house, bringing home our first dog named Daisy, the bedroom my older sister and I shared with its bunk bed and bright floral wallpaper . . . and church. Definitely, church. You might say I was born in a pew. I am certain that after my family, it was the church ladies who held me in their arms as a newborn baby.

As far back as I remember, there was Sunday school, memorizing Bible verses, and singing "Jesus Loves Me." Every week Dad, Mom, my sister, and I would walk into our church. I'd go down to that old cinder-block basement. Week after week I was told life-changing truths about Jesus and salvation from sin.

Other early memories I have include seeing my dad reading his Bible, even taking it to work with him to the fire station. I'd watch him put it in his briefcase so he could study between calls. And my mom, in the "formal" living room (kids were discouraged from entering), singing and worshiping with the radio, tears rolling down her face.

Sometime in the mid-'70s, around the age of six, I realized that all the songs and memory verses were true. The example my parents lived in front of me was something extraordinary. So I made the decision that I needed Jesus to save me. I said that prayer— the most important prayer that can ever be spoken. I said it with all sincerity and knew I was now a child of God. I knew He loved me, would help me whenever I needed Him, and He had a plan for my life. I knew that I would go to Heaven someday.

—Amy

Today's Takeaway:

(Amy's words) There has never been a time that I haven't been moved by someone's redemption story, but I don't have a dramatic "before" story to tell. After all, I was just a little kid. But every salvation story is miraculous, whether saved at five or ninety-five. All of us were sinners, born into a broken relationship with our heavenly Father and in desperate need of being rescued. Any day, at any age, can be the day of salvation when we call on Him. If it's a little girl in a church basement or a thief on the cross, God hears and answers the one who calls on His name!

Day 227

Today's Scripture:

"For God so [greatly] loved and dearly prized the world, that He [even] gave His [one and] only begotten Son, so that whoever believes and trusts in Him [as Savior] shall not perish, but have eternal life" (John 3:16 AMP.).

Today's Testimony:

I was rejected and unloved at birth. My parents wanted a boy, but God had another plan. My life with Jesus began when I was seventeen. We had just moved to a new location. Little did I know I was about to meet my future husband, who was driving the school bus that I was about to get on. Two months later, he asked me out. God brought us together. I began going to church with him and invited Jesus into my heart. Two years later, we married. Two years after that, we had our first son. Then three years later, we had our daughter.

I love my husband and our children. For the first time in my life, I knew what it was like to be loved. Many years later, I was baptized with the Holy Spirit. I was immersed in the most powerful love which has changed me forever. Each day, He is revealing Himself more and more to me.

My faith is in the message of the cross, where Jesus was crucified for our sins, and the finished work which includes, salvation, sanctification, justification, healing, deliverance, provision, protection, forgiveness, mercy, grace, peace, and more! We are complete in Jesus. He did it all for us on Calvary. Believe it! Use your faith and walk every day with Jesus. Believe in the work that Jesus provided for you on that cross. He promised to never leave us or forsake us. He has come to give us life, and life more abundantly. He is everything we need. He satisfies my heart and soul like nothing else. Life is worth living because of Jesus giving His life for us on Calvary. No one ever cared for me like Jesus.

—*Julia*

Today's Takeaway:

What a powerful testimony for Christ. He is our everything! That's why we give our hearts to Him—so we can have eternal life to know Him. We give Him our hearts and become a new creation. The more we seek Jesus, through reading and believing His Word, He becomes alive in us. That makes us new! Thank goodness, we leave the old ways behind and we strive to become more and more like Him. It may not happen overnight, but that's what prayer does—it helps us grow. I want to grow up to be like Him—do you?

Day 228

Today's Scripture:

"Let them praise your great and awesome name. Your name is holy!" (Psalm 99:3 NLT).

Today's Testimony:

When I was twelve years old, a friend from school invited me to youth group at her church. They were having a contest, and they earned points if they brought a friend, brought their Bible, and memorized Scripture. I'm a little competitive, so I thought this was cool. I stuck around, winning second place and a 35mm camera. I had a lot of fun. I liked memorizing Scripture, and I was very curious about this "God person." However, I did not understand needing to "be saved." I didn't know what it meant to have God in my heart.

At fourteen, I moved to a different city and met a new friend at school who went to youth group at her church. She invited me to a "Back to School Bash" at their youth pastor's house. I really enjoyed myself at this party, so I started attending their youth group regularly. Week after week, I would sit and listen to the various Bible lessons being taught. I would take it all in like a sponge, but still, I didn't have any idea there was more to this whole "God-thing" other than stories and Scripture verses.

It wasn't until this same friend invited me to a Carman concert that I realized there was so much more. I had no idea this concert would change my life. I thought the whole thing was amazing. I had never been to anything like it before—the music blaring, the lights flashing, and so many people, *all praising God!*

At one point in the concert, Carman began to talk to us about Jesus, and I felt something I had never felt before. I began to cry and knew I had finally found what I didn't realize I was missing. Carman asked if there was anyone who needed to accept Jesus into their heart, and invited us to come forward. Without hesitation, I moved from my seat and walked forward. That was the first day of the rest of my life!

—Tammy

Today's Takeaway:

Tammy's heart was so ready from all the great seeds that had been planted by godly youth workers. All that work paid off when they took this group to a Christian concert. She suddenly realized what it all meant!

To all the youth workers out there, thank you! This is what it's all about. You labor long hours and give up your weekends; you play games and feed pizza; you clean up messes and drive long hours—all for this one moment, when your teen comes to the realization they need Jesus. There's an army of people who serve our youth today; if you're one of them, or you pray for youth, I want to say thank you and don't stop. Don't grow weary in well-doing! There are crowns waiting for you—one of them may be made of pizza!

Day 229

Today's Scripture:

"So shall My word be that goes forth from My mouth; it shall not return to Me void, but it shall accomplish what I please, and it shall prosper in the thing for which I sent it" (Isaiah 55:11 NKJV).

Today's Testimony:

This is not supposed to be this way! My grandfather in ICU, one best friend in the hospital after a suicide attempt she made *in my presence*, the other confessing her struggle with anorexia. *Stop. It is not supposed to be this way.* Not within days of being ripped from the place I called home for so long and moving to a new town. *Stop!*

I was fourteen; I was too young to be dealing with all of this I was lost and drowning within myself. No one understood. No one could offer words of comfort. I felt hopeless.

I grew up in church, but I'd never felt so alone. I knew how to use my voice to sing worship, but I didn't know how to use my voice to ask for help. The voice in my mind spoke with wild abandon: *the other youth will not understand what you are going through. You do not matter! Open your eyes! They see your sadness and they walk right past you. You do not matter! You are insignificant and invisible. You are alone. ALONE!*

I remember vividly, on a weekday service in the middle of November, with an invited guest preacher, I sat in the back of the church and kneeled to pray with a heavy heart. I cried and begged God to let *someone* in the church see me. I knew He had promised to always keep me and hear me. So I prayed to God, "Please just one . . ."—just one person to see what was happening to me and hug me and pray with me and show me I was not alone. I remember sitting up and every single person who passed me I *willed* them to say hello to me and see me. But the service began and here I was again—alone sitting in the back row. Unseen. Unheard. Broken. Alone.

—*Nareliss*
(To Be Continued in Tomorrow's Reading).

Today's Takeaway:

I am heartbroken. I am ashamed. Surely there are times that I have walked past someone like Nareliss who needed me to see her but I was too consumed with my own needs to notice her.

Oh, God! Help us to see with Your "vision"—like we're putting on special lenses to zero in on others to see when they need us. Help us to sense when others are hurting and instantly be drawn to them. Let us not live callously, thinking of ourselves and only what is going on in our world so that we don't look around us and ask, not the polite "How are you?" but instead go deeper and ask, "The Lord put you on my heart; can I pray with you about anything?"

Let's check on "Nareliss" today! God knows right where she is; even if others fail her, He never will.

Day 230

Today's Scripture:

"Don't be selfish; don't try to impress others. Be humble, thinking of others as better than yourselves. Don't look out only for your own interests, but take an interest in others, too" (Philippians 2:3-4 NLT).

Today's Testimony *(Continued From Previous Day):*

I could not tell you what the worship or preaching was about. The voices swirling in my mind were a hundred times louder than what was around me. They all came together into one loud statement followed by silence: *Leave this church. You are not seen or loved. You are nothing.* I closed my eyes and buried my head into my hands and whispered to God, "I love You. But I cannot stay here. There's a gaping hole within me and I need help!"

God has a way of working when you are at your end. That whispered sentence was the prayer He wanted me to pour out into a cry. The minister at the front pointed me out all the way in the back and asked me to come forward. I looked around me because surely it was not me being called, but it was. I walked toward him and he leaned forward to whisper to me. He said, "God knows you like to whisper intimate truths to Him, and He wants to whisper back. He says you are not alone, that He is keeping you and hearing you; and that hole inside of you, from all the tragedy you are suffering, He is going to fill with a blinding light tonight. This is your church, this is where He planted you, and from this moment you will be surrounded, seen, and heard because He keeps His promises. He is with you and you will never be alone." And God did just that!

That night I rededicated my whole being to the Lord, and it changed my life. It engraved Isaiah 55:11 and Song of Solomon 8:6 upon my heart, and it has resounded time and time again in my life through every valley and mountaintop. God's Word will always be made true. His vow to me—to us, the Bride of His church—is unbreakable, and His relentless love pursues us and transforms us for His glory.

—Nareliss

Today's Takeaway:

Hallelujah! God spoke to the man of God and he obeyed. As a result, Nareliss gave her heart to Jesus and was changed. I'm so thankful for the obedience of both of them. Let us remember this story every time we walk into a room. Let's be sensitive to the Spirit. There could be a sister like Nareliss who is praying that God will use someone to "see" her and hug her or let her know someone cares about all she is going through. I want to be that sister. Do you? Pray that God will give you the heart to care and minister to others. That's what Jesus did everywhere He went. Let's not be consumed with ourselves—let's consider the interests of others!

Day 231

Today's Scripture:

"For with God nothing will be impossible" (Luke 1:37 NKJV).

Today's Testimony:

I was raised in the church and taught about the love of Christ and the plan of salvation. At the age of eleven I accepted Christ as my Savior.

When I was fourteen years old, I was molested by a distant family member. That onetime event changed how I perceived relationships were supposed to be and at the age of almost seventeen, I discovered I was pregnant. The father of my child and I married, and on the day I spoke my marriage vows I spoke them for life; but after nine years of marriage, due to his infidelity, we divorced. Living as a single mom raising two daughters with little help from their father was hard, but God was faithful.

A few years following the divorce, I began to fall away from the church and my walk with Christ. I made choices that were wrong and became involved in relationships that were not godly. Still, God continued to remain faithful and show His love for me in so many ways.

Finally, at age thirty-eight, I realized what the emotional impact of a onetime inappropriate act (by someone who was supposed to love me and protect me), had on me and the deep scars I carried from that experience. I cried out to God to help me, to show me what love was *supposed* to look like and help me heal from the perception of what I *thought* it was—and He did!

You may ask how this is my salvation story; but I tell you, though I accepted Christ at age eleven, He continually forgives me of my human flaws and choices. Daily I need His mercy and grace. I'm thankful He can take a broken vessel and use it.

God has blessed me with a very loving husband. He was called into ministry after a failed marriage and overcoming substance addiction. We met and became friends just after his call into ministry. I was honored to be available to help him with his studies, and over the next six years, our friendship developed into love. We were married and we now pastor a church. We were blessed with awesome mentors, and we use the different giftings God has given each of us and life's experiences we have overcome to minister to hurting individuals and be living proof that with God all things are possible.

—Eva

Today's Takeaway:

God loves broken vessels. In fact, I read once that when a potter takes the pieces of a broken vessel and breaks them into tiny pieces, he can then work them into fresh clay and make it into a vessel that is far stronger than any regular vessel ever could be. Be strong, woman of God! You may have been broken, but now you're far stronger than you ever would have been before.

Day 232

Today's Scripture:

"Since my youth, God, you have taught me, and to this day I declare your marvelous deeds" (Psalms 71:17 NIV).

Today's Testimony:

Since I was a baby, my parents have taken me to church. I go to church two or three times a week. Through Sunday school, kids' church, and youth groups, my desire and relationship with Christ has grown; especially in the last three years.

When I was in sixth grade, I joined the youth group. At this time, I was not reading my Bible, praying, or worshiping every day. The only time I would spend focusing on God was at the youth-group service on Wednesday nights, and occasionally on Sundays. When the time came around for my church's annual youth retreat, I went. The three nights there were powerful, and I dug a little deeper in my relationship with God. Little did I know that was just the start.

The year went by; I was baptized in water, serving God but still hungry for more. Soon it was time for our annual youth retreat again. When we got there, we found out it was canceled because of COVID, but that wasn't going to stop us from meeting with God. Instead, three to four youth groups got together in the hotel conference room and we had our own mini-session.

My pastor, who was with us, was the speaker. It was powerful! At the end he did an altar call. Almost everyone was in tears; people were filled with the Holy Spirit. I was praying and worshiping, and then my pastor came over and started praying over me. At that moment, I was filled with the Spirit and I knew I needed to keep steadfast faith.

When we left, they challenged all of us to the "30-30–30"—thirty minutes of praying, worshiping, and spending time in the Word. When we got back, we began the 2020 quarantine. I read my Bible every day, prayed, and worshiped. My faith grew. Instantly, I could tell a difference in my everyday life. I don't know how I was surviving without it. It just took that one little step in my life to make a difference.

—Presley (13 years old)

Today's Takeaway:

(Presley's words) As a kid, I didn't know the importance of having that one-on-one relationship with God. I just saw people getting touched and thinking, *That's cool—that's what I want.* I never took the time to look into it for that little extra step of faith that makes the relationship with God even stronger and more powerful. As kids, I don't think we understand what a relationship with God is until we start taking the steps so we can see what it is for ourselves. If you are like me, and you never had a trial that has tested your faith, don't be discouraged or feel like your story is any less worthy. Everyone's path is different, but that doesn't make your story any less powerful, because God gives each of us our own unique story.

Day 233

Today's Scripture:

"For you reach into my heart. With one flash of your eyes I am undone by your love, my beloved, my equal, my bride. You leave me breathless—I am overcome by merely a glance from your worshiping eyes, for you have stolen my heart. I am held hostage by your love and by the graces of righteousness shining upon you" (Song of Songs 4:9 TPT).

Today's Testimony:

It was somewhere near the goldfish tank that this spunky little girl with wild brown hair prayed the sinner's prayer. I don't remember the details. Actually, I don't even remember the moment or the prayer. I just know the story that my mom has told me over the years.

I've carried a lot of guilt for not remembering. Shouldn't you remember something as important as choosing to live your life for Jesus? And if I can't remember, am I even saved? Every time a pastor would say, "Remember what it was like when you first gave your heart to Jesus? Remember that passion you felt?" Uh . . . nope.

And if I was supposed to feel something special, but didn't, am I really going to Heaven or am I a deceived heathen on the highway to hell?

Not only did I not remember my story of coming to Jesus, but I also didn't have a great "come to Jesus" moment in my life. I grew up in a (mostly) Christian home and made (mostly) wholesome choices. What about all that talk about those who have been saved from much are able to love God much more because they know what they'd been saved from? That must mean I can't love God enough.

Oh, the guilt and the ridiculous lies. Oh, the *many* salvation prayers I prayed, hoping I would be saved just enough to squeeze past those Pearly Gates. *Please, sweet Jesus!*

I'm not sure when it all subsided for me, and I realized I was enough for the Lord. He simply wanted my heart and He had it. He paid the price and saved me—not by my works or striving or even my begging, but simply by His grace. His grace is more than enough. His salvation has given me the sweetest friendship I know. Friendship with the Father, Jesus, and Holy Spirit is so intimate. And the beauty of it is that it is available to each and every one of us.

—Megan

Today's Takeaway:

It's not about having an engraved certificate of the "salvation moment." It's about the love of the Salvation-Giver. Jesus just wants our hearts. When we search our hearts and "know that we know," He is there—that's when He walks with us and our friendship is sweet. Every day is a come-to-Jesus moment for those who love to come near Him!

Day 234

Today's Scripture:

"'For I know the plans I have for you,' declares the Lord, 'plans to prosper you and not to harm you, plans to give you hope and a future'" (Jeremiah 29:11 NIV).

Today's Testimony:

For a long time, I was reluctant to share my salvation story; I thought I might sound unrelatable, but over time, I've learned to savor the significance of God's hand on my life. I've definitely had my struggles, but I've served God since I was a child. God has been so good to me and kept me all of my life.

I decided to share my story now to encourage others—to help others see how wonderful our God is. I'm sharing for my daughter, her children, and each generation to come. As my mother demonstrated before me, we can do this! He has a unique plan for our success. I see that plan in my daughter's ministry; I can already see it in the lives of her young children. His favor has brought us to our current location, and His direction will lead us to our final destination.

What happens when we face adversity? God's grace will sustain us. He *knows* all and *is* all. He knew I would be in a head-on collision before I was born and gave me the strength to face it. He knew my parents would divorce when I was ten and He walked with me through it. He knew I would struggle with thyroid-related weight issues all of my life, but was there to help me. He knew I would be diagnosed with breast cancer at the age of thirty-five, on my daughter's thirteenth birthday, and that I could call on Him for my healing. He knew I would have breast cancer two additional times . . . the third time being considered inoperable. He knew He would take care of all of that and I would come out cancer-free! He knew I would, eventually, learn to trust that He always has a plan.

—*Leisha*

Today's Takeaway:

God sustains us through our entire lives if we rely on Him. Leisha has walked with Him, as did her mother. She is modeling how to trust God to her daughter and grandchildren. Her daughter is following her lead and is already serving God in ministry.

Leisha knows what to do when difficulty comes—trust God! Call on the One who has always been there to bring us through. He isn't surprised by our circumstances. He is able to give us a hope and a future. He is our Savior, Sustainer, Healer, and Guide. That is why we can trust His plan.

Day 235

Today's Scripture:

"I pray that God, the source of hope, will fill you completely with joy and peace because you trust in him. Then you will overflow with confident hope through the power of the Holy Spirit" (Romans 15:13 NLT).

Today's Testimony:

I was raised in a home where alcohol caused brutal fights within my family. I got so used to it that I kind of became numb to it. I did, however, vow to myself not to have a life like that.

I have always felt a longing to know the Lord. My uncle would talk to me about Jesus, and I was the only one who wanted to sit and listen. I would walk up to a little church by my house and one day, at the age of twelve, I decided I wanted to accept Jesus as my personal Savior. I remember how on the way home I felt like I was walking on air. I continued going to church until my teen years. Then I started to live like the world.

It wasn't until one day, because of a praying mother-in-law, that I got a phone call. It was a pastor from the local church. He asked me and my husband to come to church that Sunday. I told him yes, and we went. I don't think I have stopped attending church since that phone call.

I rededicated my life to Jesus and was filled with the Holy Spirit and have never been the same. Since living for Jesus I have peace, joy, happiness, and love that I never knew or had before Him. He has gotten me through so many difficult times in my life. I look back and wonder how I ever made it without Him—how many times He saved me from bad situations I put myself in. He is such an amazing God!

I love the passage from Jeremiah 29:11 because I feel like it describes my life: "'For I know the plans I have for you,' declares the Lord, 'plans to prosper you and not to harm you, plans to give you a hope and a future'" (NIV). He is my hope!

—*Haley*

Today's Takeaway:

Thank God for the people in our lives who are praying for us. They literally snatch us away from the enemy's plans for us. I'm thankful also for all the pastors out there who reach out again and again—calling, visiting, praying, helping, loving, and then being there to rejoice when someone is ready to come home to Jesus. How the pastor's heart rejoices!

If you've been prayed for, now it's your turn to pray for someone else. Who is it that God has shown you lately? Call their name out to Him; intercede. Then call them and ask them to come and sit with you at church.

Day 236

Today's Scripture:

"And Job took a piece of broken pottery with which to scrape himself, and he sat [down] among the ashes (rubbish heaps)" (Job 2:8 AMP.).

Today's Testimony:

Potsherds are broken pieces of pottery. Broken pottery is often thrown out. However, potsherds were used throughout Bible history. They were used for healing, such as in the scraping of Job's wounds (Job 2:8). They were used to scoop water from a cistern or fire from a hearth (Isaiah 30:14). Many were used to build a gate called the Potsherd Gate (Jeremiah 19:2). *Ostracon* is a potsherd that was used as a writing material. They are also used for historical data to describe a past generation.

I often view myself as a potsherd. The experiences in life made me feel broken. I was raised by a Christian mother. My father was formerly a minister but left the ministry to pursue drugs, alcohol, and women. My parents divorced when I was seven. We moved to a different state from my father. We were poor and were bullied for it. From the ages of twelve to fourteen, I was molested by two different adult members of my family. I was called a liar for years about the sexual abuse. I developed bulimia and was hospitalized for it at the age of fourteen. I left the church at the age of sixteen because I felt so alone, but no one reached out for me. I turned to drugs and alcohol to numb my pain.

I married my first husband at nineteen when I was three months pregnant; we eventually had two children. He was physically and emotionally abusive. I was finally able to leave, but then I ended up in another relationship with a man who was even more severely abusive. He beat me so badly one night I thought I would die. A few months later, I was finally able to leave that relationship.

—*Taylora*
(To Be Continued in Tomorrow's Reading)

Today's Takeaway:

Have you ever felt worthless? Worthy to be thrown out like rubbish? This was what led to Taylora allowing herself to be treated as worthless. I don't want any of God's girls to be mistreated, and I can feel my temperature rising when they are. Oh, but it's not over! God was right there just waiting on her to call on Him. He was with her through it all.

Are you in a tough place right now? Call on the One who is more than able to deliver you out of that place. Don't listen to the lies the enemy tells you that whatever you are enduring is because you deserve it; no one deserves abuse.

Trust the One who is able to put anything back together—even potsherds! Check on Taylora tomorrow and see what God does for her.

Day 237

Today's Scripture:

"He brought me out into a broad place; he rescued me, because he delighted in me"
(Psalm 18:1 ESV).

Today's Testimony *(Continued From Previous Day)*:

Those twelve years I was away from God, I was living in darkness. There were times I would tell myself, "I hate you." I felt like God hated me too, and that I was worthless. Those were the voices I heard for years. I was broken; I was a potsherd. How could God ever use me?

Finally, when I found myself alone again and in despair, I decided to kneel beside my bed and I repented. The feeling that washed over me, at that moment, I cannot describe! It was a feeling of returning home, a feeling of peace and safety. I felt the love of God like I never had before.

There is beauty that is found in brokenness. When something gets restored, we remark on how its beauty returned. We get excited when something that was broken is repaired. We take delight in it—God takes delight in us. Psalm 18:19 says, "He brought me out into a broad place; he rescued me, because he delighted in me" (ESV). God rescued me because He delighted in me.

I now serve in my church and in my community. My husband, a godsend man, and I are mental-health therapists. Genesis 50:20 says, "You intended to harm me, but God intended it for good to accomplish what is now being done, the saving of many lives" (NIV). I pour healing into others because God found me as a potsherd and began to use me. A place of healing began when I no longer blamed myself for my trauma. I can look back and see how God has taken my brokenness but has not thrown it away. He began to create something new and beautiful.

—Taylora

Today's Takeaway:

I am laughing at the enemy right now! What he thought he ruined, God made beautiful. Taylora is beautiful and so is her life. She's even pulling others out of the enemy's grip and helping them overcome too. It's such poetic justice! God even gave her a husband to double her efforts.

Don't you want to be used that way? Did you know that whatever you've been through, and gotten strength from God to overcome, kind of makes you better qualified to help others? How awesome is that? Think about what you've been through. Look around—who can you help who's struggling in it now? Offer to help. You've already been there and made it with God's help.

Day 238

Today's Scripture:
"I will extol [praise] the Lord at all times; his praise will always be on my lips"
(Psalm 34:1 NIV).

Today's Testimony:

I was born in Brazil and raised in a Christian family. My parents rarely missed a worship service at church. In Brazil, not everyone has a car because they are very expensive, and my parents and I had to walk thirty minutes to go to church even on rainy days. I remember one day when it was raining and a car splashed me with water. I got to church soaked and dirty, but I worshiped God anyway. My family and I kept that routine for almost twenty years, until my dad could afford a car.

My parents always taught me to worship God in all the moments. It does not matter our financial situation or health; or if we are happy, living an abundant life or not. Like Psalm 34:1 says, "I will [praise] the Lord at all times; his praise will always be on my lips" (NIV). As I was guided through the Word of God, I questioned my mom one day. I asked her if being in the church meant that I was saved. She told me inviting Jesus to come into my heart was necessary; going to church but not allowing Jesus to come into our heart wouldn't change anything.

After that day, I decided to pray the next time the pastor asked the question, "Would you like to receive Jesus in your heart"? Finally, the pastor asked the question, and I jumped from my seat and went to the front of the church. I was nine years old. I was so happy, and I felt like a new child.

Growing up, I had several invitations and opportunities to abandon my faith in Jesus, but I couldn't do it because that seed was planted in my heart and I loved Jesus. The challenges came—frustrations, losses, illness—but the victory came too. The healing, the miracles, and strength of my faith are also part of my journey with Jesus. Even moving to another country wouldn't separate my love for Jesus. The Bible says in Proverbs 22:6, "Start children off on the way they should go, and even when they are old they will not turn from it" (NIV). This is my story of how I met Jesus. I am thankful for my parents that introduced Jesus to me, and I will never let Him go.

—*Micheli*

Today's Takeaway:

What do we take for granted when we go to the house of God each week? That we can drive there if it's too far to walk just down the street? That we don't have to walk in the rain to attend? This story brings new meaning to me of praising Him "at all times"—even in a muddy, water-soaked dress. (Oh, I hope I would have done that! Would you have? Let's decide to.)

Day 239

Today's Scripture:

"You intended to harm me, but God intended it for good to accomplish what is now being done, the saving of many lives" (Genesis 50:20 NIV).

Today's Testimony:

Coming from a broken home was the least of my childhood dysfunction. By the time I was ten, I had experienced mental abuse, emotional abuse, sexual abuse, parental abandonment, parental kidnapping, and short-term foster care. My family didn't go to church, but I saw other kids my age who came from "normal" homes and went to church, and I longed to be one of them.

In sixth grade, my mom and stepdad began taking us to church. One of the girls in my class attended, and I was so excited. But at school she purposely ignored me and seemed to look down on me even more than before. Then the pastor made a comment from the pulpit one day about how the "new people" were dressed, making an excuse that they (we) probably didn't have the money to dress appropriately for church. We went out and bought new clothes that weekend, but it didn't make me feel any more welcomed or included. I rebelled, became suicidal, and no longer wanted anything to do with God or Christians.

The following year, my grandmother took the whole family to a Christmas production at a Baptist church. At the end of the night, the pastor said a salvation prayer and asked the entire church to repeat it. He asked those who had said it for the first time to come forward; I did. Some of my family mocked me for this, but for the first time I *felt* like maybe salvation, maybe Jesus, *was* for me, too. Maybe Jesus actually loved and died for people like me. It was a long journey to sanctification, healing, full surrender, and eventual growth, but to quote the Happy Goodmans' song, "I Wouldn't Take Nothin' for My Journey Now!"

—*Michele*

Today's Takeaway:

Nothing stings quite like the sting of being looked down on; I can still feel the poison of its bite right now. Somehow, even though you get over it, you never forget how it felt; some would say that means you never got over it. I say that's OK, as long as it teaches you to never treat someone else that way. When we get saved, we are taught to treat other people the way we want to be treated—it's the Golden Rule, but somehow it just gets lost on some.

Try this—become a master at imagining yourself standing in another person's shoes. Walk around in them in your mind; endure their situation, their limitations, their setbacks; then see if it helps shape your view of them. Maybe if we can get better at this, we won't be so quick to put down, mock, or judge others so harshly. We might even be willing to lend a helping hand or (gulp) even friendship!

Day 240

Today's Scripture:

"Do to others whatever you would like them to do to you. This is the essence of all that is taught in the law and the prophets" (Matthew 7:12 NLT).

Today's Testimony:

I am a seventy-five-year-old widow who would not be here today if it weren't for my salvation and my relationship with the heavenly Father. I have lived, loved, and lost lots of important people and battles in my life, but have survived them all due to my faith and the strength that comes to me from my heavenly Father.

My salvation became relevant to me when I was thirteen years old. I realized there was good and bad out in the world and I needed to make good choices; I had been under the protective influence of my parents. Now, I discovered what the other side was like, and I was terrified. There was stealing, cheating, lying, drinking, drugs, and sex out of marriage. My Christian values were strongly intact and I couldn't partake in any of these activities. I stood my ground and relied on God to see me through, and He did.

My first true lesson to be a good Christian was the Golden Rule: "Do unto others as you would have them do unto you." I always wanted to be treated nice, to love everybody (I was not a fighter, physically anyway), so I worked and prayed very hard to be honest, loving, and greeted everyone with a smile. A smile is genuine—your most precious attribute—because it's real and doesn't lie.

As I grew older, got married, and had my own family, I realized how even more important the Golden Rule needed to be applied to my family and everyday life. Not only did I want to be treated well, but more importantly I wanted my family to be treated with respect, honesty, and love. In order to teach these values to my family, I had to put them into everyday use. You can't teach by telling, you have to teach by example. So I tried to be the example of a loving, honest, and caring person, but I could not have attained the example I wanted my family to become if it hadn't been for God leading me at all times.

My walk with the heavenly Father is my heart, my strength, my soul, and my being. I always want to be a good person; I want to be doing for others and being kind "to a fault." My favorite prayer and the one I use every day, sometimes more often than once a day, is the Lord's Prayer—it says it all!

—*Lana*

Today's Takeaway:

Thank you, Mrs. Lana! If we follow the Golden Rule and the Lord's Prayer, giving our heart to Jesus, doing for others and being kind, I believe we can please the Lord and serve Him all our days. She's right; be genuine, use your smile as an attribute. Live as an example. You can't go wrong!

Day 241

Today's Scripture:

"This means that anyone who belongs to Christ has become a new person. The old life is gone; a new life has begun!" (2 Corinthians 5:17 NLT).

Today's Testimony:

Ever since I was young, I've gone to church—on and off over the years—but it wasn't until I was twenty-one years old that I finally realized my life needed a tremendous change. It was then that I really wanted to follow Christ and leave my ungodly ways behind. I asked for salvation, got baptized again, and began the closest walk yet with Him. From there, so many blessings have unfolded. There has been strife along the way, but His promises don't include anything being easy.

I testify that no matter how unworthy you think you are—your brokenness can never be too great for God. My past included nearly every sin you can think of against the Ten Commandments, but it is an exact opposite of what I live today. I was a thief, a liar, a cheater, disrespectful to my mom, had a mouth full of curses, was bisexual, promiscuous, a killer of animals, a partier, including drunkenness and getting high. I've even (unknowingly) experimented with the satanic realm via tarot cards.

Throughout the years, all of these things seemed normal; there were no immediate repercussions. That's how blind Satan can make you, thinking the acts you commit are just what "everyone is doing." All of which I cannot, will not, and absolutely do not partake in anymore.

Some people may view me differently after knowing my past, but that is of no relevance to me now, because my purpose is to show that through Him our slate can be wiped clean—our sins are forgiven. All things can be made new. Now by the blood of Jesus I have righteousness and can stand before the Father with purity.

As humiliating as my sin was to me, the Lord Almighty forgave. Truly, this could not be possible if God didn't reach His hand down repetitively to draw me back to Him and out of the grips of Satan. My walk with Him only gets better the more I let Him lead. I'm given more understanding, and I receive more of His presence. I am forever grateful for His grace and mercy because without it I would still be living a life of deception. So, if you see me in love with Jesus, know this is why—my God showed me mercy, made me new, and took me away from a path of self-destruction. He loved me even when I didn't deserve it.

—Nikki

Today's Takeaway:

Nikki has a new life in Christ. Her old ways are gone. Praise God! That's the beauty of our salvation—He washes us clean and everything in our past is gone. We have the responsibility to turn away from the things we used to do; it's His joy to forget it and help us walk forward.

Day 242

Today's Scripture:

"Forgive us for the ways we have wronged you, just as we also forgive those who have wronged us" (Matthew 6:12 CEB).

Today's Testimony:

I gave my heart to Jesus when I was a young girl. I was raised in church and went to church camps my whole life; but, as a child, at the age of nine, I lost my father to cancer, and what followed caused me to carry the label "victim."

After my dad's passing, my mom became very depressed. She was physically, emotionally, and verbally abusive to me. In addition, a family member started sexually abusing me. The sexual abuse went on for about three to four years, and the rest continued through all my teen years. I do want to note here that I know my mom loved me and we did have good times together even through those years. She even worked in the church as the drama director. She just really struggled with the sin of anger, and she had a horrible temper. Through it all, I knew Jesus had never forsaken me.

As a young adult, I got married to an amazing man of God I've had the joy of being in ministry with for twenty-five years. When we decided to start a family, we discovered I could not get pregnant. The doctors couldn't give me an exact reason why. I did have polycystic ovary syndrome (PCOS), but that shouldn't have been too big of a problem. Many women with PCOS get pregnant, usually having to take some fertility medications, which I did. Whether or not it's true, in the back of my mind, I felt that part of the reason was my childhood abuse. I was resentful and unforgiving of my abuser. Though I never did get pregnant, God blessed us with a family through adoption.

—Peggy
(To Be Continued in Tomorrow's Reading)

Today's Takeaway:

There are things in this life that we can't begin to understand. Life isn't fair and it never will be—like how one sister can have children and another can't. There is one thing we have to remember: God knows all things and He watches over us and cares about everything that touches our lives. When we bring a need to Him, we can rest assured, He hears and will work on our behalf. Sometimes the answer is not what we planned, but it's a good plan when it's His plan!

Tomorrow we'll see how Peggy dealt with her thoughts of her abuser, but for now, consider this: God knows about pain and hurt. He sees when you cry, but there will come a time when no more tears will ever be shed again. Jesus endured pain for us to be with Him on that day. Consider turning every bit of pain and sorrow—and the one who caused it—over to the One who can wipe it away. Jesus wants to heal every hurt if you'll let Him.

Day 243

Today's Scripture:

"But if you don't forgive others, your Father will not forgive your offenses"
(Matthew 6:15 CSB).

Today's Testimony *Continued From Yesterday:*

The conflict for me was that, as a Christian, I believe the Bible is 100 percent truth. I knew God loves my abusers as much as He loves me. The scriptures say in John 3:16, "For God so loved the world that He gave His only Son that WHOSOEVER believes in him shall be saved." I knew I was going to *have* to walk the road of forgiveness. If God can love us and forgive us in spite of our sins, then I knew I needed to find a way to forgive too. When Jesus was teaching us how to pray in Matthew 6:12, He said "forgive us our debts, as we have forgiven our debtors." We have to let go of both the wrong and the resentment as we forgive.

The funny thing about forgiveness is that we like to believe that forgiving someone is somehow a gift to *them*. The reality is when we forgive someone else it brings *us* the gift of freedom. I personally have found freedom in my relationships, both with God and people; freedom in my worship; and the freedom to enjoy life and all God has for me . . . *through forgiveness*. Therefore, today I can confidently say that I am *not* a *victim*, I *am* a *victor*!

—Peggy

Today's Takeaway:

This truth will set someone free who is hurting right now! Holding onto unforgiveness has been compared to swallowing poison but expecting the other person to drop dead. It doesn't work that way. When you swallow the poison, you're the one who is harmed. Jesus knew this, and that's why He teaches us to forgive so we can be forgiven. He knows unforgiveness quickly turns into bitterness.

Bitterness is a tool of the enemy to destroy you, and it will infiltrate every area of your life if allowed to stay. Get rid of it quickly on your knees! Let it go with all your heart. Let God make you a VICTOR!

Day 244

Today's Scripture:

"God has appointed in the church first apostles, second prophets, third teachers, then miracles, then gifts of healing, helping, administrating, and various kinds of tongues"
(1 Corinthians 12:28 ESV).

Today's Testimony:

Everyone I know seems to know the *exact* day, month, and year they were saved. I don't. I don't remember. I remember when I was baptized, I can even visualize it, so I know my salvation experience was prior to that. I remember when I was baptized in the Holy Spirit and can see that clearly in my mind's eye.

I often wonder why I don't remember that all-important event of salvation, but I think the most important thing is, I know I *am* saved. God's Word tells me I am; I know I asked Jesus to come into my heart. I have felt God move in my life. I've seen Him answer my prayers (not always the way I hoped or thought, but nonetheless, He answers them). And I know I'm saved because when I just simply sit and have a conversation with Him, I know He's listening, and I feel His presence. He hears my prayers and He's forever changed my life.

I don't know how many times I've heard people say, "Why doesn't God perform miracles in the church anymore?" I am literally one of God's present-day walking, talking miracles. In August 2019, I fell and broke my neck. I severely damaged some vertebrae and the nerve between the sixth and seventh vertebrae. I now have two rods and ten screws in my neck. My neck is now mostly hardware. My journey of healing continues to this day, and He is with me every step along the way.

The miracle is when I went for my second checkup, the doctor told me that with my type of break, I should be paralyzed—if not dead. She was amazed I was walking, with the help of my son-in-law. My family doctor also told me, after he looked at my x-rays, that it is a miracle I'm alive. See . . . God is still doing miracles!

—*Sue*

Today's Takeaway:

God does still do miracles! We just need to tune our eyes and ears to recognize them in this day and age of negative viewpoints and pessimism. It seems like everywhere you look, there's always someone trying to drag down the child of God. Sue is a miracle. She is saved, and so are we—that's also a miracle. Jesus rose again. What a miracle! Let's not get so bogged down in this world that we lose sight of that glorious event, which changed everything for all of us.

Day 245

Today's Scripture:

"For it is by grace you have been saved, through faith—and this is not from yourselves, it is the gift of God—not by works, so that no one can boast" (Ephesians 2:8-9 NIV).

Today's Testimony:

I was raised in a God-fearing household where the word *fear* was used more than *love*. My father was a lay evangelist for a great share of my upbringing. He talked more about the wrath of God than about the love of God. My father didn't experience the joyful life but was depressed and at times wondering if he had done enough to be saved. Over the years of growing up, I had an older sister who seemed to do everything perfectly in my parents' eyes. She got excellent grades and was constantly studying and had no time for fun. I grew tired of the constant comparison and rebelled. I was the black sheep.

Years passed, and against my parents' advice, I married a non-Christian. It didn't work out, but we had three beautiful children. After the divorce, on a weekend when the children were with their dad, my place was broken into and I was attacked and raped. Upon hearing about it, my parents stated, "If you were living a better life, this may not have happened." That statement hurt me. My thinking was that if God was going to punish me for my sins like this, then I could never win His love. I started running as far from God as I could. I spent the weekends getting drunk, going to dances, and returning home with men. I met this one guy who spent many nights and I excused it as God keeping me safe.

My children grew up, and both my boys got recruited by the Marines and were sent overseas. I worried a lot, especially not having a relationship with God. My boyfriend developed heart issues and had surgery. I was left so alone, knowing I couldn't protect my sons or keep my boyfriend from dying. I thought I was useless and good for nothing. I said to God, "Just take my life. I have nothing to live for. I'm a complete failure and nobody needs me." God didn't answer my cries in the way I requested, but my sister stopped over and suggested that I try the church in the neighborhood. I listened and went. The pastor was talking about the fact that God has a purpose and plan for your life if you believe He died for your sins and ask for forgiveness. I asked God to come into my heart and help me do what He wants me to do in the time I have left on this earth. Then God saved me. I couldn't save myself; only God's love and amazing grace could. Thank You, God!

—*Edna*

Today's Takeaway:

It's a powerful thing to think of a God who chooses to love us without any merit from us whatsoever, isn't it? But that's exactly it—it's not our goodness, at all. What a God!

Day 246

Today's Scripture:

"As the mountains surround Jerusalem, so the Lord surrounds His people from this time forth and forever" (Psalm 125:2 NKJV).

Today's Testimony:

I grew up in the Church of God. My parents, grandparents, and even great-grandparents went to the Church of God. I was told we were poor at times, but I never remember those hard times. I remember fun family events and fun church-family events. I remember spending a lot of time at the church cooking, cleaning, or even preparing for services.

I spent much of my teen years with the church youth and on the softball team. My parents showed me what it was to serve. In my young-adult life I fell in and out of church for many years, but praying parents help with that.

I went on to marry and had two beautiful girls. Later I went through divorce and endured the struggles of single parenthood, but the Lord and His church were always in my life. I struggled when my mom, who was my best friend, died. She was the world's greatest and I think I became lost for a while, but soon God became the One! He was always right there. The One I knew I needed more than any!

Years later, my stepmom passed away, and now my father has been diagnosed with cancer. I know in my heart that his time here is short, but I also know he'll go to a place where he'll never hurt and suffer again—although "Daddy's Princess" will hurt. I'm going to praise God for my dad's healing. I don't have the words to truly say all that God has done for me, but He's right there for every mountain and every valley.

—*Michelle*

Today's Takeaway:

It's true. He is the God on the mountain, and the God in the valley. Michelle knows it! I also know it; chances are, you have found that out by now too. This brings me great comfort because I know that unless I stand perfectly still and refuse to walk any further, I will eventually come to one or the other in my journey again someday. If I get to a mountain, I'll need strength to climb it—He'll supply that. If I get to a valley, He'll give me comfort to make it through it.

He is our sustainer for every phase of life. He simply must be called on. He waits to hear us call on Him. He is a gentleman and doesn't force Himself into our lives, but oh when we call—He comes to our cry! Call on Him!

Day 247

Today's Scripture:

"Trust in the Lord with all your heart; do not depend on your own understanding. Seek his will in all you do, and he will show you which path to take" (Proverbs 3:5-6 NLT).

Today's Testimony:

I cannot tell you how many times as a child that I asked Jesus to come into my heart. My parents raised us kids in church, so as long as I can remember I have always loved the Lord.

My definite salvation experience happened when I was seventeen. As life moved on over the years, I learned more and more about salvation and commitment to Jesus.

In the summer of my twenty-sixth year, every time I turned around I was getting ill. My marriage was very unstable and a lot of stress was going on, but it was during that time of my life that I began to know and to feel the presence of God with me.

One day in particular I had gotten so ill I had to just go to bed. I was so sick and saddened because I couldn't carry my share of the workload that had to be done. I started to cry out to God and ask for His help. At that point, I realized how much I needed Him to be a full part of my life.

So, one more time I asked Jesus to come into my life and be my true Savior. At this time, He began to raise me up physically and teach me the importance of letting His ways work in my life.

I love Proverbs 3:5-6 because it says it best: "Trust in the Lord . . . do not depend on your own understanding. Seek his will . . . and he will show you which path to take" (NLT).

Putting my trust in Him was all it took for Him to lead me by the hand on the true path of His salvation.

—*Peggy*

Today's Takeaway:

It seems to me that it's during times of the greatest stress in my life when I fall on my knees and cry out to God the loudest. Peggy was so sick that she had to go to bed—how miserable! I've been there; you probably have been too. Are we one-track-minded people sometimes? Do we need our problems to be magnified before we can get serious about prayer? Let's learn to live a life of prayer—to let it be our first reaction to everything. Whether it's praise or petition, be ready to lift your hands to God! He wants to hear from you—even though He knows every situation already. Open up the channels of blessing and providence.

Day 248

Today's Scripture:

"Before I formed you in the womb I knew you, before you were born I set you apart"
(Jeremiah 1:5 NIV)

Today's Testimony:

My mom was a recovering heroin addict working in a bar next door to my dad's motorcycle ministry clubhouse/coffeehouse. The Christians used to try and witness to her but she would just mock and taunt them. That is until one day she went next door and was met by the Holy Spirit. She asked for prayer, gave her heart to the Lord, and two months later married my father.

Due to an incident that happened in her past, she had suffered a horrible miscarriage and was told she would never have children. However, she soon learned God always has the final say. Not long after they were married, she became pregnant with me. When I was born I was very sick. My mom had unknowingly contracted hepatitis C from years of IV drug use and had passed it on to me. The doctors told my parents they didn't think I would make it. They sent my parents home and told them to make preparations as I wasn't expected to live, but my mom refused to accept this.

She tuned into *The 700 Club* and during their prayer time, they prayed for a very sick baby girl in a hospital, and said Jesus was cleansing her blood and making her whole. My mom received that prayer and claimed it over me. The next day the doctor called my parents and told them they needed to get to the hospital right away. My dad was expecting the worst, but my mom believed I'd been healed. When they arrived at the hospital, the doctor told them they didn't know what happened but last night the machines I was hooked up to started to malfunction and they had to remove me from them to figure out what was going on. When they did, suddenly my color changed before their eyes. They decided to run some tests. They ran the tests a few times because they could no longer find any sign of hepatitis in my blood at all—either a miracle took place or they mixed up my labs. My mom proudly chimed in, "Jesus healed my baby girl!"

—*Rebecca*
(To Be Continued in Tomorrow's Reading)

Today's Takeaway:

Rebecca's mom knew God could heal her baby because she had seen firsthand the great work He had done in her life. He had changed her heart and cleaned her up, taking away her drug addictions. She knew He was an all-powerful God!

Do you know that? Are you in need of something that requires a miracle today? I know Someone wonderful, and He loves you! Believe and trust God to work in your situation today.

Day 249

Today's Scripture:

"Repent, then, and turn to God, so that your sins may be wiped out, that times of refreshing may come from the Lord" (Acts 3:19 NIV).

Today's Testimony *(Continued From Previous Day):*

Fast-forward to me at the age of four; I came to my mom and told her I needed to be saved. She took me to my dad and he asked me what that meant (not thinking I really had a clue what I was asking). I explained salvation to them. As they led me in the sinner's prayer, I remember praying and in my mind I saw a big brown door with a red heart on it; I saw Jesus open the door and walk in. I was so excited to have Jesus in me! A few months later my dad's ministry fell apart—the coffeehouse/church and our home were firebombed by rival biker gangs intent on killing my dad. We moved and he backslid. My parents soon separated, eventually divorcing.

I started drinking at the age of eleven. I struggled with depression, anger, and eating disorders. I attempted suicide a half dozen times or more. I needed to turn back to God. My entire childhood I longed to go to church and learn/grow in Christ. But it wasn't until I became a young adult that I realized I needed to find God on my own—not wait for my parents. I began asking God to show me where to go. Oddly enough, it was in the middle of a bar dance floor when I made the decision to search. I was drunk and dancing with a girl I had known as "the church girl" from high school, when out of nowhere she said to me, "You should go to church with me sometime."

Instantly I sobered up and exclaimed, "Yes, OK! When?" I'm sure it was not the reply she had expected at all. I was just so ready to return to Christ and get out of the miserable life I was in. Long story short, I returned to God's house and rededicated my life to Christ shortly after that, and have been serving Him ever since.

—*Rebecca*

Today's Takeaway:

Rebecca was heartbroken after giving her heart to Jesus at such a tender age and looking up to her father all her life—she was shredded. It's a hard lesson to learn, sisters, but we *have* to keep our eyes on Jesus because people can fail—even our own family or leaders. We are responsible for our walk with Christ. Parents and leaders must give an account of their leadership, but ultimately, *we* must keep ourselves walking with Jesus. You can do that by keeping your eyes on Him always—in prayer, in the Word, in worship, and in fellowship with godly believers. You're a big girl—you can do it!

Day 250

Today's Scripture:

"And we know that in all things God works for the good of those who love him, who have been called according to his purpose" (Romans 8:28 NIV).

Today's Testimony:

When I was eight years old, I went to Bible camp. While I was there, I accepted Jesus as my Savior. I attended church on Sunday and went to youth group, but I never knew there was more to be had.

I married a man who was Catholic. I was happy to become Catholic because I had attended the Catholic church with my girlfriend several times, and I loved all the ceremonies. I imagined my husband and I would go to service on Saturday night and then out for supper or a movie.

I lived at that same level until I was forty years old. I never knew about a relationship with Jesus. I never really thought about Jesus. I didn't really have any unmet needs. My husband had a good job. We raised two wonderful sons. We lived comfortably and had savings in the bank with no debts.

Then one day, my husband left me for another woman. I tried to go to the priest, but since we had left the church several years before, the only advice he gave me was "get a good lawyer."

My brother invited me to go to his church. I didn't want to go, but I knew I had to at least once to get him off my back. I went to Wednesday night service because it would be shorter than Sunday. That night, I met three wonderful women. One called me the next day to see how I was doing. The other two invited me to sit with their families when I came on Sunday morning. Those three women made me feel so loved and welcomed that I didn't miss Sunday or Wednesday services from then on.

Whenever I meet someone new at our church, I want them to feel loved and wanted and *want* to come back. When my husband left I was devastated, but his leaving me became a blessing. Both of my sons came to the saving knowledge of Jesus Christ and know what it is to have a relationship with the Father; they married Christian women, and my grandchildren are being raised in Christian homes.

Seventeen years after my divorce—and my vow to never let anyone hurt me again—God brought a great man into my life. We have been married for ten years. I now have a great relationship with Jesus, who has blessed my life more than I ever imagined.

—*Linda*

Today's Takeaway:

Linda was comfortable—not totally turned away from God, not really pursuing Him either—lukewarm. It didn't work well being lukewarm; that's when her husband got interested elsewhere. Beware of the "going nowhere with God" status. It's a dangerous place to be!

Day 251

Today's Scripture:

"Being confident of this very thing, that he which hath begun a good work in you will perform it until the day of Jesus Christ" (Philippians 1:6 KJV).

Today's Testimony:

When I was asked to submit my testimony for this devotional, I burst into tears! I've often felt that my testimony wasn't good enough to help anyone; maybe you can relate. I thought about others who have a more powerful testimony than mine, but I'd been praying that the Lord would help me be able to share my story, and then I realized God was answering that prayer!

I was raised in a Christian home. Our parents faithfully took my two sisters and me to church on Sundays and Wednesdays and also to Vacation Bible School. I learned to love the Word of God and memorize Scripture there. I don't know where I would be today if those seeds weren't planted in my heart at an early age! One Sunday, my teacher was ending the class in prayer, and she asked if anyone wanted to receive Jesus Christ as their Savior. We had our eyes closed, and I raised my hand. She led our class in the sinner's prayer, and I asked Jesus to forgive me of my sins and come into my heart; I was ten years old, and in the fourth grade. I will never forget it! He gave me His joy and peace, and the whole world seemed brighter to me. Soon after that, I was baptized. When I was fifteen years old, I received the baptism in the Holy Spirit. He is truly my Helper! Presently, I sing in the choir, and serve in women's ministry.

The Lord has brought me through many things: a divorce, raising my daughter with the support of my parents, surgery for a brain tumor, and the passing of my precious parents. Through it all, He has been so faithful and good, and supplied every need!

I'm so thankful that Jesus drew me to Himself, saved me, and made me a new creation. When I fail Him, sometimes I get down on myself, and wonder if He can still use me. But one thing I know: God loves us with an everlasting love. His love is unconditional, and He never gives up on us! One of my favorite promises in the Bible is Philippians 1:6, "Being confident of this very thing, that he which hath begun a good work in you will perform it until the day of Jesus Christ."

—*Sally Ann*

Today's Takeaway:

Oh, how beautiful and comforting it is to me to read of a child that trusts in Jesus and then walks with Him all her life. This is the goal! Trust Him and walk with Him, leaning on Him through every trial that comes. Trials do come. I am sorry to say it—I wish we were all in Heaven now, but until then, we have this hope: He is with us! Thank you for testifying, Sally Ann.

Day 252

Today's Scripture:

"Whoever acknowledges me before others, I will also acknowledge before my Father in heaven. But whoever disowns me before others, I will disown before my Father in heaven" (Matthew 10:32-33 NIV).

Today's Testimony:

As a young girl, I would occasionally go with my cousins to Sunday services. I attended VBS, and went to other youth events from time to time. This gave me a foundation. I believed in God, but had never surrendered to Him—never allowed Him to be Lord over my life.

When I was thirteen, a kid from school asked if I believed in God. He was an atheist, so to seem cool, I said, "No," not thinking it was a big deal at all, and just carried on with life. Two weeks later, my cousin invited me to go to a youth camp with her. Not knowing this would change my life forever, I tagged along.

The very first night, we gathered together in the sanctuary and had awesome worship and sat down to get ready for the message. The lesson was about who Jesus is, His character, and His love for me. I learned verses that shook me to the core, especially this one: "Therefore whoever confesses Me before men, him I will also confess before My Father who is in heaven. But whoever denies Me before men, him I will also deny before My Father who is in heaven" (Matthew 10:32-33 NKJV).

That was the very thing I had done just two weeks prior! I had denied Him, and thought nothing of it. All of a sudden, it was like a bomb went off in my spirit. I realized how far I was from Him. I claimed to believe in Him, but I was still living my "own life," and desiring to be a part of this world.

In that moment of realization, I knew I had to make it right with God. I was terrified of living another moment separate from Him. I fell to my knees weeping at the altar, repenting for my sins. I declared, in that moment, that Jesus was, and forever will be, Lord over my life.

It's amazing how God can move in our lives! He puts us in the right place at the right time. He knew this was the message I needed to hear to turn my entire life around and run after Him. He truly is Abba Father.

—*Shawna*

Today's Takeaway:

Shawna thought no one knew what she'd said, but Someone did; He is always listening. Not only is He listening to what we say, He sees our posts, our searches, our tweets, our comments, our reposts. The things we do that seem so insignificant because they aren't really in front of Jesus, actually are. It's a sobering thought. That's why we have to grasp the truth that He's there all along—for the good, the bad, and the ugly. Let's do our best not to be a source of bad and ugly!

Day 253

Today's Scripture:

"When you stand to pray, if you have anything against anyone, forgive him. Then your Father in heaven will forgive your sins also" (Mark 11:25 NLV).

Today's Testimony:

One summer day, God called me His own. I surrendered my heart and life to Him, receiving Jesus Christ as my Lord and Savior. That is the day the healing began in me to move past my past.

The first thing that came was His love—knowing I was not garbage; instead, I knew I was a child of God. The King of kings loved me! Then forgiveness came; I knew God in Heaven had forgiven me, and now He wanted me to forgive. Do you know how to know when something comes from God? It's when you know it's impossible for you to do it on your own! With God all things are possible to those who put their trust in Him. Next I got married and life was good—but not for long. I endured verbal, mental, and physical abuse. I cried to God, but the marriage ended in divorce.

God spoke to me that it was time to heal, that I must forgive the person who sexually abused me, but I couldn't; I wouldn't. God showed me this scripture: "If you forgive not, then your Father in heaven will not forgive you" (see Matthew 6:15). I prayed and cried out to my heavenly Father, "I need You to help me to forgive. I will not allow this man to rob me of You and my life with You." God showed me another scripture, Matthew 5:44, which says to love and pray for your enemies and those who hurt you, but I couldn't and didn't want to pray for *him*! Romans 8:26 says in our weakness the Holy Spirit will help us to pray, that He will intercede for us. So I prayed for the Holy Spirit to pray for him through me. As time went by, I was able to pray and have compassion for him! I was finally able to forgive and get past my past, moving forward one step at a time in my heavenly Father's strength, comfort, guidance, and love.

Getting past your past requires a relationship with God through salvation—surrendering yourself to Him, realizing the root of the pain is the enemy working through the people who hurt you. Don't allow anyone or anything to steal the abundant life God has for you! It may seem impossible, but with God's help it *is* possible. I was abused, abandoned, and lived in fear, but now I am healed—I am God's chosen and free!

—Lisa

Today's Takeaway:

Forgiveness for someone who purposefully caused you desperate pain is hard—it's more than hard—it's almost impossible. That's why it often takes Jesus' strength to do it; that's OK. If you ask for help from your Father, He'll give it. Healing will come. He's the God of the impossible!

Day 254

Today's Scripture:

"God, you're such a safe and powerful place to find refuge! You're a proven help in time of trouble—more than enough and always available whenever I need you" (Psalm 46:1 TPT).

Today's Testimony:

Growing up, my parents would occasionally talk about God. They had my siblings and me baptized very young, but they never fully surrendered their lives to God. My mom was a single mother who had a drug addiction to prescription pills most of my life. Today she seems to live free of that lifestyle. My dad was a functioning alcoholic that acted from his emotions too often, mostly anger.

My parents fought nonstop, verbally and physically. They finally separated when I was around five years old, but that didn't stop the fighting. My dad would occasionally pick my sister and me up on Sunday, his day off, and take us to the bar to play pool and games while he drank alcohol with his friends. I was around ten and my sister was around fourteen. When I was a teenager, my dad told me my mom wanted to have an abortion with me, but he wouldn't allow it. I was her last child; she was thirty-six. I understood she was suffering, but ending my life wouldn't have taken away her pain.

In those years I lost my virginity. I started experimenting with marijuana and drinking alcohol at fourteen years old, developed a habit of that lifestyle until I was seventeen and caught a curable STD (sexually transmitted disease). We moved six times in one year because my mom lost everything to her addiction and my dad wasn't stable enough to support us. All of this, and more, developed immense levels of shame and self-hatred with no grasp of my self-worth. I used sex, drugs, and alcohol to mask the pain of a dysfunctional and broken childhood. There was so much abuse and neglect. My need and desire to live whole and healthy was not met until I met Jesus.

—Nicole
(To Be Continued in Tomorrow's Reading)

Today's Takeaway:

Nicole was raised in horrible circumstances; instead of Sunday school, she was sitting in a bar on many Sundays. This kind of raising understandably led to chaotic choices. Many would be ready to throw this situation out the window, but not God! He specializes in lost causes. His Word is "chunk full" of them. In fact, I think He *enjoys* the challenge!

If you have a "lost cause" you're praying for, just remember who our "specialist" is. And remember who He is up against in the race for their soul. Know that 1 John 4:4 says it's not even a fair race. Greater is God who is in us than he who is in the world. God wins! Keep praying and wait on God.

Day 255

Today's Scripture:

"God, you're such a safe and powerful place to find refuge! You're a proven help in time of trouble—more than enough and always available whenever I need you" (Psalm 46:1 TPT).

Today's Testimony *(Continued From Previous Day)*:

When I was a junior in high school, a man named Reggie Dabbs shared his story of neglect, abuse, and how he grew from it all. He invited the students to a local church to hear how Jesus changed his life. After being moved by his Jesus story, I was leaving the church when a woman stopped me before I could get out of the auditorium. She was the youth pastor's wife and invited me to come to their youth group. I accepted her invitation and decided to attend church by myself, trusting her gentleness and being curious about who this Jesus was and wanting to hear what Reggie and all those other people talked about.

Not long after seeking God, I learned that men and sex couldn't meet my needs, friends and family couldn't meet my needs, drugs and alcohol couldn't meet my needs; but when I met Jesus, He exceeded my needs. I desperately began seeking Him by reading the Bible and attending church regularly. Life has never been the same since.

Jesus redeemed my pain with a purpose and passion to save the unborn and spare women from the lies and pain abortion causes. He has blessed me with a husband and children, knowing I had no example of what a healthy home looked like.

He has held me in my uncertainty and lovingly sets me on His path for my life when I try to go my way. Even in my unfaithfulness, He remains faithful. I've found a friend in Jesus—a Healer, a Redeemer; a reason to live and share with others His love and truth, a love that doesn't change whether I'm deserving or not. In Jesus, I have found a life worth living!

—Nicole

Today's Takeaway:

Seeking Jesus turns our entire life around. Perspectives flip. Focus shifts. Priorities realign. Addictions wither. Nicole finally had peace, a loving home and healing!

That's what God trades for lost causes. He doesn't give up but instead makes something beautiful out of what used to be painful. He makes masterpieces with no flaw.

The great thing is that His masterpieces aren't just to be stared at, they are then put to use to help make other masterpieces. That's what I call *perfect*!

Day 256

Today's Scripture:

"Peter replied, 'Repent and be baptized, every one of you, in the name of Jesus Christ for the forgiveness of your sins'" (Acts 2:38 NIV).

Today's Testimony:

I trusted Christ as my personal Savior over fifteen years ago at a revival at our church. God spoke to my heart revealing to me my need for a Savior. The Holy Spirit laid on the evangelist's heart to run the invitation longer. I'm so glad he listened! I stood there during the invitation, gripping my chair in front of me, trying to convince myself that I already was saved; that I'd prayed as a child. I'd been in church for a few years then and I'd already told everyone I was—even sharing my salvation testimony with other church members. What would they think?

It's crazy to look back and remember the lies the enemy threw at me that night, trying to convince me I was OK, but deep down, I was terrified. I knew my life had never changed; I knew I'd never truly repented of my sins and asked God for forgiveness. I've never forgotten that moment of heavy conviction and turmoil in my soul. But I also never forgot the moment when I turned to my husband sitting next to me and told him I wasn't saved. We went to the altar together and with me sobbing, I accepted Christ as my Savior.

At that moment I finally knew what it truly felt like to be *forgiven*. The huge weight of sin I was carrying was *gone*! My life for the first time had peace. Jesus was finally my *personal* Savior. Many of you remember that time when God visited your soul and made you realize you needed Him, but this story is for those who, like me fifteen years ago, have no peace in their life, know something is missing, and are terrified to think where they would go if they died. I'm here to tell you, that day, I made the best decision I've ever made in my life. There is peace, joy, and an unending love that He has filled in my life. I'm far from perfect, but I'm so thankful that because of God's grace and mercy, I am what I am today. If God's calling you, please don't run. Run to Him, because just like me, I promise you will never regret giving your life to Christ!

—Pong

Today's Takeaway:

In our hearts, we know, don't we? We know if we have truly surrendered to God. If we have, there's peace and assurance. We can know we're ready for Heaven—there's no terror to think about where we'd go if Jesus returned to earth. On the other hand, if the enemy has successfully hedged us away from the truth, causing us to avoid the subject and the conviction, there will be turmoil. Only you can evaluate your soul—don't ever gamble with that! Be double sure there is perfect peace in your heart.

Day 257

Today's Scripture:

"When you pass through the waters, I will be with you; and when you pass through the rivers, they will not sweep over you. When you walk through the fire, you will not be burned; the flames will not set you ablaze" (Isaiah 43:2 NIV).

Today's Testimony:

Where to begin? I have so many testimonies I could share, but there isn't enough time or space to tell all God has done in my life! My dad and grandpa helped build the church we attended. But when my husband and I were married, soon we had two sons, got our first home, had good jobs, then our boys were in sports. We had it all; we thought we didn't "need" God.

For twenty years we were in and out of church. I realized there was a void in my life, and talked to my younger brother about my emptiness. He shared Jesus with me. From that moment, Jesus began to draw me, like a magnet. I couldn't get away from the pull of the Holy Spirit—the desire to get back to my Savior's love for me.

Four months after I rededicated myself to Him, our oldest son was murdered! He was stabbed to death at age twenty-seven. He left behind a wife and an eleven-month-old son. God knew I was going to need His strength to survive! It's the only way I did. All I knew was, nothing could ever hurt me this bad again.

That is until, years later, when our youngest son called with devastating news. He had third-stage pancreatic cancer. He was only forty-two years old. He fought like a champ for ten months. I held him until he took his last breath. He left behind a wife and two teenage children.

How does one get through such pain and tragedy? Only one way. The Holy Spirit has, indeed, been my Comforter. I hold onto the *hope* I have in the Lord—that I will be reunited with my sons for eternity. I thank God He has held me through it all.

—*Rebecca*

Today's Takeaway:

As a mother, I chilled reading this story just imagining getting this news! It would bring any mother to her knees. She would stay right there too, except that as a woman of God, there is a supernatural strength from the Holy Spirit. I witnessed this strength in my own mother after the loss of her two children in a fire. I witnessed it, but I don't pretend to understand it. I just know it's *powerful*. His presence gives peace, comfort, and strength to pick up and keep walking. It gives *hope* for Heaven!

Day 258

Today's Scripture:

"Jesus said, 'Let the little children come to me, and do not hinder them, for the kingdom of heaven belongs to such as these'" (Matthew 19:14 NIV).

Today's Testimony:

My conversion begins with my mother's influence. She accepted Christ as her Savior at the young age of seven, in an old-time brush arbor with sawdust flooring. She later told me it was during this revival that she would kneel in prayer, praying in the Spirit, having dreams and visions. It was also at this revival that she led her own father to salvation in Christ. I'm sure this was an answer to one of her mother's prayers.

As a child, I had the beautiful influence of my mother and grandmother. The godly examples they set for me have helped to shape my life, and for that, I am eternally grateful. At the age of six, I remember going to the altar several different times to be saved. Over and over again, I would walk up the aisle to give my life to Jesus, until I heard my mother advising me, indirectly, that it wasn't necessary to be saved again each time I made a mistake; I only needed to pray and repent. What a relief! Salvation is eternal! To this day, I thank the Lord for His saving grace and His mercies that last a lifetime.

Not long after that, I started attending a neighborhood children's Bible class, and that is where I made my final decision for salvation. I'm thankful I made this decision, way back then, as a little girl. It's the best decision I've ever made, and one that continues to bless and sustain me.

—Ruth Ann

Today's Takeaway:

Praise God for the wisdom and guidance that comes from godly mothers who have read the Word and know how to lead their children into a life that honors Christ. Ruth Ann was blessed with a rich heritage of a mother and grandmother who loved the Lord and lived out that love in their daily lives.

What kind of legacy are we leaving our children or family? Can those who look to us follow our example? Can they come to us for godly advice and sound wisdom? Can our friends trust that when they are with us, they'll be encouraged and built up, or does time spent with us drag them down spiritually?

Our Christian witness matters! It matters to our family who needs us to lean on, and help guide them; it matters to our friends who gain strength from our walk with Christ; it matters to those we don't even know are watching us—coworkers who know we are Christians, watching to see our language, our reactions to adversity. Our walk with God matters as much to others as it does to us.

Day 259

Today's Scripture:

"'For I know the plans I have for you,' declares the Lord, 'plans to prosper you and not to harm you, plans to give you hope and a future'" (Jeremiah 29:11 NIV).

Today's Testimony:

Being raised in the church and a preacher's daughter, I've been asked, "Do you really have a testimony? Doesn't 'preacher's kid' imply always being a Christian?" Actually, it doesn't, no matter your parents' profession or calling. God takes each person down their own journey and deals with the heart. Righteousness doesn't happen by association. I got saved as a small child and always felt His hand leading me.

As I reached my high school years, my journey had the same challenges as anyone else, and I fell into the trap of hiding my struggles. That led to a feeling of loneliness and seeking friends to fill a void that should have been filled with God. So many problems came my way—rebellion, envy, selfishness, and exhausting myself doing my best to hide everything. I reached a point that I had to make a drastic decision to change the path I was on, which was spiraling out of control. In every valley, God seemed to be there to bring light. "Consider your ways!" (Haggai 1:7 NKJV). When you step out of obedience, the blessings stop. I wanted to return to the joy, peace, and blessing that seemed to be in my life as a small child. I wrote this poem to describe this time in my life:

Touching, filling, and surrounding my heart
Being a young child, hoping to never depart,
Standing in Your presence is an unforgettable day . . .
Arms stretched around me, why would I stray?

Falling away as I got older
Waking to find I got lost in the world and led astray . . .

Lighting my path, never leaving me, never forsaking me;
Oh, how You've chosen me!
A faithful God, I'm so undeserving,
No greater love that has no ending.
My devotion, my surrender, radical love,
No less is the only choice I choose forever; I will be blessed.

—*Brittany*

Today's Takeaway:

God's hand is on Brittany. He is using her to bless others. There is a lot of wisdom in this sweet girl. Let us *all* "consider our ways." We want to be blessed, but God cannot bless disobedience, can He? He is a holy God. Let us follow His guidance and be blessed.

Day 260

Today's Scripture:

"Let all who seek You rejoice and be glad in You; let such as love Your salvation say continually, 'The Lord be magnified!'" (Psalm 40:16 NKJV).

Today's Testimony:

My journey to salvation started with my marriage to my high school sweetheart. Sadly, after ten years, my husband left me for another woman. I was so lost. I felt like I would now become this single, divorced woman that was just left all alone.

In the depths of my pain, I found alcohol. I picked a "void filler." It was available; I was in that environment as a bartender. Then as time passed, I picked up drugs. I would drive into work half-drunk, then close the bars every night. It got so bad that alcohol seeped out of my pores, and I lost my job. I was a mess.

I was still at it when I met my boyfriend years later. Once I came home to a Bible sitting on my bed. I didn't think much about it. I continued on, until one night I thought my vehicle was in park but it wasn't. I was drinking and driving, and as I stepped out of my car, the door smacked me in the head. It knocked me down, and my car almost ran me over. My friend, who was with me at the time, hit the brakes. God was with me—and this is how I know He was with me: my friend wasn't even supposed to *be* in the car with me; she had other plans and had decided to come with me instead. Had she not have been there, I would have been run over. That was the night everything changed for me. The truth sank deep that I could have died.

I had to make a choice: keep living the way I was and kill myself or someone else, or take my life back—but I didn't know how. I didn't have anyone to encourage me or to help me get into the Word of God, until I met my boyfriend's grandparents. I always knew *about* God, but I never *knew* Him. I now began to seek to know Him.

—Paula
(To Be Continued in Tomorrow's Reading)

Today's Takeaway:

What a miracle that Paula was alive! She had taken her life and many other lives for granted so many times by drinking and driving. The God of Heaven had His hand on her for a reason. He put some godly grandparents in her path. Tomorrow we will see how God uses people to speak into our lives.

Day 261

Today's Scripture:

"*I can do all this through him who gives me strength*" (Philippians 4:13 NIV).

Today's Testimony *(Continued From Previous Day):*

Soon after this, I married my boyfriend. After a couple of years, we realized we needed help to have a child. We went through our first round of in-vitro fertilization, and God blessed us with our beautiful daughter; she was born at thirty-two weeks and two days! She spent seventeen days in the NICU. The whole process made me grow in my faith.

As time went on and I was experiencing life, I realized God did all this for me. His mercy and grace were there for me at the lowest point in my life! He drew me to Him, aligning my path, allowing me to meet my husband and his grandparents—even giving me my cousin to help me through giving myself injections! Like Hannah, God blessed a barren woman with a child that she always desired. God walked me through everything. He gave me hope through our daughter. As I watched her fight for her life, pulling the oxygen mask off her little face, constantly showing us she was meant to be here, I realized, *I* was meant to be here! I decided to give my life to Christ. It was, and is, the best decision I've ever made in my life. Not long after, we were on round two of in-vitro fertilization. God blessed us again with our second beautiful daughter.

When I was faithless, God was faithful. I owe my life to Him. He saved me. He provided an exit where I didn't see one. He delivered and freed me from my addictions. He protected me. He comforted me. He has never forsaken me. He has done all this and so much more for me. I was that "wretch" He saved with His *amazing grace*! God's unfathomable, unfailing love blessed me with an abundant life. I am so thankful to be His daughter and that He loves me!

—*Paula*

Today's Takeaway:

It's a humbling experience to finally realize *all* our God has done to bring us to Him. When we see it, when we recognize our unwillingness to come to Him; we see ourselves like a stubborn toddler who runs away instead of coming to the table or climbing into the lap for storytime. Such a waste, but then He is so patient. He tries again. That level of love stings my eyes with tears and joy.

It took a tiny little hand pulling off a tiny little oxygen mask to help Paula finally realize that she was meant to be here—and her Father knew it. How beautiful.
What will it take for *you* to realize it? *You* are meant to be here. Maybe these words are just for you—your Father loves you and He always has.

Day 262

Today's Scripture:

"*You will make known to me the way of life; in Your presence is fullness of joy; in Your right hand there are pleasures forever*" (Psalm 16:11 NASB).

Today's Testimony:

I was raised Catholic and always had a reverence and fear of God. When I was eleven years old my parents were invited by a friend to go to a little Pentecostal church. They both had an amazing conversion and were filled with the Holy Spirit; I was as well, on my twelfth birthday. The power of this infilling has helped me all throughout my life.

We began going to early Mass on Sunday and then to the little Pentecostal church after that. It took about a year for my parents to let Catholicism go.

I was attending Catholic school when I learned how to play the guitar for folk mass. This was the beginning of God leading me into worship ministry. Throughout my teen years I grew in my musical and singing ability, as did my siblings. We ministered at church, on the streets, at convalescent homes, on the radio, and on television. There wasn't an idle moment to get into trouble.

When I graduated from high school, the pastor we served under asked me if I'd put off college a bit, and travel with their singing group for a year. My parents were in agreement, so off I went. The same church later asked my dad to come and work with their ministry. So a few months after I moved, my family followed.

Soon after, I met the man who would become my husband. He is a natural evangelist. Our hearts connected in our service for the Lord (and for each other). We were married and were later blessed with four amazing children. They all have musical ability. Even today I have the great treasure to worship with my kids at church. All of them love Jesus and have married believers. God has even blessed us with beautiful grandchildren.

It's in the Lord's presence that we are healed, find peace, and have the fullness of joy. I will continue to be a worshiper, and look forward to continued times of worship in His presence.

—*Robin*

Today's Takeaway:

Robin is a worshiper in a family of worshipers. It makes me think of the tribe of Levites assigned worship at the Temple. They were anointed to sing and praise. (2 Chronicles 29:30). How beautiful to see an entire family dedicated to the service of God!

There's great joy in serving Him. There's room for everyone to serve; find a need and fill it. You'll see; you'll find great fulfillment.

Day 263

Today's Scripture:

"But God showed his great love for us by sending Christ to die for us while we were still sinners" (Romans 5:8 NLT).

Today's Testimony:

Statistically, we never had a chance. My husband and I both came from broken homes. Divorced parents, abuse and instability; being tossed between homes and out on the streets way too early in life. It's no wonder both of us were high-school dropouts. Turning to drugs, sex, and alcohol seemed like the only way to cope with the amount of baggage I was carrying.

When I met my husband, I was divorced with two children and living with my mother. He worked with my brother and asked me out one day. In time, we married. It certainly didn't *feel* like God had His hand in our relationship at the time, but someone must have been praying for us. Drugs, partying, a baby, and a year and a half later, we were separated. Divorce papers were drawn up and were just waiting for my signature. During the separation, I found out I was pregnant again, and not wanting to raise a fourth child on my own, my husband and I decided an abortion was the best option. That decision led us down a dark path. The drugs and partying only got worse.

Even though I didn't know Jesus, during this most difficult point in our marriage, Jesus knew me. By the grace of God we were invited to a small church for "Friends Day." Who knew this one small invite would lead our whole family to salvation?

We kept going back to this church only for the kids. They were praying for us and asking for prayers in their children's church (which we didn't know). I believe this is what led my husband to be convicted by the Holy Spirit. I didn't feel the "nudge", but decided to follow the head of our household, and allow him to lead us closer to Jesus. Every Sunday, I would feel the tug of the Holy Spirit, little by little. And then, one Sunday, I broke down and asked Jesus into my heart. God has been working on my life ever since. I am eternally grateful!

—*Robin K*

Today's Takeaway:

I just want to thank God for all the children's church workers out there and remind you that you are changing the world—even if you don't know it right now! I also want to thank everyone who still invites people to church because *it works*—entire families come to know Christ because of it. My heart is full of gratitude for what God has done for this family.

He wants to do this for everyone. When I think of those children praying for their parents to be saved . . . I have prayed with children like this who are believing for parents' salvation; God will honor their prayers. I am soaring on this testimony!

Day 264

Today's Scripture:

"And God will wipe away every tear from their eyes; there shall be no more death, nor sorrow, nor crying. There shall be no more pain, for the former things have passed away" (Revelation 21:4 NKJV).

Today's Testimony:

I am the youngest of eight children. My father was an alcoholic, and was physically and verbally abusive. My mother fought every day just trying to survive. I was molested by my brother when I was five. Later I started to seek attention from every boy I could find. I lost my virginity when I was sixteen, and became pregnant when I was eighteen. I thought my life was over, and the only way out was to get an abortion, so I made the appointment. The next morning, my mother took me to the clinic. That was the worst day of my life.

When I was nineteen, I met my future husband, a Christian, and I knew nothing about God. When I asked him out, he told me his parents had a rule that he could not date anyone who was not a Christian. He took me to church, introduced me to Jesus Christ, and we began to date. Within a few short months, my life had drastically changed. I had asked Jesus to be my Lord and Savior.

Then he joined the Navy. I felt abandoned and retreated into a self-destructive lifestyle. I started dating a man who was in his forties. Life seemed normal again until that man no longer wanted me. I was crushed, broken, and hit rock bottom.

I went home and began to swallow a bottle of pills, but spit them out when I heard someone coming. I ran into my bedroom, fell on the floor, and began to sob uncontrollably. For the first time in my life, my mother prayed for me. The wounds of my childhood rolled out of me as I sobbed: being molested, having countless sexual partners, having an abortion, my dad not being there, and losing the one person who truly cared for me.

The next day, I reached out again to my future husband. I was nervous that he would turn me away, but God had a plan for my life. He forgave me and pointed me back to Jesus. His parents took me to church every chance they had. I went to Bible studies and stayed with his parents. They taught me about the Bible. As a result, my life was turned around and I am truly blessed. We have now been married for twenty-one years, and I'm still in love with him. And . . . I'm more in love with Jesus than ever.

—*Sarah*

Today's Takeaway:

The hurtful things that happened to us as a child are valid and real—they can't simply be treated as if they aren't there. Pain must be carried to the One who can heal it. The good news is that pain doesn't mean we have to live maimed through life—God heals and brings us through it if we give it to Him. He wants us to be free and peaceful.

Day 265

Today's Scripture:

"Go into all the world and preach the Good News to everyone" (Mark 16:15 NLT).

Today's Testimony:

From the time I was two years old I attended an old church in the country. My parents never attended, but a widow lady from the church faithfully picked me up every Sunday. I learned about Jesus and gave my heart to Him at a very young age.

This sister made sure I didn't miss anything. We attended church camps, picnics, and special music services. As I grew older, I met my husband at church.

Sadly, while I was pregnant with my third child, my husband decided to leave us. I was devastated! I stopped attending church but I would still pray to God to help me. Over time, the church was eventually sold.

Years went by and eventually I remarried. One day at work, a friend invited me to a Bible study and then to church. The Holy Spirit was drawing me to go, so I did. It was then that I rededicated my life to Christ.

After that, one day I was in prayer at home and suddenly the Holy Spirit reminded me of something I needed to pray about; I knew I needed forgiveness. After praying for God to forgive me, the Holy Spirit filled me. I felt an overwhelming presence of the Lord I will never forget. My husband, who I have now been married to for thirty years, has since asked the Lord into his heart as well.

Our Lord is so good. He is faithful. He will never forsake us, but He will always protect us. His Word is true. God is love.

—*Sandy*

Today's Takeaway:

The Holy Spirit is a Comforter who comes alongside us to help. When we have the help of the Holy Spirit, sometimes we're prompted to pray. There will be times in the life of a Christian when you miss the mark—you should have done one thing but you knowingly did another. It's at these times that the Holy Spirit will urge you and lead you to pray to ask God to forgive you.

If you listen carefully, you'll hear the guidance *before* you act. Learning to listen to the voice of the Holy Spirit is one of the greatest acts of spiritual maturity a Christian can achieve. Obeying these prompts will cause you to be able to navigate life in a much more peaceful way. You'll avoid a number of pitfalls. No wonder Sandy was filled and knew the presence of the Lord.

Day 266

Today's Scripture:

"The fear of the Lord is the beginning of wisdom; a good understanding have all those who do His commandments. His praise endures forever" (Psalm 111:10 NKJV).

Today's Testimony:

I love sharing about the One who has been my Guide, Helper, Comforter, Savior, and the endless Love of my entire life. It always feels like even before I was born on this earth, I knew Jesus. As far back as I can remember, I have talked with Him and He with me.

As a child, I lived in the South. I started school at age five in a little country school. I walked to school, not afraid of anything, just talking to Jesus and He to me. I'd been raised going to a one-room "Holiness Church," where "hellfire and brimstone" messages were preached. The church was made up of wonderful people. What I learned from this church was the fear of God that Scripture refers to in Psalm 111:10 and Proverbs 1:7; 9:10-12. It molded my heart and has never left me.

When I was between twelve and thirteen years old, we moved to the North. I met lots of new, very adventurous friends who taught me to smoke. It didn't take long before I was addicted to cigarettes. I soon remembered what I had learned from my time in that little church in the South. In fact, because of it, I became free of my smoking addiction, but I was still away from God.

Once you ask Jesus in your heart, no matter what you do, the voice of God will never leave you; He won't give up on His children. I was running from God because I wanted to be like everyone else. One night in a dream, God talked to me, but I wasn't ready to surrender. I tried, perhaps not as hard as I should have; but without someone to help me, it was difficult. Through it all, God didn't leave me. I was totally miserable and carried so much guilt. I prayed every night, "Lord, forgive me; let me live until morning and I promise I'll live for You." But, when morning came, I would forget what I promised. God's love was abounding, and He stayed by my side through it all.

—Peggy
(To Be Continued in Tomorrow's Reading)

Today's Takeaway:

My momma used to say, "If you sleep outside with dogs, you're gonna get their fleas." Peggy had been raised to live close to God but then began to hang around the "adventurous" friends who taught her a new way to live. It didn't go well.

Do you have any "fleas" around? Don't get me wrong, I'm fine with having friends who aren't saved—just not best hang-out-night-and-day friends. Your closest and dearest friends should be sisters who build up your faith.

Day 267

Today's Scripture:

"Fear of the Lord is the foundation of true knowledge, but fools despise wisdom and discipline" (Prov. 1:7 NLT).

Today's Testimony *(Continued From Previous Day)*:

Three years later, God came to me in another dream. I didn't see Him; instead, I heard a drumbeat and it was saying, "IT'S TOO LATE! IT'S TOO LATE! He has come, and you've been left behind!" I fell on my face, screaming for mercy. There was none. It was over; I was lost for eternity with no forgiveness. In all my life, I was never so lonely or scared. Finally, I woke up. After such an intense dream I surrendered my life to God and never looked back. That was many years ago, and I have never regretted giving my life to Him. I found a church and started working for God.

God then put a compassion and love in my heart for hurting people. I was led to go to a jail ministry for what I thought would be a one-time trip to help someone who invited me to go. I planned on doing it just once because I knew this couldn't possibly be the ministry for me. She and I went. Upon entering the facility, suddenly my heart broke for those women. Thirty years later, I walked out for the last time. Oh my, how God blessed me in that ministry! I have had the honor to pray with hundreds of women to receive Jesus. Once you pray and ask Jesus in your life, you will never get away from His drawing, and one day you will surrender. *Thank You, Jesus, for Your faithfulness and thank You for leading me all these years.*

—*Peggy*

Today's Takeaway:

My heart swelled wide at this. I blinked back tears and I have a feeling our heavenly Father's heart is majorly proud of this too. If you think earthly fathers get excited about their girls, just imagine your heavenly Father's pride at what His girls accomplish!

Peggy heard the warning, answered it, and never looked back. She surrendered to Him. Then she decided to follow His calling completely.

I'm here to tell you, if you want a joyful life, do what your Father has called you to do and I promise you, it's *fulfilling and exciting*. I can't promise you that other people will always understand it. But there'll be treasures in Heaven for you. That beats treasure here any day!

Day 268

Today's Scripture:

"But God loves us deeply. He is full of mercy. He gave us new life because of what Christ has done. He gave us life even when we were dead in sin. God's grace has saved you"
(Ephesians 2:4-5 NIRV).

Today's Testimony:

My story begins in a Christian home, and with godly parents. We went to church every time the doors were open. When we were small children, when church, revival, or camp meeting lasted until late at night, my mom would put a pallet on the floor for me and my siblings to sleep on. My parents taught us about the love and saving grace of God at an early age. They prayed for us, and with us, all the time.

One night when I was five years old, I gave my heart to Jesus during our family devotion and prayer. When I was twelve, and understood more about serving God, I was baptized. Later, I became a youth leader. I was filled with the Holy Spirit while on a mission trip in London, England. I continued my education and began my career as a legal assistant working for a law firm for several years. After that, I married a music minister and we're blessed with two amazing children, who are now teenagers.

I've always been active in church, in many different roles, and I'm blessed to still be serving our Lord today. I am so thankful that both of our children have accepted the Lord as their Savior. Our son was four years old and our daughter was only three when they made this decision. After our family devotion, our son looked at me and said he wanted to ask Jesus into his heart. Then his sister said, "I want Jesus in my heart too." Leading your children in a prayer of salvation is a true blessing, and I'm so grateful. It's my prayer that this will continue from generation to generation.

The Lord has been with me and my family through every joy, blessing, heartache, and struggle that comes along the way of everyday life. He has always been faithful to see us through and He has always supplied our needs. He is a faithful and loving God!

—*Robin*

Today's Takeaway:

There's nothing greater than household salvation. It's a blessing to experience it, but then it's an even greater blessing to get to pass it on to your own children. What an encouragement to see these generations go forward! This is the plan of the Bible that we strive toward. The Lord is there to help us start now if we weren't blessed with this heritage, but it's exciting to see where it can lead in the future.

Day 269

Today's Scripture:

"O give thanks unto the Lord; for he is good: for his mercy endureth for ever"
(Psalm 136:1 KJV).

Today's Testimony:

Everyone who has been saved by the amazing grace of Jesus has a story. And everyone's story is different because we are each His unique creation, "fearfully and wonderfully made" (Psalm 139:14 KJV).

I walked with the Lord for many years. I loved Him and served Him. I never dreamed I would ever stray from Him. But I began to allow circumstances in my life to cause me to slowly drift away. It was not an overnight change, it was little by little. I simply walked away from the Father's house.

I just went about, doing my own thing. Instead of experiencing the safety and peace I had in my Father's house, I found myself relying on man's form of peace. I started to depend on antidepressants to help me sleep, drinking to make me happy. Did this work? No. But I kept trying.

Finally, I came back . . . back to the only One who could save me, deliver me, and set me free. His grace is truly amazing! The moment I called out to Him, the moment I asked for forgiveness, He was there—ready to redeem my life. He forgave me and restored me. I felt like a bird set free from its cage.

Joy, peace, mercy, and His great love flooded my soul. I felt alive again! He didn't have to give me another chance to serve Him, but He did. His love amazes me, every day. I have experienced and understand, on a deeper level now, His love, mercy, and grace. And here's the best part: It's available to everyone, despite our sins and mistakes. He truly loves and cares for *us all,* and His mercy endures forever.

—*Shirley*

Today's Takeaway:

It's sad, isn't it, to think of walking with the Lord and things being so good between you—sweet worship, protection, guidance—then sometimes we pull our hand out from His and walk away. Now, because we aren't in His presence anymore, we open ourselves up to going the wrong path, stumbling in the dark, tormenting voices trying to lead us into more and more sin. Pretty soon, we find ourselves doing the very things we loathe. You would think God would be too angry at us for leaving to welcome us back if we cried out to Him, wouldn't you? I might be. But not Him. We ask for forgiveness and He comes. We may have to suffer the consequences for the choices we made, but we are fully restored to walk with Him again. How wonderful is our Father? His forgiveness cost His very blood, but He gave it. His mercy *does* endure forever.

Day 270

Today's Scripture:

"Come to me, all you who are weary and burdened, and I will give you rest"
(Matthew 11:28 NIV).

Today's Testimony:

I accepted Christ as my Lord and Savior at age fifteen; I confessed my sins and was baptized. I knew the Lord and served Him through my early life.

Then during a very bad and abusive marriage, I let my guard down and let the enemy creep into my life. I was using the excuse that I was keeping peace in the household. The truth is, I was letting the enemy take control of me, and destroy my life for twenty years.

Several years after the death of my abusive husband, I remarried. I thank God all the time for the man He put into my life. He immediately insisted that I return to God and to the church. That was where my heart truly wanted to be. I was feeling guilty, burdened, and knew I was living a sinful life. I was searching for peace. Jesus said, "Come to Me, all you who are weary and burdened, and I will give you rest."

I knew I had to go back to God, give my life back to Him, and start serving Him. I bowed down, confessed all my sins, and asked God to forgive me and accept me back as His child. I vowed to Him that I would never let the enemy take hold of my life again. I went back to church and served the Lord for many years, but I felt like I needed a closer walk with God—that I was still missing something.

Then my faith was tested. I lost my daughter to cancer; then, eleven months later, I lost my husband. I was heartbroken and burdened with a mountain of expenses. I felt like I was climbing mountains, never reaching the top—like the enemy was trying to take over once again. However, I refused to let him. In Matthew 17:20, Jesus encourages us to pray to remove those mountains in our life, for God is stronger than any mountain. He removed them and gave me peace.

After this I changed churches and renewed my vows with God. I was baptized again. God gave me peace and joy. He has provided all my needs. After a few years, I lost my son; I was heartbroken again. I was hurt, but this time I didn't feel alone. I felt peace, and knew God was in control. I have grown so much in my walk with Him; my desire is to still draw closer.

—Margaret

Today's Takeaway:

(Margaret's words) Reading God's Word every day keeps a light in my life. I thank God every day for His love, mercy, and grace. I thank Him for His promises and for the forgiveness of sin.

(My words) Margaret is eighty-five years old and her desire is to draw closer—beautiful! Let's follow her directions—read God's Word every day; it will keep a light in our life.

Day 271

Today's Scripture:

"You will seek me and find me, when you seek me with all your heart"
(Jeremiah 29:13 ESV).

Today's Testimony:

I've been born twice—once in the physical and once in the spiritual. My testimony starts as a little child. I was taken to church every Sunday by my grandparents. Church was a place where "normal" people went. Because of my dysfunctional home life, I appreciated seeing there was a better way to live. I heard the Bible stories and sang the songs. I knew there was a God, but never had a real sense of how to *know* Him.

As I grew up, I no longer went to church. I didn't have anything to do with God. I had no support at home, and no one around me to share the truth, except to tell me when I was doing wrong. In my early twenties, I remember watching a movie in which a character was dragged away by demons. That shook me because I was faced with the question, "Where am I going?" I knew I was going to hell and that caused me to start to pray. The only prayer I knew back then was, "Now I lay me down to sleep. . . ." I kept living the way I wanted to, but if I prayed before I went to bed, I thought I'd be OK.

When I started to date my now husband, I would talk with him about what his past was like, his home life, and we would talk about God, but not in a way that gave us conviction to change how we lived. When we decided to get married, he suggested a church that he went to when he was younger. He called the pastor and asked if we could get married there. The pastor told him that you had to be a member or attend regularly to be able to use the church. My husband told the pastor we would be willing to attend the church.

We didn't know that we'd walk in there and never be the same. We were just "going through the motions," but once we started to sing from the hymnal, tears started to flow from both of us. We took everything to heart and gave our lives to Jesus *that day*. We literally walked in one way, and walked out being changed forever. Shortly after we were married, we began to serve in the ministry together. Our life has been truly blessed. We have raised two wonderful boys, and have much to be thankful for. God is faithful to His Word!

—Sandy

Today's Takeaway:

Sandy and her husband may have been there just to go through motions, but God had something much bigger in mind. He had already been dealing with them and touching them. They were tender to the Spirit when they arrived.

You never know when you talk to someone where they are in their lives, God may have you set up to help someone at just the right time to touch their hearts and influence them for the Lord.

Day 272

Today's Scripture:

"The steps of a good man are ordered by the Lord: and he delighteth in his way" (Psalm 37:23 KJV).

Today's Testimony:

As the lyrics of a song by G. E. Wright says, "I was lost and undone without God or His Son." That was me. I was in my first year of marriage and pregnant when my husband announced he was drawn to give his heart to the Lord and felt called to preach. I wanted no part of it! I abruptly said, "If I wanted to be married to a preacher, I would have married one. If you do that, this baby and I are gone." My husband gave in easily and didn't pursue his call.

The next couple of years were wild; a lot of partying and fighting. Sadly, this robbed our precious son of the loving and stable environment he deserved. Our lives were a wreck. I decided to take our now three-year-old son and go on vacation, stating; "If we don't return, don't bother to look for us."

While on vacation I made a visit to my father-in-law's house; they were both born-again Christians. They were excited when I agreed to leave my son with them for a few days. I didn't tell them about our situation, but God revealed it to my father-in-law. After I picked up my son, Dad began praying in earnest: "It's in Your Word, God: 'Train up a child in the way he should go: and when he is old, he will not depart from it.' My son may only be twenty-four, but as far as I'm concerned, that's old enough. His life is a wreck and he's about to lose his family." A father's heart went into that prayer.

Tired and confused, I decided to return home. At the time, I didn't realize it was the prompting of the Holy Spirit. I later learned that on the Monday before I returned, my husband had awakened from a ten-day drunk; we were gone and he was totally miserable. He said he dropped to his knees and cried out, "God, if You're out there, I need You. I'll do anything You want me to do, I'll go anywhere You want me to go, and I'll be anything You want me to be." In His great mercy, God reached down through all the misery and ugliness of my husband's life—or rather ours—and saved him.

—Sally
(To Be Continued in Tomorrow's Reading)

Today's Takeaway:

God had His hand on Sally and her husband. He had chosen them to serve Him. He knew Sally was stubborn; He made her that way! He planned to use that gift against the enemy someday. She went on to become one of the greatest pastors' wives ever. God knew exactly what He was doing. We have to learn to trust God's plan. It may not be what we pictured but it's always interesting—and blessed.

Day 273

Today's Scripture:

"The steps of a good man are ordered by the Lord: and he delighteth in his way"
(Psalm 37:23 KJV).

Today's Testimony Continued From Yesterday:

I returned home with our son, but my husband didn't say a word to me about his salvation experience. Shortly after this, we moved in with my husband's family. I noticed my husband was different, but figured it was for the sake of our son and me. After two weeks, he said, "We're going to church tonight with my parents." I wasn't happy and threatened to take our son and leave again. He looked straight at me and said calmly, "I love you more now than when we got married, but I'm going to serve God with you or without you. The choice is yours." Then, without another word, he left the room. My threat didn't work this time, so I went "just to keep the peace." Or so I thought.

My father-in-law was an evangelist and the meeting that night was in the country in an old garage. It all seemed rather bizarre and chaotic to me, but it didn't matter. In spite of my indifference, I knew my father-in-law was praying hard for me. I was still determined not to budge, but barely had that thought crossed my mind when I felt an overwhelming emptiness in my soul. I desperately wanted to be filled with Jesus. In all the chaos going on, I found myself at the altar surrendering my life to Jesus Christ, making Him my Lord and Savior. I was born again—CHANGED! It was such a remarkable experience that it has stayed with me for over forty-six years. On our way home that night, our son began singing his own little made-up song to a sweet, heavenly inspired melody: "Thank You, God, for saving my mommy; thank You, God, for saving my daddy; and thank you, God, for saving my grandpa too." I could not have been more in total agreement. All glory to God!

—*Sally*

Today's Takeaway:

Whoa! This time Sally's husband didn't back down. Why? Because he had a dose of God's holy boldness in him this time. When you get a mandate from God, you'll be like Peter—you won't deny Christ; you'll be ready to stand up in front of a crowd and testify. (Acts 2). You'll be changed.

Sally was changed, and it changed the trajectory of her entire life—for the better. What direction are you headed today? Do you know? If you don't, you can know. Are you willing to go with God's plan for your life, or are you still holding on to your plans? His plans lead to blessing. Your plans without His guidance lead to disappointment.

It's not too late to give Him full control like Sally and her husband did. Trust Him to guide your steps. He created every path.

Day 274

Today's Scripture:

"But now, O Jacob, listen to the Lord who created you. O Israel, the one who formed you says, 'Do not be afraid, for I have ransomed you. I have called you by name; you are mine'" (Isaiah 43:1 NLT).

Today's Testimony:

When Jesus called my name, I was outside hanging up clothes on the clothesline. I heard a voice calling two or three times. I heard my name, as clear as anything, "Tina," and a few moments later, again, "Tina." Who was calling me?

I looked around. I didn't see anybody. So, I just returned to my work, hanging up clothes, but then, again, I heard Him. He was calling my name . . . two or three more times.

I ran into the house, maybe someone was in there . . . but there was no one. My kids were playing at their friends' house. My husband was at work. I thought about what had happened. Later that evening, I started looking for the Bible my mom had bought me as a Christmas present a year or so ago. I'm ashamed to admit it, but I had never picked it up or even been interested to see what was inside—not until I heard Him call my name. That changed everything. I began to read my Bible and I started going to my mom's church. It was a little bit of a distant drive, but I didn't know of any other one. It didn't take long—I got saved. I asked Jesus into my heart. I asked Him to forgive me of my sins. And I began a new life. Oh, how thankful I am that He called me by name!

—*Tina*

Today's Takeaway:

What a personal God we serve! He sees us at every moment. Not only does He see us, but He sees inside of our hearts to know when we are sensitive to His Spirit. He knew Tina was ready to hear Him call her. He knew she had a Bible that she had never opened.

How used is your Bible? Is it part of your everyday life—like your toothbrush? Or is it more of a weekly tool, like a mop? Or even worse, is it something you seldom pull out, like a Christmas tree? You'll be able to gauge a person's spiritual health on the health of their Bible—only it works in the reverse: *pristine* can mean rarely touched and unhealthy soul, whereas *ragged* can mean well-used and spiritually fit. Make it part of your normal routine to read your Bible—hopefully, as regular as brushing your teeth—and you should begin to see a change in spiritual maturity and joy serving your Lord.

Day 275

Today's Scripture:

"Produce fruit in keeping with repentance" (Luke 3:8 NIV).

Today's Testimony:

I remember it like it was yesterday—the day I asked Jesus into my heart. I was three years old. It was a Sunday night. We were in a weeklong revival at my church. The pastor had given the invitation for salvation and I remember going up with others much older than me. I remember where I stood and everything. I knew even at the age of three what I was doing. I was filled with the Holy Spirit at six—another day that changed my life.

My family went to another church when I was around eight. This church allowed my relationship with God to grow. I soon began working in the nursery, and kids ministry helping with puppets at the church. As a teen I ministered to my peers and kids as a leader—in drama, dance team, and as a puppet-team leader.

Then I experienced serious church hurt; I left the church and began to do my own thing with God. I never walked away from God, but walking away from the church wasn't the best thing either. I just didn't know any better. Later I was attending a church where the youth pastor quit, so the pastor asked me and another person to step in and lead youth. I did this for a few years until the church hired a youth pastor. During this time I grew so much in God; I truly learned who He was in ways I had never encountered until then.

After that, I attended another church that needed my help. I was working in children's ministries, praise and worship, and other areas. But then, I failed God by having a relationship outside of marriage. I got pregnant and gave birth to my daughter out of wedlock. That experience helped me understand that even when we sin, God is merciful, loving, and forgiving as we repent. So with God's help, I began the journey of being a single Christian mom. I moved forward in His forgiveness and mercy.

God has since opened the door for me to take in my nephew and niece as my own kids. He has seen me through a failed marriage and has proven Himself faithful. He showed up and provided for me and the kids not just a house, after the divorce, but a new car as well. During this time I anchored in at church, choosing to root myself by the still waters and not let the situation destroy me. I learned firsthand God truly is who He says He is—my hope and provider.

—Candace

Today's Takeaway:

The Lord loves it when His girls want to serve. It sounds like Candace enjoys serving and being useful wherever there is a need. There is nothing so rewarding as working for our Lord. If you haven't signed up for His employment, get in line. His benefits are awesome.

Day 276

Today's Scripture:

"He brought me up also out of an horrible pit, out of the miry clay, and set my feet upon a rock, and established my goings" (Psalm 40:2 KJV).

Today's Testimony:

My story starts when I was about ten years old. I was molested by a family friend. I told no one about this because I was scared *I* would be the one everyone blamed. Shortly after this, I turned to alcohol to ease the hurt and shame. This started a bad pattern in my life.

Later in high school I tried to numb the pain I felt; I wanted to feel better, so I tried partying. This only made my life worse; I got pregnant my senior year and got married a year after graduating. I settled into being a mom and a wife. Then I had two more children.

Not long after my youngest son started school, I became addicted to crystal meth. I went down that dark road for many years and lived a very wild and sinful life.

Around Christmas time I was at my lowest point. After being high for weeks straight with little to no sleep, God picked me up out of the dark and desolate pit I had put myself in. My life was out of control. I was awakened by a strange presence and heard a voice talking to me.

The voice asked me if I'd had enough—enough of trying life my way, or was I ready to try a better way? I ended up in a battered women's shelter with my future looking uncertain. Sitting in that shelter, I knew it was time to turn my life around. So one night I asked God, "Please help me! I can't do this on my own!" God heard my cry. I had filed for a restraining order and had divorce papers, but God had other plans. He saved my husband instead and turned his life around too. Through much work, my husband and I were set free from drugs and alcohol.

My life and marriage were restored. We were soon rooted in our church where I now serve in children's ministry along with my middle son. My husband and I now go out and speak at different outreaches in our community. All three of our children have graduated school and have good jobs. I thank God every day for His saving grace!

—*Amber*

Today's Takeaway:

God is a restorer of lives, of marriages, of homes, of self-worth. He takes what was ruined and rebuilds it better than it was. He is the Way-Maker! When Amber cried out for help, that set in motion the most powerful force that has ever been. The same God who spoke light into being reached down and lifted her out. That's the kind of God we serve. What do you need from Him? He's able! Don't be discouraged today. He is able to help you.

Day 277

Today's Scripture:

"The Lord directs the steps of the godly. He delights in every detail of their lives. Though they stumble, they will never fall, for the Lord holds them by the hand"
(Psalm 37:23-24 NLT).

Today's Testimony:

Life can be confusing and it can be heavy. Life is even more daunting growing up with a family that didn't quite meet the norm. I grew up with divorced parents who, from a young age, grieved the loss of their parents. Even though my home life was a bit messy and broken, God's grace was enough to cover all of the chaotic and erratic moments, even when I couldn't quite see it yet.

I grieved the loss of my grandmother who was killed in a car wreck when I was just eight years old. Her death left me asking many hard questions that I was scared to say aloud. I didn't realize God knew me intimately and already saw everything in my heart. The tragedy of losing my grandmother eventually led to my mom leaving the only church I had known, and bringing me to a new church—the one which would later bring me to "camp," and subsequently to the moment God used to change my life.

On the first night of camp, God's love and conviction brought me to the altar, sobbing my eyes out. I didn't understand why I was crying, I just knew I needed Him. All my questions, all my hurt, and all my anger were met by His love, in that one moment, and I accepted Him as my Lord and Savior.

Thank God, He didn't leave me when I was young and confused. Thank God, He didn't leave me crying at the altar. Instead, He met me right where I was, and His mercy and goodness have continued to chase after me, even now.

God has healed me not only emotionally but physically along the way. He has baptized me with His Spirit and shown me there is still more to learn. I praise Him for His grace that met me at such a young age, and continues to cover me today. Life can be crazy and heavy for us, but it is never too much for God.

—Mikalea

Today's Takeaway:

Life is crazy! The good thing for us is that God works through "crazy." He loves us in our messy, questioning, difficult places and calls us to Himself. He wants to bring us into a place of peace, calm, joy, and rest. His plans are for our good—He knows the pain and hurt we've endured and it grieves His heart to see us hurt. He's a healer of pain—every kind. I'm so glad, aren't you? He'll meet you where you are, right in the heavy places. If you'll let Him, He'll take your pain and give you peace in its place. Trust Him.

Day 278

Today's Scripture:

"So the Lord must wait for you to come to him so he can show you his love and compassion. For the Lord is a faithful God. Blessed are those who wait for his help" (Isaiah 30:18 NLT).

Today's Testimony:

I grew up in a Christian home along with my three sisters. My mom raised us to always seek God, to love Him, and to put Him first in all we do. As a child, I struggled emotionally in different areas. Over time, I was diagnosed with depression and anxiety. As I grew up, things got worse. It seemed like a never-ending battle just to survive each day.

I was always taught that God was there, that He wouldn't leave me, but deep down, I did not believe it. My mom encouraged me to face each day and to "pick myself up," but I couldn't. The depression was holding me down too tightly to get back up. I can't tell you how many types of medication I tried, but every pill only made it worse.

By eighteen, I had absolutely no hope of a future or a purpose. I wanted to give up completely and I thought of it many times. During that time, God spoke to my older sister and said that if I wanted to be healed, I had to ask Him for healing.

I am a very stubborn and strong-willed person, so asking for help is not an easy thing for me. I thought I could do it myself; but I reached a point where I just couldn't take it anymore. In the middle of the night I asked God for help. I told Him I couldn't live like this anymore. Slowly, but surely, He began to help and heal me.

Thirteen years later, I can look back on that moment with clarity. God didn't come running and pick me up off the ground just like that. It was more like I had finally looked up and saw His hand—His hand that had been stretched out, the whole time, waiting for me. He never left me, just like I had always been taught.

God gave me hope that nothing in this world had ever been able to offer. Not only did God give me *hope*, but He gave me *purpose*—to be a mom. So now I walk this life with God, my husband, and my two little boys. Hope does not come from earthly things. I ought to know; I searched for it as hard as I could, and found it *only* in the Lord.

—*Sarah*

Today's Takeaway:

God loves all His girls and He knows how to help each and every one of us, but He is a gentleman and waits to be asked for help. He is a master at mental health—He can guide us toward feeling better, toward healing. He created us and He is our healer! He loves us and wants us to be well. His Word says when we cry out to Him, He hears and answers us.

Day 279

Today's Scripture:

"Create in me a clean heart, O God, and renew a steadfast spirit within me.
Do not cast me away from your presence, and do not take Your Holy Spirit from me.
Restore to me the joy of Your salvation, and uphold me by Your generous Spirit"
(Psalm 51:10-12 NKJV).

Today's Testimony:

When I was a little girl, I remember going to church by myself. My mom or dad would drop me off at the church and go back home. They would send my brother to pick me up, but I was in the choir singing with the women. I wasn't old enough to read, but they gave me a songbook like I could, so I sang right along with them. I loved the Lord, and I wanted to be in church.

I had a happy childhood until I was violated by one of my dad's friends. I was only six years old when this man got drunk and molested me. He told me if I said anything to anybody, I would be taken away from my mom and dad and I would never see them again. I kept it a secret until about twenty years ago.

When I was nine, my dad was killed by a high-voltage power line. I still went to church, but as time went on I made some choices I have regretted. I held God responsible for my dad's death. I was angry at God and didn't attend church or pray the way I should.

Years later I got married, had a baby, and divorced. Thankfully, I was able to go back to school and gained a certificate in business, but I knew things weren't what they should be. I didn't drink, smoke, or do drugs; but I wasn't living for the Lord, either.

Years later, I met a man who treated me pretty good, so we got married; but it wasn't too long after saying "I do" that I knew I'd married the meanest man I had ever known. I decided to go back to church and surrender my whole life to Jesus. My husband didn't like it. He tried to sabotage everything I did. God kept me safe despite this man's many attempts on my life. He physically beat me, verbally abused me, attempted to drown me in a lake; one night, I even woke up with a gun to the back of my head. At that point, I prayed, "Lord, if it's my time to go, just take me home," and I went back to sleep. . . .

—*Doris*
(To Be Continued in Tomorrow's Reading)

Today's Takeaway:

The only reason I can think of for Doris going back to sleep with a gun pointed at her head is being so exhausted from dealing with this psycho that she was ready to either trust God or die. Thankfully, God was there and He still had plans for Doris. She had surrendered her life to Him and He was about to do something in her life.

Day 280

Today's Scripture:

"Now to him who is able to do immeasurably more than all we ask or imagine, according to his power that is at work within us, to him be glory in the church and in Christ Jesus throughout all generations, for ever and ever! Amen" (Ephesians 3:20-21 NIV).

Today's Testimony *(Continued From Previous Day):*

Later that week my husband said to me, "You were sleeping pretty good when I put that gun to your head the other night." I replied, "Oh, that wasn't a dream? It was real?" He said, "Yes, it was; do you want me to show you?" When he left the room to get his gun, I ran with only the clothes on my back and whatever I could grab. With nowhere to go, I slept in parks and driveways. Looking back, I am amazed at how God protected me.

In one last attempt to control my life, my husband tried to commit suicide. However, instead of death, he was in a coma for six weeks. The doctors tried to get me to pull the plug, but God said, "No."

Although God allowed him to live through this, He told me it wasn't my job to take care of him. And so, finally, I stood my ground and was able to leave that situation for good. The Lord set me free.

In trusting God, He has given me so much more than I could have ever imagined. God brought me through everything. I'm still amazed. His blessings are so great, I don't even know how to put my gratitude into words.

—*Doris*

Today's Takeaway:

I can't pretend to understand what causes people to abuse others. All I know is that God loves us, and He can heal the hurt caused by the abuse. We can take to Him every memory and every disappointment—He takes them and somehow He dulls the pain until one day we realize we barely feel its sting anymore.

One of the most important parts of dealing with abuse is being able to forgive the abuser. The best way to do that is to ask God to save the person and help them learn to live a better life. This is hard, but necessary. Freedom comes by letting go of any bitterness in your heart toward the person who hurt you. After you forgive the first time, the enemy will bring it to your mind again, and again. What can you do? Forgive them—again and again, until you stop remembering. One day you'll realize that you hardly ever remember it. VICTORY!

Day 281

Today's Scripture:

"Behold, I make all things new" (Revelation 21:5 KJV).

Today's Testimony:

As a child I was brought up in church; my mom was the pastor. It was hard at times, and I didn't always do the right thing. I didn't always walk in God's ways. And I was a difficult teen.

At the age of fifteen, I was sent to live with my grandmother, where I would live for the next twenty years. I eventually got married and had kids, but my life was falling apart. My husband and I had filed for a divorce. Then my husband got very sick and was in the hospital. I remember leaving the hospital one day feeling like the weight of the whole world was on my shoulders. I had three young daughters, and I thought my husband could die. On top of that, my dad was dying from cancer. I was at the end of my rope.

Later that day, I received a phone call from my mom, asking me how things were going. With tears in my eyes and a trembling voice, I told her about the situations I was going through, the problems I was facing, and my feelings of hopelessness. She told me I was under the conviction of the Holy Spirit. And then, she led me back to God through prayer. Oh, I am so grateful for a godly mother. That phone call changed the course of my life. I decided to drop the divorce; my husband and I decided to start over.

Several months later, we moved back to my home state. Little did I know, my dad had been praying for me to come home. That was many years ago, and since then, my life has been so blessed. It took some time and a lot of prayers, but life took a new turn. Today, I am still serving the Lord. Even though life has its ups and downs, I am truly blessed, and thank God every day. He has been there through it all, and will be, through all eternity.

—Sandra

Today's Takeaway:

What a difference a godly mother can make in your life! Actually, God can use anyone; it just seems so much sweeter when it's your mother. Sandra had struggled and struggled—she was hopeless and miserable. Her mother heard it in her voice. Thank God she had the boldness to lead her to pray to be saved. That changed everything. Somehow, centering your life on Jesus causes all the world to begin to align itself. You begin to see things more clearly and make decisions more calmly when Jesus is running your ship.

Let's not forget praying fathers—they change the world too. Sandra was truly in a "blessing sandwich" with her mom on one side and her dad on the other. I want to be on the blessing side of a phone call to someone today!

Day 282

Today's Scripture:

"I am the Lord, and there is no other; apart from me there is no God. I will strengthen you, though you have not acknowledged me, so that from the rising of the sun to the place of its setting people may know there is none besides me. I am the Lord, and there is no other. I form the light and create darkness, I bring prosperity and create disaster; I, the Lord, do all these things" (Isaiah 45:5-7 NIV).

Today's Testimony:

God chose to use the death of my father to show me just how mighty He truly is. In fact, during the three days prior to my father's passing, I remember God revealing Himself to me in so many ways. I knew He was showing me that in every season of my life, He's been there—watching and caring for me. All along, He had been preparing me for this day. The day I would realize He is in complete control.

I watched in awe as my dad left this world and entered into the presence of God. Then I started on my five-hour-long drive back home. Although my heart was breaking after losing my dad, my heavenly Father was there with me. I listened to worship music while I drove, and God comforted me. He saved me on that long drive home, sanctified me, and filled me with His wonderful Holy Spirit.

My life was changed. My thoughts, speech—everything—changed. Everything in my life was different from that moment on. I was delivered!

As I got about a mile from my home, I passed by a little country church I had passed so many times before. But this time, I felt God speaking to my spirit: *Be there, Sunday morning, 10:00 a.m.*

So that Sunday morning, I went. I not only went, I became a member of that little church. After all these years, it's still my church. Of course, things have not always gone the way I planned. I've failed many times. Like everyone, I've made some bad choices. But each time I repented, God turned me around and opened His arms with grace, patience, and forgiveness.

It still blows me away to realize the Creator of the universe is my Father. And yes, I'm Daddy's girl. I'm a child of God Almighty! Because of that, I can look forward to each day, each new chapter of my life, with hope. "With God, all things are possible" (Matthew 19:26 KJV).

—Charlene

Today's Takeaway:

How comforting to know that as Charlene needed comfort over the loss of her earthly father, she trusted her heart and life to her heavenly Father. How tender that drive must have been. His comfort and care fill our every "nook and cranny." His arms wrap us up like a big "cushy" blanket. I need that!

Day 283

Today's Scripture:

"Therefore this is what the Lord says: 'If you repent, I will restore you that you may serve me; if you utter worthy, not worthless, words, you will be my spokesman. Let this people turn to you, but you must not turn to them'" (Jeremiah 15:19 NIV).

Today's Testimony:

I was brought up in a Christian home with a long list of *do's* and *don'ts*. It was an unseen list, but it was there all the same. A lot of those *don'ts* sure looked like they'd be a whole lot more fun than the *do's* did. A few years after trying to do the right things, I decided it was time to start trying out the "don't" list.

I decided I wanted to be a smoker. I got a pack of cigarettes and, for a long time, I practiced the technique of smoking. It doesn't come naturally, you know. It is something you have to work at. Mission accomplished. I was a smoker. Then it was onto the art of swearing. I kept practicing, but I never could get those words to come out in the right places. This mission was not accomplished. I spent the next fifteen years working on the other "don'ts" from the unseen list; most of them I'll keep between God and me.

Then I started a new job in a different state where no one knew me or of my Christian upbringing. Most of these people didn't have a *do* and *don't* list, and I could fit right in, I thought. But, as they got to know me, they started referring to me as, "Hey, Church Lady!"

What was up with that? I wasn't a church lady. I didn't get it. But those words never left me. They were always in the back of my mind. *Hey, Church Lady!* They didn't say it in a degrading way; it was meant as a compliment. Not too long after this, my husband became a Christian and I rededicated my life to my Lord. Now, I am trying to live up to the "Hey, Church Lady" name—not by the *do's* and the *don'ts* of the man-made list, but through the relationship that I have with my heavenly Father and His Word. When God speaks to your heart, you can run as long and as fast as you want, but you can never hide from Him. Jonah tried, and he ended up in the belly of a big ol' fish.

Long story short, I was able to be a God-sent witness to those people without a man-made list. Not by preaching at them, but by just being me, the church lady that God had asked me to be. I was able to pray for them, but the best part was when they began giving me their prayer requests. I am very blessed. Thank You, Jesus!

—Peggy

Today's Takeaway:

I love Peggy's words, "You can run as long and as fast as you want, but you can never hide from Him." He loves you and pursues you. Don't run, stop and rest in His care. How you live in front of people makes a difference. You don't need a list for that—just a changed heart.

Day 284

Today's Scripture:

"A man's heart plans his way, but the Lord directs his steps" (Proverbs 16:9 NKJV).

Today's Testimony:

Jesus is my Lord and Savior. He is my best friend, and my relationship with Him grows deeper and sweeter each day. I remember giving my heart to Jesus as a fourteen-year-old girl in a youth service. The evangelist was talking to us about the dangers of drugs. I was determined to follow the Lord and turn away from that kind of life. I understood how important it is to guard this special relationship above all else.

I learned this life lesson again a while back. One day, I had read several Facebook posts that stuck with me. I couldn't get them off my mind. All day, these posts filled my thoughts, and even as I went to bed that night, they persisted, until finally, I was able to fall asleep. When I woke up the next morning, those same thoughts were still there. This concerned me, *Why was I dwelling on these things?*

Then the Lord led me to the Book of Proverbs, where I read about wisdom. While I was reading, I prayed that God would reveal to me what He wanted me to learn. And He did. He showed me it's *wisdom* not to allow others (their opinions, words, or even posts) to *direct* me. Only He should direct my steps, because only He knows what is best for me. No one else does.

It's so easy to be caught up in all the voices around us, but only One should be directing our thoughts, our steps, our lives. Having served God for a long time now, I've known His voice and I've followed it. He guides me in my decision-making and keeps me from making the wrong choices, which would inevitably lead me outside of His perfect will for my life. I know as I continue to seek Him, He will continue to bless me, protect me, and guide me into His perfect will.

I later watched the movie *God's Not Dead*. As I watched it, I could relate to the young lady who had questions about her beliefs, and shared them with her teacher. In my life, there are things I struggle to understand. Still, I know the One who can provide all the answers I need is Jesus. He teaches me. He directs my steps.

—*Michal*

Today's Takeaway:

It's amazing the things that will stick in your mind. They're not always the best things. Have you ever gotten the jingle to an annoying commercial stuck in your brain? Far worse than that is to get some negative comment from social media stuck there. The enemy magnifies these things and uses them to try to steer us. It takes wisdom to navigate negativity. Pray! Michal is right: Only God should direct us. Be careful who steers you.

Day 285

Today's Scripture:

"God has given each of you a gift from his great variety of spiritual gifts.
Use them well to serve one another" (1 Peter 4:10 NLT).

Today's Testimony:

When I was eight years old, my brothers and I were invited to Vacation Bible School by my neighbor (who is also a distant cousin). We attended each day, but I remember Wednesday's message the most. It was a message of love, and it moved my heart. I accepted the Lord into my heart that day.

There was a church about twenty miles from home that offered classes. I was only eight, but I wanted to go. The problem was, I had no way to get there. But God watches over His children, and He makes a way where there is no way.

My aunt had just married a man whose mother lived at the end of my road. At the wedding, she invited my entire family to church. My father quickly declined because of a bitter experience he had three years prior. But she didn't stop there. She asked, "Could your children come? I will take them."

The next Sunday, three children went to church without any parents. Oh, how I thank God for my aunt! This was the beginning of a faithful journey that lasted for years. God led me to a church where I learned the books of the Bible, memory verses, and Bible songs. This knowledge has lasted a lifetime.

My aunt came Sunday after Sunday, week after week, year after year for about nine years. She never missed a Sunday. In rain, snow, and even on holidays, she was always faithful. I remember sometimes she would drop off her family at church early, and then come back to pick up me and my brothers, and her mother. She was much like a "mom" to me at church. She helped me find scriptures in the Bible and hymns in the songbook. And I loved how my brothers and I would sit with her, as part of her family. It made us feel like we belonged—and we did.

I thank God for saving me at eight years old and for placing an example of great love in my life. My aunt passed away at the beautiful age of ninety. I pray I will show the example of love which was set for me to others who are in need. Such love that always reaches out and never ends.

—*Sandy*

Today's Takeaway:

What a beautiful life of service that Sandy's aunt lived! God will be blessing people through her life for generations to come.

This is the "earthly version" of "Well done, good and faithful servant." Let's live to hear that from our Father. Let's live a servant's life here on earth.

Day 286

Today's Scripture:

"Don't yield to your fear. Have faith in me" (Luke 8:50 TPT).

Today's Testimony:

I was eleven years old when I accepted Jesus as my Savior. I was sitting with my grandparents when I felt the need to go to the altar. I don't remember the speaker, message, or songs, but I remember the tug of the Holy Spirit calling me to follow Jesus. My grandmother was thrilled when I made that decision. I remember her wrapping her big arms around me and squeezing me afterward. Unfortunately, I didn't grow in my faith and start "following" Jesus until I experienced a series of personal challenges and tragedies—each one drawing me closer to Him. It was then I made a true commitment—when Jesus showed His love for me through my healing.

I had just had a mammogram. The next day, I received an email letting me know the results were in, and when I opened the results, the mammogram said there was a lump in my right breast.

I asked the Lord what to do about it, and He simply said to me, "Trust Me." I didn't go into panic mode with the news. Shortly after reading the results, I received a phone call from the physician's office letting me know they needed to schedule me for a repeat mammogram and ultrasound to confirm what the radiologist had found.

I asked Jesus who I could talk to about it, and He gave me the name of one friend who has stood on the Word of God for her own healing in many areas for years. She is the only one I was allowed to talk to about it. I called her, and she asked me how I felt. I told her, "It's stupid. I don't have time for it, and I don't believe it's true. I have felt nothing in my breasts." She agreed to stand in agreement with me and prayed with me right then and there. I remember telling her, "When I have that repeat mammogram and ultrasound, I want to hear, 'There's nothing there.'"

In the three weeks leading up to my repeat imaging, I stood on the Word of God for my healing like I had never done before. One day, I was reading in Daniel about Shadrach, Meshach, and Abednego, and I heard the enemy ask me, "What if God doesn't heal you?" I told him, "Even if He doesn't heal me, I WILL NOT bow to fear."

—Kari
(To Be Continued in Tomorrow's Reading)

Today's Takeaway:

Talk about standing up to the enemy! Kari answered him in faith. That's the bravest thing a Christian can do—decide even if things don't go our way, we will still serve Him. Our enemy simply doesn't know what to do with that. Faith like that stumps him and pleases God.

Day 287

Today's Scripture:

"You parents—if your children ask for a loaf of bread,
do you give them a stone instead?" (Matthew 7:9 NLT).

Today's Testimony *(Continued From Previous Day)*:

The weekend before my repeat imaging, I got a phone call from my physician's office, urging me to make sure I get the imaging done. I could tell by the tone of the caller's voice that they felt I had cancer. The night before my appointment, I was pacing my house, praying and reading through healing declarations. I don't think I have ever felt like my prayers and declarations were as powerful as they were that night. When I finished, I felt in my spirit like something had happened, something powerful.

The day of my repeat imaging, my husband had a doctor's appointment in the same city. I pulled into the hospital, and seeing the questioning look on his face, I commented I was getting a mammogram, nothing big. He went into the waiting room with me, and they called me back shortly thereafter. Throughout the entire process, I had such peace. I remember thanking God for that peace that passes understanding and telling Him I trusted Him, no matter the outcome. I thanked Him for this trial that drew me to Him, for increasing my ability to trust Him no matter what.

Soon the nurse came back and asked me to follow her. We walked into the imaging room again where my clothing was, and she said to me, "You can get dressed. There's nothing there." I immediately said, "God did this!" She looked at me questioningly, and I said to her, "GOD DID THIS! I have stood on His Word and His faithfulness throughout this whole thing, and I asked to hear, 'There is nothing there' after this appointment. You said those exact words." She left me to get dressed, and when I came out, she led me to the exit door. As she led me out, I saw her wiping her eyes.

When I got to my car, I explained to my husband what God had just done. I called my friend and told her, and she screamed, "God came through for you. Hallelujah!" We had a praise party on speaker phone.

A few days later, I was standing in my kitchen, and I asked Jesus, "Why would You do that for me? Why me?" There were so many prayers I have prayed that I felt like He didn't hear or answer for me, so why this one? I clearly heard Him say, "If you ask Me for bread, would I give you a stone?" Of course not, Lord. Hallelujah!

—Kari

Today's Takeaway:

There are times that we pray for things and God says no. That's a hard thing to hear—no matter if you're a toddler or an adult. We have to understand that God loves us, no matter what answer He gives. When He says yes, we praise Him; when He says no, we should praise Him. We can trust Him to do what's best because He loves us.

Day 288

Today's Scripture:

"For God presented Jesus as the sacrifice for sin. People are made right with God when they believe that Jesus sacrificed his life, shedding his blood. This sacrifice shows that God was being fair when he held back and did not punish those who sinned in times past, for he was looking ahead and including them in what he would do in this present time. God did this to demonstrate his righteousness, for he himself is fair and just, and he makes sinners right in his sight when they believe in Jesus" (Romans 3:25-26 NLT).

Today's Testimony:

I had an amazing childhood. My parents were traveling children's evangelists, so my whole summers were full of Jesus, cotton candy, and bounce houses. When I turned nine my family planted and pastored a church, so I have always had Jesus in my life.

Middle school and high school were much harder years for me. I had a difficult time making friends, and everyone knows kids can be mean sometimes. At the same time throughout those years, I got myself into an unhealthy relationship. This person was mentally abusive and pulled me further from God. The result of this was that I started to sin. I found myself at a dead end and felt like I couldn't go on with everything that was happening and what I was feeling. I felt stuck and was in the darkest place I had ever been. I remember crying out to God one day asking for Him to save me, and asking for forgiveness of the sins I had committed while drifting away from our relationship. I was home alone at the age of fourteen when I rededicated my life to Christ. I got back on the right track and removed myself from that toxic relationship. I made the decision to step away from people who were bad influences on me.

I started to focus on my relationship with Jesus and people who treated me well. Now I am so blessed and happy and serving God.

—*Autumn*

Today's Takeaway:

The strong foundation Autumn had from all the teaching she'd heard growing up in her children's ministry paradise came charging through in an instant. Even though she was alone, she remembered what to do when she was in a desperate place—cry out to her Father. She knew to pray and ask forgiveness. And He answered. Then everything changed. Suddenly, she had the strength to make the changes that needed to happen in her life. Way to go, Autumn!

Are you in a place where it's time to make some tough decisions? Are you struggling with the strength to do the right thing? You don't have to do it alone. Your Father helps you to "be strong in the Lord and in the power of His might" (Ephesians 6:10 NKJV).

Day 289

Today's Scripture:

"This is my command—be strong and courageous! Do not be afraid or discouraged. For the Lord your God is with you wherever you go" (Joshua 1:9 NLT).

Today's Testimony:

I remember the evening I was saved. I was watching the Billy Graham Crusade with my parents. George Beverly Shea was singing, "Just as I Am" and my heart was opened to God. I was only thirteen years old, and I was searching for peace, love, joy, and a sense of belonging. And I found it all, in Him. I prayed right then and there to be saved and for God's guidance in my life and that He would fill the emptiness I felt.

Years passed and I was looking for a church where I could feel like I was part of the family of God. A coworker invited me to her church. She and her husband picked me up and took me to their small church. Everyone was so friendly and inviting. The pastor was approachable and knew everyone by name.

He offered a baptism class. I went to the classes and after the third one, I was baptized. When I was lifted out of the water, I knew what it felt like to be a child of God. I finally felt complete, and to this day this church is my home.

I've gone through some valleys in my walk with God, but He always reminds me I am never alone. I went through a very difficult time during which many tragedies hit me, all within just weeks of each other: I was in a car accident and nearly died; I suffered the loss of my youngest son, the loss of my nephew, and the loss of my sister's husband. I nearly fell apart; and I would have if it were not for the supernatural grace and strength of my Savior.

I am so thankful I had a church family to reach out to at that time. My pastor's wife was so kind and reminded me Jesus holds us when we don't have the strength on our own. It's true. I have felt the arms of my loving Jesus hold me and comfort me, when nothing else could have. I wouldn't have made it without Him. I will never leave His side. I need Him. I am home and I belong.

—*Michelle*

Today's Takeaway:

It's no wonder God wants us to fellowship with other believers. The early church met together regularly and shared everything they had. They made sure needs were met and people were cared for. This is exactly what Michelle's church did for her. How beautiful it is when God's people serve one another!

Are you involved in a local church? You need the teaching, fellowship, care, and accountability the local church provides. Find one and be faithful. It's absolutely necessary to your spiritual health. You need them and they need you.

Day 290

Today's Scripture:

"For this son of mine was dead and is alive again; he was lost and is found"
(Luke 15:24 NIV).

Today's Testimony:

I didn't know, with certainty, that I was saved until God sent a messenger to me with a wakeup call. Being raised Catholic, I already believed Jesus died for my sins and He was my Savior. I had said the words years before, but didn't understand them fully. Then one day, while I was in my backyard pulling weeds, I looked up and saw a young man standing on the other side of the fence, looking at me. I wasn't afraid although I knew the man didn't live next door, and I never heard or saw him coming. He never told me his name and never asked mine; all he said was, "Are you saved?"

"I don't know," I answered. Then he asked me to come with him to his church on Sunday. I told him I would think about it, and started to walk away, but then I turned back and he was gone. I called my sister and asked her if I was saved. "Of course," she said "Don't you remember saying the prayer at my house years ago?"

I remembered, but I didn't know what it really meant. I told her about the man and she told me not to go with him, since I didn't know him. I prayed about it and felt like God spoke to me. I believed he was a messenger from God to help me realize what being saved meant. I realized I needed to make some changes.

I asked God for a way out of the life I was living. I had no money, no job, and three small children. I realized I had to leave the man with whom I lived. I knew I needed to "start over" with God's help. I got on my knees and asked His forgiveness, and I heard, "Welcome home, prodigal daughter."

—*Roseanne*

Today's Takeaway:

God uses circumstances and people to get our attention. At any given moment, He knows our thoughts and what's going on in our lives. He told the Samaritan woman at the well the details of her living situation. She knew she didn't know Him—*but he knew her.* There are times when He sends witnesses into our paths to help us think about Him and what we're doing. I'm so glad Roseanne listened and responded to Him. Things change for the better when we call on His name. He's always ready for a "start-over."

Day 291

Today's Scripture:

"But seek first the kingdom of God and His righteousness, and all these things shall be added to you" (Matthew 6:33 NKJV).

Today's Testimony:

Many years ago my husband and I decided to join a church. At the time, we had a two-year-old son and wanted him to be raised in a Christian home. A year later, we had another son, and then my husband accepted a job offer in a different state. After moving, we didn't go back to church, but still claimed to be Christians. A few years later, we moved back home, but still didn't reconnect with the local congregation. My husband's job was demanding and sometimes required long hours. The boys were now older and involved in all the school activities. We were "too busy" to make time for church. I realize, now, that these were all simply excuses.

Then, years later I had a horrible reaction to a medication I was taking and had to go to the emergency room. I was treated and sent home around 3:00 the next morning. I got home and went to bed, then around 7 a.m., I woke up with the most severe cramp in my right leg. I jumped out of bed, not realizing I was standing so close to the nightstand. I bent over to touch my leg and hit the nightstand, face first. It was such a bad blow that I needed medical attention.

The doctor said I was a very fortunate woman; if I had been three inches lower, I could have had a very serious injury—like a karate chop under the nose that could have killed me. It took three months to recover, and for the bruising to go away.

I began to think a lot about what would have happened if I had died. Was I really ready to go? My answer was no . . . I wasn't ready. I knew I had to not only get back in church but, more importantly, get back to the altar and rededicate my heart to Him.

I did just that! And I have been faithful ever since. I will never again let a reason or excuse keep me from my Christian walk. I know when I seek the Lord, and put Him first, then everything else will fall into place. I thank God this happened. I tell everyone that sometimes it takes a dramatic incident for Him to get our attention. In my case, I'm very glad He did.

—*Carol*

Today's Takeaway:

Carol has spoken wise words. She realized everything she used to keep her from the Lord were all excuses—and they're dangerous. They seem so innocent at the time, but they're used by Satan to prevent us from growing close to God, and from getting stronger in our faith, more powerful in our praying, deeper in our knowledge of the Word of God, more faithful in our witness to the world. See how a simple excuse can hinder you? Beware!

Day 292

Today's Scripture:

"And we know that all things work together for good to those who love God, to those who are the called according to His purpose" (Romans 8:28 NKJV).

Today's Testimony:

Can you imagine leaving Bible study, heading home, getting into the turning lane for your street when you see a driver coming straight toward you head-on? Seconds later, you realize your vehicle has been spun out of control facing oncoming traffic.

As a mother I had to quickly gather myself together as best as I could with the cries of my young sons who were traveling with me. Next, I looked up and saw a semi-truck coming toward my SUV. I didn't realize that the driver of the semi-truck was planning to use his truck to block any further vehicles from hitting me and my sons. I later learned the individual who hit me and my sons was intoxicated, driving with a suspended license without any proof of insurance.

Thank God I had given my heart to Jesus, because I knew who to call on. I was praying—grateful that, with the exception of some bruising and scars, my sons and I were alive. I didn't realize life as I knew it was about to take a drastic turn.

Quickly, I received a letter in the mail, stating there was a warrant out for my arrest related to the car accident. How could this be? I was facing jail time, fines, court proceedings, attorney fees, and most importantly looking at the possibility of not seeing my children! Satan tried to torment my mind with all the things I was being faced with, yet I desperately held onto my faith. This went on for months and finally, in the end, I came out victorious as my heavenly Father said He would be a lawyer in the courtroom, and He had the final verdict.

Immediately, after all my family had been through, then came the Covid-19 pandemic. My mother and my aunt contracted the virus. Sadly, I lost my aunt to the virus. My mother laid in the hospital on a ventilator fighting for her life. I took the stand with my three sisters that we would pray together on the phone for our mother each morning, believing God would bring her through.

—*Shamea*
(To Be Continued in Tomorrow's Reading)

Today's Takeaway:

Sometimes it seems that every trouble and trial gets unleashed in our lives at the same time. It's during these rough and rocky times that we must cling to God, like holding onto a ship's mast through a hurricane. That's what Shamea made up her mind to do. She had been saved, so she knew to trust God and believe. She and her sisters called on God.

That's the blueprint to follow—trust and obey. Trust God and obey His Word that says to pray. Trust and obey—there is no other way!

Day 293

Today's Scripture:

"The Lord watches over those who obey him, those who trust in his constant love"
(Psalm 33:18 GNT).

Today's Testimony *(Continued From Previous Day)*:

Through God's miraculous power, my mother beat Covid-19 and is alive and striving today because of our faith in God. He is a miracle worker and a promise keeper. Later my father also contracted Covid-19 and was diagnosed with kidney cancer. However, he is still living and is a miracle as well.

The enemy wanted me to keep my eyes on everything I had to deal with, but in the end I had to remember that all things were working for my good. You see, I had some things I had been praying for—closer relationships with my sisters, their salvation, and more. God worked through the daily prayers for our mother; they saw God's power as He healed our mother. After having to take time off from work to prepare for trial, I was able to start my own business. I am now the proud owner of a boutique.

Through all of the court proceedings, I witnessed so many things and I realized not everyone who is incarcerated is a criminal. From this, God called me into the prison ministry to be a witness that God is a deliverer, since He has delivered me and my family from so many things. Who would have thought that all the chaos I had to go through was going to ultimately work out for my good? I have learned to trust God with everything in me. My prayer life has changed, and I'm now a prayer warrior; I feel my faith is stronger now.

Know that if God is for you, it doesn't matter if the world is against you. God is a rewarder to those who diligently seek Him. "All things work together for good to those who love God, to those who are the called according to His purpose" (Romans 8:28 NKJV).

—*Shamea*

Today's Takeaway:

God grants victory and blesses His girls as they serve Him and trust Him. Shamea and her sisters waited on God and trusted Him. He healed their mother *and* touched their dad. Then God turned the very accident that terrified and weighed her down into a blessing in her life. She saw God deliver her and then turn it around for her good.

God knows just what He's doing to cause us to triumph. He watches over us. He used the trials she had faced to make her stronger in faith and prayer. Maybe our difficulties are worth it after all.

Day 294

Today's Scripture:

"Now faith is the substance of things hoped for, the evidence of things not seen. For by it the elders obtained a good report. Through faith we understand that the worlds were framed by the word of God, so that things which are seen were not made of things which do appear. . . . But without faith it is impossible to please him: for he that cometh to God must believe that he is, and that he is a rewarder of them that diligently seek him" (Hebrews 11:1-3, 6 KJV).

Today's Testimony:

I have given my life to Christ; I'm so thankful He saved my soul. He is my provider, my guide, and my shield. He watches over me with His love and care.

Life has been very tough at times. There are many different battles to face in our walk with God. I am a twelve-year, late-stage cancer survivor.

As of late, recent PET/CAT scans and biopsies have found my body to be cancer-free. My loving God—with all the prayers from my pastor and his wife, and the prayer warriors at my church—has brought me through. God is my healer. My life is dedicated to God and I have been so very blessed. Every day I have, I will give Him praise.

—Dora

Today's Takeaway:

It takes faith to come to a saving knowledge of Christ—we must believe God exists and that His Son hung on a cross for us, died, and rose again on the third day. It takes faith to believe He's coming back to take those who live for Him, and have Him in their hearts, to Heaven someday. It also takes faith to trust Him when we hear the scary word *cancer*.

We know God is our healer. His back was striped to pay for our healing (1 Peter 2:24). We take our needs to Him and call on Him in prayer. That's what Dora did. That's what Christians do when we need healing. We read the Word, we pray, we ask fellow believers to pray—we keep it up, and we have faith. Then we trust God's answer. Paul said, "To live is Christ, and to die is gain" (Philippians 1:21 KJV). He knew if God had another plan for him, Heaven would be a gain. That's hard, I know, but we must think about Heaven as it really is—*wonderful*. And trust Him!

Day 295

Today's Scripture:

"Let us love one another, for love comes from God" (1 John 4:7 NIV).

Today's Testimony:

It all began when I was nine. My parents were driving home from our aunt's house on Thanksgiving Day. My dad fell asleep, intoxicated, and my mom was driving and fell asleep at the wheel. We crashed about a mile from our home. I ran for help. With the grace of God, we all survived, but my dad was paralyzed from the waist down.

After that day, I went to church on Sunday with my neighbors—all kinds of churches, but I knew God was calling me there. When I was ten, my mom left my dad and all of us kids behind. My neighbors and other family friends took care of us a lot. During this time, I was molested by my best friend's dad and my life was never the same.

I was angry, hurt, and didn't have a lot of guidance during this time. I started dating and soon I became a teen mom at the age of fifteen. I married at eighteen, and was married for twenty-four years. After enduring a lot of adultery from my husband, the marriage finally ended in divorce, leaving me with the children to raise alone. I decided, since I'd been married most of my life, I'd find out what it was like to live the "single life"—the wild version.

I went through many bad days of going to clubs, partying, dating, and thinking this was how life was supposed to be. I was cheated on many times and accepted it as OK. I wanted to feel loved. Finally, one night I was with a man who left me on a back road, and I had to walk home for miles. I was almost hit by a car and thought, *What am I doing?* I got home, finally safe, and sat in my room crying for days. I asked God, "What do I do with myself?" I heard Him say it was time to reflect on my life.

I decided to leave that lifestyle behind; then I met a man of God. We talked about the Lord and it was wonderful. Eventually, we fell in love and got married. We read the Bible together. He asked me if I'd ever accepted God into my heart, and I said no. I fell in love with the stories of the Bible and he asked me if I wanted to accept Christ, and I did. I was led to Christ by my husband, and I will always be grateful for that.

—*Elsa*

Today's Takeaway:

Elsa had endured so much pain, hurt, and rejection. She began to think that was how life was supposed to be for her. How opposite to the truth! How I hate the enemy for making her believe that. Her Father tenderly waited on her to be ready to hear the wonderful truth that she was worth far more. He sent her "Prince Charming" to lead her to Him. Your Father loves you that much too. He wants to bless you like that—and even more!

Day 296

Today's Scripture:

"Christ has redeemed us from the curse of the law" (Galatians 3:13 NKJV).

Today's Testimony:

I am glad to share the goodness, faithfulness, and love of God in my life. I went to church sporadically as a child. My life started out normal. I had loving parents. We would pray and read our bedtime Bible stories at night. As a young girl, I remember going to Sunday school at church, and learning to pray.

But things got hard, quick. My father was diagnosed with terminal cancer, and from that point on, everything was centered on him. His decline was traumatic to see. But thankfully, he received the Lord on his deathbed. After that, I quit going to church. Oh, I'd go occasionally with family and friends, but there was no commitment on my part. My mom was heartbroken and suffered from depression after my father died. And then three years later, she died. Soon after, my maternal grandparents followed her home. My mother and grandparents were my spiritual witness. I felt lost without them. I felt bombarded by death. I no longer had any strong Christian influences in my life, so I was left to question, all alone, "Why, God? Why?"

I didn't hear any answers . . . *So why not party and enjoy life like the world does?* And so I did. But after "living in the world," getting married, and having a child, I wanted more. I *knew* something was missing.

I remember the day God met me on the floor in my kitchen; I cried out to Him and He forgave me. Then He provided for me. He actually *sent* someone to repair a roof I had no money to repair. From then on, I started to learn to rely on *Him* for all my needs. And there were many, many needs. My life took a few more twists and turns: more kids, divorce, alcoholism in my family, loss of homes. But in the midst of it all, God, my heavenly Father, took care of me. He picked me up and encouraged me. He carried me through. He is truly a Father to the fatherless.

In time, I found a home church. One day, I felt as if someone walked down the pew and stood next to me. And then Galatians 3:13 popped into my head. I remembered that my dad had died on 3/13, and I was reminded, "Christ has redeemed us from the curse of the law." I am so grateful to my Lord and Savior, Jesus Christ, for redeeming me.

—*Gerry*

Today's Takeaway:

There is such a painful feeling of loneliness when parents or grandparents die. Gerry must have felt like the world was ending for her. The good news is, God picks us up and carries us when we can't go on. He strengthens us until we can make it. He is the lifter of our head (Psalm 3:3).

Day 297

Today's Scripture:

*"They couldn't stand the thought of food, and they were knocking on death's door.
'Lord, help!' they cried in their trouble, and he saved them from their distress.
He sent out his word and healed them, snatching them from the door of death"*
(Psalm 107:18-20 NLT).

Today's Testimony:

My dad was my pastor. I knew everything I needed to be saved. I knew the doctrines of the church. I had already been baptized in water. I would read the Bible and teach children and teenagers.

I had witnessed many miracles in the church and in our family—people who had been miraculously healed instantly, others freed from oppression. I had also witnessed how God baptized many in the church with His Spirit. How many extraordinary and powerful testimonies had my eyes seen and my ears heard!

Now I was a young married woman with a beautiful girl and carrying another baby in my womb. My husband was a telephone-company manager. I really liked that—it made me happy to have my husband *just for our family.* I had asked the Lord from a very young age to give me a Christian man, *but not a pastor.* I had already been the daughter of a pastor; I felt that was enough. When we got married, my husband had no interest in being a pastor (or so I thought), even though he was a faithful believer and loved God.

Now on this day, as I read the Word of God, a feeling of helplessness and doom took hold of me. I saw myself before the Lord. I realized I was empty, sick, lost! I began to cry, and the clarity of a beautiful tropical day was like the clarity of my interior—of my spiritual situation! I fell to my knees and exclaimed: "Oh God, I could be lost for eternity!" I couldn't say anything else. I was just crying intensely. That was the day I *really* gave my heart to God unreservedly. God saved me! He healed my interior being.

Many extraordinary experiences happened after that time—I read the Bible with passion, I turned my issues over to the Lord. God baptized me with His Holy Spirit with the sign of tongues. God called my husband, my children, and me, to the pastoral ministry. I began to rejoice in everything our good God had planned.

—*Miriam*

Today's Takeaway:

Moments of clarity are sometimes scary, aren't they? I'm with Miriam. Sometimes I see myself (or my motives) clearly, and it's not pretty. Miriam saw and that truth drove her to cry out to God in desperation. Perfect answer to that situation! When the Holy Spirit pricks you, waste no time; surrender whatever the situation is to Him immediately. He is the answer!

Day 298

Today's Scripture:

"For just as the heavens are higher than the earth, so my ways are higher than your ways and my thoughts higher than your thoughts" (Isaiah 55:9 NLT).

Today's Testimony:

It was in the summer—June to be exact—that God put it on my heart to go back to school to be a young adults pastor. This had never crossed my mind before and was not something I had ever seen myself doing. First, I didn't like speaking in front of groups of people; and next, I was *not* living a life that was in any condition to lead a group, especially not one that involved helping young adults grow closer to God. *How could I do such a thing, God? I am not qualified for this!* But despite my feelings, I was willing to pursue what He was putting on my heart because I knew it *was* Him; but I was completely torn.

See, I believed in God, but I was *not* living for Him. In this moment where God met me, I was in a low place. I was just moments away from pursuing a sex change because I felt God had made a mistake with me and I should have really been a boy. I had felt that way my whole life and had never felt comfortable in my own skin. I had gone through a failed suicide attempt, was heavily into drinking and taking pills, and I had been involved in many same-sex relationships in the ten years leading up to this moment. So, when I say I was *far* from qualified to become a pastor, that's an understatement!

Despite all this, I knew He was calling me into ministry. And even though none of it made sense, I told Him, "OK, God, this is not by my own desires that I pursue this; but because I know for a fact it's what You're wanting from me, I'm willing to take the necessary steps, but You have to make a way because, right now, I see no way this could ever be good."

—*Sarah*
(To Be Continued in Tomorrow's Reading)

Today's Takeaway:

God's plans don't always make sense to us, do they? They won't always even make sense to the person standing beside us. That's because we see from a human perspective. We can't know what God knows. We can't see what God sees. But He does. Who could look at Sarah's life and guess God was calling her? Not even Sarah understood but that didn't matter; God understood! I'm just thrilled that Sarah had the willingness to obey Him.

Tomorrow we'll see what happened for Sarah; but right now, think about this: Are you willing to do what doesn't make sense when God directs you? It's a scary thought, isn't it? We like for things to make perfect sense, but they won't always work out that way. We have to commit to following God no matter what. Will you do that? Try today to tell Him you will give it your best to follow even when you can't understand—then give it your best!

Day 299

Today's Scripture:

"We know that God makes all things work together for the good of those who love Him and are chosen to be a part of His plan" (Romans 8:28 NLV).

Today's Testimony *(Continued From Previous Day):*

I also made an agreement with God that I would not pursue any relationships with any woman during this time; I would just focus on Him and my relationship with Him so I had no distractions, and could grow deeper in Him as I discovered where it was He was taking me. Through that obedience, God led me down this three-year journey of a deep and intimate growth in my relationship with Him. I finally got to meet the God I had heard about—the God of miracles!

He used those three years it took for me to get my degree to completely rock my world, and He allowed me to see Him for who He really is. He's an amazing and faithful Father who loves His children so much that He's willing to leave the ninety-nine to go after that one who strayed away from Him. He helped me not only to fall in love with the One who created me, but also to fall in love with the beautiful creation He made in me. He allowed me to see myself through His eyes—a beautiful woman who was unique and wonderfully made. He slowly stripped away the desires of my heart that were not of Him and he tore down every lie Satan had placed in my life. I found myself standing there in a new light, no longer recognizable to the world.

So, there I was at the end of this journey, doing an internship at a church serving in a young adults ministry. I had been given my first opportunity to speak in front of the whole church. Despite the nerves and anxiousness, I got up there and did what I knew God wanted me to do, not knowing the man God had for me was sitting in the crowd for his first time at the church. On that day my whole life changed. God brought that man to me after service, and the rest is history. On Thanksgiving Day that year, he asked me to marry him. Two years later we welcomed our beautiful baby girl into this world and are currently both assistant pastors together in our church. "With God all things are possible" (Matthew 19:26 NIV).

—*Sarah*

Today's Takeaway:

God knew His plan all along—and what a beautiful plan it was. I cried reading what He had lined up for Sarah. All that time and struggle, and *this* was what He was leading her toward. How wonderful our Father is to His girls!

Doesn't that make you want His plan for you? I do! He has plans to prosper you and not to do you harm; He wants to give you a future and a hope. I know that's what you want too. Then let's submit to Him. He's pretty great at this planning thing.

Day 300

Today's Scripture:

"For you bless the godly, O Lord; you surround them with your shield of love"
(Psalm 5:12 NLT).

Today's Testimony:

I was raised as a pastor's kid. This meant I was born in a Christian home, whether I chose that life or not. My parents didn't force me to believe, but I was required to go to any church event, participate in family prayer, and attend church every Sunday.

When I was in middle school, I started to struggle with my identity and self-worth. I didn't love myself, so I tried to find love in other things, such as inappropriate things online and unhealthy relationships with other girls my age. I started turning away from the Lord and focusing on more worldly values. These actions caused me to spiral into depression and anger.

One summer the church I was going to decided to take the youth group to summer camp. My parents had signed me up, and my best friend at the time, someone who was also caught in the things I was caught up in, decided she didn't want to go, which meant I had to go alone. At camp I was forced to surround myself with positive people who, like me, were struggling with many things, except they were happy through their pain because they trusted that God would take care of it.

One night at camp during worship, I opened my heart to God and decided I would give Him a chance. Something shifted in the atmosphere of the sanctuary that night. I found myself crying with another girl as we worshiped the Lord for loving messy people like us. I truly accepted and believed in God for myself, and I have not been the same since.

—*Rachel*

Today's Takeaway:

God loves Rachel so much. He surrounded her with His love at that camp through people who trusted Him—she could see it! Then He wrapped her up with His love in that sanctuary—she could feel it! Something did shift that night. There was a shift in her future. The enemy had to let go of his plans for her, because she made up her mind to follow God's plans for her life. No wonder she worshiped! I'm worshiping too! She'll never be the same.

Once you let go of your plans and embrace His, you'll never be the same either. Those plans will take you places you will never imagine. God will amaze you. His plans for you are BIG! OK, God, we're all in!

Day 301

Today's Scripture:

"Guide my steps by your word, so I will not be overcome by evil" (Psalm 119:133 NLT).

Today's Testimony:

As a little girl I struggled with the addictions of my mother and father, and later had to be adopted. The addictions and dysfunction from my family drove me to seek out God. I got saved and I found that He, and He alone, could bind up the wounds of my childhood.

During my teenage years I valued my gift of music. It helped me get through school, which I wasn't a fan of. As I moved on in life and grew up, I longed to be loved by a stable, godly man and was blessed when that prayer came true. I then became pregnant with our first child, only to endure a life-threatening, ruptured ectopic pregnancy that resulted in the loss of our first child. We were crushed, but continued to pray without ceasing that God would bless us with another child. Due to the ruptured ectopic pregnancy, my chances of having another child was cut in half. Would I even be able to have children now?

Praise God, He provided! We later were overjoyed with the birth of our first son, and then God once again blessed us with a second son. We couldn't believe the overwhelming grace of God. Years have passed since then, and now God even graced us with wonderful daughters-in-law and grandchildren.

By the grace of God I am a very blessed woman. That doesn't mean life has been perfect. There have been times in life that I failed God, when I felt it was not worth living. Today, however, I have committed my life to living out the plan God has for me. I know that prayers from family and friends have kept me. I've learned God is sovereign, and all things really do work together for good, according to His purpose (Romans 8:28).

—*Josie*

Today's Takeaway:

Josie didn't let the struggles of her beginning determine her ending. She held on to God and He saw her through the difficulty of her early years. I'm telling you, there is nothing like having that assurance to strengthen you through the difficult times of school. Ha! School can be a tough atmosphere!

Whom are we kidding? The job place can be a tough atmosphere at some places. Hold God's hand and let Him make you *fierce*. God and you make a majority. Be kind, but determined to be different!

Day 302

Today's Scripture:

"'*For my thoughts are not your thoughts, neither are your ways my ways,' declares the Lord. 'As the heavens are higher than the earth, so are my ways higher than your ways and my thoughts than your thoughts*'" (Isaiah 55:8-9 NIV).

Today's Testimony:

I was six years old in the second children's church service. My parents were the children's directors at the time; they led the first service and my aunt led the second. I honestly don't remember much of it, but I know I gave my heart to Jesus that morning. I didn't *feel* much different. Whenever I've been in a group that is asked to share their testimony, I've shied away because I thought I didn't have a good one. You know, the one where God revives their soul in a dramatic and amazing way? Those are the goose-bump-giving testimonies people typically want to hear. My testimony *started* with getting saved as a child—so anticlimactic. Or so I thought.

I was a "good girl" who went to church three times a week, loved serving, got good grades, and rarely did anything "bad." How boring. However, as I've matured and grown I recognize that "Amazing grace, how sweet the sound, that saved a wretch like me" was not a onetime event. It's a continual grace. We're human, and we make mistakes; even the good girls and boys—the individuals who feel like there's not much to be saved from. That's one of the most deadly lies the enemy likes to use to get us to believe we're better than what we really are—that our need for a Savior isn't that desperate.

I look back and see the hand of God in my life. I didn't recognize it at the moment, but I had a gift of discernment and others would verbalize it in this way: "You have wisdom beyond your years." I grew up hearing the quiet voice of God nudging me, and I definitely felt His conviction and correction when I did something wrong. As an adult and mother of four young children, I see the beauty in being raised the way I was. I still went through very difficult times; especially as I went off to college and continued with graduate school. I made life-altering decisions, ones I regret and wish I could change, but at the same time I'm thankful as those mistakes have made me who I am today, through God's restoration and healing.

—Rachel

Today's Takeaway:

I can't help but smile when I read about children who give their hearts to God in children's church. So much time and energy go into preparation for those services to help children understand Jesus loves them and gave His life for them. It's thrilling to hear when all that work pays off. It's the greatest testimony of all when a child comes to know the Lord and outsmarts the enemy's traps laid out for him or her and walks with God, avoiding the deep pain of horrific sin.

Day 303

Today's Scripture:

"Defend the weak and the fatherless; uphold the cause of the poor and the oppressed.
Rescue the weak and the needy; deliver them from the hand of the wicked"
(Psalm 82:3-4 NIV).

Today's Testimony:

I was a child of the '60s and was abused daily by my mom. This was so difficult for me; all I wanted was her love. When I was eight years old, I heard God audibly tell me, "*I* love you." This happened every day for two weeks. But I didn't know who God was. About a year later, I learned of God's loving gift—His Son, Jesus; and I received salvation. My home life didn't change, but my heart did. I had compassion for my mom. Christ's love filled my heart.

From there, God led me into a deliverance ministry. Now, as an adult, the Lord's call on my life is to defend the defenseless. I am passionate about seeing people set free. As a former victim of abuse, with nobody in my home to defend me, God has given me a high calling—to help the helpless.

For thirty-five years now, I have been ministering to people and seeing them set free in the name of Jesus Christ and by His power. I'd never trade my experiences for anything. What we go through makes us who we are. Our fiery trials are a purification of our faith. I'm pressing toward the mark of the high calling of God (see Philippians 3:14).

—*Laurie*

Today's Takeaway:

God has put a tender compassion in Laurie's heart because of what she went through as a child. God uses our experiences. No one will understand quite as well as she will the pain a person in that situation undergoes. God knows that and places gifts and talents in people He can use to minister to others in that situation. He calls people to bless others with their empathy and love. How wonderful!

What have you been called to do for the Lord? Are you doing it? What experiences have you been through that you could help someone with? God will give you the words to say to help them. Just make yourself available to Him. He'll open a door for you.

Day 304

Today's Scripture:

"The Lord is my strength and my shield; in him my heart trusts, and I am helped; my heart exults, and with my song I give thanks to him" (Psalm 28:7 ESV).

Today's Testimony:

I was diagnosed with severe Ménière's disease, and lost 80 percent of my hearing. This was devastating because I play the piano by ear and sing on our worship team. My ear specialist said I'd be deaf within six months. It was getting harder and harder to be on the worship team. Finally, I told our music director I was going to step down. She told me God was going to heal me. I knew that was what it would take because God had saved my soul and I walked with Him. I knew His power—He had forgiven my sins! After being off the worship team for several weeks, I heard the Spirit of the Lord say, "If you take one step, I'll take two." I told Him, "Lord, I don't want to look stupid going up there . . . I won't be able to hear." He just said, "Trust Me."

So, I started walking forward to the piano. As I walked, my ears started popping and the fullness that was in my ear was gone—the ringing, gone! I started playing the piano with the praise team. I could hear without any special devices; I knew God had healed me!

I went back to my ear specialist the following week and they ran their tests. The doctor said, "This is remarkable; you have regained all of your hearing except for 11 percent in one ear, and 15 percent in the other." He said he had never seen such a remarkable comeback and mentioned putting me in his medical journal.

This vertigo that I dealt with had gotten so bad I had to use a wheelchair, a walker, or a cane because of my balance issues. But one morning, after our pastor finished his sermon, I went up to the keyboard to play the music for the altar call. About halfway up the aisle, it was as if someone grabbed the cane right out of my hand and threw it. And it landed on the altar!

For a brief moment, I said, "Oh, Jesus, what do I do now? How am I going to make it to the front without falling?" Again, I heard, "Trust Me." The anointing of the Holy Spirit came upon me in that moment, and said, "Walk."

I started walking across the front, to the altar. I walked back and forth. My husband told me afterward, "You ran across the front, and I knew you were healed!" Well, I haven't used my cane since that day. Each day is a step, to be taken one at a time; and every day, I hear Him say, "Trust Me."

—*Val*

Today's Takeaway:

God is all-powerful! He not only can wash away all our sin, but He can miraculously heal. Val heard the Lord tell her to step out in faith—she had to take the first step. But when she did, God met her faith with healing power.

Day 305

Today's Scripture:

"Only I can tell you the future before it even happens. Everything I plan will come to pass, for I do whatever I wish" (Isaiah 46:10 NLT).

Today's Testimony:

All my life I've been in church. I've always had a close relationship with the Lord. I never understood those who didn't want to follow Jesus. Turning down love never made sense to me.

At eight years old, my mama led me in the sinner's prayer at my bedside, and God has been working on me ever since. At fourteen, I was filled with the Holy Spirit. I was given a very bold spirit, so I wanted to share the Good News with everyone: teachers, other students, even complete strangers. My daddy never allowed us to act shy, so maybe it's his fault I can talk with anyone!

My life took a real turn when, in seventh grade, I fell head over heels in love with a boy I met. You may think that's too young, but God had a plan. He said, "You have just met your husband." The problem was, he wasn't a Christian. All through school I tried my best to get him to notice me. Nothing. Confused, I decided to fast and pray. So, I came home from school and let my mom know I was fasting and praying in my room. As the hours passed, I asked God to put me in His perfect will.

Suddenly, the room changed and I heard an audible voice quietly say my name. At first, I thought it was my mom. I looked around and no one was there. Once again, I knelt down and began praying. I heard my name again. This time, I realized it was God, so I answered, "Yes, my Lord, I am your handmaiden."

Then He gave me a vision. He showed me things that were going to happen in my coming years. He warned me not to allow this boy to pull me from the church; rather, I was to pull him in.

It came to pass just as God said it would! That boy came to the Lord and we later married. I never told him about going into the ministry; I wanted him to know it was God who called him. I watched him struggle for three years until *he* got "the call." We were at our home church, on a Sunday night, and he was at the altar, weeping before the Lord. I knew the exact moment it happened, *but God knew all along.*

—*Michele*

Today's Takeaway:

(Michele's words) He has been faithful to me! I have a new directive from God—to pray for people—my heartbeat is especially for pastors' wives. Galatians 6:9 says, "Let us not grow weary of doing good, for in due season we will reap [a harvest], if we do not give up" (ESV). God knows everything we will ever face!

Day 306

Today's Scripture:

"For what profit is it to a man if he gains the whole world, and loses his own soul?"
(Matthew 16:26 NKJV).

Today's Testimony:

Raised in a pastor's home, I was saved as a young child. I attended every service possible, I knew all the songs in the "Red Back" hymnal, and was able to quote Scripture, but that didn't mean I had it all together. I was a bit shy and hid in the background. There were many things I did for the church. Still, something was missing. I'd been going to church out of tradition. I never really had that personal relationship with the Lord. I guess I allowed the church to become commonplace.

Our church had just finished a book study: *Not a Fan* (Idleman, 2011). This study had stirred something in me and my husband. The question it left us with was, "Are we a fan of the things of the world or the things of God?" One day, as I was sitting in church, the most gut-wrenching feeling came over me. Then I heard, in my spirit, the Lord say, "What are you doing for My kingdom?" Wow! What *was* I doing for His kingdom?

This is where my new journey began. I knew I had to figure out where I was falling short. I asked the Lord for total guidance and direction in my life. I began to speak His Word into my life. After talking to my husband and pastor, we started a seniors group. I still felt the Lord leading me deeper. This was a scary thing, but the Lord took control and led me—now I am an ordained minister!

The senior group is still a big part of our ministry. My husband and I are now also the discipleship coordinators at our church. We're excited that the Lord has put us on this spiritual journey with Him. If you think your spiritual walk is out of tradition, my prayer is that my testimony will help you realize you're not alone. Begin to pray the words of Jesus, read His Word, worship Him, and Christ will take you places you've never been before.

—*Rebekah*

Today's Takeaway:

It's a BIG thing to have God Almighty ask you, "What are you doing for Me?" That's not a question you could just brush off, could you? Rebekah couldn't. It hit her hard! But that's when she decided to do something. She got down to business with God. She listened to Him and when He directed, she followed. I love that!

So, what are you doing for Him? I know, I'm not God. I'm just curious. You'll never be happier than when you're doing something for Him. Try it; you'll see.

Day 307

Today's Scripture:

"Trust in the Lord with all your heart and lean not on your own understanding.
In all your ways acknowledge Him, and He will make your paths straight"
(Proverbs 3:5-6 NASB).

Today's Testimony:

Saved and baptized as a young child, God loved me through all the wrong decisions I made, and brought me to where I am today. I left home at eighteen and served four years in the U.S. Navy. During that time, I indulged in worldly pleasures. And although the Holy Spirit convicted me, I continued to ignore Him. Homesick for my family, I fell into alcoholism and wrong relationships. During this time I gave God a backseat to my selfishness.

After dating for only five months, I married a man who was raised in the Buddhist culture. I didn't know how far I had fallen. Life became a world of hurt, depression, and insecurities. I ate to comfort myself. My "friends" backstabbed me. My husband was a "husband" in name only. I knew this wasn't God's plan for me. I had searched for love in the world, and found hopelessness.

Nothing filled the void in my heart—not until I was re-baptized and rededicated my life to God. That was the day my life changed. God gave me a fresh fire, a new love for His Word and His peace. He filled me with a sense of wholeness, and He took me to the next level.

After seventeen years and one child later, it became clear my marriage was over. God was drawing me to Himself. I sought prayer and the counsel of mature Christians, who all gave me the same direction and words. Everyone and everything that was of the world was being taken out of my life.

Through it all, God never left me, never gave up on me. His love was the very thing I needed, but it took so long to realize. God is showing me to let go and to trust Him completely.

—*Renee*

Today's Takeaway:

When we walk away from God, we leave that protection of being in His will—we tend to make poor choices and go down the wrong path for our lives. This leads to misery and frustration.

How much better it is to stay with the Lord. Stay in His will. Listen to His voice to keep from choosing something or someone that will lead us to painful consequences.

So, what if you've already gotten into the mess? Now what? First, repent. Talk it out with the Lord; He will listen, and loves you. Next, assess where you are. Read the Word to get guidance on what to do. Next, get godly counsel if you need it, then anchor yourself in the church and the Word.

Day 308

Today's Scripture:

"Jesus replied, 'You must love the Lord your God with all your heart, all your soul, and all your mind'" (Matthew 22:37 NLT).

Today's Testimony:

As a child going to church with my parents, I asked Jesus into my heart. There have been times I have felt like I wandered away from Christ. At those times I rededicated my life.

My goal is to show Jesus to someone every day by letting them see Jesus in me. I know I don't always accomplish this, but with God it is possible. I keep striving toward my goal.

My greatest example in learning to live my life for Christ was my mom. She was a great woman of faith and taught me with her actions the value of having a relationship with Jesus.

My hope and prayer now is that I can be that same example for my children. It's my greatest desire that they can learn from me about the value of having a relationship with Christ the way I learned from my mom. I pray that even though I fail often, they'll be able to see God's light in me.

As for me, I will continue to read my Bible and pray so I can grow in my relationship with Christ. I hope everyone who reads this will do the same.

—*Val*

Today's Takeaway:

They say the best way to push yourself to greater heights is by setting a goal. Val has set an awesome goal for herself, to show Jesus to someone every day—not by merely letting them see her "Jesus Saves" coffee mug at work, or hearing her *Amazing Grace* ringtone, but by actually seeing her actions. You know . . . how she treats waiters, cashiers, bill collectors, or grumpy family members. This is where "the rubber meets the road."

Let's all set this goal. Let's imagine Jesus is sitting beside us at every conversation, every transaction, every meeting—oh wait, He actually is. That can be scary if we think about it. Help us, Jesus!

We can have even more motivation when we think about our children watching our every move, learning from us, from our example, learning how to live when they become adults. Do we want them to become clones of us? Would that be OK? If not, we may have some work to do. Let's strive to reach that goal—then pass me that "Jesus Saves" mug, full of creamy coffee!

Day 309

Today's Scripture:

"Day by day the Lord takes care of the innocent, and they will receive an inheritance that lasts forever" (Psalm 37:18 NLT).

Today's Testimony:

The words to the Andraé Crouch song "Take Me Back" *took me back* to a revival service, sixty years ago. It was at our family church, and every night it was packed. A mighty move of the Holy Spirit fell upon us, and many gave their heart to the Lord. On the last night, the evangelist had all the teens and children come to the altar so he could pray over us. Some started singing and praising the Lord, while others were praying and shouting. What a time we were having in the Lord!

I was only eight years old, but I remember it like it was yesterday. I accepted the Lord into my life and was so happy and excited to be saved. I shared it with everyone I saw. Two years later in that same church, I was praying with my friend to be filled with the Holy Spirit, and while praying for her, I was filled. What an awesome God we serve!

I am so thankful and blessed for the godly heritage that has been passed down to me from my grandparents to my parents. I was only two years old, and my dad already had me singing in the choir, along with my sister. Sure, we probably sounded like little chipmunks, but the point is we learned to serve and praise God at an early age.

Having the Lord in my life still puts a song in my heart. He fills me with such joy, love, and peace. He is my everything! I have been blessed to minister to children and teens, adults and seniors, the brokenhearted and those who lost loved ones. I'm thankful to *still* be singing in the choir, on our praise team, and singing solos. God has blessed me so much; He's given me a wonderful husband, two daughters and sons-in-law, and five grandchildren whom I love dearly.

Who would have thought that an eight-year-old girl could receive so many opportunities and blessings just by opening her heart to the Lord . . . sixty years ago? And the longer I serve Him, the sweeter it gets! I love the Lord with all my heart, and I pray He continues to use me and direct my path.

—*Brenda*

Today's Takeaway:

It's a blessing to walk with Jesus. It doesn't make you exempt from life's troubles; it gives you the One to turn to in those troubles. Walking with the Lord gives you the strength to face whatever comes; it gives you the wisdom to look to the Word to find answers when you don't know what to do. Walking with God also gives you joy for your journey. That's my favorite! No long-faced "mully-grubber" in this walk!

Day 310

Today's Scripture:

"Delight yourself in the Lord, and he will give you the desires of your heart. Commit your way to the Lord; trust in him, and he will act: He will bring forth your righteousness as the light, and your justice as the noonday. Be still before the Lord and wait patiently for him" (Psalm 37:4-7 ESV).

Today's Testimony:

I was raised in the church. I had wonderful parents and a safe and happy childhood. When I became a teenager, however, my life spiraled out of control. I was a disgraced, shamed, teenage pregnant girl at the age of seventeen. I went on to marry the father of my baby because I thought it would "right" my sin, but after a marriage of repeated infidelity, I finally divorced him.

Two years after our divorce, I felt like I was ready to start dating again. The night of my first date, my ex-husband called as I was being picked up by my date. Hearing a man's voice in the background, he showed up *at my home* in a drunken, jealous rage. He stabbed my date in the leg and stabbed me in the head—leaving me for dead as our four children watched in fright. But God allowed us to live.

That date and I had a relationship for three and a half years. I was smitten with him and he was my heart's desire. When the relationship ended, I was devastated. I remember grasping the edge of my dresser, pleading with God not to let the relationship end. I prayed, but my prayer wasn't answered the way I wanted.

Later on, I got into a relationship with a man who started out seemingly perfect until, little by little, he became abusive. I remember being punched in the face so hard that my face was black and swollen; my nose was broken, requiring surgery. That should have been enough for me to leave, right? I was afraid—afraid of what he would do to me and my four children if I left. In my twisted mind, I thought staying in the abuse to keep us all alive was better than being dead.

—*Rhonda*
(To Be Continued in Tomorrow's Reading)

Today's Takeaway:

The enemy loves a spiraling life; confusion and every evil work go hand in hand (James 3:16). It's no surprise that there is pain and heartbreak at every turn when he is in charge. It sounds crazy to think Rhonda would not just gather up her children and run; but the problem is, women in her position get tricked into thinking they cannot escape. She and women in her position need to have strength to overcome that lie and reach out for help.

Day 311

Today's Scripture:

"The Lord has heard my cry for mercy; the Lord accepts my prayer" (Psalm 6:9 NIV).

Today's Testimony *(Continued From Previous Day):*

Later, I remember sitting on my porch swing, praying for God to open a door and make a way for me to get out of that relationship. I vowed to serve God for the rest of my life if He would save me.

Then, after many quiet days, in the parking lot where I worked, the man slammed my head into the steering wheel, threw hot coffee on me, and beat me up as people walked by—watching, staring, and doing nothing to help. That was the day God gave me the courage to walk away and never speak to him again.

I sat up all night with a baseball bat, afraid he was coming to kill us and praying for God's protection; He heard my cry. God saved me and my children once again.

God not only heard my prayer, but He blessed me beyond measure. Just three months after my salvation, I had a new job that paid more money, a new house I was able to purchase on my own, and a more reliable vehicle. He gave me a fresh start. I quit dating because I didn't want my kids to suffer for my poor choices. I realized true love is not found in men but God. I poured myself into church, ministry, and a deeper relationship with my Lord. That was the happiest I had ever been.

After nine years of growing in my relationship with Jesus, God sent me a Christian man who loved me and my children. We had a wonderful life and my children were able to experience the love of a God-fearing, Christian father. Ten years later, he died from a battle with cancer.

Long after, I bumped into the man I had prayed for—the one that had gotten stabbed as he came to pick me up on our first date. We lived just two miles apart for over twenty years and never knew it. This man had found Jesus. God brought us back together. He is now my husband. God's timing is perfect. Although we can't always see how God is working, He is working on our behalf and orchestrates every move. He answers with the best answer!

—Rhonda

Today's Takeaway:

God brought Rhonda full circle—because she trusted Him. She let Him be in control, and that brought peace and blessing like she'd never known. I don't know about you, but I can't handle chaos and turmoil. It's a miserable life! I need mercy instead. I want calm and peace—that's found only in Christ.

Day 312

Today's Scripture:

"Trust in the Lord with all your heart, and lean not on your own understanding; in all your ways acknowledge Him, and He shall direct your paths" (Proverbs 3:5-6 NKJV).

Today's Testimony:

I grew up attending church, going to youth camps and youth events since I was five. I don't remember the specific moment when I asked Jesus into my heart; I just remember I was a young girl. I remember being baptized when I was six. Then I was filled with the Holy Spirit at youth camp, at thirteen years old. For me this testimony isn't so much about how or when I came to be saved, but rather more about when I came to really *know* Jesus.

I was born into a family that loved Jesus and taught me Jesus loves me and I could love Him too. Life was good; I had nothing to complain or worry about. My family wasn't rich—after all, my dad was a pastor—but we had everything we needed and most things we wanted. God was good.

Then it happened, ten minutes before my seventeenth birthday: my eighteen-year-old cousin, who was more like a brother to me, lost his battle to leukemia. I couldn't understand what was happening. I thought when you loved and served Jesus, things like this didn't happen. Up until this point in my life I had only known the goodness of God in good times. My faith was being put to the test—my love for Jesus and His love for me was now in question. *How? Why? What did we do wrong?* These were all questions I had. Sitting in the backseat of the car, my parents in the front, we were preparing to leave the hospital for the last time. I remember my dad asking me, "Are you mad at God?" Not really wanting to answer that question (not sure if I could say it out loud), finally, I said, "Yes, yes! I am mad at God!"

I was thinking, *I just don't understand. I fully expected God to heal my cousin, to resurrect him when the machine flat-lined. I had the faith of a mustard seed that was supposed to move mountains—actually my faith was an avocado seed; so what happened and where was God's goodness now?* My parents' answer to me was one I didn't expect: "It's OK to be mad; God has really big shoulders."

—Jamie
(To Be Continued in Tomorrow's Reading)

Today's Takeaway:

I get chills when I read this and I feel my eyes sting with tears, because I can feel the impact of the gut-wrenching truth when Jamie was told *it is OK to be mad!* God can handle your feelings—He made you. He understands anger at horrible loss. He has big shoulders and you can lean on them with your pain and your questions. Have you ever been angry at God? It's OK; He still loves you.

Day 313

Today's Scripture:

"Trust in the Lord with all your heart, and lean not on your own understanding; in all your ways acknowledge Him, and He shall direct your paths" (Proverbs 3:5-6 NKJV).

Today's Testimony *(Continued From Previous Day):*

My parent's answer to me was one I didn't expect, "It's OK to be mad; God has really big shoulders."

Almost immediately I felt relief and experienced peace. In that moment I began to know the goodness of God when life wasn't good. I wish I had a great answer as to why bad things happen to good people, but I don't. Unfortunately, we live in a sinful world and stinky and bad things happen to everyone. But I know now that trusting God when I don't understand allows the peace of God to overwhelm and protect my heart and mind from the lies of Satan.

That day the enemy told me God wasn't good after all. He told me God must not care; He must not really love me—He certainly didn't love my cousin. Satan told me my faith was not good enough. But in the backseat of the car that day, when my parents gave me permission to be mad at God, they also gave me the freedom to stop being mad and begin to trust Him. Proverbs 3:5-6 says to trust God with all your heart, to lean not on your understanding, but in all your ways acknowledge Him, and He will make your path straight. God set me that day on a path of knowing and experiencing the goodness of God in good times and bad. God is good all the time, and all the time God is good!

—*Jamie*

Today's Takeaway:

The enemy goes opposite to God. Since we know God *is* good, the enemy tries to make us think He is not, so he lies to us—especially when tragedy strikes. He tells us that bad things happening proves God doesn't love us. We must remember he is a liar and the father of lies (John 8:44).

What we *can* do is trust the God who knows everything and can give us peace through all troubles and tragedies that come our way. We know the Word says, "Even [when] I walk *through* the valley of the shadow of death, I will fear no evil, for you are with me" (Psalm 23:4 ESV). In good times He's there, and in bad times He's also there!

Day 314

Today's Scripture:

"The Spirit of the Sovereign Lord is upon me, for the Lord has anointed me to bring good news to the poor. He has sent me to comfort the brokenhearted and to proclaim that captives will be released and prisoners will be freed" (Isaiah 61:1 NLT).

Today's Testimony:

I grew up as an only child in a *good* home; not a *godly* home. Religion of any kind was not discussed. I had a brief time as a youth to hear the Christmas and Easter stories. My heart's desire was to love and be loved. I sought diligently for acceptance but instead felt unattractive, unworthy, unaccepted, unappreciated, and unwanted. My senior year in college I met a man. It was love at first sight, but he was dating another girl as well as me. After nine months of dating I told him to choose, and he chose to see us both. I told him I never wanted to see him again. That was my breaking point. I was desperate to get away from the hurt and rejection that filled me.

With one semester of college left, a box of tissues in my hand and my shattered heart on my sleeve, I walked into the army recruiting office and told them I wanted to leave as quickly as possible and I wanted to live in Europe. Ten days later I was in boot camp, followed by Germany.

At last, a new start! I quickly became very popular among the men for all the wrong reasons. It wasn't for money or gifts, but looking again for someone to love me. Each encounter took a piece of my shattered heart and turned it harder. I became bitter, angry, hateful, mean, and oh so lost. Deeper and deeper, the darkness was stealing who I was. I could make a grown man cry with my words and actions—a skill I honed to perfection. Out of the few women I did come in contact with, none would have anything to do with me. There were a handful of Christians in my unit, and because of my job they were often at my demand. I made their life miserable and labeled them "The God Squad."

—*Christine*
(To Be Continued in Tomorrow's Reading).

Today's Takeaway:

So Christine was what the world likes to call "bad news"; there are other names. She wanted everyone around her to feel as awful as she felt on the inside; she was doing a pretty good job of it. The thing is, Jesus has "God Squads" everywhere. He commands them to carry out His work and they do. Tomorrow we'll see what He can use them to do. Are you in a squad? Maybe it's time to enlist!

Day 315

Today's Scripture:

"The commander of the Lord's army replied, 'Take off your sandals, for the place where you are standing is holy.' And Joshua did as he was told" (Joshua 5:15 NLT).

Today's Testimony (Continued From Previous Day):

One exceptionally nasty day, two of the men I worked closely with had all they could take. They came into my office, shut the door, and said, "We're coming to your house tonight and you're going to accept Jesus as your Savior." I simply said "OK." They turned and ran from my office. I went home and waited, but no one came. I wasn't sure what to expect, but I was desperate and broken. I could recall nothing about this Jesus they said I was going to accept. I knew it was my last chance at life, but I didn't have a clue what that would look like. Ready to give up, I finally heard a knock on the door. Two men and one woman—part of "The God Squad" I had persecuted—were standing at my door.

They walked in grimly and sat on the couch. I could see the terror in their eyes. The woman sat in the middle with a Bible on her lap. I don't know what they expected, but what happened next wasn't it. They said one word: "Jesus." I fell to my knees and wailed—I mean big, ugly, face-in-the-carpet, loud weeping. All the hurt, all the rage, all the bitterness—all the hard scales on my heart burst. I couldn't tell you how long I was in that state, but when I raised my head they were bolted upright on the couch with eyes and mouths wide open.

I don't remember what they said except to be ready to go to church with them the next night. I didn't know what happened to me. I was joyful, content, and at peace. For the first time in my life, I didn't feel alone. I didn't quite know what to do with all of it, so I slept—deep, dreamless, peace-filled, unconscious sleep all night and most of the next day.

Soon it was time for church. I didn't know what to expect but was filled with anticipation. I just knew I wanted more of God, more of what I experienced with my face in the carpet, and I didn't care what I needed to do to get it. As I looked around I saw someone I recognized. He and his family used to live above me and I'd harass them as they came and went. My legendary parties were the reason they moved. He was the pastor. He greeted me politely, not knowing me, and then sudden astonishment hit his face as he remembered who I was. Not only did God work in my heart, he also changed my appearance. At first, no one knew it was me; I actually glowed.

I later became sergeant of "The God Squad" and married the guy from college. Today I am a Biblical counselor and ordained minister in the Church of God. I thank God every day for allowing me to be His servant.

—*Christine*

Today's Takeaway:

What a change! Peace is such a better way to live. That's why I'm in the Lord's Army, yes sir.

Day 316

Today's Scripture:

"But as for you, you meant evil against me; but God meant it for good, in order to bring it about as it is this day" (Genesis 50:20 NKJV).

Today's Testimony:

I grew up in a "normal" two-parent home, but we were unchurched. My mother believed in God, but her struggles and sin kept her from fulfilling God's purpose for her life. The freedom I received from being the youngest child of two girls growing up in the '70s and '80s, led to running with the wrong crowd, sexual sin, drinking, and using drugs. By the time I was twenty-nine years old, I was married, divorced, and had two beautiful sons. But that's not all; I was also in a full-blown cocaine addiction.

I went to a secular rehab, and when I got out, I found a small church to attend. I stayed sober for eight years. I had gotten saved, but I never completely surrendered my life to Christ. I knew about *religion*, but had no idea about the *relationship* with Jesus I was missing out on and I so desperately needed.

I married again, someone I met in the church, and we had two beautiful daughters. I also managed to put myself through X-ray school. I was happy . . . living the "church life." My husband and I were small-group leaders, I was leading Celebrate Recovery, and life seemed good to me. Then my husband had an affair and my whole life fell apart. The enemy got in and I didn't know how to get him out. I didn't know how to get rid of the demons that moved into my home. I didn't have any strength—I knew nothing of the Holy Spirit. I just wasn't strong enough on my own. So I fell, and I fell hard!

—*Leeann*
(To Be Continued in Tomorrow's Reading)

Today's Takeaway:

My mind goes to what happens when you try to hang a big, heavy picture on the wall into thin sheetrock with nothing but a straight pin. The picture won't have enough strength to hold it up and it will fall—hard and fast. There has to be some substance to hold that picture up—and that's like us. We have to have substance holding us up; that substance is the power of Jesus. If we don't have it, we'll fall—we won't stand the test of trials.

Leeann said she got saved but didn't surrender—I'm not sure there's one without the other. In Leeann's story tomorrow, we'll see the result of trying to live for God without actually loving Him enough to give Him our heart. But for now let me say, it's like a mask; it's just not real. Only real salvation will be strong enough to see us through real problems.

Day 317

Today's Scripture:

"For once you were full of darkness, but now you have light from the Lord. So live as people of light!" (Ephesians 5:8 NLT).

Today's Testimony *(Continued From Previous Day):*

I started drinking, which eventually led to using drugs again. Within two years, I was divorced, arrested twice, lost my x-ray license, and had been to two more secular rehabs. I lost the trust I had with my family, and I lost my mind. *I was lost.*

I ended up living at one of the biggest smokehouses in our metropolitan area. This is where I met the husband I have today, but we lived in active addiction and darkness for what seemed like eternity. This was the lowest I had ever been. I was miserable. Satan meant to destroy us, but God wasn't done with me yet.

My husband and I moved 800 miles away, after ten years of addiction, to a faith-based treatment center. He went to the men's campus while I went to the women's. That's where I learned Jesus loved me, wanted me, and wanted to forgive me. I learned He had a plan and a purpose for my life.

Jesus offered me joy and peace—things I didn't know anything about. All I had to do was lay it all down: my marriage, my children, my life. I had to surrender at the foot of the Cross, at His feet. And I did.

It's a continual process . . . this "laying it all down." I continue to surrender my life to Him every day. I die to myself daily. I can't do life without Christ—and I wouldn't want to.

When my husband and I completed the treatment center's program, we decided to stay in the area instead of going back where we came from. We trusted Christ with our lives. God has opened up so many doors for us. He has brought so many people into our lives—good people that we will spend eternity with. He has restored all of our relationships and He continues to bless us daily. We have a huge calling on our lives, an anointing. We have a purpose, and it's only in Him.

—Leeann

Today's Takeaway:

The enemy thought he'd won—that he'd destroyed Leeann and could use her to hurt others along the way. Ha! I love it when he's all wrong. God gave Leeann another chance. He's awesome at that. She and her husband were saved, set free, and anointed to help others. Take that, Satan!

Not only *can* God rescue the "impossible cases," He *does*! Do you think you have an impossible case, something that can't be fixed? God is able, but He won't if you don't ask. The Word says, "[We] have not, because [we] ask not" (James 4:2 KJV) So ask! Then watch and believe.

Day 318

Today's Scripture:

"Confess your faults one to another, and pray one for another, that ye may be healed. The effectual fervent prayer of a righteous man availeth much" (James 5:16 KJV).

Today's Testimony:

From a young age, I remember being brought up in church. I was blessed with godly parents who raised us in a Christian home. One time, another child in Sunday school ripped my coloring page, and I remember praying over the broken pieces of that page for God to fix it. I was taught as a small child there was nothing God couldn't do. Possessing that childlike faith in my heart led me to pray the sinner's prayer around the age of ten. Since then, I have walked with the Lord daily. I have experienced His blessings time and time again.

His healing power has definitely been experienced by our family. When my daughter was born she was rushed to the NICU and was very sick, but then was able to come home with us completely healed.

My husband had surgery and in the process of it, the doctors accidentally stapled off his bile duct; then in the surgery to repair it, they said he might have to have a feeding tube for the rest of his life or he could die on the operating table. But I said, "I have peace about this and you will be all right!" When he came out of surgery, he looked better than when he went in. He didn't have to go to ICU, he wasn't on a ventilator, nor did he receive blood."

Later, I kept telling my doctor something wasn't right (always listen to your body, ladies). Finally, the doctor ordered a CT to find an ovarian tumor the size of a bowling ball. The tumor was removed. The news I received was not what I had expected. They said I had borderline cancer. The next stop was to see an oncologist. He did a hysterectomy, but I didn't have to have chemo or radiation. I will soon celebrate eight years with no signs of cancer. Through it all, I have learned to be still and wait on Him. When God was all I had, He was truly all I needed!

—*Theresa*

Today's Takeaway:

Theresa had faith as a child and it has carried her through her entire life. She knew God could do anything, so she asked Him for help with everything. God loves for His girls to ask Him for help. He loves for us to trust Him with our lives. He loves to listen to us tell someone else, "I have peace about this." It makes Him proud. I love to make Him proud!

Day 319

Today's Scripture:

"And he said: 'Truly I tell you, unless you change and become like little children, you will never enter the kingdom of heaven'" (Matthew 18:3 NIV).

Today's Testimony:

My parents divorced when I was about three years old. My dad's parents spent a lot of time with me and my sister. They often took us to church, AWANA, VBS, and other special events. My paternal grandpa was a pastor and helped with leadership roles in the church.

A couple of years had passed, and I learned one day in Sunday school what it meant to be saved. Later that evening, I talked to my grandma about what I had learned. I wanted to be saved, but didn't fully know what to do. Then she helped me say a prayer to ask Jesus into my heart. I remember it so vividly. I was staying the night at her house, and we said the prayer together, just outside the doorway of her bedroom. I felt my body being filled with love. Afterward, I knew I had just made the best decision of my five-year-old life. I had peace and joy, like never before. It was a precious moment.

Throughout my life, my salvation through Jesus Christ has helped me persevere and overcome trials, such as physical, emotional, and sexual abuse. He has also brought me out of co-dependency and several toxic relationships.

In exchange for the old, He has given me a new life. He's blessed me with a wonderful, God-fearing husband to be my partner in this journey. I could write a whole series of books on the good things God has done and the amazing ways He has kept my heart, for the past thirty-five years, since that day I invited Him in.

John Newton wrote, "Through many dangers, toils, and snares, I have already come. 'Tis grace hath brought me safe thus far, and grace will lead me home." Oh, I am so grateful for the amazing grace of my Lord and Savior, Jesus Christ. We *all* sure need it! And I pray, daily, for His salvation to reach the lost, so that *all* His children can experience His triumphant love, like I did, that night I asked Him into my heart.

—Amy

Today's Take Away:

It was a "precious moment" when Amy's grandmother prayed with her to be saved. It was the most important moment of her life. I believe John Newton wrote under the inspiration of the Lord when he wrote about the "dangers, toils, and snares" that we've already come through and God's grace taking us through the rest of them until He leads us home. That's how it works. If we trust Him with our hearts, we are given the grace to make it all the way home. Oh, I'm ready to be there!

Day 320

Today's Scripture:

"Oh taste and see that the Lord is good! Blessed is the man who takes refuge in him!"
(Psalm 34:8 ESV).

Today's Testimony:

Having been raised in a pastor's home, with amazing godly parents, it often feels as though I came out of my mother's womb saved, sanctified, and filled with the Holy Spirit. Of course, we know this is not possible, and there have been many crises of faith over the years. One thing is for sure, I have always known the reality of Jesus Christ. I'm grateful to my parents for not only raising me in church and teaching me our faith, but further for showing me, by example, the overwhelming greatness of a relationship with Jesus Christ.

In our home it was never just words or prayers. It was a lifestyle. They shared with us as children their walk of faith, allowing us to see the hand of God so clearly and tangibly that I knew beyond a shadow of a doubt God is real, and He loved us very much. This foundation is the greatest gift any parent could ever give their child. I strive to give my own children the same pattern and foundation of faith.

I can't remember a specific date and time of conversion. There have been many altar calls, many bedside prayers. I can remember many times throughout my adolescence committing or recommitting my life to Christ, feeling the tug of conviction in my heart to live a life consecrated to God, asking forgiveness for one thing or another. As I reflect on what my testimony would be, I think it's less about those moments of conviction and more about the walk I've had with Jesus.

For me personally, the crises of faith—the questions of "why'" that we all find ourselves struggling with throughout life—have never really been about whether God is real. The questions I have faced over the years have focused on the plan. *God, why are You taking me here? God, why have You not allowed this? Or God, why have You allowed that? God, I know Your love for me, but in this moment, I am not feeling Your love.* Sound familiar?

—*Rebekah*
(To Be Continued in Tomorrow's Reading)

Today's Takeaway:

I absolutely love Rebekah's thoughts here. Your salvation is not so much about remembering a single moment in time as it is your walk with Him and what you have settled in your heart. When the tough moments in your life come and Satan challenges you to question God and His plan—what it really comes down to is questioning God's love for us: *God, if You love me, then why did this happen?* The truth is, salvation steadies you in these moments. You'll feel His presence and assurance—His love—because He's inside.

Day 321

Today's Scripture:

"Oh taste and see that the Lord is good! Blessed is the man who takes refuge in him" (Psalm 34:8 ESV).

Today's Testimony *(Continued From Previous Day):*

I often speak to people about "the puzzle." We live our life one puzzle piece at a time. As a person who loves to be in control of my own surroundings, I have many times found myself asking, begging, pleading with God to show me more of the puzzle. What I have come to know throughout my walk this far is the faithfulness of God despite circumstance. Through leaning on my heavenly Father, even though I cannot see the next piece of the puzzle, I have found great peace and unimaginable strength. I have found the joy of the Lord in the midst of sorrow, the provision of God when there seems to be no logical way.

Jesus has shown Himself to me in the most loving and compassionate ways. He has carried me through some very dark seasons in life—where I sit on the basement steps out of the earshot of my children and cry out to Him. In those moments where I feel unheard, alone, not valuable, and inadequate for the task at hand, Jesus Christ has never left me. He has stepped in and shown Himself. With each hurdle I have jumped, my relationship with Jesus Christ has grown, and deepened into an amazing picture—a beautiful puzzle that reflects the goodness of God. One of my favorite questions to ask kids in a children's church setting is, "How do you know that God is real?" As they search for the answer and offer up possibilities, I always direct them to Psalm 34:8: "Taste and see that the Lord is good! Blessed is the man who takes refuge in him" (ESV).

I know the reality of God because in my walk with Him I have "tasted of His goodness." His steadfast and unwavering faithfulness has been my constant refuge. And when the "why" questions of life come up, I remind myself and others we have tasted and we have seen that the Lord is good. He is ever faithful!

—*Rebekah*

Today's Takeaway:

God doesn't always show us the next puzzle piece, does He? He will at the right time. We can rest in the fact that the pieces at least fit, even when we don't always think they will. I personally don't like the all-black pieces—they don't give any clues as to where they go. The thing is they're necessary to the puzzle, and they make the picture more beautiful. That's kind of like sorrow—there's no going through life without it, and even though I don't like it, there's no love without sorrow. Thankfully, God is always there to see us through every dark season of life. If you walk with Him, you'll see, He is good—through trouble, through joy, through questions. Taste and see!

Day 322

Today's Scripture:

"And thou shalt love the Lord thy God with all thy heart, and with all thy soul, and with all thy mind, and with all thy strength: this is the first commandment" (Mark 12:30 KJV).

Today's Testimony:

It has always been overwhelming to me that Jesus loved me so much He freely gave His life on the cross. The realization of a love like this keeps me wanting to draw closer to Him and to never leave or forsake Him. There is no greater love than to lay down one's life. I will forever be grateful for His powerful love.

My journey has been one of loving Jesus my entire life and desiring to please Him. I was raised by Christian parents who modeled Christ-like love and faithfulness to their local church. Around the age of seven, in my Sunday school class, I asked Jesus to be my Lord and Savior. Since that time, three words describe my experience with Him—presence, power, and protection.

In my younger years, I thought serving God would be a life free from the cares of the world. As I grew older, I discovered walking with Jesus would not be without difficult days, disappointments, trials, wrong decisions, hurts, death, and tears. There would be times I wanted to quit. But His keeping power in those times drew me to Him, reminding me He was with me and I could give Him all my cares because He cares for me.

Loving God with all my heart, soul, mind, and strength has been an everyday growing experience. Mark 12:30 is my favorite verse because I know if He is first in my life, His presence will be made known. I'm so glad each morning is fresh and new, and I can feel His presence when I study His Word, pray, and spend time with Him. I feel His presence as He guides me through the day and as I strive to be more like Him.

—Joyce

Today's Takeaway:

(Joyce's words) Putting Mark 12:30 into practice every day has protected me from choices that would have otherwise destroyed me. *Thank You, Jesus, for Your presence, Your power, and Your protection. I love my life with You.*

Maybe you have bought into the world's fake news and your life is a mess. The good news is, what He has done for me, He will do for you. Take action today and embrace Christ's commandment for daily living.

(My words) What a beautiful testimony of God's "keeping" love and care. That's the part *I* love: we keep Him in our hearts and He keeps us throughout our lives—through every trial, through every victory. He's our Guide.

Day 323

Today's Scripture:

"Put on the whole armour of God, that ye may be able to stand against the wiles of the devil" (Ephesians 6:11 KJV).

Today's Testimony:

I was born and raised in church. I've always had faith and believed in God, but when I was fifteen years old I found myself wrapped up in self-doubt, insecurity, and fear. I was truly at a loss, but after a powerful youth service one night, I decided to take the big step and truly give my heart to Jesus and shift my focus upward. I didn't know it at the time, but I was about to step into some very difficult times in life. If I had not dedicated myself and my life right then to living for Christ, I wouldn't have had Him to fall back on in the hardest moments of my life.

There are days when it's easy for me to be stumped by the question, "What has God done for you?" It's not because God hasn't done a plethora of things for me; it's because I often feel they're insignificant or not big enough to be worthy of sharing with others. But just the fact that He saved me is awesome! And then I remember what He's brought me through.

My testimony is one of those things I didn't feel was great enough to share, because it's not some amazing comeback story and it's not "finding gold on the other side of a rainbow after a stormy night." It's a fifteen-year-old pastor's kid in the front row at a youth-group service deciding that I needed to change my focus and give my heart to the God who created everything. Actually, that is pretty amazing!

—*Alli*

Today's Takeaway:

I think I'd love to find gold on the other side of a rainbow after a stormy night. Ha! But even more important than that is seeing a young girl commit her heart to God—that's pure gold! Because Alli did that, she was fortified for the storms of life that were coming. She didn't realize it at the time, but she just put on lots of armor to prepare herself for that battle. That's worth telling someone about.

It's a common misconception that people only want to hear about the "deep lives of sin" testimonies. People really want to hear about the everyday victories God helps us through—because that gives them hope that God can do the same in their lives. So talk about the "plethora." We want to hear about it. It's so much better than all the negative stuff we usually hear about, right? So spill it, girl!

Day 324

Today's Scripture:

"But at midnight Paul and Silas were praying and singing hymns to God, and the prisoners were listening to them. Suddenly there was a great earthquake, so that the foundations of the prison were shaken; and immediately all the doors were opened and everyone's chains were loosed" (Acts 16:25-26 NKJV).

Today's Testimony:

Years ago, at the age of sixteen, my life as I knew it would be changed forever due to a bad decision. I don't know why I didn't just say, "No!" I knew better, but wanted him to like me. I could blame it on being naive or immature, and that would be somewhat true; but at any rate, I didn't say that little two-letter word, and now, I would pay a valuable price for many years to come.

Four months later, and sixteen weeks pregnant, we stood at the front of a church pledging our love to each other. I would soon find out my seventeen-year-old husband didn't know how to handle the stress of all this, and would take it out on me. The abuse, which started with him slapping my face, graduated to so much more. Over the course of four years, our family grew to four children, all under the age of four. But our family size was not the only thing that grew. The abuse grew. It grew so badly that it was no longer a slap across the face, but blackened eyes, being pulled down dirt roads by my hair, being choked, and having a gun to my head. I felt like my life was no longer my own, but I had four children who needed me. So what was I to do?

Even though my precious mother brought me to church as a child, I didn't know the Lord as my Savior. Being seventeen and married had allowed me to make adult decisions, so I walked away from church and everything to do with it.

Years later, my husband moved us away from my family and closer to his. Now I no longer had my mother close by to run to when the abuse happened. And I didn't have her close by to hug when my husband started having affairs with other women. My only refuge was watching Oral and Richard Roberts on television when my husband was out of the house. But little by little, the Lord started speaking to me through His Word, and preparing me for His plan—a plan for a change.

—*Marlene*
(To Be Continued in Tomorrow's Reading)

Today's Takeaway:

Sometimes the enemy can beat us so far down that we believe his lies and think we either "deserve" what we're in or that it's so deep there's no hope of it ever changing. My blood boils when I think of poor Marlene far from her mother and suffering at the hands of this abuser. But she wasn't far from her Father. He was there and He sent her hope and reminders through messages from His servants and through His Word that all wasn't lost. He still had a plan for her. He has a plan for you too.

Day 325

Today's Scripture:

"All honor and glory to God forever and ever! He is the eternal King, the unseen one who never dies; he alone is God. Amen" (1 Timothy 1:17 NLT).

Today's Testimony *Continued From Yesterday:*

It was a beautiful Saturday in August, and my younger sister was getting married, so I drove with my grandparents back home to attend her wedding. The next day, my mother asked me to go to church with her. After much nudging, I reluctantly agreed to go—on one condition. I told her, "If an elder sister in the Lord asks me to go to the altar with her, I'm walkin' out the back door!"

But God knew what I needed even before I did. The Lord had plans to give [me] hope and a future'" (Jeremiah 29:11 NIV).

The next thing I knew, the evangelist was talking directly to me. Everyone else in the church seemed to be blurred out, and I found myself walking to the altar to surrender my sin, pain, hurt, disappointments, and everything else that had been burying me down for so long now. I felt free at that moment—so much so that I walked back to my seat, grabbed my cigarettes and lighter, brought them back up, and laid them on the altar. I was done. God delivered me, right then and there.

Jeremiah 29:11 became my lifeline when my husband would come home drunk from the bar. I knew God had other plans. So, I did exactly what Paul and Silas did—I prayed and worshiped Him in my "prison." It was as if the earth quaked and the chains fell off. God never left me nor did He forsake me during all that time. After thirteen years, I knew it was time to be free from the infidelity and abuse. I was DONE being a victim, so we finally divorced.

I would love to say that after accepting Jesus as my Lord and Savior, everything got better . . . and I can! It did! My life was forever changed. Years later, I married a man of God, and we are now in ministry together. Who would have thought? *God.* And *He* gets all the glory, honor, and praise.

—*Marlene*

Today's Takeaway:

Yes, God did it! I love the fact that since Marlene said she'd leave church if a lady came and asked her to pray, God had the evangelist ask her. Don't mess with God! He runs after us because He loves us so much. He wants us to surrender all the pain and hurt. He can see the better plan and us thriving in it. How wonderful! How about we just go His way and enjoy the peace and security He offers. Yay Marlene—out of the "prison" and into "praise"!

Day 326

Today's Scripture:

*"For the vision is yet for an appointed time; but at the end it will speak,
and it will not lie. Though it tarries, wait for it; because it will surely come,
it will not tarry"* (Habakkuk 2:3 NKJV).

Today's Testimony:

I started my journey with the Lord when I was five years of age. I remember so clearly the love I had for Him. He took notice and baptized me with the Holy Spirit, and I started singing harmony with my mother. That same year we began singing as a family and traveled all over to revivals, homecomings, and camp meetings.

At the age of eleven, things drastically changed. My mother died of cancer, so that ended our family travels and singing as I knew it. God, being the awesome Father that He is, that same year began to teach me to know His voice. I was at a revival service with my oldest sister when during the altar service, the Lord spoke to me personally. He said He had specific plans for me.

At the age of fifteen, my father was in a head-on collision and died. A year later, my brother whom I adored was killed in a motorcycle accident. Shortly after, my sweet grandmother died. You can imagine how devastated I was. At this point in my life I questioned why we had so much pain and sorrow. What was going to happen to me? My sorrow started affecting my ninth-grade school work.

One night after crying myself to sleep, God sent me a dream of my future. I was standing outside and I looked up to see Him in the clouds. He motioned for me to come up to Him. I stood up on the picnic table and began to reach up. He motioned for me to look down. As I looked down I saw many people's arms hanging from my foot to the next person, and so on. I didn't understand until He told me those are the ones I would minister to in my lifetime.

Meanwhile, I needed an A for an essay in order for me to pass my ninth-grade year. I got an A+ and my essay was displayed in the showcase at school. It was titled "Reach for Success." I was involved in a teen revival where I personally brought 118 teens from my school. All of them were in the altars giving their lives to Him. God fulfilled the prophetic voice I heard as an eleven-year-old broken little girl. It all came to pass word for word. All I can say to you today is for you to hold onto the prophetic word God has spoken to you. His word does not return void. I'm still experiencing the journey.

—*Mary*

Today's Takeaway:

God had His hand on Mary. She faced heartbreaking circumstances that could have taken the song out of her heart, but God spoke to her. He had a plan to use her for His glory. He wants to use you too. Don't let fear stop you!

Day 327

Today's Scripture:

"The Lord himself goes before you and will be with you; he will never leave you nor forsake you. Do not be afraid; do not be discouraged" (Deuteronomy 31:8 NIV).

Today's Testimony:

Standing in my living room, tears streaming down my face, my whole world came crashing down around me. Tensions had been building for months until I couldn't hold it together any longer. Thanksgiving had been just a few days ago. I was at a loss . . . wasn't gratitude supposed to lift spirits and lighten hearts? After thirteen years in recovery, I somehow thought I was immune to depression and anxiety. How did I get here? The bigger question—How was I going to get out of this pit?

The pathway to depression had been carved out during my childhood. My parents fought constantly. Their arguments often turned violent. Fear gripped my brother, sisters, and me as we watched my dad beat our mother. I was determined not to do anything to make him angry. One way I found to please my dad was to make good grades at school. I was in the same grade as the children of his bosses. When my grades were high, he could brag about his daughter's report card. My focus turned from doing my best to becoming the best. I needed my dad to approve of me, which caused a tremendous amount of anxiety.

My need for approval carried over into adulthood. When failure happened, I used alcohol to numb the pain. The alcohol helped me mask my anxieties and gave me the courage to be what others thought I should be. The end result—an addiction to alcohol and a total loss of self. My addiction to alcohol and search for acceptance led to an affair that ended my first marriage.

—Donna
(To Be Continued in Tomorrow's Reading)

Today's Takeaway:

Sometimes holidays, instead of making us feel happier and lighter, only make our situations feel heavier or, even worse, cause them to come to a head. Thanksgiving is a time to look around us and pause to give thanks for all God has done, but depression and anxiety can cloud our minds so that we can't see anything but despair.

In Donna's case, the path to this moment had been years in the making with using alcohol as the "fix" to make herself feel better or get strong enough to handle what was happening. Instead of building her up, it had the opposite effect. What we can be thankful for is that there is a remedy for this. Tomorrow we'll see what happened in Donna's life, but what about your life? What "fixes" your situations when they arise? Let Jesus be your "fixer"; His Word will guide every subject. Decide to be thankful for even something small and give Him the rest.

Day 328

Today's Scripture:

"And let the peace that comes from Christ rule in your hearts. For as members of one body you are called to live in peace. And always be thankful" (Colossians 3:15 NLT).

Today's Testimony *(Continued From Previous Day)*:

My first marriage was now over due to alcoholism and an affair. What was supposed to be my happily-ever-after turned into a roller-coaster ride. A new partner did not ease my anxieties. Infidelity wrecked our lives. The final straw came when my husband said he had met someone and fallen in love. His past affairs were physical in nature—this woman had captured his heart. Anxiety fueled my thoughts. I tried everything I could think until I convinced him to stay.

In the midst of all of this, my husband lost his job. This turned out to be a huge blessing in disguise. We moved several states away for a fresh start. It was almost like God was waiting at the state line to welcome us home. We moved, and months later I dedicated my life to Jesus Christ. My husband accepted Jesus soon after. God began healing our brokenness and our broken marriage. We began serving together in the baptism ministry. It was such a joy to be with people as they prepared to make a public declaration of their faith.

Five years later, God called us to start "Celebrate Recovery" in our community. Even though I had given my heart to Jesus, I was still trying to please others to get their approval. God used recovery to help me find healing for my addiction to alcohol and my need to please others. He had performed miraculous healing in many areas of my life. I thought I was doing well. Then the break occurred. My husband and I were going through a major life change—his retirement. My anxieties resurfaced. This was not a surprise to God. He had been preparing me for this next season of life. Celebrate Recovery had been focused on combating the stigma of mental health. Because of conversations about the importance of getting help, I was not ashamed to admit I needed help. God helped me to share openly with my doctor, who was patient and kind. He has used medication, a Christian counselor, and lifestyle changes to improve my mental health.

Based on my experiences, I trust God and His promises. Today I stand on the words found in Deuteronomy 31:8: "The Lord himself goes before you and will be with you; he will never leave you nor forsake you. Do not be afraid; do not be discouraged" (NIV). He is with me no matter what.

—Donna

Today's Takeaway:

When we come to Jesus, it's not a pray-and-check-off-the-box kind of experience. Life is to be lived leaning on the Word, prayer, and fellowship of other believers to grow and stay strong in our Christian life. We can't exist on an island. We must ask for and get help when we need it; that's why our Lord provides it.

Day 329

Today's Scripture:

"Those who live in the shelter of the Most High will find rest in the shadow of the Almighty" (Psalm 91:1 NLT).

Today's Testimony:

On Sunday, I believed my husband and I had a great life. We weren't millionaires or movie stars, but we were rich in love, hope, and in the future. We had been married since a young age and had two beautiful boys. Two boys that we were told we would never bear, but the Lord blessed us, knowing I'd need them in the future.

My husband and I believed in God. We were active members in our church, tithe-payers, serving whenever we were needed. When our pastor called for a baptism service the week before, I felt led to get baptized again as I rededicated my life to the Lord. My husband cried at the baptism; it was a great day! All that week, I remember putting scriptures around my house: "You are more than a conqueror!" (see Romans 8:37). "Greater is He that is in me than he that's in this world" (see 1 John 4:4). All over my house, I was compelled to write scriptures of faith and hope.

That Sunday, we had a huge snowstorm. The next day, schools were closed. My husband had to leave for work early to go by the dealership to get an extra set of truck keys. He had just bought his first brand-new truck; he was so proud. Later that morning, my oldest son was outside shoveling the snow and I was laying down with my three-year-old trying to get him to sleep for a nap, when my son came in and said, "Mom, the police are here!" That statement forever changed my life. The officer said there had been a shooting earlier that morning, involving my husband, and he had been killed!

Millions of questions crowded my mind, but the words wouldn't come out . . . only screams. Five police agencies were involved in the shooting. When my husband pulled over, his truck was surrounded by gun-drawn police officers. A police SUV rammed into the back of my husband's truck, and the police officers, surrounding his vehicle, opened fire! My husband slumped over the steering wheel, with his foot on the gas, and his truck spun and crashed into a house. He lived for forty minutes after the shooting.

The tragic story was on every news channel that afternoon and the rest of the week. My house was swarming with relatives and friends. My mind was swirling. *How do I face this? I couldn't bear to live without him! My kids . . . what do I do? I can't face this alone!* No one understood. My words wouldn't come out. I felt like I couldn't even cry out!

—*Trina*
(To Be Continued in Tomorrow's Reading)

Today's Takeaway:

Trina was overwhelmed and blindsided. She needed to run to God. If you ever find yourself in a tornado like this, cry out to God—He's right there!

Day 330

Today's Scripture:

"He alone is my refuge, my place of safety; he is my God, and I trust him"
(Psalm 91:2 NLT).

Today's Testimony *(Continued From Previous Day):*

Starting Monday, everyone was constantly trying to comfort me and my children. They kept asking about the arrangements for my husband's viewing, funeral, and memorial dinner. WHAT? NO! Making those arrangements made things final. I couldn't keep going through this pain, loss, humiliation from lies I was hearing, and seeing the pitying eyes.

The seeds of the enemy started to grow quickly in my weakened state. By Tuesday, I knew I would never go to the funeral home on Wednesday to make the arrangements—I just couldn't do it. On Tuesday night, when my friends wanted to take my kids for the night so I could rest, my plan was set. With my fight gone, I said goodbye to my last guest and my children. With my house cleaned, I waited. At 11:47 p.m., Tuesday night, I sat in a chair in front of the clock with a loaded gun in my hand. I was determined that at the strike of midnight, I would have blessed peace and be with my husband—not tormented anymore. So I waited . . .

All of a sudden, I heard a very LOUD sound! It sounded like shattering glass and was like a cannon. It's not a sound I had ever heard before or since, which makes it so hard for me to explain. The sound shook me and scared me! It went right through me. When I looked up, my grandfather's Bible had fallen off of a shelf and hit the edge of the night stand . . . then hit the floor. That booming sound/voice was the Bible hitting the floor. Instantly I looked down. I saw the gun in my hand, and I immediately knew my intentions. The clock read 5:15 a.m.! As sure as I am here, I KNOW I didn't fall asleep. I truly believe a war was waged over my life! That war that was waged in my mind was only seconds, but with my God, it was from 11:47 p.m. until 5:15 a.m.!

The most intense feelings of calmness, peace, and love came over me. Then I began to cry out my shame for not trusting my Lord in all things. I hadn't prayed and called on Him first. I should've trusted the One who holds my eternity in His hands. I had not listened to the Way-Maker, the Healer, the Comforter. I asked for forgiveness for my weakness and vowed to serve my Lord God and His kingdom for the rest of my days.

—*Trina*
(To Be Continued in Tomorrow's Reading)

Today's Takeaway:

I don't know what the sound was, but I *know* who sent it! I'm so glad Trina was shaken back to herself when she heard it. She'd been in a fog; it's understandable but deadly. Thank God He wouldn't let go!

Day 331

Today's Scripture:

"In the same way, the Spirit helps us in our weakness. We do not know what we ought to pray for, but the Spirit himself intercedes for us through wordless groans" (Romans 8:26 NIV).

Today's Testimony *(Continued From Yesterday)*:

When a mountain of lies, grief, and life-altering situations are mounted against you, you can either call/groan to God or follow the whispers of the enemy. There have been so many signs of mercy, love, and wisdom shown to me and my boys, and I *know* my Lord was there waiting for me to call out His name. "Show me Your mercy and glory!"

When I had the opportunity to show mercy and love to the police officers who mistakenly took my husband's life, I could have done what the enemy whispered in my ear. He whispered HATE! When I had a chance to address all nine of the officers, the calming presence of the Peacemaker came over me. I had the opportunity in court to turn and pray a blessing over each of the officer's lives and the lives of their families. I asked the Lord God to bless them as they went out and came in. I prayed that everything good He had for me, to give to them too. Then, I said, "I love you all and I forgive you."

Out of the nine officers, one officer came to me and asked me how I could forgive him when he couldn't forgive himself. I spoke about the Healer, the Way-Maker, the Peacekeeper—I spoke about my Lord God's mercy and grace!

I truly feel if I would have sown the *hate,* the enemy was whispering for me, instead of God's *mercy*, then the officer would have been on his way to commit suicide because of his grief. Then he would have left a mourning wife and three children behind to struggle and cope just the way I would have. Hate breeds hate. Love breeds love. To this day, that police officer is one of my best friends! I love him and his family. We have shared many blessings, miracles, and tremendous spiritual growth together. We have both dedicated our lives to be servants of our Lord God.

My journey from that night has gone through many valleys and has soared many times over the mountaintops. I do believe my God was preparing me for that critical time in my life. Revelation 12:11 says: "They triumphed over him by the blood of the Lamb and by the word of their testimony" (NIV).

—*Trina*

Today's Takeaway:

Trina overcame through the blood of the Lamb and her testimony that she was able to give to the very officers that caused it! That is what trusting in Christ does. It takes the worst day of your life and eventually gives you the strength to be able to climb up on top of it and stand over it and declare, "You will not define me." In Christ, I am victorious over *even* this!

Day 332

Today's Scripture:

"You keep track of all my sorrows. You have collected all my tears in your bottle. You have recorded each one in your book" (Psalm 56:8 NLT).

Today's Testimony:

I was raised in a God-fearing home with parents who loved me unconditionally. I was saved at an early age, but then the preteen years hit, and I had more of a desire to "fit in" than to follow God. The desire to be accepted by my peers pressured me and I became rebellious. I began lying to my parents, going to parties, drinking, and even experimented with drugs. All the while, I was still attending church. I had the "lead role" in life—the part of a chameleon.

Then, at the age of fifteen, I was finally caught sneaking out of my bedroom window. That's when the world as I knew it came crashing in. My wise parents grounded me from everything except scholastics and church. Although I had been caught, I still managed to remain defiant, learning new ways to circumvent the rules. Lying became easier and more creative. Still, I would frequently run to the altar on Sunday to repent for what I had done on Friday and Saturday. It didn't matter how far I went, Jesus was always there helping me back up. Promises were made, but then Friday and Saturday would come again; it was a vicious circle.

Summer came that year, and I attended youth camp. That's when everything changed. One night during service, the Holy Spirit arrested me and I made a conscious decision to fully commit. I gave my heart to the Lord and became a child of God. I was tired of my role as a "chameleon."

I wouldn't be here today if it weren't for praying parents, a praying church, and an amazing youth leader who knew how to watch, listen, and guide. I was blessed with parents who remained steadfast in the Word and trusted God through it all. With God's help, I was able to stand firm and refuse to re-engage in rebellion. This was not an easy process, and I failed miserably some days. But God never let go. I had finally committed and wasn't turning back. The prayers of those who really loved me were answered.

To all those parents praying for your children, don't ever question if God is hearing your prayers. He hears every single one. Remain steadfast and trust God.

—*Sonya*

Today's Takeaway:

God isn't satisfied with a "chameleon" life for us—no more than we would be satisfied with half our bodies to be healthy and the other half to be eaten up with cancer! We can't live half-and-half and expect to be whole. God also knows if we expose ourselves to the lies of the enemy, it's only a matter of time before we are completely deceived. The only way to live victoriously for Christ is to be fully committed to Him, as Christ is to us.

Day 333

Today's Scripture:

"And this same God who takes care of me will supply all your needs from his glorious riches, which have been given to us in Christ Jesus" (Philippians 4:19 NLT).

Today's Testimony:

I grew up in a Christian family, so I was surrounded by God and the church from the very beginning. But I found myself just going through the motions. I didn't know *Him*; I just knew *about* Him. As a teenager and young adult, I turned from God. I had seen what He had done in others' lives and even in my own family, I just never experienced it in my life.

At my lowest point, I was going through a rough marriage that included verbal, mental, and physical abuse. It was then that I felt God draw me to Himself. As I was planning to leave this marriage, a scripture came to me: "'For I know the plans I have for you,' declares the Lord, 'plans to prosper you and not to harm you, plans to give you hope and a future'" (Jeremiah 29:11) . This was the first time I felt God was with me, and He continued to be with me from that moment on. I finally realized He would never leave me nor forsake me (Hebrews 13:5). I gave my heart to Him.

God helped me through each of the trials I faced—financially, as a single mother, with transportation, even daycare and a better job. He provided all I needed. Every day, He continues to show me His mercy and grace in new ways, even when I fail Him. He is such a loving Father. He continues to let me run to Him. His arms are always outstretched, ready to help, and He never turns His back on me.

I am committed to living for God instead of others. God has shown me that being a Christian is not just doing good works; it's also about faith (James 2:18). I am not perfect, but God loves me. God has never once left me. Exodus 14:14 says, "The Lord shall fight for you, and ye shall hold your peace." He has shown Himself to me in His Word. God loved me at my lowest point and He rescued me from eternal separation from Him.

—*Kathy*

Today's Takeaway:

Kathy has experienced the nearness of God. We can make it if we have Him near. He gets us through. He teaches us a better way. He gives us peace. He quiets our souls. He provides His Word so that we can hear from Him, and makes a way for us to talk to Him. He never leaves; He's always near. Heaven surely will be wonderful when we see Him face-to-face!

Day 334

Today's Scripture:

"Jesus said, 'Let the little children come to me, and do not hinder them, for the kingdom of heaven belongs to such as these'" (Matthew 19:14 NIV).

Today's Testimony:

Before I was born, my parents were married and wanted children. My mom desperately wanted a baby; my dad, however, would've settled for cats (I'm just kidding!). Anyway, my parents tried for several years to get pregnant and were not successful, so they chose to adopt. They put their names on the list and waited . . . and waited. My mom got so tired of waiting that she told her family she was taking her name off the list. The next day she called the adoption agency and told them the same thing. The woman on the other line talked my mom into staying on the list just a little longer. My mom reluctantly agreed, and later that day she got a call that the agency had a baby for them!

I always knew about my adoption growing up. I viewed it as this amazing, positive, beautiful choice that my biological mother made. Fast-forward eight years, and I got a baby sister! She is my parents' biological daughter. No one knows what changed for that to happen, but something did, and I have the most beautiful and amazing sister! Our parents raised us in church and ministry. We loved each other, and as a young girl, I gave my heart to the Lord. I grew up serving God and living for Him.

Later, when I turned twenty, I met a guy, got married, had a son, and divorced—all by the time I was twenty-four. I walked out of that situation wondering what I had done wrong. I thought I'd done everything the "right way." And yet I was, brokenhearted and raising my son alone. I was so angry at God. That's when He showed me I couldn't earn His love by what I did or didn't do—He always loves me the same. In a few years, God brought me and my son a wonderful, loving man. He loves the Lord; he is patient, loving, kind, and wants to help raise my son. We got married, had two more beautiful boys, and are raising them together—in a very wild, chaotic, beautiful life!

—Amber
(To Be Continued in Tomorrow's Reading)

Today's Takeaway:

Amber's story is too much to tell in one day. We'll continue the rest tomorrow. When I think about how Amber was so loved—by her biological mother who made the sacrifice to do what she felt was best for her baby, not for herself; and by her adopted mom and dad who endured the pain of waiting, praying and yearning for her, then raising her as their own all her life, I am overwhelmed. Amber's beautiful story reminds me of how our heavenly Father must love us all the more. What He has endured for us! It's hard for our human minds to grasp; but with all that I *can* understand of love, as a daughter, and then as a mother, His love goes *so* far beyond that!

Day 335

Today's Scripture:

"The Lord will work out his plans for my life—for your faithful love,
O Lord, endures forever" (Psalm 138:8 NLT).

Today's Testimony (Continued From Previous Day):

Christmas of 2018, my mom surprised me with a DNA test. My results came back as European, not very exciting. But then I looked in my DNA matches and saw a long list of people who shared some portion of my DNA. That was very exciting! My closest DNA match was a first cousin. You have no idea how that felt, being adopted. My brain and emotions felt like they were not even in the same body.

This began months of me asking my husband, "Does she/he look like me?" Then one day while I was looking at photos on the DNA website and Facebook, I got a new match. It was listed as a "close relative"! Because my adopted mom and my biological mom wrote letters to each other during the first six months of my life, I knew my biological mom's first name and I knew I had an older sister and I knew her name. I immediately started sobbing at the sight of their names listed and went to their profiles on Facebook. Meanwhile my sister called my mom and said, "Amber found her birth mom! What do we do?"

A few months later, I reached out to my birth mom and she responded. It was the most surreal thing I've ever experienced. She was excited to hear from me! We decided to meet face-to-face. It was like a God-directed fairy tale.

My biological mother's choice was beautiful and selfless. Adoption is amazing, but there is so much trauma that is endured from all sides. I can't begin to imagine what she must have lived through after those moments of giving up her baby. I don't know what emotions she felt, but I'm sure her heart was broken. However, she told me that when she was looking through couples in the book at the adoption agency, she saw a picture of my parents and it was like there was a light on their faces. I know God's hand was on her that day, when she picked that young couple "with the big hair." God brought us all together then; and years later through our meeting again, both my biological mom and I received healing in a way that only God could provide. I have never been this spiritually healthy and close to God as I am after that chapter in my life.

—*Amber*

Today's Takeaway:

What a story of bringing people full-circle! Amber and her adopted mom felt healing after meeting her biological mother and hearing the "rest of the story." Can you imagine what it will be like one day when we finally see our Father face-to-face? We may not understand everything now, but one day we will and He'll wipe away every tear. We'll have perfect peace with not only Him, but *all* of our family, and we will never be separated again. There's no other word for that but HEAVEN!

Day 336

Today's Scripture:

"Then they spoke the word of the Lord to him and to all the others in his house. At that hour of the night the jailer took them and washed their wounds; then immediately he and all his household were baptized" (Acts 16:32-33 NIV).

Today's Testimony:

As a young mother in the '70s, I was living a good life with my husband and five children. My husband and I both had good jobs and a nice home. The problem was we weren't saved.

One of my sons got saved at age twelve. He would ask my husband and me to go to church with him. I would go sometimes, but my husband didn't.

One night my older son woke us up and told us that his younger brother passed out and was not responding. We took him to the hospital. He was having seizures. The hospital gave us medication and sent him home. At home, he got worse instead of better.

The doctor sent him to a children's hospital. There he was diagnosed with acute panencephalitis (SSPE)—also known as Dawson disease—a rare form of brain inflammation. They told me he had one year to live.

We were brokenhearted. Crying and not knowing what to do, my husband said to me, "We've got to find help. We've got him buried in our minds. We need God!"

He asked me where I'd like to go to find a pastor to help us. I had gone to the church where my son got saved, so that is where we went. We called the pastor and he asked us to come to church Sunday. We went that Sunday night.

Church had already started when we arrived. They were playing "Amazing Grace." The pastor stopped the service and called our family down front. He asked us if we'd like to give our hearts to the Lord. Our entire family was saved that night.

I don't know how I could have lived through that time without God. My son lived seven years. The pastor preached at his funeral and titled the message, "The Little Evangelist." His life touched a lot of people.

God has been good to me all these years. My husband has gone on to be with Jesus and our son. God has given me a new Christian husband. We are happy and serving God together. I love the Lord and praise Him for all He's done for me.

—*Lavenia*

Today's Takeaway:

There is nothing more wonderful than to hear of an entire family coming to know the Lord. In Acts 16:33, after the jailer saw Paul and Silas' reaction to adversity while they were in prison, it changed his life and the life of his entire household.

Sometimes doctors tell us one thing, but God has another plan. Trust God's plan—He has information that doctors cannot begin to know.

Day 337

Today's Scripture:

"Now unto him that is able to keep you from falling, and to present you faultless before the presence of his glory with exceeding joy" (Jude 24 KJV).

Today's Testimony:

The ironic thing about my testimony is that for many years of my life I didn't believe I had one. I can't remember a time of not being in love with God. I know no one is automatically saved, but I do know as a small child my faith in God was strong. All I wanted to do was talk with Him, and according to my mother, that's what I did quite often. When I was about *four* years old, she walked in as I was praying asking God to open my ears so that I could hear Him better. During that time of my life, salvation occurred. That level of faith has carried me throughout my life.

In my sophomore year of college, I was attending a Christian university. One night at the end of my spring semester, I was telling God I felt as if I didn't have an actual testimony. You know, those "horrible pit" kind of testimonies. It made me feel so inadequate as a believer.

Well, I was in a series of extremely compromising situations throughout that weekend which, being at a Christian university with strict rules, could have gotten me expelled. (Disclaimer: I was not in any of these situations by choice, nor was I taking part, but my presence was enough to get me in a lot of trouble.) At the last event, a wild house party evolved. I sat down on the steps and asked God, "What is going on? and why am I here?" No sooner had these words left my mouth, when police showed up and I had to sneak out the back like a criminal.

I was so angry at my friends for putting me in this awful position. I could not believe almost everything I had avoided my entire life was happening in one weekend. When I returned to my dorm, I sat down, completely bewildered. Then I heard the Lord say to me, "Now unto Him that is able to keep you. . . . Your testimony is that you allowed yourself *to be kept*." At that moment my whole weekend made sense—God gave me a glimpse of the life I *thought* was a perfect testimony, when *my* testimony is that *God is truly able to do what He said He can do . . . keep me.* It sounds so simple, but it's really powerful.

—*Karien*

Today's Takeaway:

Does *being kept* by Him mean we have to be perfect? No, but it does mean asking God to help us choose to be kept by Him so others will know He is really able to do what He says. We do the asking—He does the keeping.

Day 338

Today's Scripture:

"Surely goodness and mercy shall follow me all the days of my life; and I will dwell in the house of the Lord forever" (Psalm 23:6 NKJV).

Today's Testimony:

I was not raised in a Christian home. We had a picture of Jesus in our house, and a large Bible on the coffee table. Sometimes I heard the name of Jesus, seldom in the proper context. For a while, we kids rode the church bus to attend Sunday school, but then we moved to the country, too far for the bus to pick us up anymore. That was the extent of my exposure to Jesus.

Even though my parents and family were good people, they weren't godly people. I didn't understand how God fit into a person's life. I assumed following Jesus involved a lot of rules. I imagined God to be a distant, authoritarian figure who was ready to catch me messing up, and punish me for it.

Years later, as an adult, my thoughts about God turned to curiosity. The only person I knew who could tell me about God was my brother-in-law. He talked like he knew Jesus and they were close friends. Those discussions chipped away at my self-created images of God. I learned God loves and forgives, and Jesus is both Savior and friend. But, even though I loved hearing about God, I wasn't ready to go any further.

My uncertainty about God didn't stop His pursuit of me. He kept drawing me to Jesus. This time, He worked through our daughter. When she was eight, she started asking about church. So, to appease her, we went to my brother-in-law's church. We had only attended a short time when the church hosted the movie *The Passion of the Christ*. We attended and I was humbled. I knew a little about the story of salvation, but this movie made it real. It opened my eyes to this God who loves me and wanted me to know and love Him. I accepted Jesus right there. Not only did I get saved, but soon my entire family did. We were completely changed and would never be the same.

I am so thankful for that night, because three years later my brother died from cancer. We all had peace; we knew we would see him again. I may not have started in a Christian home, but thankfully this is how it will end.

—*Tammy*

Today's Takeaway:

I understand why Tammy's heart was so full. God was faithful in His pursuit of her over the course of her life. He sent someone to patiently share Jesus with her, and to pray for her and her entire family. He wanted her to come into the kingdom of Heaven. He's doing the same thing for you. He's got people praying for you and your family right now. Whether you know it or not. He's pursuing you and caring for you. You're surrounded with love!

Day 339

Today's Scripture:

"God showed how much he loved us by sending his one and only Son into the world so that we might have eternal life through him. This is real love—not that we loved God, but that he loved us and sent his Son as a sacrifice to take away our sins" (1 John 4:9-10 NLT).

Today's Testimony:

Looking up at the sky into the infinite universe of stars and beauty, I would ask, "Why, God? Why don't they understand me? What is this life all about? What do You want me to do? If You are out there, God, I need You." This was me at age ten. I would go out at night, when I was doing my chores of burning garbage, and talk to God. I felt like no one understood me. Looking back, I see I was defiant with my parents, but at the time I thought they hated me and wanted to make me miserable. I didn't have any friends at school and felt unloved by everyone.

I was an outcast. We didn't have much money, but the other students came from well-to-do homes. I didn't fit in and was picked on a lot. I was loud and obnoxious. I'm sure I drove the nuns crazy some days. I would challenge the teachers and staff and ask questions. In catechism class, I was the student that was inquisitive about the beliefs and traditions of the Catholic faith and wanted to know why we did the things we did. I was also curious about what other people believed and why there were different churches out there.

I wasn't allowed to attend non-Catholic churches except when I would visit my one cousin. Every time I would go, I could feel something different.

As a teenager, I became very close friends with a girl whose dad was a pastor of a local church. I wasn't allowed to attend her church, but they did have a lock-in I could go to. I remember being inappropriate and chasing boys around all night, but I also remember feeling included; everyone was so nice. My friend talked with me about God and gave me a Bible. I still went to mass every Saturday. but I just stood there. I thought I was too cool now to participate and wasn't even sure if God was real.

—*Tabatha*
(To Be Continued in Tomorrow's Reading)

Today's Takeaway:

Do you realize God sees every difficulty you face? There's not a trial you go through that He doesn't understand. I think that's why God planned for Jesus to be born into a poor family—so He could understand how it would feel to have only a little. He knew what it felt like to be an outcast. He understands our questions too. He made us curious; He isn't threatened by it. Take your questions to the Word and to Him in prayer. When you're sincere, He'll guide you.

Day 340

Today's Scripture:

"Surely goodness and mercy shall follow me all the days of my life: and I will dwell in the house of the Lord forever" (Psalm 23:6 KJV).

Today's Testimony *(Continued From Yesterday):*

In college, once again God put someone in my path to show Himself to me. I had a roommate who read the Bible every night and would pray with her boyfriend on the phone. God used her to plant seeds in my life. While at college, I was in a long-distance relationship with my boyfriend. I got pregnant my first year; we got married after our daughter was born.

At this time, we didn't go to church anywhere and didn't really acknowledge God in our lives. I could feel that sense of rejection creeping into our marriage just like I'd felt growing up. My husband is an amazing man, but he also worked a lot and liked to hang out with his friends, which left me feeling alone and second-best again. A couple of years later, I had our second child.

Before Father's Day a few years later, my husband's dad said all he wanted was to have all of his sons attend church with him. My husband and I had never really gone to church together, besides weddings or funerals. We agreed we would go for his dad, but if they were "crazy," we wouldn't go back.

As we entered the church, everyone greeted us; it was so nice. Then the music started; they had a full band. I had never seen or heard anything like it. As I looked around, people were singing from their hearts and not just going through the motions—even teenagers. Then I saw some people raising their hands and I thought, *What are they doing?* As I started singing, tears flowed. I had no idea why. The church service was like nothing I had ever experienced. After the service, people hugged and loved us. When we got to the car, we were in awe. We decided to go back.

Two weeks later, we came back for another service. Again, everyone was so kind. We could feel love in the place. This time during the singing, I was sobbing. I was so embarrassed. I thought, *What is wrong with me? I don't cry in church.* The pastor talked about God's love, and at the end, he asked for anyone who wanted to receive God's forgiveness and love to raise their hand. My hand went into the air, and so did my husband's. We prayed together for God's forgiveness that day. Our life has never been the same.

—*Tabatha*

Today's Takeaway:

God had been pursuing Tabatha for years. He wanted to show her what real love felt like. She finally allowed Him. All her years of going to church had been just going through the motions. We can have a "head knowledge" of God but not a relationship with Him. Where are you today? Let God in. There is nothing else like it.

Day 341

Today's Scripture:

"I am the way, and the truth, and the life. No one comes to the Father except through me" (John 14:6 ESV).

Today's Testimony:

I grew up Catholic, and when I started going to a Spirit-filled church, I thought only the hard-core Christians went on Sunday nights. I remember one Sunday night in particular; I was sitting in the back pew. God was speaking to me that night through the preacher. I heard God tell me I didn't have to be alone, I had Him to lean on, and I could have His help whenever I asked for it. My knees started shaking nervously, I was clasping and unclasping my hands, and my eyes welled up with tears. We stood up for the closing and there was an altar call for anyone who wanted prayer. Well, I sure did.

I went to the altar, and when the preacher asked me what I wanted, it took me a few seconds to speak. Finally, I blurted out with tears in my eyes, "I want it all." He prayed with me, then I returned to my seat. After he closed the service, he remarked to every-one that I had rededicated my life to Jesus. Even though I had been in church just about all my life, that was the first time I remember *ever* deciding to dedicate my life to Him.

There was no amazing rescue from drugs, no exciting rescue from alcohol, and no dramatic rescue from sexual misconduct. I had been rescued from some of those things earlier in my life because He was loving, forgiving, and gracious enough to have His hand on me before I ever knew I wanted or needed it. So, even though I didn't have a "rock-bottom" salvation; instead, I learned to thank God for sparing me from that expe-rience. All that matters is I came to the Father through the Son.

—*Sharon*

Today's Takeaway:

Thank God, Sharon decided to be "hard-core" that night. The Lord knew she needed it all. It was time for her to give everything to Him. She not only heard the message, but she responded. How many times do we hear a message and feel like we need to pray but hesitate? Sharon was transparent before Him, and because of that, she was blessed for the rest of her life. Salvation came to her because of her willingness to respond when He called.

Don't worry about comparing your testimony with someone else's; what matters is that you tell your story to someone and explain what God has done in your life and how He can change theirs. He's a good God. He deserves the praise.

Day 342

Today's Scripture:

"For it is by grace you have been saved, through faith—and this is not from yourselves, it is the gift of God—not by works, so that no one can boast" (Ephesians 2:8-9 NIV).

Today's Testimony:

I serve an amazing God! Church has always been a very important part of my life, but something tested my faith about seven years ago that almost left me devastated.

My husband was very ill. He was in the Intensive Care Unit for a week. He wasn't getting any better. I was constantly praying to God. After a week, my daughter and I had a talk with the physician about him. We, together, made the decision to let him go home to God. Afterward, I became angry with God for not doing what I asked Him to do.

I did not step back in a church for almost a year. My granddaughters started going to church on Wednesday nights. My family started going on Sunday, but I would not. Finally, I said yes and went back to church. I have been blessed by God, but there was a part of my heart that wasn't open to God, no matter how much I tried.

A couple of weeks ago my pastor preached a sermon on God's amazing grace. I felt tears running down my face. I knew it was God saying, "I gave you grace when you were going through everything. When are you going to do the same for Me?" With tears running down my face, for the first time in seven years, I told God I was sorry for blaming Him all this time. I love God with everything inside of me! I truly understand 2 Peter 1:2, which says, "Grace and peace be yours in abundance through the knowledge of God and of Jesus our Lord" (NIV).

—*Norma*

Today's Takeaway:

There is nothing more painful than losing someone we love—except being separated from God. To have both of those things added together is almost unbearable! The natural thing to do when we hurt is look for someone to blame. The truth is that God loves His children. "Precious in the sight of the Lord is the death of His saints" (Psalm 116:15 NKJV).

At an appointed time, God receives His own. That doesn't make it easier for the people who love them—unless we remember that living in the presence of our Lord is wonderful. No pain, no problems, no more worries to face in this life for our loved one—only peace and joy! We will all be reunited and never have to say goodbye again. That will be worth it all!

Day 343

Today's Scripture:

"Cast all your anxiety on him because he cares for you" (1 Peter 5:7 NIV).

Today's Testimony:

I have grown up knowing about God and the Bible my whole life. My parents have tried their best to lead my family in a godly example. One week in my Sunday school class, one of the teachers talked about accepting Jesus into our hearts. A few days later, it really hit me; and while I was at a craft class, I decided I wanted to do it and make that decision. Right there, in school, my mom and I knelt down in the hallway and prayed. That is how my journey started. I had no clue about how amazing and hard the next years would be, and I still have a lot more of my journey to cover.

When I was five years old, I knew this girl and she did some really sad and horrific things to me. I didn't fully know or understand that I needed to tell my parents, but I knew it wasn't good. Some years later, I realized the truth of what had happened and got my courage up to tell my parents. I went into their room and told them all that had happened. My parents were so kind, gentle, and loving through it all, but still, it left me with such fear.

I remember one night I was sleeping in my parents' room on the floor. I was so scared I was shaking, but out of nowhere, I heard God's voice say to me, "I'm here." After that, I was able to fall asleep so peacefully. God was, and still is, so good to me, and His name "Comforter" fits Him so well.

God was there through it all, and a few years later, I came out of that season and started a new one. I knew that I would be just as victorious as I had been in the past seasons, and in the ones to come. Journeys are hard and can have rough terrain, but once you get to the top of the mountain, it is more beautiful than you can imagine.

—*Mataya (12 years old)*

Today's Takeaway:

Wow, so much Christian maturity in a girl so young! Her struggle was hard. I wish she could have been spared that pain, but the good thing is, her pain was not endured in vain. God does not waste our pain; when our faith is tested, our endurance grows (James 1:3). We learn to stand stronger and know He is able to make us victorious in all situations. The next time a trial comes, we find that we're a little stronger than we were the last time. That's the power of a great God.

Day 344

Today's Scripture:

"From the rising of the sun to its going down, the Lord's name is to be praised"
(Psalm 113:3 NKJV).

Today's Testimony:

I was raised in church. I am grateful to have been aware of God for the majority of my life; however, we all have to make our own choices at some point in life. I remember being five years old the first time I asked Jesus to come into my heart. I'm not sure I understood what that meant. *Jesus . . . in my heart?*

Jesus was in my heart, but I didn't see Him in my home. My family never missed a beat when it came to church. Every Sunday, Wednesday, and extra clean-up days—my family was there. However, showing up to church doesn't mean you're perfect. It also doesn't mean you have a relationship with God. My parents seemed like saints on Sundays and terrified me every other day of the week. How could they be so "holy" one day, and treat me the way they did the next? Eventually, my parents divorced when I was around eight. My mother was convinced that Jesus was the only way to stay sane, and she was correct. Even through trauma and emotional episodes, she always came back to church and missing it was not an option.

One Sunday, my mother heard that the children's pastors needed volunteers to assist them in children's church. I was all in. I still remember the way those kids worshiped, so unashamed. If *they* could, why couldn't I? Serving in children's church impacted my view of many things, including my view of everyday Christianity. The children's pastors began to be intentional toward me, inviting me to their house. They were my first encounter with lifestyle Christianity. They didn't just worship in church, but in their home. They spoke differently and responded with grace. Were they perfect? No. But, they apologized when they were wrong and strived to know God better. This relationship carried over to weekly sleepovers and rides to school. They became my safe place. They became my "pastor parents."

—Jocelyn
(To Be Continued in Tomorrow's Reading)

Today's Takeaway:

Without looking over to tomorrow's page, do you think that because Jocelyn had such a great momma, who was determined to raise her in church, and because she had such absolutely amazing children's pastors, who modeled everything a Christian should be in front of her, she automatically followed them and skipped all the problems of life? I want to say yes, but she did not skip the problems many people face. What I want you to understand first is, she got a strong foundation that helped her before she faced anything. Get your own foundation—in the Word of God—hear it preached, and read it!

Day 345

Today's Scripture:

"For the Lord God is our sun and our shield. He gives us grace and glory. The Lord will withhold no good thing from those who do what is right" (Psalm 84:11 NLT).

Today's Testimony *(Continued From Previous Day):*

My "pastor parents" were my safe place; they modeled Christian life in front of me. This discipleship caused my love for Jesus to go beyond Sundays and into every decision in my life. As I grew, so did my love for Jesus. It was up and down, but I chose Him. I will always choose Him.

The storms of "family hurts"—first love, drug abuse, and a tainted self-image—have fought for my faith. However, Jesus has always been in the boat with me, saying, "Peace, be still." The storms of my past cannot compare to the sunlight in my future.

The sunlight so far has looked like serving eighteen months as a full-time missionary in South Africa, and having both my divorced parents and "pastor family" serve alongside me for two weeks. The sunlight looks like forgiveness toward men who used me. The sunlight looks like wearing the identity of Christ and not my poor choices.

My story, I am sure, is like many others; it isn't once-saved and done. Issues continue to happen and bog me down from time to time. However, as my pastor mom always says, "You're either up or you're getting up."

What does your sunlight look like?

—*Jocelyn*

Today's Takeaway:

So now you see, Jocelyn faced many issues, like all of us. She wasn't exempt, and probably you won't be either. What will you do when the storms of life rock your boat? Don't be scared. We happen to know a Captain who isn't just experienced, He speaks to waves. I know it sounds crazy; it did to the disciples too, until they saw the waves calm. I've seen this happen in my life. I've watched my God speak peace and make waves stop when I *knew* there was no other explanation except Him. Try giving Him your issues.

If you think becoming a Christian means you'll never face problems, get victory over that lie right now. Our God doesn't keep us in a box where nothing ever happens to us; He equips us to handle it when it comes. That way, we'll be equipped to help someone else and be useful for His service.

Day 346

Today's Scripture:

"For the Lord Himself will descend from heaven with a shout, with the voice of an archangel, and with the trumpet of God. And the dead in Christ will rise first. Then we who are alive and remain shall be caught up together with them in the clouds to meet the Lord in the air. And thus we shall always be with the Lord. Therefore comfort one another with these words" (1 Thessalonians 4:16-18 NKJV).

Today's Testimony:

I was raised in the Catholic church and always believed in God, Jesus the Son of God, and the Holy Spirit, but I was not living my life as a Christian should.

About twenty years ago, my husband and I had a cabin we used as a getaway; and not being a big-time television watcher, I went to a used bookstore to obtain some books to read while at the cabin.

I found a set of books called *The Left Behind Series*. I bought volumes 1-5, and read three of them while we were at our cabin. The rest I brought home with me, and read when we got home.

There was another used bookstore where I lived, and I acquired the remaining books in the series and continued reading. As I was reading, parts of scriptures entered my mind. I had read the Bible in the past, but it had been a while.

After reading the series, I started to have dreams that I needed to repent and accept Jesus into my life. Soon I stood in my kitchen and cried out to the Lord to forgive me for all the sins I had ever committed. I wept, but soon felt freer than I have ever been. I felt light at heart. Next, I found a Bible study to attend and a church to go to. Shortly after that, I was baptized in water. I *knew* I would not be left behind!

—Maureen

Today's Takeaway:

This is thrilling to me. The power of the Holy Spirit drew Maureen through a book series! Her heart had seeds already planted and God used a powerful set of books to minister to her. I shouldn't be surprised. God uses lots of things in His service. He once even used a donkey. The bottom line is, let's be on the lookout in our lives when God is using something to get our attention. I don't want to miss it when He's trying to get my attention. Let's be sensitive to the Holy Spirit—always!

Day 347

Today's Scripture:

"For my beloved son was once dead, but now he's alive! Once he was lost, but now he is found! And everyone celebrated with overflowing joy" (Luke 15:24 TPT).

Today's Testimony:

When I was a child my father was a pastor, so I grew up in the church. At about seven years old, I remember realizing I needed to pray to be saved. I did, and I was passionate and on fire for Jesus for most of my younger years.

At the age of sixteen, some very traumatic experiences pushed me away from the church as a whole and away from God. I was hurt and angry, and I ran as fast and as far as I could from everything I'd ever known.

My heart was broken and inside me was an emptiness I had never experienced. I began to try to fill that void with anything I could. I experimented with many different drugs, I drank and partied, and became someone I didn't even recognize. I began to seek out love through sexual encounters rather than meaningful relationships. I would take broken pieces of glass and cut myself because I didn't think it was fair that I carried such pain inside and no one could see that anything was wrong on the outside.

At the age of twenty-three, I had just gotten out of a relationship when I found out I was pregnant. This was a major turning point for me, and I was determined to do right for my child. She is the biggest blessing I have ever received: beautiful, smart, and sweet. With her entrance into my world, my crazy partying days were over, but my heart was still pretty calloused from past pain.

—*Jessica*
(To Be Continued in Tomorrow's Reading)

Today's Takeaway:

Hurt and anger is a natural consequence of living. It's hard, but it's true. There's no way around it—some time or another, you will get hurt and you will get angry. When a Christian experiences these things, it's especially important to go straight to the Word of God to see how to handle it. It's hard, because every situation is different—sometimes you are wrong, sometimes the other person, sometimes a little of both. Owning responsibility isn't trendy. Genuine apologies aren't usually common. Both are absolutely necessary in a Christian's life.

Sometimes, the best thing to do is apologize for more than you're even responsible for. Bring the conflict to an end quickly. Look at what absolute heartbreak could have been avoided in Jessica's life if her hurt and anger could have been resolved. Let Christian maturity reign in your life.

Day 348

Today's Scripture:

"You shall teach them diligently to your children [impressing God's precepts on their minds and penetrating their hearts with His truths] and shall speak of them when you sit in your house and when you walk on the road and when you lie down and when you get up" (Deuteronomy 6:7 AMP.).

Today's Testimony *(Continued From Previous Day):*

When my daughter was four years old, we were driving down the road and she excitedly pointed out a billboard for the zoo. I remember they had animals walking two-by-two, a Noah's ark theme. I said as much to her, and she replied, "Who is Noah?" I said, "You know, from the Bible!" But she stared at me blankly, and my heart sank.

I don't remember the rest of that drive home, but I do remember that I set her up with toys in her room the second I got home and ran to my bedroom to fall on my knees and beg God to forgive me! I realized at that moment that I had failed her! I had not given her the foundation she needed. Even though I had made her the priority in my life, nothing else I taught her mattered if she didn't know the Bible—if she didn't know Jesus. I laid out my heart to Him that night, and peace flooded over me.

For years, I had felt the tug of the Holy Spirit on my heart and ignored it. I thought I had run too far, and it would be entirely too much work to get back to Jesus. That night I realized though I had run, He had never stopped pursuing me. All this time, He had been standing right behind me, waiting patiently for my return, with arms wide open.

—*Jessica*

Today's Takeaway:

(Jessica's words) When I surrendered my heart that night, a miraculous change took place in me. God had begun the process of deliverance and redemption in my life, but there was much work to be done.

The rest of it did not happen overnight but over time. He delivered me from drug use and addiction, and from unhealthy thoughts and habits that had been a part of who I was without Him. The more I surrendered, the more He gave me in return. He brought me a God-fearing husband whom I now have the pleasure of working beside in ministry, fulfilling our calling. I am blessed beyond all measure!

(My words) There's nothing like looking into the face of your own sweet child to make you suddenly feel the weight of responsibility of love! That made it all click for Jessica! What about you? God loves you far more than you love your child or grandchild. Isn't He amazing?

Day 349

Today's Scripture:

"For I know the thoughts that I think toward you, says the Lord, thoughts of peace and not of evil, to give you a future and a hope. Then you will call upon Me and go and pray to Me, and I will listen to you. And you will seek Me and find Me, when you search for Me with all your heart" (Jeremiah 29:11-13 NKJV).

Today's Testimony:

I didn't grow up in a Christian home. My father was an alcoholic and was very abusive to my mother. I watched her get beat up so many times. She left him over and over, but he would sober up and convince her to come back. It was hard for her back then with six children to raise alone; there was no welfare back then.

I don't remember much about my childhood before I was six or seven years old. I believe my mind blocked a lot out. Usually, we would go to my grandparents' house. I loved being with them. They went to church all the time; I believe it was around this age that I first gave my heart to the Lord.

As I grew up, I didn't get to be around my grandparents often because we moved away. Eventually, I "moved away" from the Lord too. I developed the attitude that marriage didn't have to be forever. There was no way I was going to go through what my mother did. I knew that how I lived my life was not pleasing to God, but God had always kept me safe and protected me from all my mistakes. Still, I was constantly filled with guilt from my sins.

But the Lord has a way of calling us back, and at the age of thirty-two, I rededicated my life to Him. I am seventy-two years old now. God has forgiven me and cleansed me from all my sins. I regret that I let so many years go by without trusting Him and asking for His forgiveness. I am serving the Lord and am married to a wonderful man who loves the Lord also. I realize this life is only temporary here on earth and I look forward to His coming and taking us to be with Him forever.

—Robbie

Today's Takeaway:

It's a common defense move to block out painful memories from our past. Sometimes it's easier to close doors to pain and leave everything inside. The only problem with that is, some good memories get shut up inside those doors too. It takes a lot of prayer and talking through those painful memories either with God, a counselor, or both to get through those things. Just remember, you can get through them! The main thing is to forgive the people behind those doors so the enemy doesn't have a chance to cause a root of bitterness to spring up from it and make you miserable. Robbie was able to give everything to God and ask for Him to cleanse her. She was able to forgive her father and move forward. Can you?

Day 350

Today's Scripture:

"The light shines in the darkness, and the darkness has not overcome it"
(John 1:5 ESV).

Today's Testimony:

Sunday morning, still high and drunk from all-night partying with friends, I drove cautiously to my apartment to get ready for my three-year-old niece's baptism at a local church. We weren't churchgoers, but my mom said, "God sends babies to hell if they die without being baptized." So my niece was to be sprinkled, just for safe-keeping.

Looking on from the front pew, my heart hardened with judgment, my breath harsh with hangover, my bloodshot eyes glared at the scene before me. I watched my family—the bunch of hypocrites—standing with this clueless, robed man of God. *If he knew my family, he'd never have agreed to do this,* I thought.

Suddenly, a bright, blinding light overtook the church service. A strong, male voice spoke to me: "Tracy, I love you; stop hurting yourself." I was stunned. I looked around, "What? Who are you?"

He repeated, "Tracy, I love you; stop hurting yourself." Then again, a third time: "Tracy, I love you; stop hurting yourself."

Like a light switch flipped, the church service was back. Overwhelmed with love and peace, I knew God was putting me back together, right then and there.

Ezekiel 36 feels like a chapter right out of my life—especially verse 26: "And I will give you a new heart, and a new spirit I will put within you. And I will remove the heart of stone from your flesh and give you a heart of flesh" (ESV).

Jesus rescued me from the pit of despair and destruction. Jesus set my feet upon His rock—my heart in His hands and His Light in my life. Now I live to love others with His love. When I do, I get to feel His love surround me as well, as it did in my darkest days, now overcome.

—*Tracy*

Today's Takeaway:

Does this read like a scene out of a movie, or what? Yet it is real. God did this to get Tracy's attention because at that particular moment, her heart was open to His message for her. Thankfully, she listened to Him and didn't just shrug it off as an alcoholic hallucination. God spoke words of kindness to his daughter—words that covered her in love and peace. That's His message to you right at this moment. He doesn't love Tracy more than He loves you. He knows you and your struggles, yet He loves you! Give Him your cares right now; He cares for you and longs to cover you with His wings and make you feel peaceful. Let Him carry your burden and restore your joy. Today is your day!

Day 351

Today's Scripture:

"We can rejoice, too, when we run into problems and trials, for we know that they help us develop endurance. And endurance develops strength of character, and character strengthens our confident hope of salvation. And this hope will not lead to disappointment" (Romans 5:3-5 NLT).

Today's Testimony:

I have been a Christian as long as I can remember. When I was three or four years old, I was at a church service and my mom recalls I saw people praying and told her I wanted what they had; then I asked Jesus into my heart. I was blessed to be raised in the church and a home that made worshiping God a priority. However, I was not without a thorn in my side.

My parents came to this country as illegal immigrants and didn't speak much English. As we got older, they became citizens, but many people who came from other countries had to work very hard for everything they had. There were four of us kids, and my parents both worked full-time. My mother worked days and my father worked nights, so some times we were left alone. People deal with things differently; some spend time with people they aren't supposed to or get hobbies that aren't beneficial, but I turned to food.

Growing up, I was always very overweight and dealt with social anxiety because of it. Being one of the few Hispanic kids in school, being a Christian, and also overweight, I felt alone. My anxiety continued to drive me to unhealthy habits up through college and into seminary. At one point I ballooned to 330 pounds. I had a job, a degree, and a wonderful supportive husband, but I still felt the guilt and shame of being overweight. Years into adulthood, I finally decided to try the last thing I was going to try. I truly felt like God was saying this is your time. I didn't want to just exist or feel sluggish; I decided to lose weight. There were some seriously difficult days, but with His help and guidance, I have finally regained my health. I know I have the resilience to do anything God has called me to do. If He has called you, He will equip you. Take courage and step out in faith even when you are afraid. He will walk with you through the deep water.

—*Sussy*

Today's Takeaway:

The difficult battle of weight plagues women everywhere, and it often makes us feel out of control. I am so thankful that no matter where you or I are in our battles today, we have the One who can give us victory in all things. He is the One we can bring our situations to and lay them before Him with no shame and ask for help. He never leaves us out.

Day 352

Today's Scripture:

"All praise to God, the Father of our Lord Jesus Christ. It is by his great mercy that we have been born again, because God raised Jesus Christ from the dead. Now we live with great expectation" (1 Peter 1:3 NLT).

Today's Testimony:

When I was eight years old, my friend's mom started taking me to church twice a week. Little did anyone know that I was being sexually abused by my father and physically and verbally abused by my mother. I desired to be loved and accepted by anyone. I found the true love of a Father and I accepted Jesus as my Lord and Savior at the age of nine. I knew Him and knew He would always be there for me.

As the years went by, we moved and I couldn't go to church with my friend, but I never forgot my relationship with the Lord. The abuse continued at home almost daily from both parents. I can remember being in the bed crying to the Lord as I was being abused, praying and believing He was there with me. He cared for me and saw my tears. When I was being hit, God was there. Even though I was experiencing pain, I knew I was loved and accepted by Jesus.

When I got to high school I met a fabulous Christian teacher who was sensitive to the Holy Spirit, and I came to trust her. I eventually told her what was happening at home. She reported everything to Child Protective Services, and they told my parents either they had to get help or I had to live with someone else. They chose for me to leave. Once again I felt rejected, unloved, and alone. But God helped me. He placed me with my aunt, which was forty minutes away from my school. My teacher, because of her love of Christ, took me to school every day for the forty-minute drive.

As I continued to learn what true love is by being loved by people who had the heart of Jesus, I soon learned what a real father is—one who cares and listens. Through prayer and worship, I found I could crawl up into my heavenly Father's lap and become a true "Daddy's girl."

—Corinne

Today's Takeaway:

Unspeakable abuse and suffering never go unpunished. God Almighty sees all and keeps an account. Corinne was delivered, thank God. The Lord will comfort her and heal her pain, and one day every tear will be washed away. I'm so thankful she can understand that she truly is her heavenly Father's girl.

I praise God for the teacher who listened and took action to rescue her. Do you see suffering around you? *God help us to be like the Good Samaritan, who saw and took action.*

Day 353

Today's Scripture:

"'*For I know the thoughts that I think toward you,*' saith the Lord, '*thoughts of peace, and not of evil, to give you an expected end*'" (Jeremiah 29:11 KJV).

Today's Testimony:

My story begins at age eleven when I started using drugs. By twelve, my drug addiction escalated and soon I became entangled in a bad, abusive relationship. By sixteen, I had two children. By nineteen, I was in jail. After serving my sentence, I started dating who I *thought* was the man of my dreams. We had one daughter together. However, again, I found myself in a cycle of abuse.

I started waitressing at a family restaurant where a local pastor came in for breakfast every morning. I wasn't looking for God, but after he kept inviting me, I eventually agreed to visit his church. I sat in the back and thought, *If this stuff is real, God, come get me.* I'd love to say from that point on, God restored my life and all was well; but it actually got worse. I was still on drugs, although my desires were slowly changing; it was a process. My boyfriend started going to church with me and we got married. Some good things were happening, but we still struggled with addiction.

Then four years later, my life was shattered. I found my husband in bed with another woman. Devastated, I left God and went back to drugs for two more years, until I finally broke. We were pulled over by an unmarked car. We had drugs, guns, and the driver was intoxicated and had a suspended license. I called my pastor, crying and confessing how I had gotten myself into trouble. He said, "I'm going to pray; call me back." That's it; and then I was put in handcuffs. I cried out to God in repentance, "Lord, if You let me go free, I'll never touch drugs again. I'll leave this lifestyle for the rest of my life."

Before long, the officers had everything out of my car. But then they walked up to me, released my handcuffs and said, "You're free to go." It was a miracle! What happened in the natural, happened in the spirit. I was free at last. I got saved; God restored my life. I started working at church, and eventually married the son of the pastor who had mentored me all those years. I'm now thirteen years clean, and happier than I've ever been.

—*Jessica*

Today's Takeaway:

We have a God who sticks around through all of our steps and missteps. He walks through every part of it. He won't force us, but He loves us back to Him. If the road seems very long, just remember, He never gets tired or weary with you. He just wants you in His will.

Day 354

Today's Scripture:

"Now the works of the flesh are obvious: sexual immorality, moral impurity, promiscuity, idolatry, sorcery, hatreds, strife, jealousy, outbursts of anger, selfish ambitions, dissensions, factions" (Galatians 5:19-20 CSB).

Today's Testimony:

I remember the Sunday when my mother got gloriously saved and baptized. It was December. We had just moved and I was about six years old. The men in the church chopped ice in the water to baptize her and my dad. What a day! As I was growing up, my mother loved the Lord and took us to church regularly. However, after a divorce and a remarriage, the ladies from the church were not too friendly to my mom, and after a while she stopped going. Sadly, at the time she needed Christian friends the most, none were to be found. By the time I was grown and had a family of my own, my mother had made new friends, but these friends were not the ones she should have chosen.

My mother met her new friends at a home party. The problem was, this party was to lure people into the occult. It started out by the leader saying my mom was really gifted. She could help people by charting their stars and reading their palms. The leader told her if she read the Bible first, the palm reading and star charting would actually be blessed by God. Of course, as Christians, we know this is *not* correct. In her hunger for friends and to be accepted, she fell into the trap. I showed my mother how this was not of God, but opposite to Scripture. No matter what I said, she did not listen to me.

I prayed that my mother's friends would drop her like a hot potato. Over the years, one by one they did. When the subject came up about knowing the future, tarot cards, or anything to do with this group, my mother would quickly change the subject. She knew I believed it was a sin to be involved and that she needed to be out of the group. To my knowledge, she never tried to influence my kids about the occult activities. When the grandkids were at church events, I invited her. Sometimes she went. She always said she believed in God. She had witnessed God answering many prayers in miraculous ways, including my daughter being healed of leukemia.

—Fredrica
(To Be Continued in Tomorrow's Reading)

Today's Takeaway:

I'm sad to hear all of this started with rejection from some ladies who could have shown love but instead turned a cold shoulder. How different this could have been! We all need friendship. Sometimes we only want to talk to the people we "know" or who are just like us. Jesus wasn't that way; He looked for the friendless. Let's reach out to hurting people at church, and be wise about the friends we choose.

Day 355

Today's Scripture:

"For 'everyone who calls on the name of the Lord will be saved'"
(Romans 10:13 NIV).

Today's Testimony *(Continued From Previous Day):*

As time went on, I never saw my mother openly denounce the occult. Years had passed and my mother was in poor health. I was concerned about her soul. If she were to die, how would I know if she went to Heaven? I had seen with my own eyes the excitement of when she was saved and baptized in icy lake water in December. I kept praying for God to give me a sign—something. I know it's the Holy Spirit who draws us to repentance. I kept praying for the Holy Spirit to call my mom.

I was hurrying around getting ready for a Wednesday night service, when I got a call from my mom. She was wondering if I was going to church, and if she could go with me? I nearly dropped the phone. I picked her up and we went to church. Being the sign-language interpreter, I sat up front facing the two deaf people sitting in front of me; my mother sat behind them. On the way home she said she liked the service. I was happy, but I still didn't know if she was ready to meet Jesus.

The next week, my phone rang, and my mom wanted to go with me to service again. Two weeks in a row! There was a guest speaker this time. He preached all over the Bible, as if he wasn't sure he'd get a chance again. I was sitting in front of the deaf group signing for them; my mother sat behind the group. When the end of the service came, the visiting preacher gave an altar call. This usually didn't happen in a midweek service. Because I must keep my eyes open while signing to the deaf for the prayer, I could see my mom raise her hand to rededicate her life to Christ. I was so excited! Then as the church prayed the sinner's prayer together, the Holy Spirit echoed in my ears that this was for me to be able to see my mom raise her hand and rededicate her life to Christ, so when her time came, I would *know* she went to be with Jesus, the lover of her soul.

Shortly after that night, my mother had a massive stroke and died. Although I was deeply saddened and shocked by her death, I had a joy in my heart because I knew—really KNEW that she was with Jesus, the lover of her soul.

—*Fredrica*

Today's Takeaway:

God was faithful to Fredrica's prayers. She would not give up on her mother but believed she would know beyond any doubt her mother was ready for Heaven. She got that assurance. She was even given the privilege to *see* her mother pray. How beautiful! Are you believing for God to do something for you? Don't give up! Keep trusting like Fredrica did. She stood fast and believed. You can too.

Day 356

Today's Scripture:

"I will praise You, for I am fearfully and wonderfully made; marvelous are Your works, and that my soul knows very well" (Psalm 139:14 NKJV).

Today's Testimony:

My entire life, I have been the girl that looked "different." It is impossible to look "normal" with a port-wine stain birthmark that covers half your face. When I was a baby, my parents got stares and comments. As a child, people would ask what I'd done—had I fallen off my skateboard or been hit by a baseball bat? As a child, I underwent laser treatments every six weeks for four years, but saw little results. Later, I tried all the latest and greatest makeups to cover it up, but they just felt like plaster on my face. Finally, I gave up trying to be normal.

I expected people not to like me, and was surprised if they did. I wore a fake smile, as though I was happy and confident, but it was a lie. I was broken and hurt. I felt worthless, like I didn't matter. I felt I wasn't good enough and wouldn't amount to anything. I wondered how I could be made in God's image and have a birthmark on half my face. Why would God create me to look like this?

As I went to youth group and read the Bible, I began to be real with God. He showed me who I truly was, who He made me to be. I understood that He uniquely designed me for a purpose that only I could fulfill. God used what I saw as my weakness to touch other people's lives. Outward appearances fade; it's who you are on the inside that people remember.

Live confidently in who you are in Christ, who He made you to be. Don't let the world tell you that you're worthless. See yourself as God does—as royalty, as loved, as beautifully created in His image. We are His handiwork. God specifically designed each of us the way we are for a purpose that only we can fulfill. Let's be real with ourselves, with God, and with others!

—Abby

Today's Takeaway:

Bravo, Abby! I just want to hug her and be one of her friends, don't you? There is something wonderful about being real, being yourself, that is so freeing! God has a specific plan for each of us; He puts special characteristics in each of us He can use. In Abby's case, her birthmark is something He uses for His glory to help Abby and other people see that we must look deeper than the surface.

In a society when so many seem to be preoccupied only with their appearance on the outside, let's stop and go a little deeper to what really matters. Let's go down to our hearts—first let's examine our own and lay it open before the Lord, then let's be concerned about the hearts of those around us. Now, that's real beauty!

Day 357

Today's Scripture:

*"And we know that all things work together for good to those who love God,
to those who are the called according to His purpose"* (Romans 8:28 NKJV).

Today's Testimony:

As a very young child, I was aware of God's presence all around me. The beauty of the mountains, the streams, flowers, and growing crops in the fields overwhelmed me. I walked three miles to church each Sunday to a holiness church where the pastor and his wife made me feel very welcome. They led me to know God at the age of ten. They gave me a Bible, taught me the books of the Bible, and helped me memorize many Bible verses.

My family had failed crops for three years in a row and decided to move where there was work. My whole family was excited, but I knew I would miss my church. I found another vibrant church after we moved. I worked in various roles with children, always remembering my pastor saying God was going to use me for His glory. I stayed in that church, and later met and married a Christian man who felt called to the ministry. We both wanted to build churches of people who stood on God's Word.

My husband heard about a church where there was a building but only two elderly people. Before that, I had a dream about a building that was empty. In my dream, children were everywhere. My husband said he would go to check out the church. When we got there, I knew immediately this was the building in my dream. We decided to take the church. I started seeing children riding bikes in the parking lot, so I went out with cookies. I kept inviting them and asking them to bring their moms and dads to church. In three years, we had a congregation of over three hundred. God saved, healed, and gave us workers, all while we were trying to follow God's leading through study of the Word and prayer. From the church came two preachers, a missionary to Africa, and several counselors and teachers. I thank God every day for all of them. God is faithful to His promises (see Psalm 145:13). After my husband felt the church was secure with leaders, he went on to pastor other churches. God blessed all these churches to grow in numbers and finances, but most of all spiritually.

—Joyce

Today's Takeaway:

(Joyce's words) I found that in each church, working with children was very rewarding. I taught them to worship, read their Bibles, and memorize Scripture. Nothing was a greater blessing to me than leading someone to the altar. I'll soon be eighty years old. I pray God will use me to win others to the Lord and be an encouragement to them. Someday I want to hear God say to me, "Enter in, thou good and faithful servant."

(My words) Joyce, I believe you will!

Day 358

Today's Scripture:

"Count it all joy, my brothers, when you meet trials of various kinds, for you know that the testing of your faith produces steadfastness. And let steadfastness have its full effect, that you may be perfect and complete, lacking in nothing" (James 1:2-4 ESV).

Today's Testimony:

When I was five years old, my parents started taking us to Sunday school. But when I was seven, I started telling "fibs." I felt a heaviness in my heart every time I would lie. And because of that conviction, at seven years old, I asked for forgiveness and asked Jesus into my heart. I was baptized that same summer. I remember as I was coming out of the water, I felt a rush of warm peacefulness.

Life after that was awesome. I married my best friend at eighteen, and we started building a great life and family together. But then, I lost my dad, the rock of our family, to melanoma cancer. I was shocked. I had believed, with all my heart, that he would be healed. Then to add to that, our family ran into extreme financial problems. It was such a low time in my life. I felt like I'd hit a brick wall. But still, I could hear my dad say, "Just keep the faith, Lis." Well, I did; and a few years later, we rebounded beautifully.

Life was back on track, until my husband had a near-death experience and was in the hospital for eighteen days, in an induced coma. Doctors said there was nothing more they could do. I begged God, "Please God, not again. Don't take my husband away too!" I remember lying prostrate in front of the Christmas tree, on Christmas Eve. Our girls were gone; it was just me and Jesus. I cried and yelled out, "Please God, heal my husband, in Jesus' name." I prayed for what seemed like hours. A few days later, my husband was sitting up, and talking. Doctors were so shocked.

I'm now fifty-one, and I can't say I've never messed up. But when I do, that same heaviness comes on my heart, just like it did when I was little, and it doesn't go away until I ask Jesus for forgiveness. He has taken care of me all my life. I've been blessed with a wonderful family—too many blessings to count.

I used to think I didn't have much of a testimony, but now that I put it in writing, I realize I do. I've been faithful to Jesus since I was seven years old, and He's been faithful to me every day of my life.

—Lisa

Today's Takeaway:

How powerful! I love that Lisa could feel a "heaviness" in her heart whenever she "messes up"—that is a good thing. It's the conviction of the Holy Spirit working in your life when you can feel that. It means God is drawing you. I also love picturing Lisa lying on the floor in front of the Christmas tree crying out to God. He heard her cry. I love it when doctors are shocked for a good reason, don't you? God gets all the glory!

Day 359

Today's Scripture:

"Since God chose you to be the holy people he loves, you must clothe yourselves with tenderhearted mercy, kindness, humility, gentleness, and patience"
(Colossians 3:12 NLT).

Today's Testimony:

This is my testimony: My name is Karen and I'm seventy-seven years old. I am so glad I was saved. I met my husband forty-three years ago and I was so blessed to have my mother-in-law in my life. She was an amazing woman who loved the Lord with every fiber of her being. I wanted to be like her. I had been married before and had three children. My husband's parents accepted my children and me into their family like we had always been there.

I had not been raised to go to church like I should have. I'd lost a daughter at five weeks old from SIDS—I never blamed God for that, I just figured He needed her in Heaven. I almost drowned saving my friend's son from drowning. I can't swim; I knew God had made that happen. Then I met Sam and the boys—whom I called my sons as I raised them from the ages of thirteen and eleven. That was a challenge, but we got through it. I kept listening to my mother-in-law and her love of the Lord and I wanted that. So, on Christmas Day, forty-two years ago, sitting with my mother-in-law and my sister-in-law, I accepted the Lord. He has brought me through so much.

Two years ago, I had two major surgeries. The first one was to place a cage on my spine. I had already had two back surgeries and was in a lot of pain. God guided me to a wonderful specialist who operated on me; the next day I went home with no pain. Praise the Lord! Then two months later I had my left hip replaced. Again, I went home the next day with no pain and I was in church on Sunday. I can't say enough about what the Lord has done for me and my family.

I try to stay positive and share the Lord with people so they can have what I have. I am so proud of our church and all the pastors and their spouses.

One other thing, my husband didn't go to church for over twenty-five years, but one day he started going to church with me and has not missed a Sunday since. I always joked that he had more prayer cloths under his side of the mattress than I could make a quilt with. So, if you are praying for someone to come to church, keep praying! I am so thankful to God that my husband finally came.

—*Karen*

Today's Takeaway:

Well, I don't know about you, but I love Karen and I want to go live with her! She makes me smile just hearing her words. I bet I know why her husband started going to church, so he could be with her! Let's be contagious like Karen's sweet, kind, and joyful spirit. It will point everyone to Christ!

Day 360

Today's Scripture:

"Wake up, wake up, O Zion! Clothe yourself with strength" (Isaiah 52:1 NLT).

Today's Testimony:

Growing up we were always involved in church. I can clearly remember the day I said the sinner's prayer up at the altar at church camp and I received the Holy Spirit. When camp was over, I couldn't wait to tell my parents what had happened. I knew they would be so proud.

While in my twenties, I still went to church and prayed. I knew the Lord had a purpose for me and I knew it was to sing, but I just couldn't find "my place." I left my parents' church, thinking it was the will of God. I followed different "prophecies" on what I was "supposed to do." I got into a bad relationship and I started to go down a dark path, making bad decisions for myself. I felt alone and not able to go to my parents and talk to them like I used to. Until one day, the Lord said: "Wake up, Shantell."

I knew I needed a change. I walked into my father's study and started to cry. I asked for forgiveness and pleaded to come back to their church. Of course, he said yes with open arms. It was the first time in a long time that I was able to talk to them.

Around this time, I met my husband. We got engaged exactly one year after our first date and married a year after that. He truly was an answer to prayer. Soon after we got married we got pregnant with our first child. During the pregnancy, everything was great, but on the day I went into labor, I had a migraine. I couldn't focus. The pain of both the migraine and labor was just too much, so I asked to get an epidural. The anesthesiologist had trouble administering it and punctured my spine. After I laid down, I started to lose feeling from my shoulders to my feet. My husband was comforting me because I was shaking and felt so cold. When it came time to deliver, the nurse had to help me because I couldn't move. I had to give one last push, but right then, I felt a pop in my neck!

I told my mom and husband that something was wrong. The nurse gave me oxygen and told me that I was OK, and my feeling would come back. That night, I did start to gain feeling again, but there was something else not right in my body. I told the nurses multiple times that every time I stood up, I would pass out! This went on for the next few days I was there. My husband wanted to take me to the ER but was told we would have to leave and admit ourselves!

—Shantell
(To Be Continued in Tomorrow's Reading)

Today's Takeaway:

There will be moments in your life when you will be scared—I mean "I want my Daddy!" kind of scared! In those moments, you can cry out to God and you can be assured He's there.

Day 361

Today's Scripture:

"Heal me, Lord, and I will be healed; save me and I will be saved, for you are the one I praise" (Jeremiah 17:14 NIV).

Today's Testimony (Continued From Previous Day):

I made it home, but I still couldn't sit up, go to the bathroom, or even hold my newborn. My husband took me back to the hospital, where I was given pain medication. A few days later I experienced my first seizure! Being rushed to the ER, once again, I was told pain medication triggered it. I then was given seizure medication and a CT-scan was performed. The scan revealed a shadowing of the brain with excess fluid—meaning that the puncturing of the spine caused a "spinal headache." I was given caffeine for twenty-four hours and monitored. Afterward, I felt good for just a few days but started to feel lightheaded again.

I was told I would now need to have a blood patch done on my spine to stop the fluid from leaking. After that, I felt like a brand-new person. I even put up the Christmas tree and posted pictures of my baby. However, on Thursday of that very week when I was in the middle of changing my daughter's diaper, my mind went BLANK! There were no words, not knowing whose baby this was, or how to put a diaper back on her. Somehow, I was able to do it and get her back into bed. I waited until my husband came home to tell him what happened and that I think I had a stroke!

The next night, I had five grand-mal seizures and was rushed to the Neuroscience Center and stayed at the ICU in a drug-induced coma for a week. I was given MRI's and more CT-scans which revealed that the "shadowing" was a blood clot in my sinus cavity, called a "sinus thrombosis." Multiple doctors said different things—from "I've seen this before," "She'll be OK," to "She might not come out of this," and "Say your goodbyes." My family and multiple churches were praying for me. It was like I was just sleeping. The nurses said I could not hear, but I could. I knew when my mom and dad were there praying. I could hear my sister sitting beside me crying, saying: "You just got your fairytale and the baby you always wanted, so wake up Sis."

A day or two later, I woke up to the doctors around me, my mom by my side, and my husband holding my hand. I smiled at them, but I couldn't talk yet. Doctors said it could be months, even years, before I could talk, walk, and eat solid foods again. However, in *one week*, I was able to do all the things they said I wouldn't be able to do. God walked into that room and healed me completely! The day I was released to go home was on Christmas Day. That was the best gift my family could have ever received!

—*Shantell*

Today's Takeaway:

God is a *total Healer*! There's no explaining it and no figuring it out. All we can do is rejoice in it. He paid for our healing!

Day 362

Today's Scripture:

"For He has said, 'I will never [under any circumstances] desert you [nor give you up nor leave you without support, nor will I in any degree leave you helpless], nor will I forsake or let you down or relax my hold on you [assuredly not]!'" (Hebrews 13:5 Amp.).

Today's Testimony:

I was eight years old when my single-parent mother packed all of our belongings and prepared to move all of her five children several states away. I was her youngest and the only girl.

As Mom was home packing boxes for the move, she sent us children to a kids crusade at our church. The church graciously reached out to my mother to assist her, as she was trying to get back on her feet from the trauma of being deserted and then having a divorce that she did not want.

At kids crusade, when the minister gave the altar call and began to sing "There's Room at the Cross for You," it struck a chord in my heart. I remember the feeling that I had as the song resonated in my spirit. I couldn't stop thinking (as I made my way to the front of the sanctuary to ask Jesus into my heart), *There's room for me?*

I didn't understand at the time that I was already dealing with abandonment and rejection issues from my father abandoning our family when I was two years old. The pain my mother carried spilled over to me, as we shared a room and I would hear her crying out to God in the night.

God always uses what the enemy intends for harm for our good. That same pain I would feel as my mom prayed throughout the night also served as a catalyst that taught me how to develop a prayer life, and has caused me to be sensitive to the Holy Spirit's voice as I minister, as a teacher, to the needs of others.

The scripture, Hebrews 13:5, shown above sums up my testimony of God's saving and keeping power. I am now sixty-one years old and can testify to the fact that God has never abandoned me or failed me . . . and I know that He never will.

—*Candy*

Today's Takeaway:

Candy learned the power of prayer firsthand in the most heart-wrenching way! There are few things that touch a child like seeing your mother cry. No wonder it made such a deep soul-touching impression on her heart. She saw how that cry was answered: God strengthened her mother to stand strong, and instead of buckling under, she was able to dust herself off, pack her children and things, and move to "higher ground." She made a fresh start.

You receive strength like that when you cry out to the One who has all strength. When you should "buckle," with His strength, you STAND!

Day 363

Today's Scripture:

"To every thing there is a season, A time for every purpose under heaven"
(Ecclesiastes 3:1 KJV).

Today's Testimony:

I was saved at an early age, but in my journey, I have had many faith experiences as a Christian. This is a testimony of God's faithfulness and protection over my life.

After spending a beautiful day at an amusement park in 1991, we wanted to meet up with longtime ministry friends in the area. After meeting at the church where they pastored, we decided to visit the parsonage. As we were turning into the parsonage driveway, immediately we were hit from behind by a speeding vehicle. The car was going 90 miles an hour. All of a sudden, my life stood still. I saw my four-year-old daughter fly above me in what seemed like slow motion. I immediately experienced severe whiplash. I then saw lights flashing in a dark empty space within my mind, trying to search for answers and reaching for thoughts of survival.

I woke up in an ambulance heading to an unknown hospital without my husband and two kids. Facing insurmountable fear and pain, I was in a place where my faith was being challenged. My only hope was to draw on my faith which I'd known since I was a child when I accepted Jesus Christ as my Lord and Savior.

It was during these dark moments that I felt my life hang in the balance. The next thing I felt was the Holy Spirit speaking peace into my heart that I should trust Him and everything was going to work out. The Bible says, "You keep him in perfect peace whose mind is stayed on you, because he trusts in you" (Isaiah 26:3 ESV).

While the nurse was removing glass from my eyes and ordering lab tests, the silence was deafening and the moments of pain began to overwhelm me. I was experiencing physical pain, but that didn't compare to the mental anguish that now clouded my mind. I was learning that in these moments we have to submit our prayers, cry out and wait on Him to answer. It's during these times that we pull on our previous experiences of God's deliverance and faithfulness.

—*Lisa*
(To Be Continued in Tomorrow's Reading)

Today's Takeaway:

Even in moments of sheer terror, our God is with us. Aren't you glad? Lisa would have loved to have had her family with her right then, or some of her friends to hold her hand, but that was impossible. There are times when only your heavenly Father can be with you—but let me tell you, *He's enough.* He strengthened Lisa, and He'll strengthen you. He'll bring the Word to your mind (when you have His Word on your inside) and help you just like He did her.

Day 364

Today's Scripture:

"Being confident of this very thing, that he which hath begun a good work in you will perform it until the day of Jesus Christ" (Philippians 1:6 KJV).

Today's Testimony *(Continued From Previous Day):*

The next moment I was heading to get x-rays. I didn't want to believe this was happening to me, but the Holy Spirit brought comfort and peace as I spoke in a heavenly language. The Holy Spirit reminded me to wait on the Lord, "Be of good courage, and he shall strengthen thine heart: wait, I say, on the Lord" (Psalm 27:14 KJV). Stand firm in His promises that "all things work to the good of those who love Him" (see Romans 8:28).

I learned in this time that I needed to put my faith in a God who will never leave me nor forsake me. I wanted all physical and mental pain gone immediately; kind of like a fast-food healing. I was asking God to please erase this moment in my life and let me start over; however, that didn't happen. I had to learn patience and trust Him to strengthen me during this venture through the storm. The Holy Spirit prepares us for spiritual battle and teaches us the truth that He is always with us. We may not always put it together, but I believe before we face difficult times, God has prepared us for the battle. If He can deliver Jonah out of a whale, surely your circumstances can change. Jeremiah knew God was on his side and already had it all planned out: "'For I know the plans I have for you' declares the Lord, 'plans to prosper you and not to harm you, plans to give you hope and a future'" (Jeremiah 29:11 NIV).

What I learned from this experience is that the Lord will protect us from harm. He watches over us to keep us safe. The accident could have been much worse, as my husband and two children were unharmed. I also found strength in the Lord to forgive the man that hit us from behind. The offender was an escape convict who assaulted an elderly couple and stole their brand-new Cadillac. He didn't deserve my forgiveness, but I could no longer be captivated by unforgiveness, as we are instructed to forgive those who have trespassed against us: "Let all bitterness, and wrath, and anger, and clamour, and evil speaking, be put away from you, with all malice" (Ephesians 4:31 KJV). Through the power of the Holy Spirit, I was able to overcome the unforgiveness and bitterness that this accident caused in my life.

—*Lisa*

Today's Takeaway:

This forgiveness and victory in Lisa's life is nothing short of evidence of a heart fully surrendered to Christ. We are simply not capable of that level of forgiveness on our own. This story helps me understand the scripture, "Christ in [us], the hope of glory" (Colossians 1:27 KJV). It is Christ in us that causes us to follow His example and do what only He can do!

Day 365

Today's Scripture:

"But let all who take refuge in you rejoice; let them sing joyful praises forever. Spread your protection over them, that all who love your name may be filled with joy" (Psalm 5:11 NLT).

Today's Testimony:

I've always loved the Lord since I was a little girl. My mother would have us kids go to church every Sunday morning, even though she did not go herself. That is when I accepted Christ into my heart and received salvation.

As the years went by and I became a young adult, I always had a relationship with Jesus, but I fully didn't commit myself or my life totally to Him until that one precious day.

I was in my early thirties by then, and I was sitting at the kitchen table. I would occasionally look out the door window at the beautiful landscape out back with all its natural beauty and I would think to myself, *How can anyone deny there is a God?* While sitting there, it felt like a veil was placed over my head covering my face, even though literally it was not there. The veil had small diamond-shaped holes in it that limited my sight. Just seconds later, the veil was lifted off my face. In that moment there was such a love that covered me, there were no words in the English language to describe it. I've always loved the Lord, but that's when I *fell in love with him!* From that day forward my life has never been the same.

He is my precious Savior!

—*Ruth*

Today's Takeaway:

What a beautiful vision from the Lord of having a veil placed over you that limits your vision of His glorious creation, only to have it removed to be able to see fully. One day we *will* see Him fully, face-to-face! No wonder she felt surrounded by His presence and love. When we live with Him in Heaven, we will literally be in His presence. The Scriptures say that now the angels are praising Him saying, "Holy, holy, holy is the Lord God Almighty, who was, and is, and is to come" (Revelation 4:8 NIV).

What will <u>we</u> do when we see Him? I cannot fathom it. The Scriptures say the elders will bow and cast their crowns before Him (v. 10). I imagine I would do the same, if I had any to cast. What a magnificent sight! It's a good thing we'll have a new body with new eyes by then. I don't know if I could handle this otherwise!

As this year draws to a close and we prepare for a new year, let's ask God to get our hearts ready for what He has for us in this coming time. Only He knows what's in store. Could this be the year that Jesus returns? Are we ready? Let's check our hearts and ask God to draw us near. I'm ready to *see Him*. Are you? Hallelujah!

Day 366

(In case of Leap Year)

Today's Scripture:

"If I go up to heaven, you are there; if I go down to the grave, you are there"
(Psalm 139:8 NLT).

Today's Testimony:

Through growing up in church my whole life, the pivotal moment of when I got saved was not when I was a young child in Sunday school. It was when I was older and experiencing the struggles of life for the first time.

I was fifteen; my dad was a pastor and my family had just moved to a new place. I blamed this on God and was very unhappy. I was also just coming out of a terrible relationship—one filled with lies and deceit. I felt about an inch tall and unlovable—worthless. I had made up my mind that I was done with church and done with God. I was going to finish high school and leave the church for good.

I was running, and I was running fast. I was going through the motions of church just waiting for graduation to come. It was in that dark, miserable place you get in when you're away from God. Then came the most pivotal moment of my life.

I was at a church event at our home church sitting in the sanctuary counting down the minutes until I could leave, when a young boy walked in. I didn't know at the time, but he would be the boy I would marry someday and spend the rest of my life with. At that moment, things began to shift in my spiritual life. Meeting him was completely ordained by God, and it began a healing process I didn't even know I needed.

Soon my spark and passion for God was reignited. I no longer wanted to run from God; I was running to God with everything in me. I accepted God into my heart in a way I never had before as a young child. He saved me completely. God restored my heart and restored who I was in Him. He gave me purpose and a whole new outlook on life. I was sold out for Him and I was passionate about following God.

From there God opened the door for my now husband and me to become licensed ministers and work for Him. Giving my life to God was a moment I'll never forget. When I was at my lowest, God showed up and He picked me up and used my life for His glory!

—*Tori*

Today's Takeaway:

There is no point in our lives that we sink too low for Him to reach down and pick us up and refresh and renew us. He knows where we are—and He's not scared to come after us. He knew Tori needed a "restart" and He specializes in those.

Are you in need of a restart? You don't even have to wait for them to come in from a backorder. Just call the "Boss" right now. He's in charge of hearts and He will take care of you. Why not start the New Year off RIGHT?